Discourse and Identity

'Benwell and Stokoe have produced an indispensable guide for any student or scholar interested in discourse and identity. This is a deft and highly accessible overview of a complex emerging body of knowledge. The authors move confidently, with great panache, from social theory to the micro details of linguistic analysis, taking in the latest work on spatial, virtual and commodified identities along the way. A neat and illuminating example can be found on every page, along with an important insight and an original line of argument. *Discourse and Identity* is the first scholarly map of the field and is a "must own book" for every identity researcher.'

Professor Margaret Wetherell, Director ESRC Identities Programme, Social Sciences, Open University

'Engaging with a range of current theories and methods of discourse analysis, *Discourse and Identity* offers a critical overview of the ways in which researchers have approached the concept of identity. Benwell and Stokoe draw on an impressive variety of discourse contexts, from ordinary conversation among friends to magazine advertisements, from online interaction to talk about the neighbors. While *Discourse and Identity* illustrates a number of different approaches in depth, including discursive psychology, critical discourse analysis, and several types of narrative analysis, the book's particular strength is in demonstrating the techniques and advantages of ethnomethodology and conversation analysis as tools for illuminating the workings of identity as an interactional achievement. Students and scholars alike will find the text a helpful resource in navigating the broad field of discourse and identity research.'

Mary Bucholtz, Associate Professor, Department of Linguistics, University of California, Santa Barbara

Discourse and Identity

Bethan Benwell and Elizabeth Stokoe

Edinburgh University Press

© Bethan Benwell and Elizabeth Stokoe, 2006

Edinburgh University Press Ltd
22 George Square, Edinburgh

Typeset in 11/13 Monotype Ehrhardt
by Servis Filmsetting Ltd, Manchester, and
printed and bound in Great Britain by
Antony Rowe Ltd, Chippenham, Wilts

A CIP record for this book is available from the British Library

ISBN-10 0 7486 1749 3 (hardback)
ISBN-13 978 0 7486 1749 4
ISBN-10 0 7486 1750 7 (paperback)
ISBN-13 978 0 7486 1750 0

The right of Bethan Benwell and Elizabeth Stokoe
to be identified as authors of this work
has been asserted in accordance with
the Copyright, Designs and Patents Act 1988.

Contents

Acknowledgements

We would like to thank the following people for their constructive comments and helpful advice on earlier drafts of the book's chapters: Charles Antaki, Michael Bamberg, Michael Billig, David Block, Joe Bray, Judy Delin, John Dixon, Derek Edwards, Adam Jaworski, Paul McIlvenny, Sara Mills, Mark Nixon, Jonathan Potter, Mary Talbot, Margaret Wetherell and Robin Wooffitt. From this list, we would like to thank Derek Edwards and Mark Nixon in particular, for reading more than their fair share. Thanks are also due to Mary Bucholtz and Jane Sunderland, for their support of the book from its original proposal stages. The input of all these readers was invaluable in improving the quality and coherence of the book – but of course any remaining lack of quality and coherence is entirely our responsibility! We must also thank Sarah Edwards, our editor at Edinburgh University Press, for believing that we would finish the manuscript, and patiently waiting for it.

We are grateful to John Dixon, Kevin Durrheim, Eric Laurier and Scott McCabe for giving us permission to use transcripts and photographs from their research in Chapter 6. We would also like to thank Mandi Hodges for allowing us to use an extract from her alcohol helpline data in Chapter 4. Additional thanks go to Victoria Hoadly for collecting some of the data used in Chapter 2. We are very grateful to Margaret Bennett who collected some of the data used in Chapter 7 for an undergraduate project, and for her insights into the meanings of emoticons.

We are indebted to L'Oréal, Imperial Leather and Ford for giving us permission to reproduce the advertisements used in Chapter 5. We would also like to thank Leeds Postcards for allowing us to reproduce the image used in Chapter 3 (Leeds Postcards LP91 Glorious/Senseless [1982]. We acknowledge the BBC as the source of the media data quoted in the Introduction, and Chapters 3, 4 and 6. We also acknowledge *The*

Guardian and the *London Review of Books* as the sources of personal advertisements in Chapter 5, and *The Guardian* for the spoof website discussed in Chapter 7. We are enormously grateful to Anita Klein for generously giving us permission to use one of her beautiful paintings ('Watching the Sound of Music') for the cover of this book.

Finally, an 'Acknowledgements' section would not be complete without thanking our nearest and dearest. We would like to thank Mark and Derek not just for moral support and hot dinners, but also for their immeasurable intellectual input and lively discussion throughout the duration of this project.

Data: Transcription, Ethics and Anonymisation

As a book with 'discourse' in the title, it is not surprising that we have used many different kinds of textual data in it: website materials, Internet message boards, conversations between friends, radio and television interviews and talk shows, telephone talk, talk in institutional settings, interview and focus group data, magazine advertisements, and street signs. By and large, the data are our own, which are either transcribed orthographically (verbatim) or using Jefferson's (2004a) system for conversation analysis (see below). Other data are quoted from existing published sources, for which we had no control over the transcription system used and have simply used it exactly as originally written. A variety of transcription systems have therefore been used. Except in the case of some of the media data, we have anonymised each piece of data used, in accordance with academic codes of ethical conduct. The personal names, place names and all other identifiers used throughout the book are pseudonyms. Where there is no source mentioned in the Extracts, the material has been collected and transcribed by the authors.

The Internet message board data used in Chapter 7 were taken from a public site with unrestricted access. Despite this free access, there is some debate among Internet researchers about the use of such materials. Some argue that researchers should make themselves known to 'users' in 'chatrooms' and explicitly seek permission to use the data (e.g. Cherny 1999). However, models of Internet ethics, which protect either participants' intellectual property or right to privacy, tend to assume some degree of cynical or prurient intent on the part of the researcher, neither of which we espouse. Others view 'public' discourse on the Internet as just that, public: 'such study is more akin to the study of tombstone epitaphs, graffiti or letters to the editor. Personal? – yes. Private? – no'

(Sudweeks and Rafaeli 1995, cited in Pacagnella 1997: 7). We have used these data, therefore, by anonymising names and altering explicit cues to the sites.

THE JEFFERSON TRANSCRIPTION SYSTEM

We used G. Jefferson's (2004a: 24–31) system for transcription for much of our interaction data. The system uses three columns: the left hand column contains line numbers, the middle column is the speaker's name, initial or other identifier and the third column is the talk. In the following examples, a '→' is used to indicate the line of talk that illustrates the transcription symbol.

A left square bracket indicates the point of onset of overlapping talk, and a right square bracket indicates the point at which overlapping talk ends:

71	T:	→	I've written [some things down (as well)]
72	B:		[WH- what] I've
73			written is nothing really.

Equals signs indicate no break or gap *between* or *within* turns:

| 432 | Sophie: | | >I COUld've gone < spa:.re when we was out that |
| 433 | | → | Saturday though.=I could've gone spare. |

A pair of equals signs is used when speakers' turns are broken up by the transcript but are actually through-produced:

449	Sophie:	→	not friends ↓with [but you jus' go]=
450	Chloe:		[You jus' go you]=
451	Sophie:	→	= [up,]
452	Chloe:	→	= [all right.]

Numbers in parentheses indicate time elapsed to the nearest tenth of a second:

77	T:		Rhight,
78		→	(0.6)
79	T:		Okay:,

A dot in parentheses indicates a brief interval of less than a tenth of a second:

> 39   T: →   I did <u>say</u> at the lecture (hm) (.) here's a

Underlining indicates stress, via amplitude or pitch:

> 44   T: →   *°Right.°* (0.2) *°'kay.°* C'd those who <u>have</u>
> 45   read it,

Colons indicate prolongation of the immediately prior sound:

> 31   J: →   I thought it was jus' the um:: Lenin's

Combinations of underlining and colons indicate intonation contours. Underlining indicates where the sound is 'punched up'. If the colon is underlined, the pitch rises on the colon. Here, the letter 'e' in 'week' followed by the underlined colon indicates a 'down-to-up' contour:

> 40   T: →   here's a <u>h</u>andout read it before next we<u>:</u>ek.

If the letter preceding the colon is underlined, the pitch rises on the letter and the overall contour is 'up-to-down':

> 444   Sophie: When we was in Echoes.
> 445   Chloe: →   Y<u>e</u>:ah,

Up and down arrows indicate shifts into especially high or low pitch:

> 13   T: Say you're <u>r</u>eading it, (0.4) at ho:me an'
> 14   somebody at ho:me says t'ye, (0.3) ↑↑what's
> 15   →   ↑↑that ↓sto:ry abo:ut ↑you're ↑reading.

A full-stop indicates 'falling', or final intonation contour rather than the end of a grammatical sentence.

A comma indicates continuing intonation rather than a clause boundary.

A question mark indicates rising, or questioning intonation, and an exclamation mark indicates an animated tone.

'¿' indicates rising intonation, though slightly weaker than a standard question mark.

Words in capital letters are especially loud sounds, relative to the surrounding talk:

455   Sophie: →   ↑THE did ↑↑THAT to me!

Degree signs are used to enclose talk that is especially quiet, relative to the surrounding talk. Double signs indicate whisper:

33   J: →   Collection °cos you:- °
34   (0.4)
35   J: →   °°Obviously not°°

An asterisk indicates a 'croaky' or 'creaky' voice quality:

36   T: →   WEll yeah *bu-* (.) uh- ↑never ↓mind.

A boldface consonant indicates a 'hardened' or 'dentalised' sound:

83   To: →   Um:: (0.3) I jus' put (0.6) i:t °°seems to°°

'<' indicates a hurried start:

14   Lou: →   It just [seems] so unfa;;ir. <I mean=

A dash indicates a cut-off:

10   Ger: →   Y'know, this-

'Greater than' and 'less than' symbols surround talk that is noticeably speeded up, or slowed down, relative to the rest of the talk:

1.   Slowed down:

427   Jodie: →   <antibiotics,>

2.   Speeded up:

432   Sophie: →   >I COUld've gone< spa::re

A dot-prefixed row of 'hhh' indicates an in-breath, and a row of 'hhh' indicates out-breath:

1.   In-breath:

7	Jan:		Ye:s ye:s
8			(0.2)
9	Jan:	→	[.hhhhh]

2.   Out-breath:

| 27 | T: | → | Hhhh |

Breathiness is indicated by 'h' within words:

| 8 | T: | → | WHhat is the Aleppo Button about, |

Plosiveness, associated with laughter or crying, is indicated by 'h' in parentheses:

| 1 | FC: | → | Bu' they seem to have their music (0.7) s(h)o:: |
| 2 | | | lo:ud |

A pound-sterling sign indicates 'smiley' voice or suppressed laughter:

| 420 | Sasha: | → | Anna you're £not allowed to £drink. |

Laughter particles are written as 'heh', with longer laughter indicated by more 'hehs':

422	Ryan:		You're <↑not allowed to drink too mu:ch.>
423			you're on antibiotics. ((From a distance))
424			(0.2)
425	Jenny:	→	Heh [heh heh

Empty parentheses indicate untranscribable talk. The longer the space between the brackets, the longer the untranscribable talk. Words in parentheses are the transcriber's best guess at what was said:

20	J:		Was it- I di'n't real- [I thought it was just =
21	T:		[WEll okay:, right =
22	J:	→	=[Lenin's trousers ( )] (okay.)

List of Figures and Tables

Introduction

We start this book, *Discourse and Identity*, with a stretch of discourse, which has some interesting features with regard to identity. It comes from a television programme, popular in the UK at the time of writing, called 'What Not To Wear'. In this programme, two fashion 'experts' (Trinny Woodall and Susannah Constantine) teach an unsuspecting member of the public how to dress 'properly'. The programme's format involves secret filming of the participant for several weeks beforehand, which the presenters then play back and discuss with her all the bad clothing choices she has made. They teach the participant rules about how she should dress for her shape, age and so on, before sending her out to buy clothes with cash provided by the programme.

In the extract below, Trinny and Susannah are playing the secret footage of the participant, Jane, in various settings of her everyday life. They point to successive failures in Jane's choice of clothes. At the start of our clip, they get to their main point: Jane isn't wearing anything feminine:

Susannah and Trinny watching the footage

Jane: 'I think I've just given up . . .'

Trinny: 'We've got to haul it out . . .'

Figure 1 'What Not To Wear' (BBC Television)

Susannah: There's NOTHING feminine! We haven't seen anything feminine or . . .

Jane:	I'm wearing a *skirt* there! (points at large television screen showing secret footage of Jane wearing a knee-length grey skirt)
Susannah:	Yeah but it's SO. . . . (sighing).
Trinny:	I *know* (tutting) but I've never seen anyone make a skirt look so . . . nondescript.
Jane:	I think I've just given up somewhere along the line to be honest.
Trinny:	Yeah, yeah.
Susannah:	Yeah.
Jane:	And now I am over thirty I really *have* given up.
Trinny:	It's a tragedy that you would resign yourself to this. You know.
Susannah:	Mmm.
Trinny:	'Cos it will only get worse.
Jane:	Oh gosh.
Susannah:	Today it's different, you're in red and you're smiling and you're vivacious and your eyes are lighting up and . . . it's so different.
Trinny:	The *real you* is *so* different from the image you're portraying and if it's inside you we've got to get it and haul it out, Jane, and, you know, put it on the outside.
Susannah:	It's the mental side has gotta change and your attitude.
Jane:	(Nodding) Sounds like a really painful . . . transformation actually.

Jane points out that, in the secret footage, she is in fact wearing a skirt – something feminine. However, the presenters sigh and tut – Jane may be wearing a skirt but in a 'nondescript' way. Jane accepts that she may have 'given up', and accounts for her poor choice of clothes in terms of her age ('now I am over thirty'). The episode ends with Susannah and Trinny defining the 'real' Jane in terms of her clothes: the 'real' Jane is mostly buried behind grey, drab, nondescript, unfeminine clothes. The presenters' task is to 'haul' what they see as the 'real' Jane 'inside' her to the 'outside' for everyone to see.

This short extract raises a number of questions about identity: its nature, its location, who can know it, what it looks like, how it could be manipulated and so on. So, to start with, we might 'read' identity off what we can see, commonsensically, from the pictures of the interaction and the transcript. The speakers are all 'women'. They are relatively 'young', though not 'teenagers'. They are 'white'. The presenters' accents sound 'upper middle class'; Jane sounds 'educated' and 'middle class'. We presume they are all 'English', and we know Jane is 'heterosexual' – she has a male partner. The three participants are not 'friends', but have another kind of relationship (for example, 'expert' and 'novice'). Trinny and Susannah are 'television presenters', or 'journalists', or 'style gurus'. Each of these categories can be further unpacked. Are they 'women', 'girls', 'female', 'ladies'? Are they 'young', 'middle-aged', 'thirty-some-things' or 'old'? Are the presenters 'snooty', 'assertive' or 'bullies'? Is Jane a 'victim'?

As we can see, an indefinably large number of terms may be used to describe persons. These 'terms', and the practice of 'description', are both *discourse phenomena*. Different descriptions may be produced, in which some 'identities' are emphasised and others are ignored or down-played. Each of the categories listed above implies another, such as that to be a 'woman' contrasts normatively with 'man', 'young' contrasts with 'old', 'heterosexual' contrasts with 'lesbian' or 'bisexual' and so on. However, not all of our speculative identity-relevant categories are clearly present in, or relevant to, the transcribed extract. We can easily spot gender ('We haven't seen anything feminine'), and age ('now I am over thirty') because the speakers explicitly mention these. We can see the relevance of some 'identities', such as 'expert' and 'novice', in the content of what the participants say. Other things have to be implied or more heavily interpreted. Issues of class, ethnicity, sexuality and so on, are not directly attended to by the speakers (at least in this part of the programme), yet we might contemplate their relevance. For example, a recent analysis of 'What Not To Wear' focused on social class antagonism and the way women are publicly humiliated for failing to live up to middle-class standards (McRobbie 2004).

The participants talk as if there is a 'real you' on the 'inside', out of sight, contrasted with a public identity display that may or may not correspond with it. This idea is central to many contemporary theories of identity: identity as an 'essential', cognitive, socialised, phenomenologi-cal or psychic phenomenon that governs human action. Typical questions based on this understanding include 'what' identities people possess (for example, are they masculine or feminine?), how they may be distinguished from one another (for example, what are the criteria for categorising people in terms of class?), and how they correlate with a variety of social science measures (for example, do people of different sexual orientations behave differently?). It is assumed that although people may present themselves differently in different contexts, underneath that presentation lurks a private, *pre-discursive* and stable identity. People should know who they 'really' are, and if they do not, they may need the help of experts, therapists, gurus and so on to reveal that knowledge. In the data above, the real Jane is 'so different' from the image she portrays. Occasionally, the exterior performance matches the interior reality: the red top Jane is wearing in the above sequence matches her happier, vivacious 'real' identity.

An alternative understanding of identity is as a public phenomenon, a performance or construction that is interpreted by other people. This construction takes place in discourse and other social and embodied conduct, such as how we move, where we are, what we wear, how we talk and so on. These ideas underpin a different strand of identity theory from the 'interior' account above. It is common to read about a 'discursive' and 'postmodern' turn across the social sciences and humanities, within which theories of identity have undergone a radical shift. Crucially, identity has been *relocated*: from the 'private' realms of cognition and experience, to the 'public' realms of discourse and other semiotic systems of meaning-making. Many commentators therefore argue that rather than being *reflected* in discourse, identity is actively, ongoingly, dynamically *constituted* in discourse.

From this broadly 'social constructionist' perspective, there is no such thing as an absolute self, lurking behind discourse. A constructionist approach examines people's own understandings of identity and how the notion of inner/outer selves is used rhetorically, to accomplish social action. Although discourse is not all there is in the world, we understand who we are to each other in this public and accountable realm. There is no way 'through' discourse to a hidden reality, even though we might talk *as if* there is. Constructionist approaches do not therefore simply replace an 'inner' self with an 'outer' one. Rather, it is the very idea of an *inner* self and its *outward* expressions that is constructed, metaphorically, as we can see in the above extract. The presenters talk on the basis that Jane's performance of who she is does not match the 'real Jane' hiding behind the clothes. But the very notion that there is a 'real Jane', whether 'inside' or 'outside', *is itself* a production of discourse. Who we are to each other, then, is accomplished, disputed, ascribed, resisted, managed and negotiated in discourse. This is the starting point for the book.

There are already numerous books written about the discursive construction of identity. Our book sits alongside these titles, but aims to do something slightly different. Many existing books are *theoretical accounts* and arguments about discourse-based approaches to identity and their limitations, but these do not deal with empirical analysis (for example, Harré 1998; Michael 1996). A large subset focuses on the analysis of *one particular identity category*, such as gender (for example, Bucholtz, Liang and

Sutton, 1999; Johnson and Meinhof 1997; Litosseliti 2006), sexuality (for example, Cameron and Kulick 2003; Livia and Hall 1997), age (for example, Coupland and Nussbaum 1993; Nikander 2002), and ethnic and national identities (de Fina 2003; Joseph 2004; Wodak et al. 1999). Another type of book focuses on explaining different *approaches to understanding and analysing identity* (for example, Tracy 2002; Williams 2000). Some choose a *particular setting* for identity construction, often institutional environments (for example, Carbaugh 1996; Gubrium and Holstein 2001; Lecourt 2004; Matoesian 2001). Finally, there are a number of books that examine a range of identity categories and their construction from a *particular analytical perspective*, such as critical social psychology (for example, Shotter and Gergen 1989), psychoanalysis (for example, Hollway and Jefferson 2000), ethnomethodology (for example, Antaki and Widdicombe 1998a; Malone 1997), positioning theory (for example, Harré and Moghaddam 2003) and narrative approaches (for example, Brockmeier and Carbaugh 2001).

This book takes a different approach. A key aim is to examine identity construction across a wide variety of discourse contexts. Rather than starting with a particular identity category, setting or analytic method, each chapter examines a different *context of construction*: different discursive environments in which *identity work* is being done. These include *everyday* conversation (for example, talk between friends, on the telephone), *institutional* settings (for example, news interviews, university websites), *narrative* and stories (for example, stories told in interviews, in the media), *commodified* contexts (for example, personal advertisements, magazines), *spatial* locations (for example, in neighbourhoods, on the beach) and *virtual* environments (for example, in chatrooms, on message boards). Across the chapters, we aim to show *how* researchers, including ourselves, identify identity construction in a wide range of spoken and written talk and text and images. We therefore adopt a strong practical orientation throughout the book. We describe and demonstrate a range of discourse and interaction analytic methods as they are put to use in the study of identity, including 'performative' analyses, conversation analysis, membership categorisation analysis, critical discourse analysis, narrative analysis, positioning theory, discursive psychology and politeness theory. We aim to give readers a clear sense of the coherence (or otherwise) of these different approaches, the practical steps taken in analysis, as well as potential problems and criticisms.

Within the broad field of discourse and identity, we find numerous, often near-synonymous, terms for 'identity', including 'self', 'selfhood', 'position', 'role', 'personality', 'category', 'person formulation', 'person description', 'subjectivity', 'subject', 'agent', 'subject position' and 'persona'. Some terms are connected to particular theories or traditions (for example, 'subjectivity' is often associated with psychoanalytic accounts, 'person formulation' is used in conversation analysis). Due to the sheer lack of agreement across different traditions, we make no special distinction between terms, but use them interchangeably, perhaps favouring a particular term if it is used in the method or theory being surveyed. Generally, we understand the term 'identity' in its broadest sense, in terms of *who people are to each other*, and how different kinds of identities are produced in spoken interaction and written texts.

Overall, we hope that our choices of literature to review, methods to describe and demonstrate, data to analyse, and debates to engage with, provide a clear and comprehensive account of contemporary writing about discourse and identity.

THE BOOK'S ORGANISATION

Throughout the book, we adopt an interdisciplinary approach, drawing on work not just in our own disciplines of English language and linguistics (Benwell) and psychology (Stokoe), but also in sociology, ethnomethodology, critical theory, feminism, philosophy, cultural studies and human geography. The fact that we have different academic histories, and work in different disciplines, is both a virtue and a tension. Readers may detect our personal preferences as we discuss and evaluate different theoretical and methodological approaches to the study of identity. And, like any book, our choice of what to review, what to emphasise, what to criticise, what to praise, and what to ignore is based on these preferences. We have tried to avoid an overly polemical tone, but have probably failed to do so at moments throughout the book. We also want to note at this point that, despite having no intentions to do so, we discuss 'gender' identity more than any other category. This is partly because so much of the empirical work on identity construction focuses on gender, but also because we both have backgrounds in gender research. However, we hope that readers will see the relevance and applicability of all our examples to other identity categories, whatever the context.

We have divided the book's seven chapters into two broad sections. Part I contains four chapters: (1) *Theorising Discourse and Identity*, (2) *Conversational Identities*, (3) *Institutional Identities* and (4) *Narrative Identities*. Part II contains the remaining three chapters: (5) *Commodified Identities*, (6) *Spatial Identities* and (7) *Virtual Identities*. The first part of the book, in addition to exploring three different sites for identity construction, is also where most of our explanations of, and debates about, analytic *methods* are located. Chapter 1 is *theoretical*, and provides an overview of the history and development of discourse-based theories of identity. The next three chapters show how identity is analysed within different methodological frameworks, and in different kinds of discourse data. Chapter 2 is the first empirical chapter, and it contrasts two approaches to the analysis of identity in *everyday conversation*, 'performative' and 'ethnomethodological'. The methods of *conversation analysis* and *membership categorisation analysis* are explained in some detail, alongside numerous examples. Chapter 3 introduces another method, *critical discourse analysis*, and contrasts it with conversation analysis in the study of identity construction in *institutional settings*. Finally in Part I, Chapter 4 discusses a range of *narrative* analytic methods, including *psychoanalysis*, *positioning theory*, *critical discursive psychology* and *ethnomethodological analyses*.

In Part II, we focus on three more sites of identity construction, further illustrating the methods introduced in Part I. However, we pay less attention to methodological debates in Chapters 5 to 7, and more to understanding the *context* of identity construction that each one examines. Each of our chosen sites of identity construction – commodified, spatial and virtual – has recently become the intellectual focus across a variety of disciplines. In addition to a 'turn' to *discourse*, identity theorising has also been influenced by 'turns' to *spatiality* and *virtuality* (in an increasingly multi-modal, digital world), and to *commodification* (in a consumer and globalised society). These sites have therefore been chosen not as inert backdrops for the analysis of identity, but for the theoretical and empirical debates they provoke about their nature as entities separate (or not) from any other realm of social life.

CONTENTS AND THEMES

In Chapter 1, we survey the history and development of identity theorising, charting the broad paradigmatic shifts in accounts of identity from the sixteenth century onwards. We start by describing early treatments of identity as a personal, internal *project of the self*. The 'self help' books that are found on the shelves of modern bookshops, as well as television programmes like 'What Not To Wear', treat identity as something that must be *worked* on. We trace the history of this understanding of identity through its incarnations during the Enlightenment period, followed by the Romantic Movement. We consider the introduction of psychoanalysis at the start of the twentieth century, with its focus on the psyche as the basis for identity, before ending our historical review with a discussion of modernity and postmodern theories of the self, and their similarities to and departures from earlier approaches.

We then move on to contrast early notions of personal, subjective identity with the idea that identity is an intersubjective *product of the social*. In the second half of the twentieth century, sociologists, social psychologists and linguistics commentators began to be interested in the notion of group or collective identities, with which people identify and claim – or resist – membership, and define who they are in relation to others. We point out that although these group accounts emphasise the social aspects of identity, they retain an internalised understanding of a pre-discursive self. The turn to poststructuralism resulted in the rejection of 'internal' accounts in favour of 'constructionist' approaches, as described briefly at the start of this Introduction. This leads us into a discussion of the contemporary theories of identity on which this book is mainly based, including discursive, ideological approaches rooted in cultural and critical theory as well as theories of performativity.

In the second half of Chapter 1, we introduce the discursive methods for analysing identity on which the rest of the chapters are based. First, we discuss the micro-level, radically empirical method of *conversation analysis*, and its ethnomethodological roots. We consider how 'identity' is to be understood and analysed from this perspective, in sharp contrast to the heavily theoretical accounts discussed in the first part of the chapter. The analysis of 'identity' rests on the occasioning of identity categories (for example, nurse, Catholic, heterosexual, man) or person descriptions more generally, in talk: how identity categories crop up, how they are 'oriented to' or noticed by speakers, and what the consequences are for the unfolding interaction. Conversation analysts work closely with interactional data, and resist pre- or post-theorising about the political, historical or macro-cultural implications of any interaction being analysed. Similar understandings of identity are found in the next method, also ethnomethodological in its basis: *membership categorisation analysis*. The third method discussed, *discursive psychology*, also has its roots in conversation analysis and ethnomethodology, as well as social studies of science and language philosophy. A similar, micro-level approach to identity can be found in discursive psychology – something that unites the first three methods we discuss. So, in the data extract at the start of the chapter, a micro-level analysis might focus on the kinds of identity categories that are made relevant to the interaction, the kinds of conversational turns they occur in, and the kinds of social actions that are accomplished by them. Jane's invocation of her 'age' – an 'over thirty' identity – happens at a particular moment in the sequence of interaction and it *does something*: it is part of an account, begun in her previous turn, that responds to the criticisms of her clothes by Trinny and Susannah.

The next three methods are united by a different theme: the combination of micro-level analysis and macro-level theorising. In a variant of discursive psychology called *critical discursive psychology*, attention to micro-level detail is supplemented with a macro-level layer of analysis in order to focus on the historical, social and political contexts of identity construction. Identity is analysed as a discursive performance that is connected to wider systems of cultural meaning-making. In our data, this might produce an analysis of the kinds of cultural knowledge that are needed to understand fully what being 'over thirty' means for a woman at the start of the twenty-first century. A similar kind of analysis might be found in narrative studies, depending on the particular approach taken. For *narrative analysts*, identity is constructed in the stories we tell about ourselves; in fact we are 'storied selves'. Narrative analysts examine the structure of narratives (for example, beginnings, middles, ends), as well as the cultural narrative genres that connect 'on the ground' stories (such as Jane's stories about herself) to wider 'master narratives' (for example, 'narratives of self help'). These 'master narratives' are sometimes called 'discourses' or 'interpretative repertoires' in other traditions.

Finally, we discuss *critical discourse analysis*, an interdisciplinary method that combines micro- and macro-levels of analysis to expose the ideological workings of language. Critical discourse analysis is an explicitly political approach, which is dedicated to uncovering societal power asymmetries, hierarchies, and the oppression of particular groups. It aims to identify how 'discourses' operate to sustain these hierarchies. With regard to our data, a critical discourse analyst might start, as McRobbie (2004) does, with a theoretical account of 'self-help' genres and the class antagonism they promote, as well as a feminist position on the way dominant discourses of femininity and sexuality are constructed in an all-powerful media industry. Such an analyst would then look for evidence of these different kinds of political processes in the detail of the talk.

Two important themes emerge in Chapter 1. The first is a series of common 'dualisms' in theorising about the self and identity. For example, as we have already seen from our discussion of the data extract, identity theories often split along either 'essentialist' or 'constructionist' lines. Essentialist theories locate identity 'inside' persons, as a product of minds, cognition, the psyche, or socialisation practices. From this perspective, identity is a taken-for-granted category and a feature of a person that is absolute and knowable. In contrast, constructionist theories treat the term 'identity' *itself* as a socially constructed category: it is whatever people agree it to be in any given historical and cultural context.

Constructionist approaches investigate how people perform, ascribe and resist identity, and how what it means to 'have an identity' is produced in talk and text of all kinds. It is not surprising that this book, with its focus on *discourse*, generally adopts a constructionist approach, although, as we discuss in Chapter 2, this is not always a straightforward position. Another prevalent dualism in identity theories is between 'agency' and 'structure'. The issue here is to do with whether people are free to construct their identity in any way they wish (the 'agency' view, in which the individual *has agency*, is *an agent* or *agentive*), or whether identity construction is constrained by forces of various kinds, from the unconscious psyche to institutionalised power structures (the 'structure' view, in which 'subjects' are restrictively positioned within existing 'discourses', for example, as 'client' or 'therapist' in 'therapy discourse'). Macro-level analytic approaches (for example, critical discourse analysis, positioning theory) tend to be closer to the 'structure' view, whereas micro-level methods (for example, conversation analysis, discursive psychology) rarely engage with the terms of this dualism at all.

The macro-micro debate, the second main theme in Chapter 1, crops up in each of the next three chapters. In Chapter 2, we contrast two broad approaches to the analysis of mundane conversations between people in various everyday settings. We start by unpacking the notion of 'constructionism', and then investigate how 'identity performance' is translated in empirical studies. Our examples focus on the performance of femininities and masculinities, in the talk of women and men friends. We discuss a number of data extracts and the analysts' interpretation of them, showing how they *locate* and subsequently analyse their participants' identity work. We discuss potential problems with performativity approaches, particularly the way they tend to reproduce precisely the essentialist understandings of identity they claim to reject. We then move on to contrast these approaches with an alternative way of analysing identity based in conversation analysis. We discuss the basic aims and concepts of the method, including the specialised transcription system. We also discuss some common criticisms of conversation analysis, particularly its 'restricted' notion of context and its lack of political engagement, as hinted at in our discussion of Chapter 1 above. Next, we discuss the related method of membership categorisation analysis, before moving on to illustrate both approaches and the way these ethnomethodological techniques allow us to see how, in the details of everyday conversation, people display who they understand each other to be.

Chapter 2 deals entirely with identity work in mundane, ordinary talk. We therefore discuss identity categories based on familial and other 'everyday' relationships, such as 'friend', 'partner', 'father', 'son' and so on. In contrast, Chapter 3 focuses on institutional identities, such as 'interviewer', 'customer', 'teacher' or 'student'. A key theme of this chapter is how we pin down what is 'institutional' about these identities. What makes talk and text institutional – its location in an institutional context, the fixed institutional identities it presupposes, or its emergent goal-oriented nature? We start by describing conversation analytic studies of institutional interaction, and discuss the debates about what counts as 'institutional' versus 'ordinary' talk. We also discuss the contribution of membership categorisation analysis to our understanding of institutional interaction. These methods are often thought to neglect the historical and contextual dimensions of institutional talk, which some argue are central to its definition. Critical discourse analysis is an approach that addresses these issues and is introduced in the next section of the chapter. We describe its history and concepts, and demonstrate the techniques of its linguistic analysis through a case study of university publicity texts. We show how identity is represented and positioned in these texts, in relation to current theories and ideologies of higher education. We conclude the chapter with a comparative analysis of some university tutorial interaction, first using conversation analysis, followed by a second reading using critical discourse analysis. In this way, we show the relative contributions of each method.

In Chapter 4, we review the eclectic set of methods that comprise narrative analysis. We start the chapter with a brief discussion of the roots of narrative inquiry, which is followed by an illustration of a basic analytic technique based on the identification of narrative structures. We then move on to explain the concept of 'narrative identity', and what a narrative approach adds to our understanding of discursive identity construction more generally. Following this, we discuss and evaluate a variety of methods for collecting narrative data, including the 'narrative' or 'biographic' interview. Our first empirical example demonstrates the identification of broad narrative themes in interview data. The second example combines discourse analysis with psychoanalysis, and the third draws on positioning theory. All of these techniques merge an analysis of stories as they are told with macro-level interpretative resources, such as 'cultural plot lines' or 'master narratives', and show how identity is constituted between these textual 'layers'. We then contrast these methods with an ethnomethodological approach that focuses on the turn-by-turn organisation of narrative tellings and identity ascription. Finally, we discuss some examples in which the analysts combine macro- and micro-levels of analysis, including from a critical discursive psychological perspective, and debate the issues that emerge from reading data in this way.

Chapter 5 focuses on the analysis of identities in an increasingly 'commodified' society. Commodification is a process that has had a profound influence on the way identities are conceptualised. We start by discussing the impact of cultural concepts of commodification (for example, 'consumerism') on theories of identity, and note a tension between 'structure' and 'agency' accounts. Some explanations treat people and their identity positions as passively controlled by economic conditions and the power and rhetoric of advertising. In contrast, other theories suggest that people actively construct their identities by deriving their own meanings for the things they buy, or resisting the positions offered by advertising texts. Following the theoretical overview, we analyse some 'texts of consumption' in women's magazine advertising as a key site for identity work and the production of normative, heterosexual femininity. Next, we examine a different kind of identity construction, the 'self-commodification' practices of personal advertisements. We identify an 'anti-commercial impulse' prevalent both in responses to advertisements and even within advertisements themselves. One manifestation of this impulse is men's resistance to the 'feminised' realm of consumerism, which we demonstrate in an ethnographic study of readers and their responses to men's magazines. This study also addresses the often-neglected voice of the consumer in the analysis of commodified identity. Across the chapter, we draw on a range of methods including critical discourse analysis and critical discursive psychology.

In Chapter 6, we investigate another 'context' for contemporary discourse and identity research: talk and text in material locations of space and place. In a book with 'discourse' in its title, it may be surprising to find a chapter that deals with the ostensibly 'non-discursive' realm of space. The chapter has a dual focus: on the construction of *space in discourse*, but also space as the *location for discourse*. In addition to language data, we consider a number of other practices and semiotic domains, including signs, photographs of people's activities in particular locations, and embodied gestures and other conduct in interaction. Discourse researchers are often criticised for ignoring the 'materiality' of the 'real world', or the role of 'the body' in interaction and identity construction. This chapter goes some way to redressing the balance, but also shows how 'the real world' is not 'real' beyond the social practices that construct and maintain it as such. Moreover, 'the body' is not separate from verbal interaction, but an aggregate part of it. We start the chapter with a discussion of the way space channels human activity along identity lines, before discussing the theoretical backdrop of the 'spatial turn' across the social sciences and humanities. A basic idea is that *who* we are is intimately connected to *where* we are, and that places can be moral sites of power struggle, exclusion and prejudice. We then investigate how identity is constructed in and through a street sign, in narrative accounts of place, and in ethnomethodological analyses of neighbour interactions. Towards the end of the chapter, we analyse extracts from a televised neighbour dispute about the location of a hedge, in order to illustrate the embodied and multi-modal nature of identity work in space.

The final chapter (Chapter 7) investigates identity construction in 'virtual' interactional environments. In Chapter 6, we discussed the *locatedness* of identity construction, a neglected theme in discourse and identity research. 'Location' also plays a central role in the ways in which 'virtual identity' has been theorised. In particular, we consider the notion of 'cyberspace' as a *dislocated place of words*, and explore how the absence of *face-to-face* interaction impacts on identity construction. For example, a common assumption about cyberspace is that 'who we are to each other' is potentially limitless. Unseen and unheard, we can be whoever we want to be: *what we write is who we are*. On the other hand, we demonstrate how Internet users actively construct a sense of material location and embodiment through the use of various textual devices. Within the literature on 'computer mediated communication', key debates include how we define 'virtual', and if and how 'virtual identity' differs from 'real identity'. We start the chapter with a discussion of the 'virtual turn' and its impact on identity theorising. Some research suggests that computer mediated communication has particular and unique linguistic characteristics and defining features, and we describe and illustrate these with data collected from message board discourse. We conclude the chapter with a case study of 'newbie' identity construction (a member's term for first-time message writers) in our message board data, focusing on the strategies used by both 'newbies' and 'regulars' to do the business of displaying who they are to each other: another process of identity construction in discourse.

PART ONE

Approaches

CHAPTER I

Theorising Discourse and Identity

The concept of 'identity', according to Taylor (1989), was unthinkable before the sixteenth century: the pre-modern, feudal era in Europe. Today, it is a heavily theorised, academic concept that is a paradigmatic product of its historical conditions, formulated and reformulated in strategic ways by the period or movement under which it arises and the preoccupations of its theorists. Early formulations of identity were the rarefied preserve of philosophers; more recently the topic has made unprecedented strides into the popular realm, permeating everyday talk and practices, from self-help literature to the pseudo-therapy of television chat shows. At the time of writing, in early 2005, an Internet search on 'identity' reveals a preoccupation with 'identity fraud', 'identity cards' and 'identity theft', all of which point to a common-sense use of the term as something that people own; a personal possession that can be authenticated or falsified.

In this chapter, we survey both diachronic and synchronic developments in identity theorising. We explore some of these introductory themes, and chart broad paradigmatic shifts in identity accounts from the sixteenth century onwards. We move from early treatments of identity as a self-fashioning, agentive, internal *project of the self*, through more recent understandings of *social and collective identity*, to postmodern accounts which treat identity as fluid, fragmentary, contingent and, crucially, *constituted in discourse*. The latter part of the chapter is devoted to explicating discursive accounts of identity. We propose that discursive approaches may reconcile some of the most entrenched dualisms characterising identity research. They are, for example, able to explicate the processes by which people orient to consistency in their accounts of themselves and other people (underpinning the view of identity as 'fixed'), whilst simultaneously showing that identity is contingent on the local conditions of the interactional context. Similarly, identity may be a matter of being 'subject' to, or taking up positions within discourse, but also an active process of discursive 'work' in relation to other speakers.

IDENTITY AS A PROJECT OF THE SELF

A brief scan of the books lining the 'psychology' or 'self-development' shelves of any large bookshop reveals a profound commitment to the notion that identity is an issue of agency and self-determination: that the individual is a 'self-interpreting subject' (C. Taylor 1989). From the numerous self-help titles advertised on the Internet bookseller, Amazon.com, you can purchase: *Change your Life in Seven Days*; *Developing the Leader Within You*; and *Reinventing your Life*. Magazines encourage us to 'Be the Best You Can Be' or take '50 Steps to a Brand New You'. In our hunt for challenges to the dualisms outlined in the Introduction to the book, we need look no further than the concept of 'self-help', whereby consumers are invited to find 'true' selves by active *reinvention* (Simonds 1996).

This notion of identity as a 'project of the self' has a long pedigree, beginning with Enlightenment rationalism and idealism, sustained through Romantic notions of personal self-fulfilment and improvement, and nostalgically retained in everyday life, despite theoretical challenges within recent critical accounts of 'late' or 'high' modernity, postmodernity and globalisation. The first recorded use of the word 'identity' appears in 1570 as 'identitie', meaning 'the quality or condition of being the same in substance, composition, nature, properties, or in particular qualities under consideration; absolute or essential sameness; oneness' (*OED* 2002). It appears, then, that the notion of identity as a unified, internal phenomenon has its roots in the word's etymology, and the everyday meaning has not changed much since its first use.

The Enlightenment self

Until the beginning of the Early Modern period, the dominant status-based social model that characterised both medieval and classical eras had meant that there were 'stark limitations on who had the right or ability to participate in even highly limited forms of self-fashioning' (D. E. Hall 2004: 6). A challenge to these limitations on human agency was established during the Renaissance, and reached its zenith in the era of the Enlightenment in the eighteenth century. The basis of the Enlightenment movement was faith in the ability of human reason, and it emerged out of the humanism characterising the Renaissance two centuries earlier.

This humanist perspective was intimately tied to a growing secularisation, the use of reason, experimental scientific method and an emphasis on individuality. The individual was conceptualised as a 'self-sufficient subject of action endowed with instrumental rationality' (Gil 2000: 54).

Two key thinkers paved the way for the ideas culminating in the Enlightenment: Descartes (1596–1650) and Locke (1632–1704). Descartes is chiefly associated with rationalism and the notion of 'disengaged reason' linked to secularisation and freedom from a larger cosmic or moral order, but also 'self mastery through reason' and whereby *cogito* (thought, cognition) is elevated above all else (Taylor 1989: 143). Locke's work is connected to empiricism: the belief that all knowledge derives from observation, rather than *a priori* reasoning. The self is therefore created by the accumulation of experience and knowledge in the mind. Descartes's separation of mind from body prepared the way for a subjectivity independent of external influence. Additionally, Locke's emphasis upon the reflexive capacity of the mind, isolating aspects of subjective experience and subjecting it to objective control, facilitated the construction of the 'sovereign subject' or 'human agent who is able to remake himself [sic] by methodical and disciplined action' (Taylor 1989: 159). The key principle of 'reflexivity' espoused by both these thinkers is one that centrally underpins the project of the self. Although Descartes's critical, deductive rationalism and Locke's radically detached, inductive empiricism seem at odds, both facilitated the creation of a model of identity which has dominated popular understandings ever since the Enlightenment: that of identity as an instrumental 'project of the self'.

The Romantic self

The Romantic movement of the first half of the nineteenth century was a self-conscious reaction to many elements of the Enlightenment, and thus responsible for refocusing questions of identity. The disengaged rationalism and empiricism of the Enlightenment gave way to an anti-empirical, expressive individualism, which, Taylor (1989: 234) argues, has generated 'what is perhaps the dominant outlook of Western technological society'. Within Romanticism, the subject is theorised as an expression of something innate, but predicated on sensibility and feeling rather than cognition. This self-expression was closely allied with 'Nature', which many Romantic poets and writers theorised as an extension of, or in harmony with, the self. This Romantic conception of an 'inner impulse or conviction which tells us of the importance of our own natural fulfilment' (Taylor 1989: 369–70) can be traced through to contemporary, late modern and populist notions of the 'true', 'authentic' self enshrined in a thousand self-help books and magazines, and underpins the ideal of self-fulfilment at the expense of political engagement often deemed to be a feature, or even crisis, of late modern society.

However, Romantic expressivism was not simply engaged with self-fulfilment as a form of pleasure or hedonism. It was also strongly imbued with morality. The uniqueness of each individual was attached to notions of responsibility to fulfil one's destiny. Again we are reminded of the prevailing view of identity as a 'project of the self'. Later in the nineteenth century, this Romantic view of identity was influential in the work of Smiles, the Victorian reformist, who preached individual reform and self-improvement in his publication *Self Help* (1882).

The psychodynamic self

During the early twentieth century, the life of the individual mind as a defining feature of identity was developed in the massively influential work of Freud (for example, 1927), the founder of psychoanalysis. Freud had two main aims: first, he was interested in charting a genealogy of individual minds and constructing a scientific method by which to describe the workings of the psyche. Secondly, he was concerned with therapeutic intervention on individual patients and the arguably conservative accomplishment of 'normative' psychosocial behaviour. Despite Freud's focus on the internal workings of subjectivity, his emphasis upon socialisation processes within the family and their impact upon the psyche brought a social element into his account. Freud's ideas have been taken up enthusiastically in a variety of disciplines. Critical, literary and narrative theorists have applied his observations about the sublimation of desire, and the influence of the unconscious upon conscious thought, to the study of literary texts (for example, Ellman 1994). Some discourse analysts, having previously resisted treating language as a window on the mind (where cognitions, psychodynamic constructs, and so on, 'exist'), are increasingly combining discourse analysis with psychoanalysis to investigate the 'defended psycho-social' subject (for example, Hollway and Jefferson 2005; see Chapter 4).

Another psychoanalytic theorist, Lacan (for example, 1977), was interested in accounting for the way in which subjects come to recognise or identify themselves and integrate into social life. Unlike Freud, however, Lacan situated this identification process in the discursive realm. Lacan theorised that a key stage in the socialisation of the infant is the acquisition of a shared system of discourse (the 'Symbolic Order'). Like Freud, Lacan attempted to account for the way the fluid and chaotic unconscious of early infancy is reined in and subjected to the illusion of coherent and bounded identity. In this process, which Lacan called the 'mirror' phase, the subject is able to conceive of itself as whole, but simultaneously 'othered' or alien. This imposes a comforting illusion of unity, coherence and distinctiveness. It also, however, entails conformity to shared social rules (Freud's workings of the ego upon the unconscious and Lacan's account of the entry into the Symbolic Order); the price paid by the subject for this illusion of coherence (although see Billig (2005) for a controversial critique of the academic credibility of Lacan's work).

D. E. Hall (2004) points out that agency has an ambivalent status in psychoanalysis. On the one hand, it provides an 'objective' description of the psyche that may lead to an instrumental, reflexive intervention of the self *upon* the self. On the other hand, it constructs a version of the self that is both at the mercy of unconscious drives, and also subject to available positions in discourse. This contradiction is embodied in the argument that psychology is instrumentally oriented to an ideal of social 'normalisation'. In other words, a client of psychotherapy labours under an illusion of self-directed intervention, whilst being directed to a set of normative behaviours institutionally prescribed by the discipline of psychoanalysis (Brenkman 1994).

N. Rose (1990) develops this observation, situating his account of psychoanalysis firmly in the ideological realm. For Rose, psychoanalytic discourse has a *colonising* effect: it reproduces knowledge rather than revealing 'inner truths'; it is constitutive rather than revelatory. This has clear resonances with Foucauldian readings of psychoanalysis as a discursive regime that reproduces its own meanings. Michael (1996: 21) similarly surveys authors who have analysed the way the 'orthodox psychological models of the individual . . . have served in the entrenchment of particular identities', and Parker (1997: 484) observes that 'subjectivity which is elaborated in the discourse of Western Culture usually takes on a psychoanalytic character, whether we like it or not'. We return later in the chapter to the notion that identity is constituted through discursive regimes, and shaped by available positions in discourse.

The postmodern self

Modernity fragments; it also unites. (Giddens 1991: 189)

Woodward (2002: 16) describes the twentieth-century subject as 'an over-socialized self, which nonetheless has *internalized* its own conformity'. Late modern identity is bound up with both *challenge* and *conformity* to essentialism, and throughout its texture we can also trace lines left by the earlier movements. On the one hand, theorists of modern identity emphasise concepts such as 'fluidity', 'migration', 'diaspora', 'crossing' and 'decentring'. On the other hand, much attention is paid to individuals' strategies for shoring up an authentic sense of self in an uncertain world, including the revival of traditions of 'self-improvement' and psychoanalytically-inspired explorations of the self.

The modern era in which we currently live has been defined as de-industrialised 'high', 'late' or 'post' modernity (end of twentieth/early twenty-first century), and frequently characterised by fragmentation, relativism, a merging of the public and private spheres and a decentring or 'dislocation' of the self (Laclau 1990). The processes of *globalisation* arguably compound this dislocation. Such processes are characterised by faster and closer connections across geographical space (Giddens 1991), and an increase in the mediation of experience by, for instance, mass printed and electronic media (Grodin and Lindlof 1996). The consequences of such mediation for daily subjectivity might be, for instance, the juxtaposition of entirely disparate events or intrusion of distant events into the everyday consciousness of ordinary people. 'Live 8', the 2003 invasion of Iraq, or the reality TV show 'Big Brother', for instance, are mass-mediated, international and national events, whose characters, activities and images infiltrate and dominate everyday conversations and consciousness over temporary periods. Baudrillard (1988) develops this theme in his theory of 'hyperreality': the creation by media processes of an autonomous realm governed by 'the sign' or image which dismantles the distinction between reality and representation. He identifies television and electronic media (to this we add magazine culture) as key sources for such cultural transition. Perpetually immersed in myriad signifiers and images, the self is subsumed and *substituted* by this bricolage of imagery.

By extension, 'lifestyle' and commodification takes on special significance for modern identity construction under Western late capitalism. Critics have argued that the consumption of goods has become a substitute for the genuine development of the self, or has even led to a virtual *commodification of the self*: 'Consumer society is market society; we are all *in* and *on* the market, simultaneously customers and commodities' (Bauman 2004: 91). *Commodified identities* (see Chapter 5) offer up a paradoxical space for the agency of the subject, facilitating both creative potential and self-defining possibilities via consumption, but also subjecting identities to the laws of the market.

As we have so far seen, a number of theorists engage with the condition of identity in 'high' or 'late' modernity with varying degrees of optimism about its 'fluid' or 'fragmentary' nature, conceptualising it variously as a 'crisis of identity' (Erikson 1968) and an anti-essentialist reformulation of the self with incredibly liberatory potential. As a late-modernity 'pessimist'. Bauman (2004: 32) uses the term 'liquid modernity' to refer to a 'world in which everything is elusive' and identities are 'the most acute, the most deeply felt and the most troublesome incarnations of *ambivalence*'. Further accounts embody a more positive stance towards modernity, and reveal an interest in people's abilities to accommodate these new demands and exploit their creative potential. The radical and creative potential of postmodernity is illustrated by a number of anti-essentialist frameworks, facilitated by the global and fragmented conditions of postmodernity: *queer theory* (Bersani 1995; Butler 1990) and concepts conceived within postcolonial theory, such as *diaspora* (S. Hall 1995), *hybridity* (Bhabha 1994) and *crossing* (Rampton 1995). These frameworks will be addressed in more detail shortly.

Giddens (1991: 5), however, rejects the view that late modernity is simply fragmentary. He flags up 'unifying features of modern institutions', though with the caveat that such unity is not essential but constituted by 'coherent, yet continuously revised, biographical narratives'. Giddens's work belongs to an emerging tradition of sociological thought that theorises identity in the context of movements of *counter-modernity* or even *anti-modernity* (Latour 1993). In a society overshadowed by an overwhelming sense of personal insecurity, fragmentation and *risk*, Beck (1992) argues that we respond to the loss of these traditional certitudes by the process of 'constructed certitude' realised, for instance, by affiliations to identities such as gender, nationalism and religion. 'Constructed certitude' is a means of shoring up a clear and unified sense of identity or ideology and achieved in part by casting out or ignoring ambiguity or complexity. It is akin to Giddens's notion of 'ontological security', a belief in one's psychic coherence and 'wholeness', which relies on a process of sequestration of chaotic or anxious elements including madness, sickness and death, sexuality and global crisis.

Giddens's (1991) account of the self in the late modern age represents a modern return to the more traditional model of the 'rational agent model' of Locke and Descartes, partly against the grain of the constructionist accounts that predominate in contemporary social theory. His theories of how individuals achieve ontological security have already been outlined and are unambiguously illustrated by the modern activities of self-help and therapy in the popular sphere (see Cameron 2000). What distinguishes Giddens's 'reflexive project of the self' from earlier instantiations, however, is a crucially critical or sceptical element about the degree of agency enjoyed by the subject. This more recent form of reflexivity might be deemed 'critical reflection' – incorporating an awareness of the contingent, constrained nature of subjectivity, shaped by the forces of consumerism and enjoying what Giddens makes clear is a fragile kind of certitude dependent upon evasion and denial. Nonetheless, Giddens has attracted considerable criticism from historically-minded scholars for the way he sidesteps issues of socialisation, context and history (and the notion of being *subject* to available discourses). Later in the chapter, we consider recent reflexive and discursive accounts that *do* pay attention to historical and contextual processes.

Whilst accounts of identity as a 'project of the self' often situate the reflexive self within some kind of social context, a more radically social version of identity, in which the self comes to be *defined* by its position in social practice, can be found across a range of diverse theories. It is to these that we now turn.

IDENTITY AS A PRODUCT OF THE SOCIAL

One cannot be a self on one's own. (C. Taylor 1989: 36)

The idea that identity is an *intersubjective*, rather than merely subjective, matter was addressed by Hegel in *The Phenomenology of Spirit* [1807] (1977). Using the analogy of a struggle between 'lord and bondsman', Hegel hypothesised that external factors, such as the social world, prevented the consciousness from being entirely free or autonomous, but required an imagining of and sometimes submission to an 'other'. The 'recognition' process which is crucial to identity therefore arises through participation in social life: '[A]n individual's self-consciousness never exists in isolation . . . it always exists in relationship to an 'other' or 'others' who serve to validate its existence' (D. E. Hall 2004: 51). Hegel's social view of identity represented an important conceptual shift which has bequeathed an influential legacy for more recent accounts of identity, and which, as we shall see shortly, came to influence some discursive views of self. This formulation of identity as a *social location* paved the way for theories, particularly in sociology and sociolinguistics, in which the self is defined primarily by virtue of its membership of, or identification with a particular group or groups.

In the second half of the twentieth century, sociological accounts of identity were characterised by a concern with *collective identities*. Group labels, such as 'adolescent', 'black', 'working-class', were taken to be indisputable identity formations, often serving as social variables against which forms of social behaviour or linguistic usage could be measured. Collectivist accounts remain extremely influential in traditional sociology, psychology, economics, variationist sociolinguistics, marketing and the popular imagination. Indeed, a commitment to one or more of these 'labels' is invariably the most common response to the question, 'Who am I?' It is only recently that the homogeneity implicit in this version of identity has been challenged, and whilst singular labels persist, they are increasingly acknowledged to *intersect* in multi-dimensional ways (for example, Eckert 2000). Howard (2000: 382) refers to these as 'theories of intersectionality', and remarks that they are often prompted by politically motivated identity work, such as coalitions between marginalised groups. Nevertheless, despite the complications to 'group identity' that intersectionality brings, identity is still being theorised as pre-discursive, unified and essential. A number of scholarly approaches rely on this 'collective' view of identity, including 'social identity theory' (within social psychology), and variationist sociolinguistics (within language studies).

Social Identity Theory

A key theory of group identity is 'social identity theory' (SIT, and the related 'self-categorisation theory'), developed by the psychologist Tajfel and his colleagues (see Tajfel 1982; Tajfel and Turner 1986) in the social cognition tradition of social psychology. Within SIT and SCT, social identity (as opposed to personal identity) is defined by individual identification with a group: a process constituted firstly by a reflexive knowledge of group membership, and secondly by an emotional attachment or specific disposition to this belonging. The emphasis in Tajfel's work lies in the social-cognitive *processes* of membership, and the way that 'belonging' is both initiated and sustained, rather than in the form of named collectivities outlined above.

/Social identity theory explores the phenomenon of the 'ingroup' and ~Rationale~ 'outgroup', and is based on the view that identities are constituted through a process of *difference* defined in a relative or flexible way dependent upon the activities in which one is engaged. Put simply, the ingroup is the one to which an individual 'belongs' and the 'outgroup' is seen as 'outside' and different from this group. So, for example, we, the authors, might, whilst teaching or marking essays, perceive ourselves to be members of the lecturer 'ingroup', but view students as an 'outgroup'. People strive to maintain a positive social identity, partly by making favourable comparisons between the ingroups and outgroups. This process of social categorisation is achieved cognitively by such operations as attribution and the application of existing schemas relating to the group, and sees its operation serving particular social and psychological goals, such as boosting self-esteem (R. Brown 2000). Another central idea is that outgroups are more easily and reductively characterised than ingroups, such that ingroup identification often leads to stronger stereoptyping and prejudice towards outgroups.

From the perspective of SIT, identity is something that lies dormant, ready to be 'switched on' in the presence of other people. Social identity memberships therefore have something of a causal relationship to actions and behaviour. It has been criticised for this treatment of identity as a cognitive, pre-discursive and essentialist phenomenon (for example, Antaki, Condor and Levine 1996; Widdicombe and Wooffitt 1995). A similar understanding of identity is produced in a linguistics-based approach to group identity: variationist sociolinguistics.

Variationist sociolinguistics

Within the field of sociolinguistics, an approach known as 'variationist' focuses on the relationship between social identity and language use. Work in this tradition often involves long-term ethnographic and participant observation methodology, in which researchers chart the distribution of linguistic variables (for example, features of accent, syntactic or morphological patterns, conversational features such as question types) across a population (often but not exclusively geographical) and attempt to identify patterns of correlation with social factors such as 'sex', 'age', 'register', 'social class' and 'group identification'. Key studies in this field include Trudgill's (1974) Norwich study, which mapped the correlation of variables such as the [ŋ] endings on verbs (for example, 'going', 'singing') with social variables of sex and social class. Sociolinguistic approaches have also been employed in language and gender research in an attempt to identify systematic differences between men's and women's language use, focusing on such variables as non-standard grammar, accent, lexis and code-switching and aspects of turn-taking such as interruption and overlap, modality and mood (for an overview, see Coates 2004).

Variationist sociolinguistics theorises identity in a similar way to social identity theory, as a pre-discursive construct that correlates with, or even causes particular behaviours: this time language behaviours. Whilst empirical studies provide a rigorous description of the distribution of language variables, they have been criticised for their attempts to *interpret* the social significance of such a distribution. In most variationist work, the relationship between the two entities (social identity and linguistic behaviour) is deemed to be *causal*: for instance, being a woman leads to a greater convergence to standard grammar, increased politeness and forms of solidarity in talk and behaviour. This formulation has been challenged from a number of quarters. For Cameron (1997: 59–60), it is an example of the 'correlational fallacy', by which one description is yoked situationally and often coincidentally to another and assumed to

offer an *explanation* of social or linguistic behaviour. For social constructionists, the labels themselves are crude and monolithic, usually defined
by biology (for example, sex and age) and imposed by analysts (for
example, social class), rather than being provisional identities that people
themselves negotiate in talk. Whilst such critics would not necessarily
attempt to dispute the formal, descriptive status of categories such as
'male' or 'student', they *do* challenge the implicit assumption that such
categories always operate to define 'identity' for social beings themselves.
Similarly, patterns of linguistic variation do not necessarily reflect or
define identity simply because they emanate from those to whom a social
label may be conveniently attached. A person may speak with a pro-
nounced Scottish accent, but we cannot be confident that this is an
expression of 'Scottish identity'. A man may regularly use vernacular
forms and swear, but we cannot be sure that this is a reflection of 'masculinity'. What variationist approaches arguably do is carve the world
into a series of finite categories into which their object of study is then
moulded and shaped.

Challenges to group accounts

In recent years, in both psychology and sociolinguistics, there has been
something of a backlash against the notion of an internally located, group
or collective identity. Some approaches have sought to destabilise the
essential, permanent, unified quality of group categories, whilst preserving the sense of personal and subjective investment such categories
apparently hold for people. For example, Lave and Wenger's (1991)
'Communities of Practice' (CoP) theory has been taken up in sociolinguistics to challenge the essentialist categories of variationist methodology whilst acknowledging the shared experiences of social beings in their
contexts of local communities of social practice. Eckert and McConnell-
Ginet (1998: 490) define CoPs as 'an aggregate of people who come
together around some common endeavour'. CoPs are defined by social
engagement rather than location or population, and thus describe social
collectives that are meaningful to those participating in them, rather than,
say, the analyst's more abstract categorisation. They also reorient identity
to social practice and talk, rather than pre-given, essential identities, and
treat an individual not as a member of a singular group, but rather as
'an actor articulating a range of forms of participation in multiple communities of practice' (ibid.). Examples of such communities might
include work colleagues, a class at school, or a neighbourhood watch committee, and may be usually permanent (for example, the family) or transient (for example, a training camp).

More radically destabilising challenges to 'group' identity can be found in poststructuralist and sociolinguistic theory. *Queer theory* (for example, Sedgwick 1993) for instance, has come to signal not only challenge to the constructions of normativity around sexuality, but challenge to 'legitimate' or 'dominant' notions of identity more broadly (D. E. Hall 2004). *Diaspora* represents the identities of those moving between cultures 'unsettling the assumptions of one culture from the perspective of the other' (S. Hall 1995: 48). In recent poststructuralist trends within postcolonial theory, the term has come to be decoupled from an essential ethnic or homeland identity to refer to a dynamic and heterogeneous notion of community (Brooker 1999). *Hybridity* is defined by Bhabha (1994) as an aesthetics of identity which uses the Bakhtinian motif of hybridity (where two discourses are 'mixed' in one utterance) to destabilise traditional binaries and myths of cultural homogeneity. Though often used as a shorthand for a fusion of cultural identities, hybridity has been theoretically implicated in the hegemonic (rather than coercive) imposition of dominant, colonising power upon a colonised community. *Crossing* is a sociolinguistic term (Rampton 1995) that refers to interethnic linguistic adoption of styles or codes of talk of an outgroup (to which one is not thought to belong), which, whilst marginal, is nevertheless associated with covert prestige. Thus members of various adolescent ethnic groups will 'cross' between Punjabi, West Indian Creole and 'stylised Asian English'.

However, whilst the poststructuralist turn has resulted in the dismantling of essentialist notions of identity, there may be laudable political reasons for their maintenance. Aside from achieving a sense of subjective security, often in the face of postmodern narratives of crisis and fragmentation, the membership of a specific, named collectivity may be a *marked* and politically motivated strategy to make oneself and one's interests 'visible' and 'included' (Spivak 1990). Referred to by Woodward (2002) as the 'political dimension of the self', the concept of 'group identity' is given renewed credibility and vigour by *identity politics*. Identity politics, in its liberal, leftist form, is most associated with marginal, oppressed groups, whose historically marked and 'othered' status led to a concept of historical group subjectivity and is thus central to feminist, gay and civil rights movements. **Northerners, Thatcher**

Identity politics is not, however, without its critics. It has been argued, for instance, that collective self-identifications simply legitimise the conditions of inequality that give rise to them in the first place (Wilmsen and McAllister 1996). Those who view social identity as 'acts of power' – that is, an affirmation of the self through suppression, exclusion or oppression of the 'other' – also experience a conundrum when attempting to

Rationale or politics Chapter

conceive of marginal identities in this way. In attempting to promote the self, we cannot fail to denigrate the other, even where the other is traditionally dominant and hegemonic. This is an argument faced, for instance, by radical feminists and black activists and often realised in the form of backlash. Linked to this view, but with a slightly different emphasis, is the formulation that social identity is an inscription in discourse, and therefore of itself, prescriptive, limiting and unelective, rather than something politically empowering. All of these views are poststructuralist in orientation, stressing the constructed and oppressive dimension of identity, and thus pose a serious challenge to identity politics. Without *some* form of a politics of 'difference', however, it might be argued that we face a toothless and irresponsible dismissal of discrimination, which however theoretically constructed and contingent, has felt and material effects (Daly 1978; Fanon 1952). Finally, a rejection of identity politics is linked to the neglect of the often passionate identifications people make with existing collectivities, and the extent to which these identifications contribute to their subjective sense of the self.

In an influential essay, 'Who needs identity?', S. Hall (2000) argues there is a political need to exploit a notion of identities (or 'subject positions') within discourse, whilst acknowledging that these are temporary attachments, rather than essential 'cores' of self. Hall recognises that ideology and hegemonic practices operate to impose order and stability upon the indeterminate play of signifiers in the discursive field: 'The unity, the internal homogeneity, which the term identity treats as foundational is not a natural, but a constructed form of closure' (p. 18). This closure is, in turn, tied intimately to political questions of identity. In order to understand the process by which subjectivities are 'gendered', 'sexualised' or 'racialised', we need to retain an appreciation of the necessary regulatory fiction that is identity and identification. Within some postmodern traditions, this 'fiction' is arguably accommodated by the way in which group identification and subject positions become conversational *categories* that may be invoked as a resource in discursively produced identities.

IDENTITY, IDEOLOGY AND DISCOURSE

A discursive view of identity can be realised in two ways: as a discursive performance or construction of identity in interaction, or as a historical set of structures with regulatory power upon identity. We begin with the latter formulation. In our historical summary of identity accounts, we have seen that two particular models predominate: that of the sovereign subject fashioning his or her own identity, and the individual psychological subject battling unconscious forces, cognitive mechanisms and schemas. Towards the end of the twentieth century, however, a strong trend emerged to reconfigure the subject as something sociocultural and sociohistorical: an *unfinished product of discourse*. This 'discursive turn' in critical and cultural theory engaged with potential impediments to self-determination, which had never previously been adequately addressed. This section, then, represents the 'other side of the story': the subjected, structured self, produced via a set of identifications in discourse.

The Marxist critic, Althusser (1971) theorised how people come to accept and even internalise existing social relations and norms. His infamous metaphor of *interpellation* describes how the subject comes to be produced within discourse:

> [T]he subordination of the subject takes place through language,
> as the effect of the authoritative voice that hails the individual . . .
> a policeman hails a passerby on the street, and the passerby
> turns and recognises himself as the one who is hailed. In the
> exchange by which that recognition is proffered and accepted,
> interpellation – the discursive production of the social subject –
> takes place. (Butler 1997: 5)

Like Althusser, the Italian political theorist, Gramsci (1971) saw power located not only in repressive institutions such as the police and the army, but also in the bourgeois culture industries, such as the arts, the media and education. Whilst the repressive institutions wielded power via coercion or oppression, the culture industries organised relations of power by persuasion, consensus and complicity. Hegemony, as a practice of power, operates largely through discourse: 'a way of representing the order of things which endowed its limiting perspectives with that natural or divine inevitability which makes them appear universal, natural and coterminous with "reality" itself' (S. Hall 1982: 65). Subjects give their consent to particular formations of power because the dominant cultural group generating the discourse persuades them of their essential 'truth', 'desirability' and 'naturalness'.

Althusser and Gramsci paved the way for Foucault's (1972) 'discursive production of the subject'. In Foucault's account, identities (or 'subjects') are regarded as the product of dominant discourses that are tied to social arrangements and practices. Foucault went further than Althusser in attempting to decentre or even erase the individual subject by focusing not so much upon the *process of identification*, as upon the actual discourses presumed to form the basis of subjectivity (Mills 1997).

The implications of this model for the operation of power are immediately apparent. If our identities are inscribed in available discourses, then these processes may operate to reproduce social inequalities, what Howard (2000: 385) terms the 'ideological constitution of the self'. In this account, the development of the individual becomes a process of acquiring a particular ideological version of the world, liable to serve hegemonic ends and preserve the status quo. Identity or identification thus becomes a colonising force, shaping and directing the individual. *1. Rationale or Methodology*

This type of discursive model implies an anti-essentialist view of identity, since it presumes all meaning to be situated not within the self, but in a series of representations mediated by semiotic systems such as language. For Derrida (1976), there is nothing beyond the text: reality is always representation, and therefore it is language that *constitutes* the 'I' of the subject and brings it into being through the process of signification. Similarly, in Laclau and Mouffe's 'Discourse Theory' (for example, 1985), they argue that social space (including identities) as a whole must be treated as discursive. In both theorisations, the self is no longer an essence, but a *description*. In turn, this challenge to the status of identity as essential and unified has led to its theoretical reconfiguration as constructed and fragmentary. The transient identifications we make with myriad, conflicting texts are deemed incapable of sustaining a coherent and stable selfhood.

The arguably one-sided model of identity outlined above, in which the subject is treated as a mere effect of discourse and ideology rather than an initiator of action, has prompted some modifications or challenges. This critique is twofold. On the one hand, the Foucauldian view of the 'subjected' self is deemed to sustain a paradox: 'Subjection consists precisely in this fundamental dependency on a discourse we never choose but that, paradoxically, initiates and sustains our agency' (Butler 1997: 2). On the other, this is a depressingly ineffectual version of the subject (what Eagleton [1996: 146] terms a form of 'self-incarceration'). We will deal with each of these criticisms in turn.

Butler (1997: 3–4) argues that links between theories of power and the domain of the psyche have been neglected 'in both Foucauldian and psychoanalytic orthodoxies . . . [and] we cannot presume a subject who performs an internalisation if the formation of the subject is in need of explanation'. This point is echoed by S. Hall (2000), who also identifies this paradox in Althusser's theory of interpellation, whereby for a subject to be capable of 'being hailed' it must have some kind of psychic coherence and existence prior to discourse. Hall's response to this conundrum is to attempt to reconcile the *external* discursive realm as described by Foucault, and the 'psychic acts of identification' as illuminated by psychoanalysis. For S. Hall (2000: 19), 'identity' is the meeting point, or the point of 'suture', between:

> on the one hand, the discourses and practices which attempt to 'interpellate', speak to us or hail us into place as the social subjects of particular discourses, and on the other hand, the processes which produce subjectivities, which construct us as subjects which can be 'spoken'. Identities are thus points of temporary attachment to the subject positions which discursive practices construct for us.

Though Foucault's early works 'offer a formal account of the construction of subject positions within discourse', they reveal 'little about why it is that certain individuals occupy some subject positions rather than others' (S. Hall 2000: 23). S. Hall employs the term 'identification' to embrace both discursive and psychoanalytic realms: the subject is not merely 'hailed' in a purely passive sense, but reflexively recognises and invests in the position.

The political toothlessness of a Foucauldian account of identity is addressed by Butler (1997), who attempts to evade the inevitable association between constructionism and linguistic determinism. Her 'solution' to this paradox is to theorise agency as 'exceed[ing] the power by which it is enabled' or as 'the assumption of a purpose unintended by power' (p. 15). In this account the subject is never fully determined by power, but neither is it fully determining. A similar solution, via the process of reflexivity and 'meta-awareness', is proposed by D. E. Hall (2004: 55), who argues that 'the possibility that one can gain control over that which has controlled one's consciousness *by becoming conscious of that dynamic of control* is the premise of most twentieth-century theories of politicized subjectivity'. Such a premise underpins the method of critical linguistics (the precursor of critical discourse analysis, see pages 43–5), in which detailed engagement with the workings of language, and an assumption that ideology is a result of particular configurations of lexico-grammatical items, may entail a certain empowerment for the analyst/subject.

Identity and performativity

Butler's response to Foucauldian accounts of identity is similarly addressed by her earlier theory of 'performativity', which theorises identity and, more specifically, gender, as discursively produced and 'performative' (Butler 1990). Like D. E. Hall, Butler is interested in reconciling psychoanalytic and Foucauldian traditions; indeed, she allies herself to a tradition of psychoanalytic-inspired French poststructuralist feminism. Here, the gendered subject is situated in, and endlessly produced through, discourse and therefore lacking in existential coherence and stability.

Butler's basic premise is that identity is a *discursive* practice, a discourse we both inhabit and employ, but also a *performance* with all the connotations of non-essentialism, transience, versatility and masquerade that this implies. It is an ostensibly appealing account precisely because it seems to allow us to dispense with the model of fixed, essential gender, governed by rational agency. Indeed it has been taken by some to imply a plural model of endless, limitless gender. However Butler has resolutely criticised those who take her theory to imply such liberatory freedoms: a subject may not transcend the gendered discourses within which it is situated: '[T]here is no gender identity behind the expressions of gender; that identity is performatively constituted by the very "expressions" that are said to be its results' (Butler 1990: 33). Nonetheless, she does engage with the view that subjects may enjoy performative agency through the repetitive 'iteration' of signs or acts: stylised, conventionalised gender performances which are informed by the authority of historical, anterior voices. Whilst the constraints of these pre-constituted histories mean that identity will not necessarily be the ideal product of social goals, nor the reflected process of social action, at the same time the very *repetition* that inheres in the performance of gender identity guarantees the *possibility* of change. Each new performance may entail the introduction of new elements: intertextual borrowings, resignification, reflexivity and disruptive tropes such as irony. In this way, Butler reformulates Foucault's 'unnuanced' account of the subject and reconfigures it in a way that is able to accommodate concepts of both structure and agency. A similar theorisation of discourse is described by Fairclough (2004: 141) who describes texts as instantiations 'which draw upon and instantiate the system', but because they may be located in new and potentially inexhaustible ways in social life, they are 'channels for socially driven changes in the language system'.

An earlier framework, also relying upon a dramaturgical metaphor, is Goffman's (1959) work on 'impression management' or 'the presentation of the self'. Goffman's work on the interactionally-produced self has its roots in the work of the American Pragmatists in the first half of the twentieth century, such as Mead (1934). Mead analysed the self as situated in everyday life and therefore theorised identity as contingently produced through interaction. This theoretical perspective was further developed in *symbolic interactionism* (Blumer 1969), which moved beyond Mead and the Pragmatists to address the 'how' of identity by analysing manifestations of the social self empirically. Like Butler, Goffman views interaction as a 'performance' shaped by the demands of the setting and addressee and constructed to maintain a mode of presentation consonant with participants' goals. In this way, identity for Goffman is a discursive process contingent upon the interactional context in which it occurs. Unlike Butler, however, Goffman's sense of 'performance' is unproblematically agentive, premised on a rational, intending self able to manage carefully an often idealised, consistent persona or 'front' in order to further his or her interpersonal objectives.

In this section we have surveyed the performative and postmodern turns across critical and cultural theory during the latter part of the twentieth century, in which formulations of identity underwent a fundamental transformation. The Foucauldian-inspired account of identity as an 'effect' of discourse challenges the view of the agentive self, whilst the performative view of identity as an actively constituted, performed discursive achievement challenges the premise of essential identity. Additionally, our discussion included critiques of the Foucauldian view of the subject as one that problematically managed to erase 'identity', despite its evident salience and political importance for participants in everyday life.

However, empirical studies of identity are relatively rare in the humanities and critical theory, despite the enthusiastic use of the term, 'discourse'. Recent efforts to encourage theoretical accounts of subjectivity to engage with the specifics of social contexts have prompted a more productive dialogue between critical theory and discourse analytic methods (for example, McIlvenny 2002). A discursive paradigm has now spread across the disciplinary spectrum, evidenced in the Foucauldian-inspired *critical discourse analysis*, the constructionist, anti-cognitivist approach of *discursive psychology*, the studies by *narrative analysts*, and the work of *conversation analysts* and *ethnomethodologists*. These different approaches share a focus on the central role of language and interaction as the site of identity *work*, although they vary in the extent to which 'identity' is actually theorised or treated as an analytic priority. Discourse-based approaches generally describe identity as a fluid, dynamic and shifting process, capable of both reproducing and destabilising the discursive order, but also one in which people's identity work is analysed in talk. It is to these discourse-based frameworks that we now turn.

DISCOURSE, INTERACTION AND IDENTITY

Self-consciousness . . . exists only in being acknowledged. (Hegel [1807] 1977: 111)

We have already encountered Hegel's contribution to the view that identity is a response to the activities of others, and this is the early philosophical position that comes closest to a 'discursive accomplishment' view. Hegel's contribution is usefully summarised by Williams (2000: 21):

> Human selves and their identities are not substances sedimented
> prior to persons' relationships with one another, but are
> constituted as properties only in and through the forms of human
> subjectivity that arise from and inform that participation and
> those relationships.

This perspective is echoed by Taylor (1989: 36), whose intersubjective concept of the reflective self adopts a Bakhtinian view of dialogism in which individuals are continuously formed through conversation or imagined conversation: 'I am a self only in relation to certain interlocutors . . . a self exists only within what I call webs of interlocution.'

In the previous section, we outlined the view of the historically-produced subject, but noted that most of the 'grand' theories of discourse outlined above engage in only the slenderest of ways with actual situated examples of language use, neglecting both linguistic detail and empirical evidence: *how* exactly are identities discursively produced or performed? What is the process or *mechanism* by which the individual speaker takes up positions in discourse to which they have been summoned? We also addressed the limitations of the Foucauldian account and its neglect of the agency of the subject. In this section, we argue that interaction-based theories of identity are capable of accommodating a number of these problems and paradoxes, such as the agency/structure dualism, or the apparent incompatibility of postmodern conceptions of fluid and shifting identity with the social investment in authentic, stable identity. These include 'micro-' level empirical approaches such as ethnomethodology, conversation analysis, membership categorisation analysis and discursive psychology, as well as the 'macro' methods of narrative analysis, positioning theory and critical discourse analysis. These approaches play a central analytical role in the remainder of the book: we discuss each of these just briefly in the remainder of this chapter, and in more detail in subsequent chapters.

Conversation analysis and ethnomethodology

Conversation analysis (CA) emerged in the 1960s and 1970s in the work of the American sociologist, Sacks, and his colleagues Schegloff and Jefferson. Sacks's aim was to develop an alternative to mainstream sociology: an observational science of society and social action that could be grounded in the 'details of actual events' (Sacks 1984a: 26). CA involves the study of technical transcripts of recordings of everyday and institutional talk of various kinds, focusing on the turn-by-turn organisation of interaction. It has developed into an influential programme of work with many findings about how conversation works.

Here is a quote from Sacks (1984b: 413), describing the basic aim of his project:

> The gross aim of the work I am doing is to see how finely the details of actual, naturally occurring conversation can be subjected to analysis that will yield the technology of conversation. The idea is to take singular sequences of conversation and tear them apart in such a way as to find rules, techniques, procedures, methods, maxims (a collection of terms that more or less relate to each other and that I use somewhat interchangeably) that can be used to generate the orderly features we find in the conversations we examine. The point is, then, to come back to the singular things we observe in a singular sequence, with some rules that handle those singular features, and also, necessarily, handle lots of other events.

This quote is strongly suggestive of CA's roots in ethnomethodology (EM): literally, 'the study of people's methods', a programme developed by another sociologist, Garfinkel (1967) which was, in turn influenced by the phenomenological philosophy of Schütz (for example, 1962) and Goffman's (for example, 1959) work on the interaction order. Garfinkel's basic idea was that people in society, or *members*, continuously engage in making sense of the world and, in so doing, methodically display their understandings of it: making their activities 'visibly-rational-and-reportable-for-all-practical-purposes' (Garfinkel 1967: vii). Language was central to the EM project of explicating members' methods for producing orderly and accountable social activities. For Schegloff (1996a: 4), talk is 'the primordial scene of social life . . . through which the work of the constitutive institutions of societies gets done'. It is through talking that we live our lives, build and maintain relationships, and establish '*who we are to one another*' (Drew 2005: 74, emphasis added). This last point hints at why CA can be a useful method for studying identity.

EM/CA adopts an indexical, context-bound understanding of identity, in which the self (if it is anything) is an oriented-to production and *accomplishment of interaction*. The sequential organisation of turns provides the 'context' for talk. This focus upon the situated context first prescribed in symbolic interactionism is more radically realised in EM/CA. A policy of 'ethnomethodological indifference' (or 'bracketing') means that analysts reject prior theories as resources for understanding the social world (Garfinkel and Sacks 1970). This means that in any study of 'identity', analysts do not assume its relevance ahead of their analysis. Instead, the focus is upon what members orient to in talk. As a key proponent of this position, Schegloff (1992a: 192, emphasis in original) writes:

> Showing that some orientation to context is demonstrably relevant to the participants is important . . . in order to ensure that what informs the analysis is what is relevant to *the participants in its target event*, and not what is relevant in the first instance to its academic analysts by virtue of the set of analytic and theoretical commitments which they bring to their work.

For Schegloff, claims of identity relevance, and, say, any forms of power or inequality that might be associated with them, must be demonstrably linked to particular actions in talk. Given that an individual person is categorisable via an infinite number of possible identity choices (for example, lecturer, mother, cellist, academic, Catholic and so on), the 'problem of relevance' means that analysts must attend to what is demonstrably relevant to participants 'at the moment that whatever we are trying to produce an account for occurs' (Schegloff 1991: 50), and inspect the talk for what is *consequential* for speakers. In a key paper, Schegloff (1997a) argues that approaches like critical discourse analysis, which often presuppose the relevance of identity categories (gender, ethnicity, class and so on) and power asymmetry, obscure what is actually happening in interaction by imposing the analysts' political and theoretical agendas onto the analysis. As Heritage (2005: 111) suggests, the aim of CA is to show 'context and identity have to be treated as inherently locally produced, incrementally developed, and, by extension, as transformable at any moment'.

So rather than assuming that a transcript will represent a 'synchronic snapshot' (Antaki et al. 1996: 477) of a stable consistent, immutable self, CA charts the identity work of shifting selves, contingent on the unfolding demands of talk's sequential environment. The idea that identity is an accomplishment, or performance (discussed throughout this chapter), can be traced to Garfinkel's (1967) work on the 'passing' of the male-to-female transsexual, 'Agnes'. In particular, contemporary arguments about gender identity as a performance are arguably rooted in his study of the 'managed achievement of sex status in an "intersexed" person' (p. 116). Through a case study of Agnes, Garfinkel aimed to make studiable the forms of common-sense reasoning that people use to produce themselves as gendered beings, as well as the recipes that regulate the 'seen but unnoticed' production of gender. Thus his task was to 'understand how membership in a sex category is sustained across a variety of practical circumstances and contingencies, at the same time preserving the sense that such membership is a natural, normal, moral fact of life' (Zimmerman 1992a: 195).

Despite the constructionist overtones of Garfinkel's work, EM/CA does not start out with a particular theoretical position on identity or its ontological status. The similarities and differences between ethnomethodology and postmodernism/social constructionism are hotly debated (for example, Hester and Francis 1997; Wowk forthcoming). However, EM/CA seems to avoid the essentialist assumptions of group accounts by showing *that and how* speakers occasion shifting, 'contradictory' identities and category memberships. Moreover, the empirical emphasis of CA presents a possible solution to those theorists anxious to delineate a theory of subjectivities as they emerge in discourse, and who find this element neglected in Foucauldian accounts. The fine-grained, turn-by-turn, indexical analysis is able to answer *how* precisely subjects 'fashion, stylize, produce, "perform" these positions in discourse' (S. Hall 2000: 27), and show practically and empirically how 'subject positions' are occupied in discourse (Wilkinson and Kitzinger 2003).

Membership categorisation analysis

Another approach rooted in ethnomethodology and Sacks's (1992) lectures on conversation is membership categorisation analysis (MCA). Whereas CA focuses on the turn-by-turn sequencing and organisation of talk, MCA also pays attention to the situated and reflexive use of categories in everyday and institutional interaction, as well as in interview, media and other textual data. Sacks focused on the local management of speakers' categorisations of themselves and others, treating talk as *culture-in-action* (Hester and Eglin 1997). His ideas were based around the membership categorisation device (MCD), which explains how categories may be hearably linked together by native speakers of a culture. He provides this now-classic example taken from a published collection of children's written stories: 'The baby cried. The mommy picked it up' (Sacks 1972a). Sacks claimed that we hear links between 'mommy' and 'baby', specifically that the mommy is the mommy of the baby. He provided an explanatory apparatus that allows this 'fact' to occur: the MCD. In this case, the MCD of 'family' allows the categories 'mommy' and 'baby' to be collected together. Categories (including 'members') are therefore linked to particular actions ('category-bound activities') or characteristics ('natural predicates'). Moreover, there are conventional expectations about what constitutes a 'mommy's' or 'baby's' normative behaviour, such that absences are accountable.

One way in which the categorisation process occurs is via the rich inferential resources, carried in categories, that are available to members of a culture. For example, a woman may be categorised as a 'mother', 'wife' or 'daughter'. Each of these categories carries with it a set of category-bound activities, predicates, or 'rights and obligations' that are expectable for a category incumbent to perform or possess (Watson and Weinberg 1982). As Widdicombe (1998a: 53) writes:

[T]he fact that categories are conventionally associated with activities, attributes, motives and so on makes them a powerful cultural resource in warranting, explaining and justifying behaviour. That is, whatever is known about the category can be invoked as being relevant to the person to whom the label is applied and provides a set of inferential resources by which to interpret and account for past or present conduct, or to inform predictions about likely future behaviour.

The analytic interest focuses on the multitude of potential identity ascriptions available to members of a culture and:

which of those identifications folk actually use, what features those identifications seem to carry, and to what end they are put . . . Membership of a category is ascribed (and rejected), avowed (and disavowed), displayed (and ignored) in local places and at certain times, and it does these things as part of the interactional work that constitutes people's lives. (Antaki and Widdicombe 1998b: 2)

Both EM/CA and MCA have been influential in the development of the next approach we discuss, discursive psychology.

Discursive psychology

The term 'discursive psychology' (DP) was first coined by Edwards and Potter (1992) in their book of the same title. DP's roots lie in a variety of theoretical-philosophical and empirical traditions. In addition to ethnomethodology and conversation analysis, these include the language philosophy of Wittgenstein (1958) and Austin (1962), constructivist approaches to human development (for example, Vygotsky 1978), and social studies of science (for example, Gilbert and Mulkay 1984).

DP's original goal was to unpack, critique and 'respecify' (Button 1991) the topics of social, developmental and cognitive psychology, and their methods of investigation (Edwards and Potter 2001). It therefore aimed to challenge mainstream psychology in much the same way that ethnomethodology and conversation analysis challenged mainstream sociology. DP comprises a fundamental shift from treating psychological states (for example, anger, intention, identity) as operating behind talk, causing people to say the things they do. In this way, DP challenges the traditional psychological treatment of language as a channel to under-lying mental processes, and the experimental study of those processes. Instead, it studies how common-sense psychological concepts are deployed in, oriented to and handled in the talk and texts that make up social life. Thus language is not treated as an externalisation of under-lying thoughts, motivations, memories or attitudes, but as *performative* of them. Note that these are not *ontological* claims about the status of 'inner minds' or 'external realities': the focus is on 'how descriptions of persons and their mental states are tied to, or implied by, descriptions of actions, events, and objects in the external world' (Edwards 2004: 186). The external world, or people's traits and dispositions, are treated by speakers as common-sense evidential resources for making inferences, building descriptions, resisting accusations of interest and so on.

DP understands discourse as *action oriented*, whereby actions are to be analysed in their situated context rather than as discrete units of activity (Potter 2003). Discourse is both *constructed*: people talk by deploying the resources (words, categories, common-sense ideas) available to them; and *constructive*: people build social worlds through descriptions and accounts thereof (Wetherell 2001). DP therefore examines members' *situated* descriptions of persons, categories, events and objects, drawing heavily on conversation analysis for its analytic method. It investigates, for example, how 'factual' descriptions are produced in order to undermine alternative versions, to appear objective and reasonable or weak and biased, and deal with the speaker's and others' motives, desires, intentions and interests (Billig 1987; Edwards and Potter 1992).

In terms of identity, DP has followed one of two main trajectories. First, in its original EM/CA-based formulation, several writers have combined Sacks's (1992) work on membership categorisation devices with sequential conversation analysis to examine the way social identities are claimed, resisted and otherwise put to use in interaction (for example, Antaki and Widdicombe 1998a; Dickerson 2000; Edwards 1998; Kerby and Rae 1998; Rapley 1998; Widdicombe and Wooffitt 1995). A second strand of identity-relevant work is more closely aligned to the poststructuralist and sociology-of-science approach in Potter and Wetherell's (1987) discourse analysis, developed more recently as *critical discursive psychology* by Wetherell and her colleagues (for example, Reynolds and Wetherell 2003; Seymour-Smith, Wetherell and Phoenix 2002; Wetherell and Edley 1999).

In a response to Schegloff's (1997a) position piece on conversation analysis, Wetherell (1998) rejects what she sees as a 'pure' CA approach, arguing that talk represents only a partial fragment of social life. Her proposed solution is a 'synthetic' approach to analysis, which combines CA-inspired attention to conversational detail with wider macrostructures and cultural-historical contexts. The resulting analytical approach is a 'genealogical' one which aims to trace normative practices, values and sense-making through both historical and synchronic intertextual analysis: 'The genealogical approach . . . suggests that in analysing our always partial piece of the argumentative texture we also look to the broader forms of intelligibility running through the texture more generally' (Wetherell 1998: 403). Analysts therefore claim to 'reach above' the text on the page (or start with macro social and political concerns) to make connections with the wider systems of meaning-making that people draw on. People may orient to, or position themselves against the 'interpretative repertoires', 'subject positions', 'ideological fields', 'discourses' (and so on) that the researcher claims are running through the textual data. As Kiesling (forthcoming) argues, people's discourse is incomprehensible unless we import some extra-textual, or *intertextual* (cf. Benwell 2005), resources. Holstein and Gubrium (2000: 3) similarly advocate combining ethnomethodological approaches with more Foucauldian inflected discourse analysis: '[A]s varied and inventively distinct as [stories of the self] are, they are stories "disciplined" by the diverse social circumstances and practices that produce them all'.

Researchers in this 'critical' tradition adopt the language of postmodernism in their descriptions of identity as multiple and conflictual, rather than unitary and coherent. A major contribution of discourse analytic work in social psychology was to celebrate *variability* as a feature of discourse, which seems to fit well with the postmodern notion of the multiply shifting identities that are on display in talk (Potter and Wetherell 1987). As Reynolds and Wetherell (2003: 496–7) suggest:

People's discourse tends to be highly variable and inconsistent
since different repertoires construct different versions and
evaluations of participants and events according to the rhetorical

demands of the immediate context. This variability allows for
ideological dilemmas to arise as people argue and puzzle over the
competing threads and work the inconsistencies between them.

However, Edwards and Stokoe (2004) argue that it would be a mistake to
take multiplicity as a claim about selfhood per se, that selves are generally
fractured and fleeting. In fact, consistency is crucially important to
people, not as an empirical generalisation about how consistent or variable people actually are, but as a participants' concerted accomplishment:
'[C]onsistency is a strongly sanctioned normative requirement for being
a sensible, accountable, rational, reliable human being . . . Fixity versus
multiplicity are not best used as rival ontologies of the self' (pp. 501–2).

   In addition to Wetherell's 'critical discursive psychology', there has
also been a shift amongst some discourse analysts in social psychology
towards psychoanalysis as a tool for theorising subjectivity. There has,
therefore, been a recent retreat backwards to using language to access the
'interior' world of subjectivity, or psychic reality (for example, Frosh,
Phoenix and Pattman 2003; Gough 2004; Hollway and Jefferson 2005).
This is because of criticisms some have about the inability of discourse-
based approaches to deal with the 'inner' unconscious mind, as well as the
phenomenological world of experience. We discuss the work of Hollway
and her colleagues in more detail in Chapter 4, in which we also examine
Wetherell's blend of macro- and micro-levels of analysis.

Narrative analysis and positioning theory

Another approach that combines macro- and micro-levels of analysis is
narrative analysis. However, as we will see in Chapter 4, 'narrative analysis' cannot be easily defined, as there are many different versions that have
developed in different academic disciplines with different theoretical
roots. Broadly speaking, narrative theorists argue that we live in a 'storytelling society' through which we make sense of our lives and the events
that happen in it (Denzin 2000). And, it is increasingly argued, it is in narrative tellings that we construct identities: selves are made coherent and
meaningful through the narrative or 'biographical' work that they do.

   The roots of contemporary narrative inquiry lie in literary theory, sociolinguistics, psychology and anthropology. Most narrative work adopts a
constructionist understanding of discourse, or narrative, as constitutive
of 'reality'. Selves and identities are therefore constituted in talk, and so
in narrative as 'storied selves' (Sarbin 1986). Through storytelling, narrators can produce 'edited' descriptions and evaluations of themselves
and others, making identity aspects more salient at certain points in the

story than others (Georgakopoulou 2002). Narrative researchers examine the kinds of stories narrators place themselves within, the identities that are performed and strategically claimed, why narratives are developed in particular ways and told in particular orders. Additionally, many narrative researchers examine the link between the immediate context of storytelling (that is, in a narrative interview, in a published text) and the wider 'master' narratives, or cultural story lines of which the local story is a part.

In recent years, and particularly within critical psychology, narrative analysis has been combined with another approach that attempts to make connections between macro-'discourses' and micro-levels of interaction: *positioning theory* (PT) (cf. Bamberg 2004; Davies and Harré 1990; Harré and van Langenhove 1991; 1999). Positioning theorists examine the co-construction of identity between speaker and audience. 'Positioning' refers to the process through which speakers adopt, resist and offer 'subject positions' that are made available in discourses or 'master narratives'. For example, speakers can position themselves (and others) as victims or perpetrators, active or passive, powerful or powerless and so on. The narrative of 'heterosexual romance' makes positions such as heroic prince/passive princess, or husband/wife available, and tells us what sorts of events do and do not belong to that narrative. People position themselves in relation to these subject positions, engaging in the 'discursive practices through which romantic love is made into a lived narrative' (Davies and Harré 1990: 53). PT posits an intimate connection between subject positioning (that is, identity) and social power relations, such that the analytic approach attends to identity work at the micro conversational and macro socio-political levels. However, like practitioners of critical discourse analysis, positioning theorists argue against a wholly agentless sense of master discourses in which identity construction is constrained by a restrictive set of subject positions available. Instead, they claim that people may resist, negotiate, modify or refuse positions, thus preserving individual agency in identity construction (Bamberg 2004; Day Sclater 2003).

Again, we discuss both narrative analysis and PT in some detail, with several empirical examples, later in the book. We now turn to our final framework for investigating the links between discourse and identity: critical discourse analysis.

Critical discourse analysis

Critical discourse analysis (CDA) is a Foucauldian-inspired, interdisciplinary branch of linguistics that attempts to explore the ideological workings of language in representing the world. CDA begins from the determinist premise that language is not a neutral or transparent medium that unproblematically reflects an objective reality. Rather, it is a form of ideological practice that mediates, influences and even constructs our experiences, identities and ways of viewing the world. Early incarnations of CDA, such as *critical linguistics* (Fowler et al. 1979; Kress and Hodge 1979), tend to adopt the intentionalist assumption that strategic 'word-smithing' is employed by writers and speakers. In this way, they treat discourse as a system of options from which we make choices, which are frequently linked to specific ideological effects.

Within CDA, identity is constituted in the grammar of language, both at the level of representation, in terms of the relationship between text and reader or conversational participants, and also in terms of the 'expressive' dimension that reveals a subject's attitudes and ideologies (Fairclough 1989). This expressive dimension has been characterised by Fairclough (2003) as an element of 'style', or 'way of being' and as incorporating both 'social' and 'personal' identity. More recently, CDA has been committed to identifying existing *discourses* associated with particular practices or institutions which may operate 'interdiscursively' across a range of contexts (for example, Chouliaraki and Fairclough 1999; Wodak and Meyer 2001), such as the language of the marketplace 'colonising' a public sector institution such as the university (Fairclough 1993). The assumption is that such discourses may operate as points of identification, to be taken up, ascribed to, or inculcated by social actors. CDA therefore has the explicitly political agenda of raising awareness about the ideological frameworks informing language choice, and the way that subjects may be constructed, represented and positioned by discourse, particularly in institutional contexts.

Two key assumptions underpin the practice of CDA. The first is that analysis should be based on a close engagement with the language of texts. The second is that language is a context-bound and social phenomenon and can be properly understood only by paying due attention to the social and cultural contexts in which it occurs. Like other methods we have discussed, CDA therefore attempts to forge links between 'micro' and 'macro' contexts, arguing that a complete analysis of discourse involves detailed engagement with a textual product ('text'), a consideration of the wider discourses in which the text is situated ('discursive practice'), and an analysis of the context of socio-cultural practice ('social practice'), such as production, transmission and consumption (Fairclough 1995).

Despite its ostensibly Foucauldian premise, CDA and its practitioners (particularly Fairclough) are clear that the Foucauldian account presents an abstracted and exaggerated version of the powerless 'subject'. Like positioning theory, CDA rejects this overly determinist account for failing to engage with the details of language as situated practice (Fairclough 1994). In this way, Fairclough echoes many of the concerns expressed by critics such as S. Hall (2000) and Butler (1997) and outlined earlier. By engaging with social *practice* in its situated linguistic contexts, and with scope for both compliance and resistance in our reception of discourse, he argues that we problematise 'any schematic view of the effect of discourse upon the constitution of, for example, social subjects' (Fairclough 1994: 61). In his recent work, Fairclough (2003: 159–60) again problematises this determinism, particularly in relation to identity. He describes a dialectical relationship between 'discourse/representation' and 'style/identification', by which discourses are 'inculcated' in identities, in a more agentive and on-going process of identification.

Nevertheless, CDA remains an approach firmly rooted in a historical, political and ideological view of the social world and explicitly deals with 'big' concerns such as power and social structure, and for this reason 'identity' in CDA, whilst realised at the micro-discursive level, tends to be treated as an index or expression of an ideological position (for example, 'student as consumer' [Fairclough 1993], 'father as baby entertainer' [Sunderland 2000]). As a 'top down' approach, it has been criticised for bringing *a priori* categories to the analysis that are 'known' to be relevant to interaction (whether in terms of representation or the position and intentions of the producer), and in this way arguably takes identity categories (such as 'gender') for granted. A more detailed explication of CDA can be found in Chapter 3 (*Institutional Identities*) and applied examples can be found both there and in Chapter 5 (*Commodified Identities*).

Beyond 'discourse' and identity

There are a number of debates about the different approaches to interaction analysis listed above, which we mention briefly here and discuss in more detail in relation to empirical examples throughout the rest of the book's chapters. These debates can be partitioned along two broad lines, both to do with particular understandings of language, what the analysis of discourse and interaction can and should be, and what might be, metaphorically speaking, 'beyond', 'beneath' or inaccessible in discourse. These concerns attend to what some see as an over-reliance on *discourse and the immediate interaction context* as the site for identity analysis, which, it is claimed, produces an impoverished analysis that fails to deal adequately with subjectivity, experience and the unconscious. Relatedly, it is argued that discourse approaches to identity neglect the material reality of the body and its relevance to social action. Bodies, it is argued, unlike discourse, are not *shared*, which introduces a crucial element of autonomy into an account of embodied identity (see Coupland and Gwyn 2003). We attend to this issue of identity work in the 'material' world, and the multiple semiotic fields of gesture and interaction, in Chapter 6 on *Spatial Identities*.

Because of these concerns, many analysts include *something other* than what discourse itself tells them about the identities being constructed within it. The 'something other' goes in one of two (or sometimes both) directions. In the new psychoanalytic tradition, analysts claim to 'look through' language and into the 'interior' world of the unconscious mind, to 'the divided psychosocial subject of unconscious conflict; a subject located in social realities mediated not only by social discourses but by psychic defences' (Hollway and Jefferson 2005: 147). Alternatively, as we have seen in 'macro' analytic approaches such as critical discursive psychology, narrative analysis, positioning theory and critical discourse analysis, analysts look to the discourses and ideologies that seem to be echoed in the immediate discourse context, using their cultural knowledge and theoretical-political concerns as interpretative resources. Both of these positions result in identity analysis that contrasts with the 'micro' analytic approaches of conversation analytic and discursive psychological approaches discussed earlier, in which 'going beyond the data' is to engage in what Schegloff (1997a) calls 'theoretical imperialism'. We have already mentioned the contrasting positions of Schegloff and Wetherell (1998), a key debate that we return to at relevant junctures throughout the book.

CONCLUSION

In this chapter, we have tracked the development of discourse and identity as a field of study with distinctive ways of theorising and investigating identity. Within our synopsis of identity accounts, we now find ourselves at a point where the book's main themes and preoccupations take off. The following chapters each take a different context for identity construction, and consider a range of analytic methods for identifying identity work in different kinds of discourse data. A commitment to an empirical and discourse-based understanding of identity enables us to explore the way in which dominant cultural understandings of identity categories are maintained, reproduced and normalised in everyday texts and practices of interaction. It enables us to put some 'flesh' on the bones of an abstract, theorised notion of 'identity', in ways that are empirically rich, methodologically grounded and compatible with some of the most exciting critical theoretical ideas to emerge at the turn of the twenty-first century.

CHAPTER 2

Conversational Identities

This chapter contrasts two approaches to the analysis of identity in conversation: *performativity* and *ethnomethodological* approaches. We have chosen to focus on just those studies that analyse identity in *everyday* interaction. This cuts out a large literature based on interview or focus group talk and studies of institutional settings. It is probably fair to say that the majority of discourse-based work analyses identity construction in interviews and focus groups, particularly in the study of gender identity, sexuality and ethnicity. Some of this interview-based work is discussed in Chapter 4 (*Narrative Identities*) and Chapter 5 (*Commodified Identities*). Identity practices in institutional talk are explored in Chapter 3 (*Institutional Identities*), Chapter 4 and Chapter 6 (*Spatial Identities*).

Let us start by considering some data, which come from a conversation between friends before embarking on a night out together:

Extract 2.1: VH: 3: 90–111 Simplified transcript

Dawn:	We need to go in three quarters of an hour.
Elena:	Okay.
Marie:	Oh MAN I haven't even gone out and I'm sweating like a rapist!
	(Laughter and 'horrified' reaction)
Marie:	I'm really hot!
Elena:	You two have got to stop with that phrase.
Marie:	Has anyone – has anyone got any really non sweaty stuff.
Dawn:	Dave has. But you'll smell like a man.
Kate:	(Laughs)
Marie:	Right has anyone got any feminine non sweaty stuff.
Kate:	I've got erm roll on.

We started this book with the notion that identity inhabits not minds, but the public and accountable realm of discourse. Identity is *performed, constructed, enacted* or *produced*, moment-to-moment, in everyday conversations like the one we have in our example. What can we say that is relevant to identity about the above conversation? At the grossest level, we might *inform* readers that the speakers are identity-categorisable in 'obvious' ways: they are friends, students, young, women, white, middle-class and so on. Much sociolinguistic and psychological research starts with these categories as variables that can be correlated with behaviours, including language behaviour.

However, the discursive approaches discussed in Chapter 1 study the way identity is constructed *in* discourse. From this perspective, analytic observations about the data are likely to focus on the *performance* of femininities in these women's interaction, or the shifts between traditional, 'appearance-oriented' femininity alongside more contemporary 'laddish' versions. Positioning theorists and critical discourse analysts might speculate about the 'discourses' that circulate in a culture (for example, 'discourse of appearance', 'discourse of heterosexual femininity'), which open up different subject positions for speakers to take up and resist (for example, 'traditional' versus 'progressive femininity'). Finally, ethnomethodologists might focus on how speakers categorise themselves and each other as types of persons (for example, 'man', 'rapist', 'feminine'), the actions accomplished by their category choices, and the turn-by-turn organisation of talk in which they are generated.

We start the chapter by examining empirical examples of the *performativity* theories discussed in Chapter 1, focusing on how ideas about identity-as-construction are analysed. Some of the problems with this approach are then discussed, before we move on to describe the first of our *ethnomethodological* (EM) approaches, conversation analysis (CA), as a different method for studying identity. We explain the basic concepts of CA and its roots in ethnomethodology, and then do the same for our second ethnomethodological perspective: membership categorisation analysis. Finally, a range of examples from key studies are presented, which aim to give readers a clear understanding of how different analysts identify identity in their conversational data.

PERFORMING IDENTITY IN CONVERSATION

Within the extensive literature on discourse and identity, the construction of *gender*, above all other identity categories, has produced an enormous body of work in recent years. For this reason, our discussion of 'performativity' approaches focuses on the construction of gender. But the illustrations and arguments apply equally to any other identity category one cares to investigate.

A unifying theme in discourse and identity research is the rejection of the 'essentialist' position that identity categories – including gender – are fixed, unitary properties of individuals. In contrast, constructionist researchers locate identity in the public realms of discourse and semiotic systems. From this perspective, identity is:

> ... not a universal of nature or culture but a question of performativity. (Barker and Galasiński 2001: 87)

> ... best viewed as the emergent product rather than the preexisting source of linguistic and other semiotic practices. (Bucholtz and Hall 2005: 588)

> ... the repeated stylisation of the body, a set of repeated acts within a rigid regulatory frame which congeal over time to produce the appearance of substance, of a 'natural' kind of being. (Butler 1990: 33)

> ... produced and sustained by human agents in interaction with one another. (Hare-Mustin and Maracek 1990: 533)

Much of this research has its 'social constructionist' roots in postmodernism, poststructuralism and literary theory, drawing heavily on the language of discourse and performativity in, for example, Foucault (1972), Butler (1990), and Bauman (2004). How researchers understand constructionism is crucial to how identity is subsequently theorised and analysed (Stokoe 2005). As this chapter contrasts performativity/constructionism with CA/EM, it is important to note that despite their surface similarity, 'EM/CA is not social constructionism' (Wowk forthcoming). This is a matter of considerable debate, with some writers emphasising the similarities between the two perspectives and others pointing out irreconcilable differences (for example, Button and Sharrock 2003; G. Watson 1994).

CA grew in close association with EM, and both CA and EM are often aligned with constructionism and thus anti-essentialism (for example, Buttny's [1993] 'conversation analytic constructionism'). Lynch (1993: xiv–xv) argues that both EM and versions of constructionism based in the 'sociology of scientific knowledge' (SSK) share a focus on the investigation of knowledge production. Both take an anti-foundationalist stance by 'seeking to describe the "achievement" of social order and the "construction" of social and scientific "facts", and both "explicitly renounce the use of transcendental standards of truth, rationality, and natural realism when seeking to describe and/or explain historical developments and contemporary practices" ' (ibid.). Additionally, the SSK concept of methodological relativism parallels ethnomethodology's efforts to 'point to some of the ways in which the world is *rendered* objectively available and is *maintained* as such' (Heritage 1984: 220, emphasis in original). Both EM and SSK place reality temporarily in brackets, adopting the position of 'ethnomethodological indifference' (Garfinkel and Sacks 1970: 63) in order to study how people maintain a sense of a commonly shared, objectively existing world.

With regard to identity, Kitzinger (2000: 170) writes: 'CA (while not compatible with essentialist feminism) is entirely compatible with (indeed, offers a method for) social constructionist, postmodern and queer theories which treat gender and sexuality as accomplishments rather than as pre-given categories.' Constructionism and EM both argue that things that we treat as 'facts' are discursive constructions or locally managed accomplishments, in which the object of study is the 'situated conduct of societal members in order to see how "objective" properties of social life are achieved' (West and Fenstermaker 1993: 152). Both argue that identity is not an individual attribute or role but an 'emergent feature' of social interactions.

However, some ethnomethodologists stress that EM/CA 'takes no position on the continuum between realism and social constructionism (or any other dualisms either) and is, if anything, a-constructionist' (Wowk forthcoming). In particular, EM does not take up a particular ontological position with regard to the nature of 'reality'. Instead, it 'respecifies' (Button 1991: 6) issues of what is real and authentic, including what is 'true' about identity, as matters for 'members' themselves to deal with. For EM, then, it is a 'basic mistake' to assume that we need to 'adopt a theoretical stance on "reality" at all' (Francis 1994: 105), partly because preoccupations about ontology inhibit close analysis of members' practices (Button and Sharrock 2003). It is interesting, then, that criticisms of CA approaches to the study of identity often point to its perceived 'extreme' constructionist/relativist or anti-essentialist stance (for example, Holmes and Meyerhoff 2003). But it is not clear that CA practitioners regard themselves as 'constructionist'.

We return to this and other debates about CA later in the chapter. For now, we flag the argument that not all 'constructionisms' are the same, and therefore should not be aligned with – or rejected – lightly. However, we move on now to examine some empirical translations of 'constructionism' and 'performativity'. We start with examples of the construction of feminine and masculine identities. Following these illustrations, we discuss some of the problems that arise in such analyses of identity construction.

Performing feminine identities

Our first example of identity construction is taken from the interactional sociolinguistic work of Coates (for example, 1996; 2003), who has written extensively about the performance of masculinity and femininity. Her work provides a rare example of the analysis of identity construction in everyday conversation. Coates collected data by asking participants to tape record themselves in everyday settings, whenever they felt comfortable to do so. Her analytic approach draws on Foucault's (1972) notion of 'discourses' and 'subject positions', and her focus is on the 'construction of gendered subjectivity', the 'construction of femininity' (Coates 1999: 123), and the performance of heterosexuality and hegemonic masculinity. For Coates, femininity is 'contradictory and precarious', as evidenced in the way, for instance, girls 'experiment with a range of discourse styles and subject positions' (ibid.).

The following extract comes from a friendship group comprised of, Coates tells us, 'white, middle-class girls'. Here, three 16-year-old girls are talking about the appearance of another girl, Sarah, who is trying on make-up. Note Coates's (1996: xii–xiv) use of a non-standard 'musical score' transcription system, in which square brackets indicate the start of overlap between utterances, a forward slash indicates the end of a tone group, and the broken lines indicate that turns within it are to be read simultaneously.

Extract 2.2: From Coates 1997: 286

GWEN:	doesn't she look really nice/
KATE:	yes/
EMILY:	she DOES look nice/

| GWEN: | [I think with the lipstick |
| KATE: | you should wear make-up [more often. Sarah/ |

GWEN:	it looks good/ [Sarah your lips . s- suit lipstick/
KATE:	[
EMILY:	yeah looks [nice/

GWEN:	((I'm saying)) what you said- big lips suit [lipstick
KATE:	ooohh yes/ [[share it
EMILY:	[you should be [a model

GWEN:	yeah/ looks good to me/ Sarah you look really nice/
KATE:	yeah/
EMILY:	models have big lips/

Coates focuses on the way these girls *do* or *perform* their identity, in the way they present themselves as gendered beings. She argues that the culture we live in offers an extensive range of ways of being, 'but all of these ways of being are gendered. These possible selves are not different kinds of person, but different kinds of woman [or man]' (1997: 285). Coates points to a number of identity-relevant features in the data:

1. the overt compliments that Gwen, Kate and Emily give to Sarah, as part of the routine friendship-maintenance work done in the group;
2. the co-construction of a shared world in which it is normal to wear make-up as part of 'doing femininity';
3. the high status afforded to looking 'nice' or 'good', having 'big' features, and looking like a model.

Coates argues that this sequence works to produce a particular kind of appearance-oriented, traditional, heteronormative femininity. However, she gives examples of many other kinds of gendered subject positions taken up across her data. For instance, the women and girls' 'discoursal range' includes factual/scientific, medical, maternal, repressive/patriarchal, romantic love, liberal and resistant/feminist, each of which 'give girls access to different femininities' (1999: 129). In general, their talk is characterised by a range of linguistic patterns, including sustained topical talk, supportive rather than interruptive overlapping talk, and the frequent use of minimal responses and hedges. Coates (1996) concludes that women's talk is like a 'jam session', and functions to develop the cooperative 'connectedness', solidarity and support of their friendship.

Performing masculine identities

The following example comes from another of Coates's (2003) studies, this time of men's conversations. The conversation takes place between four men, all carpenters, who are having a drink in a pub after work. One of the men, Alan, is telling a story:

Extract 2.3: From Coates 2003: 65

1	should've seen Jason on that digger though
2	yeah he . he come down the ((park)) part
3	where it's- the slope
4	then he's knocking down the front wall
5	and there was this big rock
6	and he couldn't get out
7	so he put a bit more . power on the thing

8   and . and the thing- the digger went <<SCOOPING NOISE>>

9   it nearly had him out <LAUGHS>

10   he come out all white.

Coates presents the responses to Alan's story in a separate transcript:

8	Alan:	it nearly had him out/ <LAUGHS> he come out all white/
	Chris:	<LAUGHS>
	Kevin:	<LAUGHS>
	John:	

9	Alan:	
	Chris:	<LAUGHS>
	Kevin:	I bet that could be dangerous [couldn't it/
	John:	(([hurt himself/))

10	Alan:	
	Chris:	
	Kevin:	if it fell [on your head)) it's quite-
	John:	[he- you know/-

11	Alan:	
	Chris:	<LAUGHS> [can I have some
	Kevin:	[it's quite big/ [
	John:	[he crapped himself/he [crapped himself/

12	Alan:	
	Chris:	pot noodles please Kevin <<SILLY VOICE>>
	Kevin:	<LAUGHS> [no/
	John:	[did he have to sit down

13	Alan:	he- he- well . he was quite frightened [actually/
	Chris:	[
	Kevin:	[
	John:	and stuff? [I know/

14	Alan:	cos- cos- [well yeah/
	Chris:	was it for you as well [mate?
	Kevin:	
	John:	I must admit-

15	Alan:	((well I still-))
	Chris:	did you go a bit white as well then did you?
	Kevin:	
	John:	god/

16	Alan:	
	Chris:	<u>don't get</u>
	Kevin:	
	John:	he was thinking 'god please don't wreck it'/

17	Alan:	
	Chris:	<u>any blood on it</u>/<SARCASTIC>
	Kevin:	is that the one with all the loa-

| 18 | Kevin: | lots of different things on it? |

[Discussion continues about different types and sizes of diggers]

Coates analyses the structure of the participants' stories, drawing on Labov's (1972) method of narrative analysis (see Chapter 4). She emphasises the speaker's gender in her analyses, claiming that the stories cannot be analysed 'without being aware of the gender of the narrators. They are men's stories, not stories in general [and] . . . one of the things they are doing is performing masculinity' (Coates 2003: 34–5). She contrasts this with women's storytelling, which she argues focuses on more ordinary and mundane topics (for example, comfortable shoes, buying a sundress) than the men's topics (for example, contests, violence, heroism, skills – although we might ask what is more mundane than diggers, pot noodles and 'shitting' yourself!). Men's stories 'perform dominant masculinity' via their choice of topic, focus on action, lack of hedging, competitive style, and use of taboo language (p. 110). Women's stories perform 'ideal femininity' (p. 111) through the choice of personal topics, displays of sensitivity, and telling stories cooperatively in sequences that orient to the importance of mutual understanding and friendship.

Coates argues that the 'digger' story, via its themes of power and machinery, 'constructs a dominant version of masculinity, where masculinity is bound up with physical strength' (p. 66). She points out that while Kevin and John 'orient to Alan's move to bring Jason's fear into focus', Kevin's comments about the danger of machinery are 'met by taunting from Chris' (p. 67). Chris's turn in lines 11 to 12 'can I have some pot noodles please Kevin', which is uttered in a 'silly voice', is the kind of thing that might be said by someone with a relative lack of power (for example, a child to its mother). Coates writes (p. 68):

By saying this, is Chris implying that Kevin's utterance *I bet that could be dangerous couldn't it if it fell on your head, it's quite- it's quite big* would be more appropriate in the mouth of a care-giver or food provider, i.e. in the mouth of a woman? Certainly, Chris seems to be trying to humiliate Kevin, to position him as being cowardly or a wimp, or being unmasculine. Perhaps by producing an utterance as irrelevant as this, he is implying that Kevin's utterances are equally out of place.

Coates further suggests that Chris finds Kevin's remarks threatening to his masculinity. Alan's turn (line 13), in which he admits to being 'quite frightened', is littered with false starts, hedges and hesitations, indicating a lack of comfort in delivering his answer. Chris then 'predictably . . . has a go at Alan with the direct challenge *was it for you as well mate?* . . . [to which] Alan replies *well yeah*, with his *well* again signalling that this is a dispreferred response' (p. 68). Chris's 'aggressive', 'face-threatening' turns at talk are evidence of his performance of 'hegemonic masculinity'. Overall, Coates claims that it is difficult for (these) men to discuss feelings of vulnerability, due to the 'peer pressure' that 'works to silence those who try to voice alternative masculinities' (p. 69).

Problems with performativity

Coates's work provides a clear example of what the *theory* of *identity-as-construction* might look like in empirical analyses of everyday conversational data. However, there are several problems with studies (and Coates is just one example) that identify themselves as constructionist, or as looking at gender-as-performance. First, they often make essentialist-sounding claims (implicitly or explicitly) about the way *women* perform *femininities* and *men* perform *masculinities* (Stokoe 2005). Many studies *start* with men's or women's talk as data, be it conversational or interview based, and *then* examine how masculinity and femininity are constructed within it. For instance, in Coates's examples, men perform masculinity by talking about commonsensical 'men's stuff' – fighting, machinery, power and contests – but it is not clear that the participants themselves treat it as 'men's stuff'.

What we have, then, is a tautology, in which researchers 'start out "knowing" the identities whose very constitution ought to be precisely the issue under investigation' (Kulick 1999: 6). Such constructionist studies therefore arrive at somewhat non-constructionist conclusions, leaving what Velody and Williams (1998) call a 'realist residue'. Moreover, there is no notion in such work that people are *not* performing gender: if the data do not look like standard femininity or masculinity the 'finding' is that gender identity is not what we thought it was, or that it is variable, inconsistent, postmodern, multiple or fragmentary (Edwards and Stokoe 2004). Thus the performance of gender is explained or accounted for in a circular fashion. Coates starts with gender categories and does not get very far away from them. These problems apply equally to studies of other identity categories, such as sexuality, class, ethnicity, age and religion.

Performativity studies therefore rely heavily on *analysts'* rather than *participants'* categories: on analysts' assumptions about what the speakers are doing rather than on what the speakers display to each other as relevant to their conversational business. In Coates's data, 'gender' and sexuality are the identity category analysed, yet the speakers are presumably lots of other things as well: students, Catholics, white, Jewish, middle-class, sons, daughters, pianists, British, Tories, bartenders and so on. Although we could argue that all discourse data are produced by people who can be gender-categorised, this is not enough to make gender *relevant* every time. Why is gender the omni-relevant category, and not any other? And at what point does gender *stop* being relevant? Stokoe (2005) argues that to impose a gendered reading onto data is doubly problematic: not only does it weave features of social life into data that may not appear concurrently relevant to speakers themselves, but it also precludes a focus on other potential relevancies.

So far, we have discussed one approach to analysing identity in discourse: the study of performativity in everyday conversation. We have discussed some problems with this kind of work, including the problem of assuming what identity is, and how it is relevant to talk, before analysing the data. In the next two sections, we consider an *ethnomethodological* approach to analysing everyday conversation and its key methods: conversation analysis (CA) and membership categorisation analysis (MCA). We start with CA's basic concepts and procedures, including Jefferson's transcription system. We also discuss some criticisms of CA, before moving on to MCA and its important contribution to understanding identity. Finally, we discuss a number of examples of empirical work in this contrasting tradition.

CONVERSATION ANALYSIS

As discussed in Chapter 1, CA is a method of analysing talk-in-interaction that emerged in the 1960s and 1970s in the work of Sacks and his colleagues, Jefferson and Schegloff. It involves the collection and transcription of audio and audio-visual recordings of conversation, which form the basis for investigating how the social order, including whatever topics and concerns are made relevant, are organised and managed as talk's practical business, or matters in hand. CA started out with Sacks's study of an 'institutional' setting (telephone calls to a suicide prevention centre), and this has remained a theme in CA work (see Chapter 3), but a great deal of work has been conducted on 'ordinary' conversations, often telephone or dinnertime talk.

CA uses *naturally occurring* data rather than what it regards as 'surrogates for the observation of actual behaviour' (such as interviews, observation, fieldnotes, invented examples or experiments), because such data are too much a product of the researcher's manipulation, direction and intervention (Heritage and Atkinson 1984: 2). CA also uses a unique method of transcription developed by Jefferson (2004a), which displays in its techniques what kind of approach CA is likely to be. Jefferson uses a modified version of standard orthography, which aims to capture how people say what they say. Her transcripts therefore incorporate information about the timing and placement of talk, intonation, prosody, speed, pitch, breathiness, laughter and so on. Before we go further into the chapter, it is necessary to explain these conventions, so that those unfamiliar with the system will know how to 'read' the data we discuss.

We return to the extract we introduced at the start of this chapter, but this time retranscribe the friends' conversation using Jefferson's system (see 'Data: Transcription, anonymization and ethics'):

Extract 2.4: VH: 3: 94–6

```
94    Marie:    <Oh ↑↑ma::n >I 'aven't e'en< gone OUt and I'm sweating
95              like a, (0.4) [rapist,]
96    Kate:                   [ Man. ]
```

The Jefferson system shows us that Marie's turn starts hurriedly (<), the word 'man' is delivered at a high pitch (↑↑) and the 'a' vowel sound is elongated or stretched (ma::n). Marie's words '>I 'aven't e'en<' are delivered more quickly than the surrounding talk, and there is increased volume and emphasis on 'OUt'. There is a 0.4 second pause before she utters the word 'rapist,'. Both the 'a,' before the pause and the word 'rapist,' have a comma at the end, indicating continuing intonation rather than a clause boundary. The full stop at the end of Kate's turn 'Man.' indicates a falling, or final, intonation contour rather than the end of a grammatical sentence. We can see that Kate overlaps the end of Marie's turn, such that they say 'rapist' and 'man' at the same time. Finally, line numbers are added, which helps analysts and readers identify target lines.

CA is sometimes criticised for this kind of microscopic focus on talk and perceived neglect of nonverbal behaviour. However Drew (2005: 78) points out that CA is also conducted on video recorded data that includes 'facial expression, gaze, posture, gesture, and so forth . . . in the sequential management and organization of interaction' (for example, Couper-Kulhen and Selting 1996; C. Goodwin 2003). Indeed, Schegloff (2005) has recently widened CA's unit of analysis, from '*talk*-in-interaction' to 'talk-and-other-conduct-in-interaction' – or *practices*-in-interaction – to capture the notion that CA conducted on videoed interaction captures its embodied nature (see Chapter 6 for an illustration). Having described the basic approach of CA, and its transcription system, we now move on to describe and illustrate some of its key concepts.

Basic concepts in CA

Drew (2005) provides a clear description of four basic CA concepts that underpin the study of talk's patterns and practices. First, a fundamental observation of Sacks and his colleagues (Sacks, Schegloff and Jefferson 1974) was that conversations are made up of *turns*, and that these are arranged one after another. Sacks et al. produced a model for how turn-taking works, a 'simplest systematics for the organisation of turn-taking', on the basis that talk is organised locally by and for participants. Turns are built out of *turn construction units* (TCUs), which can include single words, clauses, phrases or sentences, which are put together to do inter-actional work. TCUs are not definable outside of how they work in sequences, but are 'productions whose status as complete turns testifies to their *adequacy as units for the participants*' (Schegloff 1996b: 112, emphasis in original); that is, their *action* potential for participants. Thus the size of a turn – the number of incrementally-built TCUs – depends on what a turn is designed to do. A key issue for conversationalists is when a turn is complete, or about to be completed (a *transition relevance place*). Speakers need to know, throughout their own and others' turns, *when* to speak and *what is relevant* to say and do next.

The second basic concept, *turn design*, is to do with what goes into a turn. This depends on what action the turn is doing, and what is needed in terms of the 'details of the verbal constructions through which that action is to be accomplished' (Drew 2005: 83). The third concept is that conversation is not 'just talk'; it achieves *social actions* like inviting, accusing, joking or offering. This means that 'when we study conversation, we are investigating the actions and activities through which social life is conducted' (ibid.: 75). Speakers 'analyse' the prior speaker's turn, the result of which 'can be found in the construction of their fitted,

responsive turn' (ibid.: 75): what CA calls the 'next turn proof procedure'. CA therefore examines how speakers *orient* to whatever has gone
before and to what might come after. Heritage (2005: 105) describes three
CA claims about how participants *orient to interaction*:

1. Speakers address themselves to the preceding talk, demonstrating
   'responsiveness to context by producing a next action that a previous
   one projected';
2. 'In doing some current action, participants normally project (empirically) and require (normatively) that some next action (or one of
   a range of possible next actions) should be done by a subsequent
   participant';
3. 'By producing their next actions, participants show an understanding
   of a prior action and do so at a multiplicity of levels – for example, by
   an acceptance, someone can show an understanding that a prior turn
   was complete, that it was addressed to them, that it was an action of a
   particular type (e.g., an invitation), and so on. These understandings
   are (tacitly) confirmed or can become the objects of repair at any third
   turn in an on-going sequence. Through this process they become
   mutual understandings created through a sequential architecture of
   intersubjectivity'.

Antaki (1995) provides the following example. If a speaker says, 'Would
you like a biscuit?', their turn at talk can be treated by the recipient in a
number of ways. However, whatever the recipient says will be treated by
the speaker as a response to their offer (for example, 'Well, I just had one';
'I'd like one'; 'How dare you!', or they could remain silent). All of these
responses demonstrate a differing understanding by the recipient of the
action done in the first turn. As Sacks et al. (1974: 728) write:

> It is a systematic consequence of the turn-taking organization of
> conversation that it obliges its participants to display to each
> other, in a turn's talk, their understanding of other turns' talk.
> More generally, a turn's talk will be heard as directed to a prior
> turn's talk, unless special techniques are used to locate some other
> talk to which it is directed.

The final concept discussed by Drew (2005) is *sequence organisation*.
Conversational turns do not exist in isolation; they are connected with
each other 'in systematically organized patterns of sequences of turns'
(p. 89). An example of sequence organisation is the *adjacency pair*.
When one speaker takes a turn, they do a *first action*, such that the recipient is expected to respond with a turn that delivers a *second action*

paired with the first one. Examples of adjacency pairs are 'assessment/agreement', or 'offer/acceptance'. The production of the first part of an adjacency pair produces a context for the second part by making it *conditionally relevant*. That is to say, anything produced next is, for participants themselves, inspectable and accountable as an instance of that second pair part. So, on issuing an invitation, any response to it will be hearable as relevant to it, as being some kind of acceptance, rejection, stalling manoeuvre, account for non-acceptance or whatever.

Preference organisation (see Pomerantz 1984) is mainly a feature of these second pair parts. Second parts (acceptances, refusals and so on) are normatively provided for, in that there is an interactionally rather than psychologically defined 'preference' for one kind of response rather than another. For example, offers and invitations are normatively accepted rather than rejected. Rejection is marked as 'dispreferred' via the use of various discourse markers such as delay in producing the rejection and the production of an 'account' for it. Thus, normatively, participants account for rejections but not acceptances. However, if acceptances are accounted for in some way, they become marked as interactionally meaningful, as in some way unusual or special.

A demonstration

In order to illustrate these basic concepts, let us return again to our friends' conversation:

Extract 2.5: VH: 3: 104–7

```
104   Marie:    ↑Has ↑anyone- (0.2) ↑has ↑anyone got any really non:
105             sweaty stuff.
106   Dawn:     Dave has. but you'll smell like a ma:n,
107                   (0.9)
```

First, we can see that *turns are being taken* between Marie and Dawn, one after the other. Marie's turn is comprised of one *turn construction unit*. It starts with, '↑Has ↑anyone-', which we can see from the rest of her turn is the start of a *question*, which is also possibly a 'pre-request'. This in itself is not a TCU – it is not yet 'respondable' because no action has been completed. This does not mean that the words 'has anyone' could never comprise a complete TCU – any word(s) can, depending on the sequence. Here, however, Marie's turn starts with a 'repair', a feature of interaction that has been analysed extensively (for example, Curl 2005; Schegloff 2000). Doing repair involves a set of practices through which speakers orient to and resolve problems in speaking, hearing or understanding in talk. On line 104, the cut-off on 'anyone-' is a 'self-initiated' 'repair initiator'. Marie then produces the 'repair' itself within the same turn, by recycling her original turn beginning and finishing off the TCU. Her turn ends with falling intonation, it is grammatically complete, and is *treated as* complete (that is, as having accomplished its *action*) by Dawn, who takes the next turn. Thus the end of the word 'stuff.' is the first possible point of completion of the TCU, and constitutes a *transition-relevance place.*

Dawn's turn comprises two TCUs: 'Dave has.' and 'but you'll smell like a ma:n,'. The first TCU is the second pair part to the *adjacency pair* set up by Marie, and it shows us that Dawn has understood the first pair part to be doing a *question.* Dawn's first TCU is an *answer* and is the preferred turn: note that it is delivered straightforwardly, without delay, and with falling intonation (see Pomerantz 1984 for examples of 'dispreferred turn shapes'). However, Dawn adds another TCU, 'but you'll smell like a ma:n,', which qualifies and attends to 'Dave has' as maybe not fulfilling what Marie is looking for. Let us see what happens next:

Extract 2.6: VH: 3: 107–1

```
107                         (0.9)
108   Kate:       Eh [↑huh heh]
109   Marie:      [Right  has] anyone got any ↑fe:minine non sweaty
110               stuff.
111   Kate:       I've ↑got um:::, (0.6) roll on,
```

The gap at line 107, despite being less than a second long, is nevertheless quite a long time in conversation, and indicates an interactional glitch or trouble. As Kate starts to laugh, Marie reformulates her request, from '↑has ↑anyone got any really non: sweaty stuff.' to 'right has anyone got any ↑fe:minine non sweaty stuff.' We can see that, in her second go at the question, the word 'really' is replaced by 'feminine', and is produced with a hearable increase in pitch and emphasis. This replacement, together with the addition of 'right', displays her understanding of the problem with her previous question. Again, Marie's turn is the first part of another adjacency pair, to which Kate provides the preferred second pair part. We might also note the identity implications of these turns in that, for these speakers, smelling like a 'man' (when one is a 'woman') is treated as a trouble source, a laughable thing and something that needs attending to and fixing.

Participants' orientations and the problem of relevance

The essence of conversation analysis is, then, in questioning *how* conversational actions are accomplished as the systematic products of sequentially ordered interaction rather than *why* they are performed. A further characteristic of CA and ethnomethodology is that analysis is grounded in what participants do and say, rather than in what analysts take to be relevant as a function of their hypotheses, research questions, politics or theory. Therefore, CA does not rely on 'accounts they [the participants] pass on to anthropologists through interviews or an analyst's rendition of speaker's intentions' (M. H. Goodwin 1990: 6). Instead, 'the goal of analysis is to see how participants themselves analyse and "classify" the business that a turn in dialogue is attending to' (Widdicombe and Wooffitt 1995: 81).

This final point is particularly important for any CA study of identity. In our earlier discussion of Coates's studies of gender identity, we noted that her method built 'gender', an already-known explanatory category, into her analysis before the start. In contrast, Schegloff (1991; 1992a) suggests that to warrant an analytic claim that a particular identity category is relevant to any stretch of interaction, plus any forms of power/inequality that may be associated with them, the analyst must be able to demonstrate that such identities are linked to specific actions. There are two key issues for Schegloff:

1. *The problem of relevance*: Given the indefinitely extendable number of ways any person may be categorised, which from the range of identities is relevant? The answer is to go by what is demonstrably relevant to participants 'at the moment that whatever we are trying to produce an account for occurs' (Schegloff 1991: 50).
2. *The issue of procedural consequentiality*: If we can establish that a particular identity category is relevant, can we see that it is consequential for participants, in terms of its trajectory, content, character or organisational procedures? Does it have 'determinate consequences for the talk?' (Heritage 2005: 111).

If we take Schegloff's recommendations seriously, it means that analysts cannot claim the relevance of any identity category unless it can be shown that it does some business for the interacting parties. This means that:

> CA has an uncomfortable time with analysis in more abstract political terms, where the analyst may want to claim that two people are acting as they do because one is a man and the other a woman, and so on – even though there is no evidence in the

interaction (or even no interaction) that the category of 'gender' is relevant to *them*. (Antaki 2003)

This point has provoked substantial debate, particularly among feminist researchers, about CA's perceived 'narrow', 'limited', 'restricted' focus on participants' orientations at the expense of using background, contextual or political knowledge 'beyond the transcript' to inform analysis (for example, Holmes and Meyerhoff 2003; Wetherell 1998). Bucholtz (2003: 52) argues that CA's notion of indigenous context is severely limited because it means that 'only the most blatant aspects of gendered discourse practice, such as the overt topicalizing of gender in conversation, are likely candidates for Schegloffian analysis'. The argument runs something like this: people do not always make their referencing explicit, and the workings of power and oppression are often necessarily implicit, so a CA analysis cannot deal with such issues that would be of concern to feminists. Some CA writers have challenged this (see the section on 'unnoticed identities' at the end of this chapter). Their arguments suggest that it is only by attending to micro-level detail that we avoid reducing analysis to an over-theorised gloss that does not deal with what people are actually doing in talk (Widdicombe 1995; Wooffitt 2005).

Having explained the basic methods of CA, and some relevant debates regarding the analysis of identity, we now move on to discuss the second ethnomethodological approach to identity analysis: membership categorisation analysis. Following this, we discuss a number of examples that draw on both analytic frameworks.

MEMBERSHIP CATEGORISATION

In addition to the sequential analysis of talk, Sacks also developed a particularly identity-relevant theme in his work on 'membership categorisation devices' (MCDs). This has since been developed into a second analytic approach: *membership categorisation analysis* (MCA) (see Chapter 1). Since their inception, CA and MCA have often been discussed as separate methods, with CA arguably the prominent approach to studying talk-in-interaction. One reason for this perceived split is that those who took up Sacks's work on the MCD, which appeared early in his writings, have been criticised by Schegloff (1992b, 2002) for misunderstanding the legacy of Sacks's work. Schegloff has, in turn, been criticised for taking CA in a too-mechanical direction that fails to capture the spirit and breadth of Sacks's ideas, particularly its ethnomethodological basis. Others have aimed to integrate sequential analysis and MCA (for example, D.R. Watson 1997).

Politics aside, the basic 'difference' (if there is one) between CA and MCA is that whereas CA's explicit focus is on the turn-by-turn sequencing and organisation of talk, MCA is 'concerned with the organisation of common-sense knowledge in terms of the categories members employ in accomplishing their activities in and through talk' (Francis and Hester 2004: 21). As well as examining categories in ordinary conversation, MCA has been used to study a variety of discourse types including newspaper texts (for example, Eglin and Hester 1999), television and radio debate (for example, Leudar, Marsland and Nekvapil 2004), various institutional settings (for example, Wowk 1984), and interview data (for example, C.D. Baker 2004; Watson and Weinberg 1982).

In addition to the 'The baby cried' discussed in Chapter 1, another presentation of the MCD appeared in one of Sacks's (1972b) studies of telephone calls to the suicide prevention centre. One utterance found in these calls, said by the caller addressing the counsellor, was 'I have no one to turn to'. Sacks noted that this sounded like the caller had searched for someone, failed to produce a person to help them, but yet was, at that very moment, talking to someone they *had* turned to. He points out that when a person is in trouble, there is a set of people that one has a *right* to turn to, and another that one does not. Sacks called these classes of categories of persons *Relationship proper* (Rp), which would include people like family and friends, and *Relationship improper* (Ri), which would include strangers. Schegloff (2002: 12) suggests that 'the key point in understanding "no one to turn to" was the case in which the person with the strongest claim to be turned to would, by virtue of the trouble to be reported, be removed . . . from the category that made them turn-able to in the first place'. For instance, in the case of an adulterer, the partner is the most obliged and entitled person to turn to. But if adultery is the *trouble*, 'were it disclosed to the spouse, [it] could be grounds for the spouse to remove themselves from the category' (ibid.). And although the person cannot talk to a 'stranger' about their problems ('stranger' being in the class called Ri), the caller can turn to a category-member from the collection K (standing for 'professional knowledge'), in this case, a counsellor.

Sacks claimed that we need an apparatus for understanding the deployment of these kinds of categories in ordinary talk: the MCD. We described in Chapter 1 two parts of the MCD: a collection of *categories*, and some *rules of application*. Examples of *categories* include man, anarchist, teacher, Australian, guitarist, prostitute, lesbian and so on. Because a person can be categorised in a multitude of ways, the actual category used can do subtle inferential work. Categories that 'go together' are organised into *collections*, such as male/female, or teacher/doctor/lawyer. The practical reasoning by which categories and their inferences 'go together' is not, however, a strictly linguistic or logical kind of entailment. Rather, it is a common-sense, normative practice in which inferences and implications are generated and managed in actual stretches of talk, with regard to particular states of affairs or narrative accounts (Stokoe 2004).

In addition to the notions of *category-bound activities* and *predicates* outlined in Chapter 1 (see D. R. Watson 1978), Sacks's machinery includes a number of rules of application, which we summarise here. These include the *economy rule*, which means that even though numerous categories can potentially characterise a person, it is treated as referentially adequate to label anyone with just one. If two or more categories are proximately used to categorise two or more persons (for example, father and daughter), and both belong to a standard collection or MCD (for example, family), then the *consistency rule* applies, which means we hear the people referred to as members of the same family, as each other's father and daughter. Some categories are *duplicatively organised*, or have a 'teamlike' property, where members are normatively expected to have specifiable obligations to each other, like in families, sports teams, workplace groups and so on. Non-duplicative MCDs include the general set of 'occupations' (farmer, secretary and so on). Similarly, categories often sit together in paired relationships that Sacks called *Standardised Relational Pairs* (SRPs, such as 'mommy' and 'daddy', 'husband' and 'wife'), each with duties and obligations in relation to the other. Categories are also *indexical*, which is to say that their use 'takes a good part of [their] colour from the local surroundings' (Antaki 2003). Terms like 'his' and 'they' are clearly indexical because their reference changes in each context of use, but, as Antaki (2003) points out, less obvious examples like 'cyclist' can be understood differently according to their particular interactional environment: 'It can mean a professional sporting cyclist, if we are talking about the Tour de France; or a vulnerable kind of road-user, if we are talking about road safety; and so on.'

Like CA, MCA does not start by theorising about how categories are used in the abstract; rather, it studies their situated use. The 'problem of relevance' discussed earlier therefore applies equally to the study of membership categories. MCA does not assume from the outset which identity categories will be relevant to any interaction. As Schegloff (2002: 30) argues, we need evidence that the 'participants' production of the world was itself informed by these particular categorization devices . . . that the parties were oriented to that categorization device in producing and understanding – moment-by-moment – the conduct that composed its progressive realization'.

The aim of analysis is thus to explicate the actions being done by the particular categories that are used in talk. According to Sacks (1992, vol. 1:

40–1), 'a great deal of the knowledge that members of a society have about the society is stored in terms of these categories', which means that they are *inference rich*. Inferences may be picked up, developed or countered in subsequent turns. Sacks notes how categories can be implied, along with their inferential upshots, by mentioning some category-incumbent features. So merely by listing the (identifiably Jewish) names of those on trial for 'economic crimes' in the Soviet Union in the early 1960s, those names could be 'seeable as belonging to Jews. And you could leave the rest to everybody's routine procedures: "See? Jews are economic criminals, as everyone knew"' (Sacks 1992, vol. 1: 42).

Since category membership can be implied like this, we can see how it gives rise to a kind of *subversion* procedure (see Edwards 1991; 1997a). Sacks discusses how a suicidal man uses descriptions such as: 'I was a hair stylist at one time, I did some fashions now and then, things like that' to imply for himself the possibility of a homosexual identity. Later, the psychiatric social worker asks about his sexual problems, and the man ties sexuality to occupation ('You probably suspect, as far as the hair stylist and, uh, either one way or the other, they're straight or homosexual, something like that'). Sacks (1992, vol. 1: 47) claims that 'there are ways of introducing a piece of information and testing out whether it will be acceptable, which don't involve saying it.' People can therefore imply possible or provisional identity categorisations, of themselves or others, and inoculate themselves from the interactional consequences of overt categorisation: category membership is deniable. As Edwards (1997a) suggests, the semantic nature of categories, with labels and a set of incumbent, typical or associated features, lends them to being invoked implicationally, in the management of accountability. Again, this provides a functional basis for categories to have those semantic properties, rather than, say, fixed and definitive properties and membership.

CA and MCA

It is clear that categories have a crucial part to play in any study of conversational identity. Sacks's original observations about categories and identity, coupled with Schegloff's detailed method for analysing the sequential environments where categorisations happen, have encouraged a generation of researchers to concern themselves with the detail of interaction, and with 'the complex and variegated way in which identities are constituted in, and also help to constitute, everyday social actions' (Schenkein 1978: Williams 2000: 133, cf. Hadden and Lester 1978). CA and MCA provide methods for analysing identity that are based in systematic analyses of social action in everyday settings. They encourage researchers to put aside their preconceptions about what might intuitively or commonsensically be happening in interaction and focus instead on the detail of members' concerns and orientations.

We move on now to consider some examples of research that have used CA and/or MCA to study the production of identity in everyday conversation.

IDENTITY IN INTERACTION

The topic of 'identity' has engaged conversation analysts for some time. The majority of research has concentrated on 'institutional' rather than everyday settings, although we should note that 'everyday' identities can be occasioned in 'institutional' settings and vice versa (see Chapter 3, *Institutional Identities*). Before moving on to some examples, we return briefly to our earlier discussion of the relationship or otherwise between constructionism, the ontology of the self, and CA/EM.

Ethnomethodology and identity

We noted near the start of the chapter that, despite surface similarities, the ethnomethodological basis of CA does not supply the same understanding of the *performance of identities* that is found in the constructionist accounts discussed earlier in this chapter. In performativity/constructionist accounts, we find reference to identi*ties*, in the plural, as multiple and variable, *rather than* fixed, singular and rigid. What these kinds of descriptions do is produce *rival ontologies of the self*: the self is *either* multiple *or* fixed; constructed *or* essential (Edwards and Stokoe 2004). In everyday life, people tend to think of themselves *as* stable, consistent kinds of persons rather than a product of fleeting, shifting identities. However, ethnomethodologists argue that 'by asserting a *plurality* of realities [and therefore identities], constructionist[s] divorce themselves from a (purportedly naïve) common-sense view that there is *just one reality*' (Hester and Francis 1997: 96, emphasis in original). Ethnomethodologists therefore criticise constructionists for subverting and ironising 'participants' sense of the integrity of their world' (G. Watson 1992: 1). That is, people generally treat 'identity' as a real thing that they can know about themselves and other people, and are not generally sent into a 'metaphysical spin' about their own ontological status (Francis 1994).

In contrast to constructionism, then, the ontological status of the self is of no particular interest in CA/EM. Instead, the focus is on members' orientations to identity *as* (un)stable, (in)consistent, (in)coherent, and so on

(Edwards and Stokoe 2004). This view is articulated clearly by Widdicombe (1998b: 202–3) and worth quoting in full:

> Conversation analysts are keen to point out that they make no intentionalist assumptions; they do not, in other words assume an underlying self who brings about the actions accomplished in interaction. Nevertheless, the emphasis on interaction would seem to have several advantages in relation to the problems of the ontological status of the self, and of how to produce a social vision of selfhood without denying human agency . . . conversation analysis provides in rich technical detail how identities are mobilized in actual instances of interaction. In this way, conversation analysis avoids the problem of 'how subjects are positioned' or come to be incumbents of particular identities without the need for a theory of self. That is, instead of worrying about what kind of concept of self we need to explain how people are able to do things, conversation analysis focuses on the things they do. Agency, in the sense of an action orientation is thus intrinsic to the analysis without locating it in self-conscious intentionality, cognitive process, or in abstract discourses.

CA studies of identity do not therefore involve speculation about theory, discourses or power. Instead, they investigate *how* people display identity, in terms of ascribed membership of social categories, and the consequences of ascription or display for the interactional work being accomplished.

Antaki and Widdicombe (1998b) set out five principles of an ethnomethodological approach to identity. First, 'for a person to "have an identity" – whether he or she is the person speaking, being spoken to, or being spoken about – is to be cast into a category with *associated characteristics or features*' (p. 3, emphasis in original in this and following examples). This refers to Sacks's observations about categories, inferences and so on, such that for any given category there will be a list of actions, beliefs, feelings and obligations normatively associated with it. Second, 'such casting is *indexical and occasioned*' (p. 3), which means that the use of any category will only make sense in its local setting. Third, the practice of casting '*makes relevant* the identity to the interactional business going on' (p. 3). In other words, when a category is used in conversation, speakers may be oriented to its use, and this can, in turn, have an effect on the trajectory of the talk. Relatedly, 'the force of "having an identity" is in its *consequentiality* in the interaction' (p. 3) – what it allows, prompts or discourages participants to do next. Finally, all of these practices are 'visible in people's exploitation of the *structures of conversation*' (p. 3).

Varieties of identity in CA and MCA

Tracy (2002) describes several possibilities for understanding what 'identity' can mean for interaction analysts, including 'obvious' kinds of 'master identities' (such as gender, class, ethnicity), as well as 'interactional identities' (such as the roles people inhabit in particular contexts), 'relational identities' (such as friend, wife, partner) and 'personal identities' (such as people's personality and characteristics).

Other kinds of interaction-relevant identities include what Zimmerman (1998) calls 'discourse identities', 'situational identities' and 'transportable identities'. 'Discourse identities' are those that people inhabit in the course of talk's practical activities, such as story–teller/story–recipient, caller–called, repair–initiator, questioner and so on: 'In initiating an action, one party assumes a particular identity and projects a reciprocal identity for co-participants' (p. 90). 'Discourse identities', or *turn generated categories* in MCA, may therefore be generated by a turn-type (Psathas 1999 – see Chapter 3). For example, at the start of a telephone call, the adjacency pair 'summons–answer' occurs, in which the phone rings (first pair part) and then the person who has been called answers the phone (second pair part). The parties orient to each other in terms of the categories 'summoner–caller' and 'answerer–called'. Since the summoner initiates the call, the category has particular obligations and rights associated with it, such as giving a reason for the call. If they do not, it is likely to be noticeable, and the summoner may be accountable for not fulfilling their category-bound obligations.

'Situated identities' are those that come into play in a particular situation. So, in a telephone call to an emergency service, in addition to the 'discourse identities' of caller–called, identities such as 'citizen-complainant' will be displayed and oriented to. 'Transportable identities' are 'latent identities that "tag along" with individuals as they move through their daily routines' (Zimmerman 1998: 90). Examples include 'male', 'young' or 'white' (what Jayyusi [1984] calls 'perceptually-available categories'). However, Zimmerman (1998: 91, emphasis in original) suggests that:

> it is important to distinguish between the registering of *visible* indicators of identity and *oriented-to* identity which pertains to the capacity in which an individual should *act* in a particular situation. Thus, a participant may be *aware* of the fact that a co-interactant is classifiable as a young person or a male without orienting to those identities as being relevant to the instant interaction.

So, there are a number of ways of understanding 'identity', and many of these subcategories are rather different from the more 'obvious' identity categories like gender and ethnicity.

In the following examples, we use the term 'identity' in its broadest sense of *who people are to each other*. Our aim is to demonstrate the methods and procedures by which analysts identify identity work in everyday conversations. We start with two examples of 'categorial identities' in telephone conversation, in which speakers produce membership category-based identities for themselves and others. Next, we discuss what Sacks calls 'operative identities', in which identities are transformed within an episode of dinnertime talk. The third example focuses on 'relational identities', and analyses episodes from the friends' talk we introduced at the start of the chapter. Finally, we consider the concept of 'unnoticed identities', and discuss ways of analysing presupposed identities that are not explicitly articulated. This returns us to the key issue for a CA approach to identity: the problem of relevance.

Categorial identities

Many CA studies are based on analyses of telephone conversations, which have two immediate advantages for their analysability: they are easy to record, and the speakers have only the other person's voice to cue them into the turn-taking machinery (rather than the situation in face-to-face conversation). The speakers and analysts are therefore in the same position with regard to the interaction's intelligibility. The first example comes from Antaki's (2003) analysis of the following call from the 'Holt' corpus.

Extract 2.7: Holt 2: 3 in Antaki 2003

```
1   Mary:    One three five?
2                (.)
3   Les:     Oh hello, it's um: Lesley Field he:re,
4   Mary:    Oh ↑hello:,
5   Les:     Hello, .tch.h I hh↑ope you don't ↓mind me getting in
6            touch but uh- we metchor husband little while ago at a
7            Liberal meeting.
8                (0.3)
```

When making introductions, as Lesley is doing here, speakers choose how to describe themselves in order to make sense of the call and what it will be about. Antaki notes that Lesley gives her full name, 'Lesley Field', inviting the recipient to recognise her on such a basis. This particular *person reference practice* tells us something about the closeness or other-wise of Lesley's relationship to Mary: they are familiar, perhaps acquain-tances, but not close friends, sisters and so on (Schegloff 1996c). Lesley further adds that 'we m<u>e</u>tch<u>o</u>r husband little while ag<u>o</u> at a <u>L</u>iberal meeting' (lines 6–7). Her second turn therefore sets up two categorial identities: first, the 'we' implies membership of a team-type category, such as 'husband–wife'. Although 'we' could also suggest other teams (for example, mother–daughter, or friend–friend), by categorising the person they met as Mary's 'husband' we get a sense for which collection of categories is being invoked.

Second, the MCD 'political affiliation' is invoked through the explicit use of a category from the device: 'Liberal' (a former political party in the UK). Given the many ways that Lesley might have done this description and basis for calling, the fact that she did it this way 'means that Mary is to understand Lesley as calling on those two bases, and gives Mary a sense of what basis she herself is now expected to speak – a member of her own husband-and-wife team, and someone with Liberal sentiments. How these are relevant to the call, we don't know yet, but they set up a footing for it' (Antaki 2003). This example shows us that categorial identities are occasioned in talk not randomly but to do specific social actions. Antaki focuses on the use of explicit lexical items ('husband', 'Liberal'), along with their place in the conversational sequence, to analyse the identity practices in this extract.

Here is a second example, from another telephone call (Schegloff 2002).

Extract 2.8: TG, 6: 01–25 in Schegloff 2002

```
01  Bee:    nYeeah, .hh This feller I have-(nn)/(iv-) "felluh"; this
02          ma:n. (0.2) t! 'hhh He ha::(s)- uff-eh-who-who I
03          have fer Linguistics [ is   real ]ly too much, 'hh[h= ]
04  Ava:                         [Mm hm?]               [Mm [hm,]
05  Bee:                                                    [=I
06          didn' notice it b't there's a woman in my class who's a
07          nurse 'n. 'hh she said to me she s'd didju notice he has
08  →       a ha:ndicap en I said wha:t. Youknow I said I don't see
09          anything wrong wi[th im, she says his ha:nds.=
10  Ava:                     [Mm:.
11  Bee:    =.hhh So the nex' cla:ss hh! 'hh fer en hour en f'fteen
12          minutes I sat there en I watched his ha:n(h)ds hh
13          hh[.hhh=
14  Ava:      [ Why wha[t's the ma[tter   ] owith (his h'nds)/(him.)
15  Bee:               [=She    [meh-]
```

```
16   Bee:     .hhh t! 'hhh He keh- He doesn' haff uh-full use uff hiss
17            hh-fin::gers or something en he, tch! he ho:lds the
18            chalk funny=en, .hh=
19   Ava:     =Oh[:        ]
20   Bee:         [hhHe-] eh-his fingihs don't be:nd=en,
21            ['hhh-
22   Ava:     [Oh[::        ]
23   Bee:         [Yihknow] she really eh-so she said you know, theh-
24   →        ih- she's had experience. 'hh with handicap' people she
25            said but 'hh ih-yihknow ih-theh- in the fie:ld.
```

This sequence is analysed within a paper by Schegloff (2002), which focuses on Sacks's work on categories. Schegloff criticises contemporary MCA work for misunderstanding Sacks's original aims for MCDs. He suggests that MCA risks engaging in 'promiscuous' analytic practices by importing the 'common-sense' knowledge needed 'for the argument-in-progress' (Schegloff 2002: 36). To avoid this, he argues, the analysis of categories, predicates, and so on must be 'grounded in the conduct of the parties, not in the beliefs of the writer' (ibid.). An issue for Schegloff concerns the kinds of things that are properly treated as MCDs, as well as what counts as a category. The issue is not whether writers 'can or should make a category out of it' but whether 'parties to the conversation do so, and, if they do, what that sounds or looks like' (ibid.).

The above extract is littered with category terms, such as 'felluh', 'ma:n', 'woman', and 'nurse'. Additionally, the 'feller/man' Bee 'has fer Linguistics' is described as having 'a ha:ndicap' (line 8). However, Schegloff claims Bee is not *categorising* the 'feller', 'just' *describing* him. He argues that, in MCA terms, the consequential category work comes later. At line 24, Bee makes 'handicapped' *into* 'a category term in a manner quite distinct from the usage or practice at line 8 . . . Its members are referred to with plural terms; common-sense knowledge gets deployed about members of the category – people like that try even harder, they are harder markers, and so forth' (p. 39).

However, we suggest that other features of this conversation are equally interesting for the category work being done. It is not clear how any stretch of talk can be 'just' description, given that all words are categories, and that every word uttered could always have been otherwise formulated. For example, in her first turn, consider Bee's work in describing/categorising the feller/man/fer Linguistics:

```
01   Bee:     nYeeah, .hh This feller I have-(nn)/(iv-)"felluh"; this
02            ma:n. (0.2) t! 'hhh He ha::(s)- uff-eh-who-who I
```

```
03              have fer Linguistics [is    real]ly too much,  ˙hh[h=    ]
04  Ava:                          [Mm hm?]
```

Bee's turn includes a number of cut-offs, repair initiators, repairs and alternative ways of categorising the person being described. She *orients* to her use of the first category, 'feller' in the repair initiator. 'This feller I have-', such that ' "felluh" ', uttered in a 'quotation voice', tells us what is to be repaired and 'ma:n.' is a same-turn replacement category: Bee therefore *treats her own choice of category* as problematic. This is not 'just description'. Her 'person formulations', or category choices, are not neutral in terms of what they are accomplishing. At line 2, she starts to produce her description of his hands ('He ha::(s)'), but again abandons this and inserts further details about the man (who she has for Linguistics). Again, this tells us that Bee is treating her own description of the man as not sufficiently adequate for Ava to recognise him, or recognise the context of her description relevant to what is coming next. And it is after this additional information that Ava produces a 'continuer' ('Mm hm?'), which does the work of saying 'I understand, carry on'.

Operative identities

The next example comes from Sacks's (1992) work on categories and sequences. The conversation takes place between Ethel and Ben (a middle-aged couple), their son Bill (at whose house the conversation takes place), and Ethel and Ben's stepfather-in-law, Max. Ethel and Ben are trying to persuade Max to have some tinned herring they are eating for lunch. We have edited the lengthy original to focus on the identity-relevant sections:

Extract 2.9: From Sacks 1992, vol. 2: 318–20

```
Ben:     Hey this is the best herring you ever tasted I'll tellyuh
         that right now.
             (1.5)
Ethel:   Bring some out//so thet m- Max c'd have some too. =
Ben:     Oh boy.
Max:     = I don'wan'ny
             (0.5)
Ben:     They don' have this et Mayfair but dis is//delicious.
[. . .]
Ethel:   Ouu Max have a piece.
Ben:     This//is,
```

Ethel: Gesch//macht.

Ben: -the best you ever tasted.

[. . .]

Ben: Yer gonna be- You better eat sumpn becuz yer g'be
            hungry before we get there Max,

Max: So.

                (0.5)

Ben: C'mon now I don' wanche t'get sick.

Max: Get there I'll have so//mething.

Ben: Huh?

Max: When I get there I'll eat.

Ben: Yeah butche better eat sumpn before. Y'wan'lay down'n
            take a nap? =

Max: = No,

Ben: C'mon.

                (1.0)

Ben: Y'wan' sit up'n take a nap? B'cuz//I'm g'n take one,

( ):   ( )

                (1.5)

Ben: -inna minute,

                (1.0)

Ben: Det's, good.

                (2.0)

Ben: Det is really good.

                (1.0)

Ethel: Mm//m.

Ben: Honestly.

                (4.5)

Ben: C'mon.

                (1.0)

Max: ((very soft)) (I don't want.)

Ben: Max, please. I don' wanche t'get si:ck.

Max: I (won't) get sick,

[...]

Ethel: Max doesn't know what he's missin'.

Bill: He knows,

Ben: I don' wan' him tuh get sick I wannim tuh eat.

Max: ( )

                (1.5)

A striking feature of this conversation is Ethel and Ben's repeated assertions that Max should eat some of the herring. Sacks tracks the different *actions* done in the repetitions, from Ethel's initial *request* to bring some for Max, through several *offers* that he has one piece, to Ben's 'quasi-*threat*' that he may be sick if he does not eat something. Sacks (1992, vol. 2: 327) claims that these shifts are closely connected to 'some changes in identities of the parties'. He writes (pp. 327–8):

> What I mean by changes in identity doesn't have to do with changing from identities they had at the beginning to identities that they didn't have at the beginning, but it's changing of *operative identities*, where the identities they end up with are identities they have in the world, but that they weren't employing earlier on. And we'll find that the sequence of offer-transforms operates via a series of identity changes that progressively provide further transforms. That is to say, at the various rejection points, in order to proceed one has to find not simply another offer-form to proceed with, but a form which is usable for and by the one to whom you are offering.

Early in the talk, the basis on which offers are made invoke nothing more about the parties' identities than that they are eating dinner together: Ben and Ethel's offers are based on the fact that they have eaten the herring and liked it, and there is someone co-present who has not.

Sacks invites us to consider Ethel's activities in the sequence. Ethel is not the host: she is the mother of the host, and wife of the man who made the initial announcement about the herring. However, Sacks suggests that because the 'hostess' is not there (that is, Ethel and Ben's daughter-in-law), she is the only adult female present, which accounts for why she 'takes over the business of having the snack brought out' (p. 328). Moreover, Ethel has it brought out for Max, her stepfather-in-law and recent widower. It is these category incumbencies that entitle her to make the instruction to Ben and make it in its precise form: to bring it out in aid of Max. Not anyone can say things like: 'Bring it out . . . so X can have some.' These actions are do-able by virtue of the series of relationships that are in play, such as whose place it is, who is being referred to, who is being instructed, and so on.

After Max rejects the first offer, Ben and Ethel move on to reformulate it, 'under various relationships that parties might have to each other' (p. 329). More specifically, Sacks tells us that Max is a recent widower, and that Ben and Ethel, 'his kids, so to speak', are making relevant their responsibility for his care. If Max's wife was present, it might be up to her to insist he eat. So it is not just that Max is old – it is that he is old *and widowed*. Because of this, Ben and Ethel have 'come to figure' that they are responsible for him (p. 328):

> If he was offered some food and turned it down when his wife was sitting there, it would never occur to them that he's going to get sick . . . and it would just pass by. Maybe the wife would say something, maybe she wouldn't but if she didn't, that would be that. When he turns it down and he's now a widower, they can see their relationship involved in it, and find that they have to go on insisting.

Thus the series of offers made by Ben and Ethel enact the nature of their relationship with Max (p. 330):

> Their re-offers can be specifically turning him into a 'stubborn old man' that they are responsible for, i.e., that he doesn't take care of himself. In part, then, the person he becomes in the sequence, the person they have got to take care of, is an identity that the sequence brings into focus.

Sacks discusses Max's series of refusals offered during the course of the sequence as doing something like principled resistance: he will 'get them to recognize that they can't force him to do things or he's going to be turned into their little boy' (ibid.). However, Sacks is gloomy about the outcome of this conversation, in which Max's identity, a 'naturally evolved object', becomes 'an old man' and a 'burden'.

Sacks's analysis shows clearly how identities can evolve in conversations like this one (ibid.):

> We want to see how it is that the burden he ends up as being can be the product of some series of ways that he is pushed into doing, things like being obstinate, stubborn, laconically rejective, by virtue of the way that things are re-insisted for him extendedly, are not ever re-insisted for anybody else.

Nevertheless, one important point that readers may have spotted is that many of the identity categories Sacks uses in his analysis are not explicitly formulated in the data. How, then, can we understand and go along with Sacks, in the light of Schegloff's requirements about relevance and procedural consequentiality? Many would argue that these kinds of impositions are equal to the imposition of gender we saw in Coates's work. However, Williams (2000: 133) argues that:

> formulations of names for events, objects or persons have specific kinds of consequences, and that is why they are not always done, why indexicals can often be found in places where formulations would have been logically, if not, interactionally appropriate. The issue is that explicit formulations are interactionally consequential in ways that indexicals are not.

In other words, the fact that Ben and Ethel do not use the categories 'old man', 'widower', 'burden', and so on (which might initiate an argument or back-and-forth insulting) means that the implications of their activities remain deniable ('We didn't *say* you are a burden, Max!'). An indexical for 'being a burden', therefore, might be 'I don' wanche t'get si:ck.' We return to this issue at the end of the chapter.

Relational identities

The above example shows how speakers can ascribe particular identities to themselves and each other, as well as resist them. In the next example, we delve further into Sacks's ideas about how people display their relationships through the occasioning of *relationship categories* and the duties and obligations that are bound to incumbents of those categories: 'relational identities' (Tracy 2002). Pomerantz and Mandelbaum (2005) suggest that any CA study of relationship identity categories, such as friend–friend, mother–daughter, and so on, must address the following questions:

1. 'How does explicitly invoking a relationship category operate with respect to accomplishing a locally relevant conversational action?' (p. 150). Given that people do not generally declare the nature of their relationship explicitly ('I'm your friend'), what kinds of sequential environments do explicit formulations of such categories crop up in, and what actions do they accomplish?
2. 'How does performing certain conversational actions relate to enacting incumbency in specific relationship categories?' (ibid.). People can be held accountable if they do not engage in the activities bound to whatever category they are an incumbent of. For example, if two 'friends' meet each other in the street, they will normatively do what counts as appropriate greeting activities for members of that category. If they fail to engage in such conduct, they will be accountable for their missing activities.

An example of these kinds of activities is provided below, in another extract from the friends' talk discussed earlier in the chapter. The participants are chatting as they prepare for their night out:

Extract 2.10: VH: 1: 431–58

((music thumping in background))

```
431                        (9.0)
432   Sophie:   > I COUld've gone < spa::re when we was out that Saturday
433             though.=I could've gone spare. (.) when he,- (.) you
434             reme:mber when he jus' kinda like wa:lked pa:st.
435                        (0.8)
436   Sophie:   An' said hi: an:: jus' walked off.
437                        (1.2)
438   Chloe:    Y[eah.        ]
439   Sophie:    [YOU KNOW] how say like you see people y[ou know]=
440   Chloe:                                             [What on]=
441   Sophie:   =[   but   ] aren't really friends with,
442   Chloe:    =[Saturday?]
443                        (0.2)
444   Sophie:   When we was in Echoes.
445   Chloe:    Ye:ah,
446   Sophie:   An' y'know how sometimes y'see frie::nds,
447                        (0.6)
448   Chloe:    Oh:[:   ye::ah    ]
449   Sophie:      [Like people y'] not friends ↓with [but you jus' go]=
450   Chloe:                                          [You jus' go you]=
451   Sophie:   =[up,    ]
452   Chloe:    =[all right.]
453   Sophie:   Yeah an' walk off.
454                        (0.2)
455   Sophie:   ↑HE did ↑↑THAT to me! I thought that is so fuckin'
456             ru:de,
457                        (0.3)
458   Chloe:    That is ru:de.
```

Pomerantz and Mandelbaum (2005: 152–3) argue that 'in performing locally relevant conversational actions or activities, participants incorporate explicit relationship categories anticipating that recipients will draw on their understanding of the activities, motives, rights, responsibilities and/or competencies associated with incumbents of the category.' In the above extract, Sophie is recounting an incident in which she displays an understanding of the kinds of activities that are category-bound to 'friend'. She does this by contrasting the appropriate activities of 'friends' with the actions of one of her (unnamed) friends, as part of a complaint about him. Her complaint therefore turns on what 'friends' should and should not do when they meet each other. Her descriptions of this man's activities include that he 'jus' kinda like wa:lked pa:st' (line 434), and 'said hi: an:: jus' walked off' (line 436). As Sacks (1992, vol. 1: 585) claimed, 'the fact that activities are category-bound also allows us to praise or complain about "absent" activities'. Sophie spells this out, by reasoning that while these kinds of activities may be appropriate for people that you 'aren't really friends with' (line 441), for this man to do it is 'fuckin ru:de,' (lines 455–6). Chloe ratifies this assessment with a second, 'That is ru:de.', produced as *objective* and independent of Sophie's *subjective* assessment (see Edwards forthcoming; Wiggins and Potter 2003).

The participants' complaint depends on a shared understanding, displayed between Sophie and Chloe (particularly in their co-construction of what people who are not friends do, between lines 449–53), of the rights and obligations that are expectable of 'friends'. In Pomerantz and Mandelbaum's terms, the participants' display of shared knowledge and ratified assessment with regard to this subject also functions to establish/maintain their own incumbency in the relational pair 'friend–friend'.

In addition to explicit uses of relational category terms, Pomerantz and Mandelbaum suggest that people enact membership of relational identity categories 'by engaging in conduct regarded as appropriate for incumbents of the relationship category and by ratifying appropriate conduct when performed by the cointeractant' (p. 160). Members of the relationship 'friend–friend' can do this by, for example, discussing one's own personal problems and showing interest in the other's, making reference to shared experiences and so on. Here is another extract from the 'going out' corpus. One of the participants, Ryan, is just leaving (lines 404, 407 and 422 sound as though they come from another room in the house):

Extract 2.11: VH: 5: 396–35

396	Ryan:	Righ' guys yous have a good ni:ght,
397		(0.5)
398	Jenny:	Thank you [::, ((sing-song voice))
399	Ryan:	[N' be safe.
400	Anna:	Okay,=
401	Sasha:	=°Yeah.°
402		((Door banging))

```
403                     (0.6)
404   ?:        (      [    )              ] ((From a distance))
405   Ryan:            [Don't let her drink] too much.
406                     (0.5)
407   ?:        (°You what,°) ((From a distance?))
408   Jodie:    Mm[m.
409   ?:          [No.
410   Sasha:      [Oh no.
411                     (1.2)
412   Ryan:     O̲:h  [ (safe.) ]
413   Jodie:          [How can] we STO̲:p her.
414   ?:        >Eh [heh heh<
415   Jodie:        [To be fa̲:ir¿
416   ?:        >> Heh heh <<
417                     (0.7)
418   ?:        Mm.
419                     (0.5)
420   Sasha:    Anna you're £n̲ot a̲llowed to £d̲rink.
421                     (0.3)
422   Ryan:     You're <↑n̲ot a̲llowed to drink too mu̲:ch.> you're on
423             antibiotics. ((From a distance))
424                     (0.2)
425   Jenny:    Heh [heh heh
426   Anna:         [[↑↑I kno:[:w.
427   Jodie:                 [< anti[biotics,> that was v̲ery posh Ryan.  ]
428   Jenny:                       [↑Go:::d ↑uncle Ryan in the hou̲::se,]
429                     (1.5)
430   Anna:     He's quite se::xy. when he's domineering.
431   ?:        Huh-hoo:::[:
432   ?:                  [Eo:::::h.]
433   ?:        [UUURghhhhh ((vomit sound))
434   ?:        [UUURghhhhhhh[hh
435   ?:                      [↑↑Heh heh
```

What is interesting about this extract are the relationship categories in play, such as friend–friend/partner–partner, and how the participants orient to and manage their membership of these different categories through conversational actions. First, at the start of the sequence (lines 396–401), Ryan turns at lines 396–99 ('Righ' guys yous have a good ni̲:ght,' and 'N' be safe') accomplish the actions of parting/closing and displaying concern, and are taken up by the rest of the group, not just his partner Anna. Thus all parties are fulfilling the category-bound duties of offering and receiving concern and farewells, here as a group of 'friends'.

Second, Ryan's turns at lines 405 and 422–3 enact his 'partner–partner' relationship to Anna. His instruction at line 405 ('Don't let her drink too much') displays an entitlement to comment on and constrain Anna's behaviour, as well as an understanding that, as her 'friends', the others are also entitled to have a say about the amount she drinks. After an initial acceptance of his instruction (lines 408–10), the friends jointly display their knowledge of Anna, as someone who is not likely to be constrainable on this matter, via some irony and teasing. At line 420, Sasha reformulates Ryan's instruction in an ironic way ('Anna you're £not allowed to £drink.'), the irony detectable in the use of a 'smiley' tone and deliberate emphasis. This occasions Ryan to reformulate his earlier instruction at line 405. He firstly downgrades it, with emphasis on 'mu:ch' (line 422), and then provides an account for his initial instruction ('you're on antibiotics'). Ryan therefore treats his initial instruction as something accountable, something that he is not straightforwardly entitled to do. This may be occasioned by the other participants' responses, which again are ironic and deal with the *action* of doing instructions, rather than their contents ('<anti[biotics,> that was very posh Ryan.' and '↑Go:::d ↑uncle Ryan in the hou::se,').

What we can see here, as we saw in our earlier example of 'operative identities', is the participants' emergent categorisation of Ryan as going beyond the rights and obligations of his category entitlements as 'partner'; in fact, he is being a bit heavy handed. He has, in effect, become '*uncle* Ryan'. After a long pause, Anna attempts to account for Ryan's actions, saying 'he's quite se::xy. when he's domineering.' (line 430). This turn does several things. First, note it is sayable by Anna: she is entitled to comment on his 'sexiness' by virtue of her relational category membership as his 'partner'. It therefore continues to maintain these categories' incumbencies. Second, 'he's quite se::xy.' places Ryan back into the category 'partner' and removes him from 'uncle'. Third, 'when he's domineering.' maintains some solidarity with her friends, and formulates the upshot of their earlier ironic teasing: that he is being heavy handed. However, Anna's juxtaposition of 'sexy' and 'domineering' is also ironised by Anna's friends: they react with mock–disgust and horror.

One final identity-relevant suggestion about the extract above is that it reproduces *unnoticed heterosexuality* (Stokoe and Smithson 2002). We discuss this notion in the final section.

Unnoticed identities

Kitzinger (2005: 222) argues that many classic CA findings are based on analyses of *heterosexual* speakers, 'who reproduce, in their talk, a normative taken-for-granted heterosexual world'. Although speakers do not usually announce their sexual orientation, she suggests that the 'heterosexuality of the interactants is continually made apparent', albeit in an *unnoticed and unquestioned* way (pp. 222–3; p. 223):

> They are simply allowing their heterosexuality to be inferred in the course of some activity in which they are otherwise engaged. I suggest that this very inattentiveness to heterosexuality as a possible identity category, and the ease with which interactants make heterosexuality apparent without being thereby heard as 'talking about' heterosexuality, both reflects and constructs heteronormativity.

Kitzinger searches a number of CA corpora for speakers' use of categories and person reference terms, such as family and kinship terms, to see how these practices imply heterosexuality. Her first observation is a simple one: the topical content of the talk is often about heterosexual relationships. In the extract discussed above, Ryan and Anna enact a heterosexual relationship, and the other participants engage in some kind of assessment or evaluation of it.

Kitzinger also describes conversations in which unacquainted speakers use heterosexual kinship terms (for example, 'husband', 'mother-in-law', 'wife'), thereby presupposing heterosexuality. For example, from the 'Holt' corpus:

Extract 2.12: Holt: 1: 6 in Kitzinger 2005

```
01   Les:    Could you:r husband call on my mother in law please
02                  (0.4)
03   Les:    a:nd uh have a look at he:r um: (1.0) .h her
04           bathroo:m,
```

In this call, in which Lesley has called a plumber, she assumes she has made contact with the plumber's wife. She therefore 'formulates her request so as to display both her recipient's presumed heterosexual marital status, and her own, via her selection of "mother-in-law" as a person reference form' (p. 239). Kitzinger also suggests that although this person reference form is not selected '*in order* to display Lesley's marital status' – it does something specific in this sequence – it nevertheless 'gives off' a public, heterosexual identity.

The problem of relevance revisited

Our empirical examples – of *categorical, operative, relational* and *unnoticed* identities – illustrate CA's approach to analysis. The relevance of identity work is grounded in the endogenous orientations of speakers themselves, and tied to the accomplishment of specific actions. However, there are some differences between the ways this organising principle is actually executed. First, in Antaki's (2003) and Schegloff's (2002) analyses of 'categorial identities', as well as in our first example of 'relational identities', we can see how culture and its categories ('husbands', being 'handicapped', being 'friends') are produced in talk: speakers occasion categories and person formulations in ways that are 'procedurally consequential'. Although the analysts need to know the English language to understand these interactions, they do not need to import, 'promiscuously' in Schegloff's terms, prior personal beliefs about what might be going on, and why, to produce their analysis.

However, in Sacks's (1992) analysis of 'operative identities', as well as in our second example of 'relational identities', we can see that the analyst imports some kind of cultural knowledge in order to identify features and activities in the talk as category-bound to or implicative of, say, 'burden' or 'partner'. The analysis may make intuitive sense, but it is not entirely clear that the participants are operating with *precisely those* categories as relevant (and, as we discussed earlier, *precise categories* – 'partner', 'girlfriend', 'other half', 'the missus' and so on – are crucial). Of course, the fact that we cannot be clear about relevant categories is what gives language practices their *defeasibility*. In other words, the idea that Max is a 'burden' (or, as we discussed earlier, that Sacks's suicidal man was 'homosexual'), remains *provisional* and *deniable*.

In Kitzinger's (2005) study of 'unnoticed identities', she adds a different kind of cultural knowledge to her sequential analysis of kinship categories – a layer of ideological commentary about the wider political consequences of particular person descriptions. It is unclear whether her analysis is an example of Schegloff's (1997a) 'theoretical imperialism', or a translation of his recommendation that political commentary is legitimate as long as it does not precede 'technical' analysis. This taps into wider debates within feminism and CA about what counts as 'making relevant', 'participants' orientations', and so on, in interaction (Kitzinger 2000; Speer 1999, 2005; Stokoe

2000a; Stokoe and Smithson 2001; Stokoe and Weatherall 2002; Wetherell 1998). However, despite the subtle differences between the CA examples discussed above, there is a clear contrast between these examples and the 'performativity' approach discussed at the start of the chapter. In Coates's (for example, 1999) examples, 'gender' is used as an *a priori*, *explanatory resource* for analysis. And although she identifies what are plausibly 'category-bound features' of gender (for example, wearing lipstick is tied to being female; riding diggers is tied to being male), Coates starts with a ready-made theoretical grid (that gender is constructed, that discourses 'position' speakers and so on) and then searches for symptoms of her theory in the talk of men and women.

We return to these debates in the next two chapters as we continue to contrast macro- and micro-level methods of analysis.

CONCLUSION

This chapter has described, illustrated and evaluated two broad approaches to analysing identity practices in everyday conversation. We started with empirical studies of identity *performativity*, which comprise a large section of the literature within the broader field of discourse and identity. The theory that identities are performed or constructed in discourse is a truism across the social sciences, and we examined some particularly clear examples of how this theory can be studied in actual examples of everyday talk. We also discussed some criticisms of the approach, including the tendency to presuppose the relevance of identity categories rather than systematically explicating their constitution in discourse.

Next, we described a different approach to everyday identity analysis based in *ethnomethodology*, and its two related methods of conversation analysis and membership categorisation analysis. From this perspective, analysts need a clear warrant for claiming the relevance of identity categories to any stretch of interaction, one that is based in participants' own understandings and orientations. We also summarised some commonly perceived problems with these approaches, including CA's criteria for 'relevance', as well as for its lack of interest in 'macro' issues like politics and the 'invisible' workings of power. However, CA has a principled case for its apparent 'lack of interest' in these topics: that it provides an essential basis for analysing participants' oriented-to, practical concerns, while avoiding pre-theorising the analysis according to analysts' interpretative schemas and interests.

In the next chapter, we address these debates more closely, as we investigate identity practices in institutional settings, and compare CA to another method of interaction analysis: *Critical Discourse Analysis*.

CHAPTER 3

Institutional Identities

In this chapter, we consider how to define and analyse 'institutional identities'. This is a less straightforward task than might initially seem the case. Does 'institutional identity' refer to fixed, pre-discursive and complementary pair roles, such as 'doctor and patient'? Does it refer to *any* identity that is displayed in talk oriented to institutional goals or activities? Is it possible to identify 'institutionality' linguistically? Do we need prior knowledge of institutional encounters to understand them?

We discuss two main approaches to understanding the links between institutions, discourse and identity. Ethnomethodological and conversation analytic (CA) approaches argue that 'institutionality' or institutional identities are emergent properties of talk-in-interaction. In contrast, critical discourse analytic (CDA) accounts argue that the way people interact in social situations reflects existing macro-social forces. Any analysis of institutional interaction starts with a critique of institutions as structures that embed power relations within them. Institutional identity is therefore a function of these existing relations. The tension between these two approaches is summarised usefully by Mäkitalo and Saljö (2000: 48):

> Analysts interested in institutional talk . . . face an interesting dilemma when it comes to the problem of how to account for the relationship between structural and enduring features of institutions and interactional dynamics. At a general level, this issue concerns how talk is occasioned by organizational structure, and precisely what is 'institutional' about talk. This relation between stable communicative practices and in situ talk is often understood as a matter of trying to connect 'macro' (social structure) with 'micro' (talk) or, alternatively, the 'present' with the 'historical'.

The related questions of whether there is a distinct linguistic register or sequential organisation associated with 'institutional talk' (as opposed to 'ordinary talk') have exercised many analysts over the years. We can ask what makes institutional talk *institutional* – its organisation, people's orientation to institutional goals, lexical choices; or is it simply the setting – that it is talk that occurs in an institutional space?

We start the chapter by considering definitions of institutions, before moving on to examine conversation analytic and membership categorisation (MCA) approaches to the study of institutional identities. We discuss a number of features of institutional talk, as identified by conversation analysts, and illustrate these features with empirical examples. We consider and problematise the distinction between 'institutional' and 'ordinary' talk, and examine some of the debates about 'pure' and 'applied' work within CA itself. Next, we discuss related but distinct work on institutional identity within MCA, before moving on to contrast CA/MCA with CDA. CDA is argued by some to address those aspects of context, history and intertextuality neglected by ethnomethodological approaches. We explain the roots and methodology of CDA, before illustrating the approach using a case study analysis of a university promotional text. Finally, we contrast CA and CDA by producing competing analyses of a stretch of university tutorial interaction, to show readers what each approach can contribute to the study of institutional identity.

DEFINING INSTITUTIONS

'Institutions' are difficult to define. Commonly they are associated with physical buildings or organisational settings, such as hospitals, schools or law courts. Institutions are intrinsically bound up with *power*, and are often seen to serve the interests of powerful groups (for example, the government, the media). Agar (1985: 164) defines 'institution' as 'a socially legitimated expertise together with those persons authorized to implement it'. This suggests that institutions can comprise *any* powerful group and are not restricted to material locations. Agar's definition also sets up an expectation that institutions produce binary and asymmetrical roles: the 'expert' (or institutional representative) who is invested with institutional authority, and the 'non-expert' (usually the 'client'), who must accommodate to the institutional norms.

The idea that institutions automatically wield enormous power, crushing individuals' speaking rights and imposing unnatural bureaucracy upon everyday events, is informed by certain theorists (for example, Althusser 1971; Habermas 1987). These versions of 'institution' assume a coercive and one-sided imposition of power from one dominant party upon an unwilling and subordinate second party. However, other accounts adopt a more complex definition of power, treating it as a phenomenon that is achieved by persuasion, consensus and complicit cooperation, rather than coercion and oppression (for example, Foucault 1972). Similarly, Gramsci (1971: 12) introduced the concept of *hegemony* ('the "spontaneous" consent given by the great masses of the population to the general direction imposed on social life by the dominant fundamental group') to explain the way social groups sustain their prominent position in cultural life.

Another theorist to point to the 'productive' potential of institutional power is Giddens (1981: 67, emphasis in original), who argues: '[A]t the heart of both domination and power lies the *transformative capacity* of human action.' This is illustrated by Mayr's (2004) study of a prison's 'cognitive skills course', in which a programme designed to change offenders' thinking and behaviour also permitted self-reflection, creativity and resistance. The traditional view of institutional power has also been challenged within the field of Organisational Discourse Studies, which views organisations as 'comprised of paradoxical, fluid and contradictory processes and practices' (Grant and Iedema 2005: 49). These 'productive' views of power provide a theoretical lens through which to approach the analysis of institutional interaction. By construing power as a *process* or *action*, it is possible to analyse it as an interactionally-produced, moment-by-moment phenomenon. The analyst can chart the ways people are 'enlisted' by, demonstrate complicity with, negotiate or resist institutional agendas.

Having considered some definitions of what institutions are, we now move on to examine how these ideas about institutions may be explored empirically, starting with conversation analytic (CA) and membership categorisation analytic (MCA) research on institutional interactions.

CONVERSATION ANALYSIS AND INSTITUTIONAL TALK

Despite its interest in everyday talk, CA's roots lie in Sacks's study of an institutional setting: telephone calls to a Los Angeles Suicide Prevention Centre. However, there is a distinction in CA between 'ordinary' and 'institutional' talk. In Chapter 2, we focused solely on the former: everyday conversation occurring on the telephone, or at friends' houses. Ordinary talk (henceforth OT) is defined as 'forms of interaction that are not confined to specialized settings or to the execution of particular tasks'

(Heritage 2005: 104). The organisation of OT has been found to contrast systematically with institutional talk (henceforth IT). For example, in IT, participants have institution-specific goals to accomplish, and the kinds of contributions that can be made are constrained. The practices of ordinary conversation (as 'master institution') are therefore used and adapted in more 'specialized and restricted' contexts (Heritage 2005: 406). Hutchby (2005) alludes to a 'continuum' of institutionality: from the restricted speech exchange systems found in courtroom settings or news interviews, to radio phone-ins and counselling, in which 'there is no normatively sanctionable departure from conversational turn-taking, simply a mutual orientation to the tasks at hand'.

CA research has identified a number of recurrent features that characterise institutional talk, and by extension, identities in institutional contexts (Drew and Heritage 1992; Gunnarsson, Linell and Nordberg 1997; Thornborrow 2002). We move on now to review some of this work, organising our discussion under three thematic headings: *asymmetrical speaking rights*, *macrostructures and goal orientations* and *identity alignment with institutions*.

Asymmetrical speaking rights

> The institutional character of the interaction is embodied first and foremost in its *form* – most notably in turn-taking systems which depart substantially from the way in which turn-taking is managed in [ordinary] conversation. (Heritage and Greatbatch 1991: 95)

One of the most common observations about institutional dyads, particularly those involving the 'standardised relational pair' of 'institutional representative' and 'client', is that the institutional representative normatively has the right to *ask questions*. This has been observed in many institutional environments, including education (for example, Benwell 1996), medical encounters (for example, Frankel 1990), courtrooms (for example, Atkinson and Drew 1979), helpline interaction (for example, Potter and Hepburn 2003), psychiatric assessment (for example, Antaki 2002), news interviews (for example, Greatbatch 1992) and neighbour mediation (Edwards and Stokoe 2005).

In OT, talk's topics, speaker order and turn allocation are unpredictable. In IT, however, these things are organised differently from the outset – explicitly and predictably. Some types of IT, such as classrooms and news interviews, have pre-allocated turn types. One party, such as the teacher or interviewer, asks questions, and the other party answers.

Such implicit organisational rules may be displayed 'in the breach': for instance, 'client'-initiated questions are generally dispreferred and sanctioned in some way (Frankel 1990). The phenomenon of breaching can be analytically useful since it tells us that 'the rules that we initially hypothesize from empirical regularities in the participants' actions are in fact rules that participants recognize that they *should* follow as a moral obligation' (Heritage 2005: 117).

For example, studies of news interviews reveal context-specific turn-taking patterns. Whilst the news interview is a forum in which both parties *may* be 'powerful', they are constrained by speaking rights tied to their respective institutional roles. A key feature is that interviewers (IR) do not state their own opinions and thus tend to ask questions rather than make statements. Furthermore, they avoid any kind of evaluative comment, even in the form of minimal response tokens – their task is to elicit opinions and information from the interviewee (IE) on behalf of the audience. This is due to a legal constraint on broadcast journalists to maintain impartiality in news coverage (Greatbatch 1998). Therefore, unlike the three-part sequence of 'Initiation–Response–Evaluation' found in classroom interaction (Mehan 1979), there is no third turn. The sequence runs 'Question–Answer–next Q–A', and the lack of IR response contributes to the accomplishment of neutralism (Clayman 1992; Greatbatch 1998). To achieve a critical interview then, it is necessary for IRs to find ways of managing the institutional constraint of neutralism. This may be achieved by the strategy of 'formulations', in which the IR glosses what the IE has just said:

Extract 3.1: From Harris 1991: 85

IR: Are you saying Neil that the uh nightmare or the Labour nightmare – if you like
– of Britain becoming a sort of land-based aircraft carrier – for want of another
word – are you saying this has at last come true?

Other strategies, illustrated with data we recorded from a BBC radio news interview (between the interviewer, John Humphreys and the former Conservative leader, Iain Duncan Smith) include:

Embedding provocative propositions within questions:

Extract 3.2: BBC Radio 4 'Today', October 2003

JH: Isn't there a bit of dignity involved in all of this and shouldn't the leader of the
opposition at least uh respect the proprieties here?

Quoting sources to express an evaluative view:

Extract 3.3: BBC Radio 4 'Today', October 2003

JH: What they're saying is you may have had a bit of a breathing space as a
       result of yesterday but there is still you still have to prove yourself

*Asking questions which anticipate answers known to be opposite to
interviewee's stance:*

Extract 3.4: BBC Radio 4 'Today', October 2003

JH: Is there not an argument that says you've given it a good shot you've
       tried it now for a couple of years you simply haven't carried the party with
       you?

These strategies mean that a formally neutral stance can still embody
negative evaluations or criticism. In Harris's example, formulations
served not only to make the positions in the interview clear for the sake
of the listeners, but are also a powerful site of meaning *creation* and can
promote the IR's agenda.

The IE, in contrast, is obliged by the goals and rules of the news interview to *answer* the IR's *questions*. However, *avoiding* answering the question is often a key aim for IEs, and is a common criticism levelled at
politicians (Harris 1991). For this reason, IRs often use closed 'yes–no'
questions, so that IE failure to produce a response creates a noticeable
absence. Since the institutional constraints of news interviews mean that
the IR is likely to control the agenda, the interviewee (IE) adopts strategies for gaining control. These include shifting the agenda before and
after an answer, or not answering at all by changing the topic (Greatbatch
1998). News interviews therefore place particular institutional constraints, some more explicitly sanctionable than others, on the respective
'discourse identities' (Zimmerman 1998) of IR and IE. However, both
parties employ conversational strategies to limit the disadvantage
imposed by these institutional 'rules'.

Macrostructures and goal orientations

Another common feature of IT is that it is driven and structured by institutional goals and agendas. This makes IT less open-ended than OT,
and produces a predictably sequenced, generic macrostructure. Although
OT may also possess structural features such as openings and closings,
these aspects are generally more fluid than in IT. If asked to reorder
a jumbled-up sequence of institutional talk, such as a service encounter,

most people have no difficulty recognising the correct sequence of turns, such as 'greeting', 'service request', 'transaction', 'leavetaking' (Ventola 1987). A jumbled-up sequence of casual conversation, however, is likely to prove much more challenging to return to its original sequential organisation.

The structural organisation of an institutional encounter is built from a regular sequence of particular kinds of turns. For example, in Zimmerman's (for example, 1992b) studies of telephone calls to the emergency services, the overall structure is: opening → request → interrogative series → response → closing. Each part accomplishes a particular action and pursues a particular interactional goal. Here is an extract from his data:

Extract 3.5: From Zimmerman 1984: 214

```
 1   911:   Midcity Emergency::,
 2          (.)
 3   C:     U::m yeah (.)
 4          somebody just vandalized my car,
 5          (0.3)
 6   911:   What's your address.
 7   C:     three oh one six maple
 8   911:   Is this a house or an apartment.
 9   C:     I::t's a house
10   911:   (Uh-) your last name.
11   C:     Minsky
12   911:   How do you spell it?
13   C:     M I N S K Y
14   911:   We'll send someone out to see you.
15   C:     Thank you. =
16   911:   =Mmhm=
17   911:   =bye.=
18   C:     =Bye.
```

In this call, lines 1–3 comprise the opening, lines 4–5 the request, lines 6–13 the interrogative series, lines 14–16 the response and lines 17–8 the closing. The caller's description of trouble in line 4 is treated as the first part of a request–response adjacency pair (Heritage 2005). After the series of question–answer pairs between lines 6 and 13, the call taker 'grants the request and is thanked as a "benefactor"' (p. 121). Zimmerman (1992b) suggests that, although the calls vary in length, particularly during the interrogative sequence, the overall structure remains constant across his data. Both parties are oriented to particular institutional goals and subgoals, 'and each is jointly constructed (or co-constructed) by both participants in terms of the constituent tasks of the call' (Heritage 2005: 121).

Heritage (2005) argues that the aim of producing a structural description of an institutional encounter is not to pin down every section of it, nor to claim that each part of the sequence will occur each time or in the same way (speakers often return to previous parts of their interactional task previously treated as complete). However, the issue of whether or not it is possible to describe the macrostructure of IT with any degree of reliability is a contentious one, which tends to divide opinion along disciplinary lines. For practitioners of CA, IT, like any other speech event, is a locally managed event constrained only by participants' orientation to prior and subsequent turns. In contrast, as we will see later, critical discourse analysts assume that IT exemplifies the principles of 'genealogy' (Foucault 1977), 'genre' (Bakhtin 1986) or 'iteration' (Butler 1990) in language. Speech events are treated as *historicised artefacts*, inherited from anterior uses and regularised by ritual public practice (see also similar ideas in genre analysis, for example, Bhatia 1993). This historical dimension has implications for *agency* since it implies that IT and texts are determined by *a priori* scripts, rituals and agendas.

Identity alignment with institutions

A final characterising feature of IT can be found in the devices used by participants that display a specific alignment with the institution. A clear example is role categories such as 'teacher' or 'judge', although such titles are rarely verbalised explicitly in institutional talk, roles being more commonly indicated by the use of titles or modes of address, such as 'Sir/Miss' (teacher) or 'M'lord' (judge).

Drew and Sorjonen (1997: 97) also identify *person reference* as a means of enacting institutional identity: 'participants may display their orientation to their acting as incumbents of an institutional role . . . by using a personal pronoun which indexes their institutional identity rather than their personal identity'. The most common forms are the first person plurals 'we' and 'us' (for example, 'We are a company of international insurance and pensions consultants'). Other examples of institutional alignment include 'setting-specific, situationally appropriate' lexical choice (p. 99). This can include specialised vocabulary, although 'jargon' is by no means the only institutional use of lexis. In a study of expressions of concern in calls to a child protection helpline, Potter (2005; see also Potter and Hepburn 2003) demonstrates how certain lexical choices may accomplish institutional business without being 'specialised' or 'technical'. The expression of concern (for example, 'I'm a bit concerned . . .') has a number of institutional functions in the telephone sequence, including prefacing and projecting an extended narrative and displaying the caller's stance. It also 'manages a fundamental epistemological asymmetry': the caller has knowledge of suspected abuse, but the child protection officer has knowledge of institutional procedure (Potter 2005: 15).

IT has also been distinguished from OT by the way in which different *pragmatic* meanings or inferences tend to arise from types of utterances. For example, teachers' questions in classrooms tend to do the action of 'testing' rather than 'information seeking'. In medical encounters, questions such as 'How are you?' lose their 'small-talk' status and are treated as more literal elicitations of a description of symptoms. Finally, Heritage (2005) notes that the institutional imperative to preserve neutrality in news interviews means that a knowledge receipt token (such as 'oh') is avoided. However, this absence is not taken to mean that the interviewer has not heard or acknowledged the turn, as it might in OT. An alignment to these pragmatic implicatures is also a means of expressing institutional identity.

Complicating the institutional versus ordinary talk distinction

The following extract is taken from a service encounter in a post office:

Extract 3.6: From Carter and McCarthy 1997: 92

1	<S01>	Can I have a second class stamp please Les?
2	<S02>	You can . . . there we are
3	<S01>	[Thank you
4	<S02>	[And one penny thank you
5	<S01>	That's for me to spend is it?
6	<S02>	That's right
7	<S01>	I bought a new book of ten first class when I was in town today
8		and I've left them at home in me shopping bag
9	<S02>	Have you?
10	<S01>	And I've got one left
11	<S02>	Oh dear [laughs]
12	<S01>	Bye
13	<S02>	Bye

In this sequence, in addition to the request–response sequence at lines 1–2, the customer initiates a new sequence after the institutional task is complete (line 5). This social/humorous sequence is not obviously 'institutional' or part of the 'business at hand'. Such sequences support the argument that IT is a distinct register, identified by types of turn, propositional and structural features, in and out of which speakers move. However, the 'social' sequence might also be understood as aiding institutional objectives: humour and interpersonal connections may ease a transaction, particularly within an institution underpinned by community principles.

In the following example, Drew and Sorjonen (1997) examine a telephone call between Kate and Jim, employees in a US state administrative office. The purpose of the call is work-related business and institutional tasks. Despite expectations of the setting, goals and participants, they begin the call with a sociable, 'off-business' sequence:

Extract 3.7: From Drew and Sorjonen 1997: 93
Jim: And a lo:vely day it is
Kate: Oh:, isn't it gor[geous=
Jim: [Yes

Following this, Kate's turn is still ostensibly 'sociable' but an element of institutional orientation emerges:

Extract 3.8: From Drew and Sorjonen 1997: 93
Kate: =I snuck out at lunch
          It's [really [difficult to come back

Kate's formulation, 'I snuck out at lunch', orients to the 'proper' institutional alignment, which she briefly rebelliously departs from. In this way 'an institutional flavour is imparted to their talk' (p. 94) even within 'sociable' sequences. Later in the call, there is a marked and noticeable shift to 'official business':

Extract 3.9: From Drew and Sorjonen 1997: 93
Jim: pt .hhhhh [What's up
Kate: [Well-
Kate: Well, I've had a call from Paul toda:y and after he called, I
          checked with your-terminal over there and they said our
          order's not awarded . . .

Thus in institutional settings, speakers may move in and out of IT and OT (Stokoe 2000b). Institutional identities cannot be assumed to be omnirelevant simply by virtue of the setting (Zimmerman and Boden

1991). Whilst there is some evidence of institutional orientation in Kate's turn, there is nevertheless an observable distinction between the 'social chat' of the opening sequence, and the 'work business' of the later phase. Talk in ostensibly institutional settings can therefore be 'non-institutional'. The example shows us that institutional identities are not omnirelevant, and that institutionality is oriented to and produced by interacting parties.

CA research requires a clear warrant for classifying talk as 'institutional'. Analysts should not presuppose institutionality and institutional identities, but find evidence in the talk that these are relevant participants' concerns. In the following section, we explore some of the debates within CA, particularly between 'pure' CA, which challenges the premise of institutionality as a shaping generality, and 'applied' CA, which assumes the relevance of institutional goals and agendas in order to discuss critically professional practice and process.

'PURE' AND 'APPLIED' CA

Central to CA's approach to 'institutionality' and 'institutional identity' is the idea that such phenomena are not extrinsic to the interaction under analysis (Schegloff 1991). This view challenges an essential distinction between IT and OT, for seeing 'restrictions' as an independent phenomenon (that is, the power of the professional over the client), and for the formalising, generalising view this implies. Indeed, many conversation analysts argue that the *institutional setting* of talk can be a misleading determiner of what actually occurs in such settings (for example, Edwards and Potter 2001).

Another distinction in the CA literature is between 'basic' (Heritage 2005) or 'pure' and 'applied' CA (Ten Have 1999). 'Pure' CA treats conversation *itself* as an institution and is concerned with explicating generalities about the mechanics and intelligibility of social action. Furthermore, some reject the pursuit of generalities in IT, arguing that, when subjected to systematic analysis, IT frequently contains non-generic elements, or generic elements associated with other types of talk, as well as insufficient evidence of distinctly different patterns. As Hester and Francis (2001: 207) argue, 'what we find to be deeply problematic is the foundationalist character of the claim that such structures provide for the recognizable production of given institutional settings and actions'.

These observations encourage the question: Is the institution in the *interaction* or the *setting*? As Heritage (2005: 107) observes, 'institutional talk can occur anywhere, and by the same token, ordinary conversation can emerge in almost any institutional context'. As we saw earlier, casual conversation often occurs in ostensibly institutional environments. At the same time, Drew and Sorjonen (1997) argue that the *context* of the 'sociable sequence' (amidst work talk and in a work setting) functions to display institutional identity. Central to these debates is 'where one locates the "centre of gravity" for understanding interactional phenomena: in the local interaction and its procedural infrastructure itself, in the general institutional arrangements, or in the institutionalized power of one category of participants over another' (Ten Have 2001: 5).

In contrast to 'pure' approaches to IT, Ten Have (1999: 162) describes 'applied' CA as a method devoted to studying 'interactions with an institutional purpose'. In other words, *applied* CA is inextricably bound up with the goal of identifying IT as a form of talk distinct from OT. The predominant focus is on sequence or interactional organisation, discourse roles and turn-types or activity types. For example, in West's (1984) research on doctor–patient interaction, she focuses on the way 'directive–response sequences' are formulated differently by male and female physicians. Directives were accomplished via different grammatical constructions, including *imperatives* ('Give me your coat'), *permission directives* ('May I have your coat?'), and *hints* ('Are you hot?'). West found that male physicians used 'aggravated directives' such as *imperatives*, *need statements* ('Yuh nee:d tuh get the *as:prun* into yuh sorda make it *to*:ler'ble.'), *want statements* ('I *do* wan' cha tuh go ahead an' *get* that Li:ght Salt'), *quasi-question directives* ('*Oka:y*, wull, why don' cha jump up on the table') and *directive by example* ('Ah'd prob'ly lay off till about *Thurs:* day') (pp. 93–6). In contrast, female physicians used *mitigated* forms, such as *proposals for joint action* ('Let's talk about cher press:ure fer a minnit 'r two'), *singular suggestions* ('[A]n then maybe yuh can stay away from the dihsserts . . .'), and *permission directives* where the physician seeks out the patient's permission to be directed: ('Could I have yer pho:ne number? An' give yuh a ca:ll then . . .' (pp. 98–101).

West then considered the *procedural consequentiality* of doctors' directive choices, focusing on moments where they attempt to get the patient to undress for a physical examination. Male physicians using aggravated directives were least successful in eliciting compliant responses from their patients; mitigated directives used mostly by female physicians were far more successful. The implications of these patterns and their relationship to institutional identity are clear: an aggravated form of directive 'emphasizes the distinction between the speaker and the addressee and asserts the speaker's authority to be issuing commands in the first place' (p. 108).

West concludes her study with observations about the medical profession more broadly, indicating that her research achieves part of its value in prescriptive suggestion: 'Should these findings hold in larger systematic samples of physicians, they might prove useful in explaining why patients are more satisfied with women physicians . . . and less likely to sue them for malpractice' (p. 109). Applied CA's practical, outcome-oriented emphasis is also emphasised by Ten Have (1999: 162), who suggests that such work 'support[s] efforts to make social life "better" in some way, [and] provide[s] data-based analytical suggestions for, or critiques of, the ways in which social life can be organized'.

Despite a differing emphasis from pure CA, applied CA is equally committed to a 'bottom-up' approach to the data, avoiding assumptions that institutionality is a prior constraint that determines what can and cannot be said. The notion of 'orientation to context' is, nevertheless, one that sets applied CA apart from pure CA and has prompted some critical debate. For example, Hester and Francis (2000: 397) argue that Drew and Heritage's (1992) notion of talk as 'context-shaped' implies that '"context" is some entity which acts upon participants and constrains their actions in a given setting', and is therefore actually similar to conventional sociology.

So where do these debates leave the question of the location of institutionality and institutional identity? Are they in the setting or the talk? Applied CA often focuses exclusively on sequence, turn-allocation and distribution of turn type as a means of pinning down the quality of 'institutionality'. However, ethnomethodologists such as Hester and Francis (2000: 404) reject this focus, arguing that institutionality 'is not to be found in any *formal properties* of the talk in and through which these activities are conducted. Such recognizability is a *situated accomplishment*, and involves a reflexive relationship between utterances, situated identities, and other circumstantial particulars.'

If 'context' cannot be determined in advance but is locally produced, there can be no 'hard and fast distinctions between institutional and non-institutional realms' (Ten Have 2001: 6). This conclusion is taken up most radically by Hester and Francis (2001), who question the very idea of an IT research programme because of its incompatibility with CA's ethnomethodological principles: *institution* is arguably a sociological rather than a members' category. Yet even if we accept that 'institutionality' or 'institutional identity' is something that people orient to in talk, how do we go about analysing this without reverting to generalities about predetermined role entitlements? The neglect of 'situated identities' or 'membership categories' in some forms of applied CA, in favour of sequential analysis, is redressed in the next section.

INSTITUTIONALITY AND MEMBERSHIP CATEGORISATION ANALYSIS

So far, we have seen that CA rejects the idea that the institutionality of an interaction is determined by its setting. However, some writers argue that CA's distinction between OT and IT relies too heavily on distinguishing sequential patterns in different speech exchange systems. Hester and Francis (2000) argue that many features identified as characterising IT are also found in OT, such as asymmetrical turn length. They also criticise conversation analysts for *invoking as resource* features of the talk they claim are constituted *in* it (for example, role categories), and therefore not adhering to CA's own criteria for relevance (see Chapter 2). Instead, Hester and Francis suggest, analysts base their observations on 'unexplicated membership category or identity analysis' (p. 399).

Membership categorisation analysis (MCA, see Chapter 2) provides an alternative ethnomethodological method for understanding what is 'institutional' about IT. In IT, categories enable interlocutors to establish and share highly specialised and expert cultural knowledge in pursuit of particular institutional goals: '[O]ne can argue that institutions "think" in terms of categories . . . and that they act on the basis of categories to pursue their tasks' (Mäkitalo and Saljö 2000: 59). MCA studies have been carried out in many institutional contexts including relationship counselling (Edwards 1998), newspaper reports (Eglin and Hester 1999), neighbour mediation (Stokoe 2003), police interrogations (D. R. Watson 1983; Wowk 1984); meeting talk (G. Hall and Danby 2003), news interviews (Fitzgerald and Housley 2002), and educational talk (He 1995).

A central aim of MCA is to explicate the mutually informing relationship between *categories and sequence*. For example, in a study of telephone calls to a ski school, Psathas (1999) demonstrates how categories get generated in particular kinds of turns. As we explained in Chapter 2, an example is the 'summons–answer' sequence at the start of a phone call, in which the caller (or 'summoner') makes the call and the called is the 'answerer' of the summons. Thus the interaction generates the category pair of caller–called, or summoner–answerer. These *turn-generated categories* are not mere functions of sequence; they also contain an orientation to membership categories regarding the person called (for example, friend, mother, wrong number). These orientations are realised through the propositions and forms of turns, such that they are appropriately 'recipient-designed' (D. R. Watson 1997).

Fitzgerald and Housley (2002) demonstrate the relationship between category and sequence, and how talk relies on the categorial identities built up sequentially within it. In their study of call-in radio programmes, they suggest that two key categories, 'host' and 'caller' are 'omnirelevant' (p. 581). So although the categories are locally invoked (for example, when 'host' introduces 'caller'), they are 'background' categories that organise the programme and whose 'omnirelevance' is clear from programmes titles (for example, 'Call Nick Ross'). The 'host' performs a range of category-specific actions, such as introducing the topic, introducing the callers, inviting them to speak, and managing the transitions between callers. Furthermore, the category 'host' is tied to certain *sequential* procedures, such as asking questions at 'organizationally relevant times' (p. 585). In contrast, 'caller' is a category that shifts in line with the organisational procedure of the show. When a caller is introduced by name and location, they are moved from 'occupying the category "next caller" from anonymous caller waiting, to what can be termed a "call-relevant identity"' (p. 586). For example:

Extract 3.10: NR[FE: 15: 94(3)] (Fitzgerald and Housley 2002: 586)

```
01   H:   Frances Smith from from Birmingham what do you think
02   C:   urhh . . . I . . . feel that the age of consent should stay at . . .
```

The host also takes up a variety of category incumbencies over the course of the talk, including 'call recipient', 'host of a radio show', 'introducer' and 'questioner'. In turn, the production of these categories gives rise to relevant co-memberships: 'call maker', 'caller to a radio show', 'introduced' and then 'questioned'.

Fitzgerald and Housley move beyond the omnirelevant, institutionally-embedded and 'topically empty' categories of 'host' and 'caller' in order to address how category knowledge of the caller (given by the caller prior to going on air) is invoked as a further index of identity and a means of achieving other interactional business, such as focusing the call or moving the caller on:

Extract 3.11: NR[FE: 15: 94(1)] (Fitzgerald and Housley 2002: 590)

```
01   H:   Ray Andrews from Thurrock in Essex do you think gays
02        should uhh pushed of [sic] from their sexuality until they're
03        twenty one
          (1.0)
04   C:   well no . . . I would go further than that I mean I'm
05        virtually sixty years of age and I can remember Uhh over
06        those years I was appalled in fact when when they made
07        it . . . when removed it from being illegal urhhhm you know
```

```
08          its what's hhehhehehehe[heheheh    ]
09   H:                          [why does it] worry you
10   C:   I was in I was in fact the person who said I believe in
11          altering the age and as far as I was concerned it be
12          altered to ninety providing they got the permission of
13          both parents uh [that's how strongly I feel about it      ]
14   H:                        [are you the leader of the Conservative]
15          group on your council . . . I'm trying to place=
16   C:   =yes Thurrock borough counc[il    ] is down in Essex here
17   H:                                [yup]
18   C:   and I'm the leader of the conservative group
19   H:   why does . . . why does homosexuality appal you so so much
20   C:   well think of it (.) use one's imagination you know you
21          perhaps unwittingly go into a pub or bar and you find out
22          err to your err that that it is habited by these people
```

The host asks the caller a question (lines 14–15) about his category membership, using information that has not yet been broadcast (that he is the leader of a Conservative council). The information has relevance at this sequential juncture: the caller has produced a contentious opinion about the age of consent for gay people (lines 6–7), and gone on to make a joke about this. The host's intervention refocuses the trajectory of the caller's turn, moving from expressing to justifying opinion. The host's use of categorial information further highlights the argument that categories and sequences work together to accomplish institutional action.

In this section, we have seen how MCA provides a crucial supplement to the sequential preoccupations of CA, and illuminates the phenomenon of situated institutional identities. Yet in the above sequence, we might note that Fitzgerald and Housley refer to something we have come *not* to expect in ethnomethodological research, the concept of *omnirelevant* identities. This concept is warranted in this context by its 'local' invocation and presence in the show's title. In contrast, however, omnirelevance is frequently presupposed by critical discourse analysts interested in exploring IT as embedded in historical processes and structures of power and authority. Indeed, the very features deemed by some to define institutionality – history, context, discourses, ritual and regulation – are what make CA and IT uneasy allies.

We now turn to critical discourse analysis (CDA) as a broad school of approaches that have been almost exclusively dedicated to an exploration of institutional discourse and settings. We start by demonstrating what some would argue are the limitations of a CA approach to

IT, and then discuss briefly the history of CDA. Next, we explain some basic concepts and procedures in CDA, before illustrating the approach with a case study of institutional identities in written discourse.

CRITICAL DISCOURSE ANALYSIS AND INSTITUTIONALITY

Extract 3.12: From Cicourel 1992: 296

1	PA:	(?) (low voice level) Is this the same one (we?)
2		(ya?) did yesterday?
3	IDA:	No. This is the eye lady
4	PA:	(?)
5	IDA:	Cellulitis
6	PA:	Oh
7	IDA:	With group A strep . . . in shock
8	PA:	In shock. (Slight rise in voice level) How about that.
9	IDA:	I[t?] was gonna be interesting I if she didn't
10	MR:	I I'm (?)
11	IDA:	have bacteremia but (laughing and voice level
12		increasing) now she's had I bacteremia

In this extract, three participants are involved in discussing the medical condition of another party (the 'eye lady'). Whilst the specialised language suggests a medical context, Cicourel (1992) suggests that our understanding of the interaction is partial without further contextual knowledge, such as the professional medical identities of the three speakers. The acronyms 'PA', 'MR' and 'IDA' denote specific medical roles ('Pathology Attendant', 'Medical Resident' and 'Infectious Disease Attending'), and each has a different level of expertise in the interaction. The roles of the speakers also invoke a set of institutional procedures: the PA is consulting with MR and IDA about laboratory findings after MR and IDA have interviewed the patient and discussed the case. The opening line thus assumes coherence with an activity done the day before. Cicourel expands the ethnographic context further to illuminate the extract. MR's prior interview with the patient, reproduced in Cicourel's analysis, is informed by his medical school training (for example, the association between 'cellulitis' and 'group A strep' can be traced to a specific sequence of instruction the physician will have absorbed in textbooks, lectures and laboratory settings). Cicourel argues that the talk presupposes 'analogous prior forms of socially organized experiences' (p. 308). Our understanding of the organisational conditions and sociocultural significance of this extract depends upon this knowledge of a series of 'interpenetrating communicative contexts' within which the talk is situated.

This analysis demonstrates the limitations of CA. Hak (1999) argues that CA's exclusive focus on transcribed video and audio recordings restricts and determines the kinds of questions that can be asked about institutional processes and identities. Many procedures of institutions are embedded in 'the wider context of institutional practices and ideologies', rather than in talk itself (Roberts and Sarangi 1999: 390). This criticism of CA is often found in CDA (for example, Hak 1999) and critical discursive psychology (for example, Billig 1999a, 1999b; Wetherell 1998). CDA is committed to the principle that the meaning of a text cannot be exclusively derived from the text itself. It is therefore dedicated to explicating the *interdiscursive*, *intertextual* layers of social and historical practices within which texts are embedded (for example, Fairclough 1992). Wider contexts can constitute interpretative resources for analysts, many of whom may not have the same access to expert knowledge or understanding from a participants' perspective. A CA analysis of a medical encounter is therefore deemed to produce an impoverished account of a patient's holistic experience of illness, which is unable to address the complexity and subtlety of institutional practices. Others more sympathetic to principles of ethnomethodology (for example, Silverman 1999) argue that whilst it is not improper to look 'beyond' talk, the import of ethnographic information that answers the 'why' question should come *after* the 'how' of situated interactional analysis to avoid a determinist reading.

The objective of CDA to furnish interaction analysis with a broad consideration of context is, however, only one part of its rationale. CDA's attention to wider 'discourses' corresponds with anti-empiricist trends in critical analysis (Parker 2004). In other words, CDA rejects CA's empirical basis. As Fairclough (2004: 116) writes, 'the "empirical" is what is available as knowledge of the real and the actual. However, the real and the actual cannot be reduced to the empirical, i.e. one cannot assume that what is known exhausts what is'. CDA is therefore committed to abstract and necessarily programmatic theories and paradigms of social and political life as guiding principles for analysis – something that CA firmly eschews.

Theoretical and methodological underpinnings of CDA

The status of CDA – as a theory, a method, an approach – has been much debated, with particular emphasis given to the interdisciplinary or transdisciplinary nature of its inquiry (Chouliaraki and Fairclough 1999; Weiss and Wodak 2003). Van Dijk (2001) is clear that CDA is not a sub-discipline of discourse analysis, nor a single method or theory, but a critical perspective for doing research. This perspective has a common interest in the role of language in the transmission of knowledge, the consolidation of hegemonic discourses and the organisation of institutional life; and much work in CDA implicitly treats identities as effects of the ideological work performed by discourse.

Fairclough (1992) cites a variety of sources, including Marxism, the Frankfurt School, Habermas, Bakhtin, critical theory and poststructuralism, as underpinning CDA's epistemology. Interdisciplinarity is promoted via CDA's commitment to mediating between the social and the linguistic, and by a desire to theorise the social as more than a mere contextual 'backdrop' or 'determiner' of texts. However, whilst its interdisciplinarity is embraced by CDA's practitioners, it is criticised by its detractors for producing analyses that are not accountable to any one method. The range of approaches is emblematic of the eclecticism and pluralism of the term 'critical discourse analysis' itself. For instance, Wodak's (2001) 'Vienna school' adopts a 'discourse-historical' approach, which emphasises the historicity and genealogy of discourses and combines this with ethnographic methods in order to produce a comprehensive model of context. Van Dijk (1998), by contrast, favours a 'socio-cognitive' framework, which theorises the relationship between social systems and individual cognition. Furthermore, Scollon's (for example, 2001) micro-sociological work includes nonverbal semiosis in the analysis of the 'nexus' of practices coalescing in moments or spaces of social life (see Chapter 6).

Under the following sub-sections we will take the component parts of 'critical discourse analysis' separately (critical, discourse and analysis) in order to scrutinise the rationale and principles of the approach.

Critical

In CDA, the term, 'critical' connotes 'critique' (Weiss and Wodak 2003: 14), and relates to CDA's interest in 'revealing' the way language mediates ideology, particularly in social institutions, and the 'ideological functions of language in producing, reproducing or changing social structures, relations, identities' (Mayr 2004: 5). Such analyses, therefore, have an awareness-raising, interventionist and unapologetically political goal, and these preoccupations are borne out by the range of topics carried out under the auspices of CDA: race and racism (Van Dijk 1991), gender and sexism (Lazar 2005), the media (R. Fowler 1991), marketisation (Fairclough

1993), national identities (Wodak et al. 1999) and the processes of capitalism and neoliberalism (Chouliaraki and Fairclough 1999).

CDA treats ideology as a set of effects in discourse – a form of social representation that systematically organises the world into patterns, which, in turn, facilitate the agendas and values of particular groups. For example, consider the two contrasting newspaper front pages below, produced during the period of war between Argentina and Britain over the Falkland Islands. The sinking of the UK ship HMS *Antelope* is constructed in sharply differing ways by the right-wing *Daily Mail* and the left-wing *Morning Star*, through different lexical choices. 'Blaze of glory' constructs the British troops as heroes, thus legitimating the war. However, 'senseless sacrifice' makes clear the paper's anti-war stance.

Leeds Postcard: LP91 Glorious/Senseless 1982

Figure 3.1 'Glorious/senseless death of the *Antelope*' (Leeds Postcards)

'Critical' is also a term that CDA turns back reflexively upon itself by making clear its analytical presuppositions (Barker and Galasiński 2001). Whilst critics of CDA point to the politicised and therefore compromised stance of the 'objective' analyst, CDA researchers argue that it is impossible to exclude the analyst's values from the research, and indeed there are often good political reasons for not doing so (Billig 1999a).

Discourse

'Discourse' is a wide-ranging affair in CDA, since it is theorised as a multi-modal, intertextual mediator of social life. Discourse and context are mutually constitutive: language both constructs social and political reality and is also constituted or conditioned by it. Fairclough (1992) theorises a three-dimensional framework for analysis: 'discourse' as text (the words spoken or on the page), as discourse practice (the processes of text production such as the discourse drawn upon) and as social practice (the institutional circumstances of event, production and reception of texts). In this model, the micro contexts of discourse are seen not simply as 'contained' by macro contexts, but work in a dialectical relationship. The notion that specific discourse events can shape larger political or ideological structures is given particular prominence, leading to a rather determinist slant: discourse may be responsible both for maintaining and challenging the status quo. For instance, consider this sentence spoken on UK news radio just before the 2003 Iraq war:

Extract 3.13: BBC Radio 4 'Today'
It seems that the move towards military action is now irresistible.

This statement encodes particular ideological assumptions through lexico-grammatical choices. For example, the nominalisation of possible actions ('the move' and 'military action') conceals agency and makes the actions seem inevitable, fatal and even natural. Additionally, the positive connotation of 'irresistible' suggests the actions are desirable. CDA also focuses on the way listeners are positioned, and how such statements contribute to the broader public perceptions about the justification, inevitability and agency of war.

The assumption that discourse, or 'semiosis' (Fairclough 2004), is an element of social practice, dialectically interconnected with other elements, has led to CDA's triple emphasis on *intertextuality* (the 'quotation' of one text by another), *interdiscursivity* (the movement of particular registers, styles and discourses), and *recontextualisation* (where textual or stylistic elements associated with particular speech events are seen to be 'relocated' in, or to 'colonise' new contexts).

Analysis

Any attempt to mediate between the social and the linguistic causes difficulties in the 'operationalisation' of the research process, since sociological and linguistic categories tend to be incompatible (Weiss and Wodak 2003). One of the main challenges of CDA is to bridge the gap between *discourse and context*, and *micro and macro*, and attempts have been made to reconcile sociological and linguistic approaches without reducing one to the other. As we have already noted, some researchers address this challenge by 'triangulating' methods to include large quantities of information about the historical, social and political contexts of the texts under scrutiny. The intertexual and interdiscursive connections between them and comparisons are then identified (for example, Reisigl and Wodak 2001). Whilst macro-level theory is employed, it is not applied unquestioningly or deductively to illuminate data. Rather, an 'abductive' approach is advocated, involving constant oscillation between theory and data.

In CDA's language analysis, discourse is treated as a system of lexico-grammatical options from which texts/authors make their choices about what to include or exclude and how to arrange them. The most influential linguistic framework in CDA is systemic functional linguistics. SFL views language as a semiotic system structured in terms of strata (for example, semantics, grammar) that are connected via a process of 'realisation': lexico-grammar 'realises' semantics, the linguistic 'realises' the social. SFL focuses on patterns of language that reflect broader concerns about power, ideology and social organisation, and argues that language forms *realise* these elements of social context. In this way 'the social is built into the grammatical tissue of language' (Chouliaraki and Faircough 1999: 140).

In the next section, we describe a practical framework for linguistic analysis, combining SFL concepts with more general categories employed in CDA. This is a necessarily simplified summary (for more detail see Fairclough 2003; Halliday 1994; Mayr 2004). Elements of this framework will be taken up again in Chapter 5.

LINGUISTIC METHODS IN CRITICAL DISCOURSE ANALYSIS

CDA and SFL theorise both discourse and lexico-grammar as 'functionally grounded' and multifunctional (Chouliaraki and Fairclough 1999: 140). Halliday (1994) identifies three *metafunctions* of language that operate simultaneously:

1. *Ideational*: How is the world represented? Who is responsible for processes and actions? How are opinions and ideologies encoded in discourse?
2. *Interpersonal*: What relationships are suggested between conversational participants or between text and reader? Is language formal or informal? Is social distance implied? Is there an attitudinal dimension?
3. *Textual*: How is the text organised and how are its parts connected? Are aspects of information foregrounded or backgrounded? Is there any significance to the layout or visual appearance of the written text?

These metafunctions correspond to three variables within the context of situation:

1. *Field*, which is realised by the ideational metafunction;
2. *Tenor*, which is realised by the interpersonal metafunction, and;
3. *Mode*, which is realised by the textual metafunction.

In turn, Halliday identifies three 'networks' from a broader grammatical system, operating at the level of the clause, that realise the three metafunctions:

1. *Transitivity*, involving participants, processes and circumstances, and corresponding to the ideational metafunction;
2. *Mood and modality*, involving clause structure types: declarative, interrogatives, imperatives (mood) and expressions of commitment and obligation and attitudinal markers (modality), and corresponding to the interpersonal metafunction, and;
3. *Theme*, involving patterns of information foregrounding, and corresponding to the textual metafunction.

The relationships between these different systems or strata are set out below. The arrows represent the movement of 'realisation' between levels of analysis. SFL has a less dialectical conception of the relationship between social context and language than CDA. It also assumes a movement by which context is realised by metafunction and metafunction is realised by lexico-grammar:

Table 3.1 Relations between systems

Context of Situation		Metafunctions		Grammatical Systems
Field	→	Ideational	→	Transitivity
Tenor	→	Interpersonal	→	Mood and modality
Mode	→	Textual	→	Theme

A final framework also associated with SFL, but operating *above* the level of the clause, is that of *cohesion* (the expression of logical connections between parts of a text). Cohesion also realises the *textual* metafunction. We now unpack the three grammatical systems in more detail.

Transitivity

Transitivity refers to the grammatical representation of relationships between participants, processes and circumstances in a clause. Halliday

(1994) sets out a typology of processes that correspond with particular participant identities. The following scheme is adapted from his work, as well as from Fairclough (2003) and Toolan (1998):

Table 3.2 Transitivity

Process Type	Participants	Circumstances
Material	*Actor (agent) and Goal*	*e.g. Time, Manner, Place*
e.g. *The children* (actors) *crept* (material process) *away* (circumstance)		
e.g. *The university* (actor) *will diversify* (material process) *its income streams* (goal)		
Mental	*Experiencer and Phenomenon*	*e.g. Time, Manner, Place*
e.g. *He* (experiencer) *believed* (mental process) *them* (phenomenon) *at the time* (circumstance)		
Relational 1	*Carrier and Attribute*	*e.g. Time, Manner, Place*
e.g. *The university* (carrier) *is* (relational process) *currently* (circumstance) *in good shape* (attribute) [this is a characterising formulation and cannot be reversed: 'in good shape is the university']		
Relational 2	*Token and Value*	*e.g. Time, Manner, Place*
e.g. *Kathy* (token) *is* (relational process) *the tallest child in the class* (value) [this is a defining formulation and can be reversed: 'the tallest child in the class is Kathy']		
Verbal	*Sayer and Verbiage*	*e.g. Time, Manner, Place*
e.g. *They* (sayer) *said* (verbal process) *it wouldn't work* (verbiage)		
Existential	*Existent*	*e.g. Time, Manner, Place*
e.g. *There is* (existential process) *no place like home* (existent)		

A final useful participant type is *beneficiary* which may occur in material processes:

> *He* (actor) *did* (material process) *it* (goal) *for me* (beneficiary).
> *He* (actor) *gave* (material process) *me* (beneficiary) *the book* (goal).

and also verbal processes:

> *He* (sayer) *told* (verbal process) *her* (beneficiary) *it wouldn't work* (verbiage).

Whilst it would be misleading to ascribe particular functions to these process and participant types out of context, it is notable that within material processes involving two animate participants, relations of power may be implicitly inscribed by the relationship between *actor* and *goal*, as in: 'The teacher (*actor*) taught the pupils (*goal*)'. Another observation about material processes is that they may be *transitive* (that is, take an object) as in the previous example, or *intransitive* (take no object, for example: 'The teacher taught for ten years', where 'for ten years' is a *circumstance*). Actors in intransitive processes are represented as having less of a material effect upon the world or environment. Transitive processes have the potential to be active ('The teacher taught the pupils') or passive ('The pupils were taught by the teacher'). In passive constructions, the actor, and thus agency, can be deleted ('The pupils were taught well').

Indeed, one of the most striking uses of language to represent power and role relations is through manipulations of agency at the grammatical level. Scientific texts, and, by extension, texts purporting to relay neutral facts, strive for objectivity by using passive, impersonal constructions. These can take various forms, such as passive constructions with the omission of an agent – the person *doing* the action ('Measures will be put in place to achieve these goals'). It can be achieved with *existential* processes ('There is a commitment to review and change work processes across the university'), and by the use of *nominalisation*, which is a type of grammatical metaphor involving the transformation of verb processes into nouns ('Improved research *performance*, particularly *growth* in research income, is a priority'). This means that agency is avoided and the process is backgrounded or even presupposed in the message. *Relational* processes are also commonly employed in 'factual' discourse, since they are suggestive of evidential, existential facts about the world ('The university is currently in good shape').

Van Leeuwen (1996) elaborates on this participant aspect of the transitivity framework in a model of representation of social actors that has clear applications for the analysis of identity in texts. Expanding the function of 'participant' beyond the merely grammatical, van Leeuwen establishes a number of 'sociosemantic' categories. First, *activation/passivation* may be realised by traditional active or passive voice, but can also be implicit in possessive pronouns (for example, 'my teacher' passivates 'me', whereas 'our intake' activates 'us'). Second, in *inclusion/exclusion* the actor may be omitted (for example, agency deletion) or mentioned but backgrounded (for example, in parenthesis). *Functionalisation* refers to identification by virtue of what one *does* ('farmer', 'lecturer'). *Identification* can be done by virtue of what one *is* including *classification* ('black British'), *relational identification* ('husband') and *physical identification* ('the red-headed woman'). Finally, the strategy of *genericisation* makes the identity generic rather than specific ('The child develops this skill from an early age'; 'Postgraduate students represent a key income stream').

Mood and modality

Mood is realised at the level of formal clause structure, and refers to choices between *declaratives* (related to the functional category of statements), *interrogatives* (related to the functional category of questions – either *polar yes–no* questions or *wh-type*) and *imperatives* (related to the functional category of commands). Modality refers to expressions of commitment to the truth or obligation of a proposition. Modal items adopt a variety of grammatical forms, including *adverbs* ('possibly', 'certainly', 'perhaps'), *modal verbs* ('could', 'must'), *participal adjectives* ('it is required'), *verbs of cognition* ('I feel', 'I believe'), and *copular verbs* ('is', 'seems', 'appears'). Moreover, modality may express certainty and strong obligation ('high' modality: *must, should, definitely, always*) or uncertainty and weak obligation ('low' modality: *could, possibly, perhaps, kind of, may*).

Mood and modality have particular relevance for representations of identity and interpersonal relationships. Mood choices, for instance, may be useful in illuminating *discourse roles* – who asks questions, who issues commands? The choice of imperative and interrogative mood in written texts may be an index of social proximity, familiarity and involvement with an implied audience. Modality is an expressive category that denotes speaker/writer attitude or judgement and which also embodies interpersonal or rhetorical functions, such as the softening of a contentious opinion or face-threatening act ('We *may* have to review your role'), or the strengthening of a persuasive action ('We *must* tackle fundamental issues').

Theme

Halliday's (1994) framework of *theme and rheme* explains how certain aspects of clauses are foregrounded. Theme is the first grammatical element of a clause, and usually contains 'given' or familiar information. For example, *'The university* must reaffirm its commitment to remain research-led'. In this example, 'The university' is the given information and the remainder of the clause is what is 'new' (the 'rheme'). This kind of patterning, whereby the subject of the clause is also the theme, is the most common clause structure, and is thus called the 'unmarked' theme. However, when a different clause element (for example, an adverbial phrase) constitutes the theme it becomes 'marked' and gains greater textual prominence. In the following example from a university document, the marked theme is a complex adverbial phrase which foregrounds the reasons for a restructuring exercise:

Extract 3.14: University document

In order to enhance the university's reputation, increase its quality and ensure a sustainable future, the university's senior management team has identified four key corporate goals.

The choice of a marked theme can serve an ideological function: the university is proposing a potentially disruptive and unpopular set of new strategies and therefore needs to highlight the good reasons behind the exercise, rather than foregrounding the role of the actors in setting the agenda.

Having explained these three main grammatical systems, we finish our description of CDA's analytic methods by discussing some other features that, while not part of the SFL model, are commonly applied in CDA. We discuss, in order, *vocabulary and collocation*; *metaphor, metonymy and synecdoche*; *presupposition*; *pronouns*; and *intertextuality/ interdiscursivity*.

Vocabulary and collocation

Fairclough (1989) suggests that ideological differences between texts can easily be spotted via their encoding in vocabulary choices. This is possible because words do not carry unitary and consistent meanings: they have an etymology, a history, connotations, personal associations, metaphorical uses and meaning derived from the surrounding context. Fairclough argues that words are 'ideologically encoded' when they reveal traces of the author's or speaker's identity (for example, 'subversive' encodes a right-wing perspective when used critically; 'solidarity' reveals a left-wing perspective when used positively). Similarly, certain words, depending on their context, may constitute sites of struggle for meaning and value, such as 'militant', 'socialism' and 'politically correct'. Words may also be markedly formal or informal, evaluative and expressive (for example, the word 'terrorists', 'mercenaries' or 'freedom fighters' – and many other terms – can be used to refer to a group of 'soldiers').

Collocation refers to common combinations of words that tend, statistically speaking, to keep company with one another. The juxtaposition of an identity category with another element with evaluative connotations ('teenage rampage' or 'embattled community') may have the effect of inflecting (or 'infecting') the identity category via association. Collocation can take on routinised phrases in public discourse (e.g. 'Tory sleaze', 'single mother', 'bogus asylum seekers', 'loony left') and thereby carry encoded ideologies.

Metaphor, metonymy and synecdoche

Ideology can be deliberately encoded into systems of metaphor, a figurative use of language whereby one word stands in for another to imply a relationship of similarity. Lakoff and Johnson (1980) argue that systems of metaphorical representation shape our cognitive processing of events (but see Edwards 1997a for a discursive reworking). An extended metaphor used consistently through a text can achieve ideological ends. For example, disease metaphors (Fairclough 1989: 120) can be used to describe social problems or unrest ('Anti-social behaviour has spread like cancer in our cities'). This form of 'moral panic' enhances the 'problem' and makes it simultaneously more threatening and anonymous (Cohen 2002). Metonymy refers to the substitution of a word by one of its attributes ('the crown' to refer to a 'monarch'), whilst synecdoche substitutes a part for the whole ('wheels' for a 'car'). C. Fowler (2005) argues that synecdoche is a common device in travel writing, where the cultural identity of an unfamiliar ethnic group is frequently 'reduced' to one of its cultural practices. In her example, the game of 'buzkashi' played in Afghanistan is repeatedly used as a synecdochic metaphor to characterise the 'lawless' and 'brutal' sociocultural and political identity of Afghans. Another type of metonymic substitution that impersonalises and therefore backgrounds the social actor is *objectification*, in which a person is substituted with a place or organisation with which they are associated (Van Leeuwen 1996). Thus 'the university', 'the department' or 'the government' operate as a means of obfuscating the actual roles of individuals in particular actions or decision-making processes.

Presupposition

Presupposition is pervasive in language. It refers to the presumed knowledge a recipient needs to make full sense of a text. This can seem 'obvious' ('Cats have fur and a tail'), but frequently it draws on cultural frames and assumptions with an ideological bias. The naturalisation of certain collocations works as a form of presupposition – 'Get trouble-free holiday insurance' – which presupposes that getting holiday insurance is usually problematic. In the following example from the same university document (Extract 3.14), the reader must accept the 'benefits' of the proposed restructuring in order to understand the proposition ('Mindful of the benefits of de-layering, delegation and devolution, the university will review and change its structures'). Alternatively, the reader may resist the presupposition: CDA emphasises the contingent conditions in which a text will be received, and stresses the possibility that intended meanings may be misread, negotiated or rejected.

Pronouns

The pronoun system provides another fruitful site for CDA. The way people use pronouns, particularly in addressing recipients, has implications for their interpersonal relationships and the way the receivers are positioned. For instance, Fairclough (1989) notes that newspaper editorials frequently use the 'inclusive we', which presupposes agreement with the reader and the authority to speak for others. Fairclough also notes the use of 'informal you' in mass communication as a form of 'simulated personal address'. Fairclough and Wodak (1997) analysed pronoun use in speeches by former British Prime Minister, Margaret Thatcher. 'We' was sometimes used *inclusively*, to convey solidarity with the general public ('We do enjoy a standard of living that was undreamt of then'), and sometimes *exclusively* to convey an institutionalised sense of 'we', the party ('After we returned to power'). This shifting pronoun use achieves an ambiguity about whether subsequent uses of 'we' are inclusive or exclusive. In discussing the decision to go to war with Argentina over the Falkland Islands, she uses 'we' in a way that could denote the government, but is strongly suggestive of a more inclusive spirit ('When part of Britain . . . was invaded of course we went we believed in defence of freedom').

Intertextuality/interdiscursivity

Finally, at a level of analysis above the clause, CDA traces the effect of other texts and other styles or registers in texts and interactions, and describes the resultant *hybridisation* of discourse. This is a particular strategy of CDA, due to its preoccupations with the transformation of orders of discourse and colonisation of one discourse practice by another. Fairclough (for example, 1995) has focused particularly on the colonisation of various spheres (the private, the public) by what he terms 'marketisation' or 'commodification', and this will be elaborated in more detail below in relation to the British higher education system. However, it is also possible to find *other* discourses colonising those of the sphere of commerce and advertising. For instance, Bertelsen (1998) demonstrates how post-apartheid discourses of black emancipation in South Africa were quickly appropriated by advertisers: '*Foschini* (fashion house): You've won your freedom. Now use it. Get a Foschini's credit card today'.

Having explained a variety of CDA's analytic procedures, we now move on to consider its relevance for the analysis of institutional identity.

CRITICAL DISCOURSE ANALYSIS AND IDENTITY

For CDA, identity is firstly a *representation* in language (the 'ideational metafunction' discussed above), and particular frameworks such as transitivity, vocabulary, identification and metaphor can be employed to analyse its construction. Secondly, identity is a *position* within discourse (the 'interpersonal metafunction'), and details such as pronoun use, presupposition and mood can show how language constructs and positions the recipient. Finally, the *expressive* dimension of language (straddling 'ideational' and 'interpersonal' metafunctions) conveys alignments with particular political or evaluative positions, and can be analysed by attention to modality, attitudinal vocabulary and collocation.

Beyond the micro focus of language choice, Fairclough (2004: 105) asks how discourses come to be internalised in social practices: 'How does it come to be enacted in ways of acting and interacting, e.g. organizational routines and procedures including genres, and inculcated in the ways of being, i.e. the identities of social agents?' This question involves particular theoretical and methodological difficulties for CDA discussed earlier: the problem of mediation between social life (including identity) and language. Is subjectivity merely an 'effect' of discourse, a position we are impelled to take up? Or is identity a conscious and rhetorical expression or construction in language – an emphasis supported by the way analyses often presume 'intended' meanings? Chouliaraki and Fairclough (1999: 1) argue that CDA aims to break down the traditional opposition between 'interpretivist' and 'structuralist' social science, in favour of 'constructivist structuralism': 'a way of seeing and researching social life as both constrained by social structures and an active process of production which transforms social structures'.

To illustrate how CDA analyses identity, we examine its construction in the promotional texts of a UK university. Universities as institutions are increasingly considered to be under threat from market forces. This 'shackling of universities to economies' (Chouliaraki and Fairclough 1999: 9) is one example of the transformation of discourse orders characterising late modernity, involving changing economic relations between state, institution and student (Fairclough 1993). A shift to a market forces-led model of higher education (HE) coincides with a more instrumental framework in universities, which 'come increasingly to operate (under government pressure) as if they were ordinary businesses competing to sell their products to consumers' (Fairclough 1995: 141). Symptoms of these shifts include the abolishing of student grants in the

UK, the introduction of student fees in England, the competitive sourcing of funding from the private sector, the creation of internal markets where departments compete for students, and managerial approaches realised in staff training and appraisal. Education has become an 'industry' concerned with producing, marketing and selling cultural and educational commodities to 'clients' or 'consumers' and mired in a culture of corporatism (Readings 1997). Fairclough (1993) concludes that relations between universities and their students have been transformed: where once the university was the authority selecting students, now students are clients choosing universities. Students have become consumers, shopping between courses and institutions, with the aim of becoming employable. Knowledge has therefore become a product. This sort of instrumentalism has frequently been seen to represent a crisis of values for many academics and educationalists (for example, Gumport 2000).

This macro sociological and economic context of British HE is relevant to any critical discourse analytic study of its texts. The following example is taken from the homepage of a UK university (anonymised as 'Anytown' and 'AT'). We demonstrate how CDA can illuminate the construction of a particular set of relations between the institution, the students and society more broadly: how macro issues are realised in micro contexts of discourse.

Extract 3.15: 'Anytown' University Homepage

Anytown – the professional university at the heart of England

Anytown is one of the UK's leading universities for graduate employment. Approximately 97% of full- and part-time students graduating from the university in 2003 entered employment or went on to further study within six months of graduation. The Sunday Times University Guide, September 2004, states that Anytown has 'one of the consistently lowest rates of graduate unemployment of any university'.

This strength derives from our close links with over 6,000 employers across the world. Many of our students spend up to a year on work placements, gaining skills and experience that give them a real competitive edge at graduation.

Our strong links with employers make us ideally placed to design and deliver courses relevant to society's future needs.

Our goal is to be the university of choice for students who want to gain the skills, knowledge and self confidence to succeed in their chosen profession, within an environment committed to student support and the student learning experience.

In the 2004 institutional Quality Assurance Agency review, Anytown received the highest commendation for its consistent commitment to supporting students and their learning, for its student-centred approach, and for the way AT continues to drive forward the employability agenda to the benefit of its students and other stakeholders.

We attract students from across the globe and our total student population of around 26,000 is made up of approximately 21,000 undergraduates and 5,000 postgraduates.

Our teaching is underpinned by strong research. All of our research units were rated as nationally or internationally important in the last Research Assessment Exercise, and four gained the coveted '5' Grade. This result makes AT one of the leading 'new' universities in the UK.

Our entry requirements are consistent with our high expectations and we remain one of the most popular universities in the country in terms of applications received.

Our first observation is the way the text constructs the university as an *attractive product or service*. Positive lexis with high modal value ('one of the . . . leading', 'highest commendation', 'strong research', 'one of the most popular') is combined with quantification discourse ('97%', 'within six months', '6,000 employers'), presenting a product with indisputable value. This is precisely the kind of discourse – reminiscent of advertising genres – that we anticipate from commercial sectors and is typical of much university publicity material.

In terms of identity construction and interpersonal relations, the use of *pronouns* is revealing. Like much of the material analysed by Fairclough (1993), the university is personalised via the first-person plural 'we'. However, because there is no direct address to potential readers ('you'), the effect of 'we' is to construct a corporate identity for the university. In other words, there is no sense that 'we' is inclusive of an audience. The ambiguity of the target addressee is suggested in the shifts between positioning students as *part* of the enterprise by the use of the possessive 'our' ('Many of our students spend up to a year on work placements'), and positioning them as external, but *potential* members ('Our goal is to be the university of choice for students who want to gain the skills, knowledge and self confidence to succeed in their chosen profession'). The first type of construction suggests that potential employers may be targeted ('Our strong links with employers make us ideally placed . . .').

In order to persuade potential 'customers' of the value of its product, the university invokes authority from external sources, such as *The Sunday Times*, the Quality Assurance Agency and the Research Assessment Exercise (UK government bodies that evaluate university teaching and research). Citing sources is a common device for establishing the credibility of an account, and adds market value to the university. This pattern of evidencing the university's credentials is further supported by grammatical constructions that suggest that qualification comes objectively from elsewhere, rather than simply being a claim the university makes for itself: 'Our strong links with employers make us ideally placed . . .'. Here the university ('us') has become the object or *goal* of the process, suggesting that their 'ideal placement' is a product of self-evident forces ('Our strong links with employers'). This pattern is repeated later in the text ('This result makes AT one of the leading "new" universities in the UK').

Unlike the texts studied by Fairclough, there is little evidence of a conversational register (with the exception of 'a real competitive edge' which is slightly colloquial), and in this sense, the material is an example of the way in which universities construct themselves as serious, corporate bodies, whose language reflects their professional status. In this way, then, it is the 'corporate' identity of the university that is the marketable commodity. The impersonal, factual and professional tone is further supported by a high level of relational processes ('Anytown is'; 'Our goal is to be'; 'Our teaching is underpinned'; 'we remain one of the most popular universities'), which connotes uncontestable factuality.

The text, like many pseudo-factual, formal types of prose, contains a high incidence of *nominalisation*, which, as we argued before, is a way of transforming processes into entities, with a resultant loss of participants and thus agency ('graduate employment', 'further study', 'Our goal', 'student learning experience', 'student centred approach'). This pattern, along with the mention of abstract qualities such as 'skills' and 'experience', constructs a discourse of education as *product* of which students are beneficiaries. This is also borne out grammatically ('skills and experience that give them a real competitive edge') where students are the beneficiaries of the clause. Nominalisation thus becomes a metaphor for the broader instrumentalisation of universities, in which knowledge is a product rather than a process. A further effect of nominalisation is to remove the potential for the university to be an actor of material processes, which reduces or obfuscates its agency. This is a trend associated with the entrepreneurial and democratising discourse used by universities and noted by Fairclough (1995: 158) as 'a corresponding decline in the implicit (unspoken) authority of the institutions over its applicants, potential students and potential staff'.

Finally, evidence of *interdiscursivity* or *recontextualisation* is provided in the inclusion of expressions and terms from managerial or corporate discourse ('students and other stakeholders', 'drive forward the employability agenda'). The precise context of 'stakeholders' is ambiguous, implying both that the students themselves are 'stakeholders' in the 'business' of the university, but also that 'others' are likely to benefit from the university's 'employability agenda'. This reveals an interesting dual ideological discourse at work, in which students are positioned both as 'customers', whose 'stake' in the university will improve their prospects in the job market, but also as 'marketable products' whose skills and education will benefit industry and the production process (Phillips 1989).

Having explored CDA perspectives on institutional identity in some detail, we end this chapter where we began: in debates between CDA and CA about the best way to analyse institutionality.

COMPARING CONVERSATION AND CRITICAL DISCOURSE ANALYSIS

In this section, we juxtapose CA and CDA analyses of an extract from a university tutorial. We focus on how institutional identities are produced in interaction, and explore any correspondence between these identities and those constructed in the promotional material discussed above. The extract comes from an English Literature tutorial in a UK university. T is the tutor, the other participants are students:

Extract 3.16: University tutorial
((Tutor has been explaining postmodernism))

```
 1   T:    >↑WHat I'd like you< to do:, (0.8) imme:diately
 2         is to spe:nd (0.3) 'bout a mi:nute >an' a half.<
 3         (0.4) <wri:ting do:wn:.> the answer to this
 4         question.
 5               (0.4)
 6   T:    Which you might well be a:sked by somebody.
 7               (2.0)
 8   T:    WHhat is the Aleppo Button about,
 9               (2.4)
10   T:    (Y-) write as <DEtailed> a response to that >as
11         you can< without consulting anybody else:
12               (5.9)
13   T:    Say you're reading it, (0.4) at ho:me an'
14         somebody at ho:me says t'ye, (0.3) ↑↑what's
15         ↑↑that ↓sto:ry abo:ut ↑you're ↑reading.
16               (0.9)
17   J:    I *didn't re:ad* the Aleppo Bu:tton,
18               (0.3)
```

19	T:	O:h::.
20	J:	Was it- I di'n't real- [I thought it was just=
21	T:	[WEll okay:, right =
22	J:	=[Lenin's trousers ( )] (okay.)
23	T:	=[don't you write anything t(h)hen]
24		(0.2)
25	S?:	Didn't read it either.
26	S?:	£neither did I£ heh:::
27	T:	Hhhh
28		(0.6)
29	T:	Handouts that nobody reads. ↑h:mmm.
30	?	(.hhhh)
31	J:	I thought it was jus' the um:: Lenin's Trousers.
32		(0.2)
33	J:	Collection °cos you:- °
34		(0.4)
35	J:	°°Obviously not°°
36	T:	WEll yeah *bu-* (.) uh- ↑never ↓mind. (0.2)
37		okay.
38		(1.3)
39	T:	I did say at the lecture (hm) (.) here's a
40		handout read it before next we:ek. (.) >bu'
41		anyway.< (0.3) some of us have *read it* I take
42		it.
43		(0.5)
44	T:	*°Right.°* (0.2) *ᵒ°kay.°* C'd those who have
45		read it, (0.6) write down, (0.9) the: answer to
46		that que:stion.
47		(1.4)
48	T:	So that we can enlighten: (0.2) people who
49		ha:ven't¿
50	S?:	°Heh heh heh heh heh heh°
51		(4.2)
52	T:	You might want to skim: through it¿
53		(3.33.7) ((papers rustling throughout
54		this time))

Conversation analysis

A conversation analytic reading of this sequence might start by considering the actions being done in each turn, and pairs of turns, such as instructing, questioning, answering and accounting. The sequence begins with the tutor formulating and reformulating the day's task (lines 1–15). Note that the long gaps between his turns (lines 5, 7, 9, 12) are not treated by the students as places for taking a verbal turn: all parties treat them as part of the tutor's turn in which the action of instructing is not complete until line 15.

After another gap (line 16), Jo takes a turn. But this turn is an account for non-compliance with the task, rather than a directly task-oriented action. Jo's turn initiates a new sequence (lines 17–43), and, although it is about the topic of the task, problematises rather than carries it out. Indications of trouble can be seen earlier in the tutor's formulations of the task. The first formulation (lines 1–4) is added to incrementally (lines 6, 8, 10–11), possibly due to the lack of uptake from the students at transition relevance places (lines 5, 7, 9). Lack of uptake does not just mean in terms of talk but other practices, such as beginning to write. After another long gap (line 12), the tutor reformulates the task. The second formulation is quite different from the first. It is observably less formal, shifting the task from the university setting to an imagined home place ('Say you're reading it, (0.4) at ho:me') with an imagined questioner ('↑↑what's ↑↑that ↓sto:ry abo:ut ↑you're ↑reading.'). The tutor therefore produces a contrast between categories of place (the 'university' versus 'home') and kinds of reader ('academic' versus 'lay'), with the 'lay' reader being actively voiced via large shifts in pitch.

Jo's dispreferred turn at line 17 ('I *didn't re:ad* the Aleppo Bu:tton,') is not mitigated with an account for her lack of preparation, at least initially. After a gap, the tutor responds with 'O:h::.'. This response token indicates an interactional glitch at this point: Jo's prior turn is newsworthy and unexpected. However, the intonation contour with which it is delivered does another action; it is hearably negatively evaluative. Indeed, it produces an account from Jo 'I thought it was just [Lenin's trousers ( )](okay.)', which is formulated after two abandoned turn beginnings: 'Was it– I di'n't real–' (lines 20–2). Her turn orients to the tutor's expectation that it was incumbent on the students to prepare for this tutorial – displayed in his task formulation and response token (lines 8, 19) – and that lack of preparation is an accountable matter. Her account is overlapped by the tutor's receipt of it ('WEll okay:,') and his formulation of a new instruction ('right don't you write anything t(h)en'). The 'WEll' indicates further interactional trouble, but his new instruction is ambiguous: the laughter particle at the end ironises it, but it is a logical–factual observation that without preparation Jo cannot do the task. It could be a reward (less work for Jo!), or a subtle (but defeasible) reprimand.

At lines 25 and 26 two other students report their non-preparation, taking the opportunity at a sequential location in which it might be 'safe' to do so – being the second person to report lack of preparation is not as tricky as being the first. The first student's admission is hearably 'smiled' and laughed through. The tutor's outbreath (line 27), although possibly evaluative like 'O:h::.', does not treat their reports as news. However, no further accounts are forthcoming. The tutor's formulation 'Handouts that nobody reads.' is done like an observation, with the '↑h:mmm.' a kind of puzzlement token (line 29). It is also ironic and somewhat scep-tical – handouts are designed and given out to be read, an *obvious* task requirement. This is followed by another account from Jo (lines 30–5), probably delivered at this point because her first attempt occurred in overlap. Jo therefore orients to the need to get the account hearably 'in the clear' for the tutor, treating the tutor as someone to whom she is accountable.

The first part of Jo's account recycles the earlier formulation of her understanding of the task ('I thought it was jus' the um:: Lenin's Trousers. (0.2) Collection'). However, she begins to add an increment to the turn: '°cos you:- °', possibly starting to attribute her error to the tutor. Interestingly, this part of her turn is delivered with a noticeably lower volume and is abandoned. After a pause, she whispers '°°Obviously not°°' (line 35). It is unclear whether the tutor has actually heard this, and whether his turn at line 36 is responsive to it or her earlier attribution of the error to him. However, '°°Obviously not°°', accomplishes a variety of things: it orients to the routine order of the tutorial in which the tutor's version is the 'correct' one, it orients to the hierarchical relationship between tutor and student such that challenges are uttered quietly or even designed not be heard, and yet it does the action of challenging – perhaps something that is relevant to the other students present. The tutor begins to respond to Jo's challenge, but he abandons it twice ('WEll yeah *bu-*', 'uh-') before moving to close this sequence ('↑never ↓mind. (0.2) okay.'). However, after another long pause, he reinstates the sequence ('I did say at the lecture (hm) (.) here's a handout read it before next we:ek. (.)'), asserting that his previous instructions were correct, and that the error, and thus the accountability, is the students'. This turn explicates the tutor's earlier presupposition that the students have done some prepara-tion for the tutorial. The tutor therefore embodies the role of someone in a position to issue instructions for the students to receive and act upon.

The incremental TCU ('>bu' anyway.<') functions to end this sequence, and the tutor moves on to ask whether 'some' of the students have read it, formulated as a closed question to which he presumably received some nodding agreements (line 43). At line 44, the tutor signals the start of a new sequence ('*°Right.°*'). He rescues the task by parti-tioning the students into two categories – those who 'have' read the text and those who 'ha:ven't¿': 'good' students and 'bad' ones – pitting one group against the other evaluatively but humorously (lines 41–9). It is again unclear whether the low-volume laughter at line 50 is designed to be heard by the tutor, but after a long gap (line 51) the tutor reformulates the task once more: 'You might want to <u>skim</u>: through it¿' The gap is functionally ambiguous: is he relenting and allowing the students who have not prepared a chance to be brought back into the fold? Or does he suspect that *none* of them has prepared, and that 'skimming the text' is the only way of recovering the task at all?

The tutor sets temporal limitations on the new task of 'skimming': after three minutes he restarts the tutorial and nominates a student to talk (line 58). At this point there is further interactional trouble:

Extract 3.17: University tutorial continued

[3 lines omitted]

```
58  T:    Paul. Do you kno̲w this story.
59             (2.1)
60  P:    >No.<
61             (0.2)
62  T:    You *don't right.*
63             (0.3)
64  T:    B̲riony.
65             (1.0)
66  B:    .tch °hehhh [        hehhh° ] ↑heh
67  S?:              [°hehhh hehhh hehhh°]
68             (0.2)
69  T:    Whatever you've got. ((coughs))
70  B:    Well-
71  T:    I've written [some things down (as well)]
72  B:                [    WH-   what    ] I've
73         written is nothing really.
74             (0.5)
75  B:    But that doesn't hinder enjoy̲:ment'.
76             (0.5)
77  T:    Rhight,
78             (0.6)
79  T:    Okay:,
80             (0.4)
81  T:    Tom?
82             (1.1)
83  To:   Um:: (0.3) I jus' put (0.6) i:t °°seems to°° be
84         a- (0.3) a series of experiences: (0.5) an':
```

```
85          (0.7) reminiscence-ces.
86              (0.5)
87  To:    Uh- of a- (0.2) of a- (0.4) °°s-°° (?) of a
88          character. .hhh
89              (0.4)
90  To:    The uh- Aleppo Button seems to link them
91          somehow.
92              (0.4)
93  To:    °°Seems°° (0.5) °°to.°°
94              (0.6)
95  T:     Uh-[huh, ]
```

Paul's response is delayed and dispreferred: he does not know the story despite having been given some time to read it. The tutor leaves Paul's response noted and unaccounted for, and nominates a second student. Briony's response also indicates trouble: it is delayed and prefaced with laughter. However, the tutor treats her laughter as the preface to an answer, rather than as the preface to an account for non-answer ('Whatever you've got.'). Briony's next turn contains more trouble, it starts with 'Well-' and is abandoned, at which point the tutor adds an encouraging comment that he has 'written [some things down (as well)]' (line 71). The tutor receipts her eventual contribution with a turn that indicates that more might expectably be forthcoming – note the continuing intonation on 'Rhight,' (line 77). After a gap, he delivers another possible continuer ('Okay:,'), but Briony does not take another turn.

The tutor moves on to nominate a third student (line 81). A pattern is emerging in the long gaps that occur between tutor nomination and the named student's turn (lines 59, 65, 82). However, each of the tutor's 'summons' produces a different second pair part. Paul produces an unmitigated, unaccounted for and speeded-up dispreferred '>No.<'. Briony's turn is also not straightforwardly 'preferred', in that it is prefaced with laughter and hesitation. The start of Tom's turn is hesitant ('Um:: (0.3) . . .'). The first part is littered with repair initiators (lines 84, 85, 87, 90), repetition (lines 83, 90, 93), minimisation ('I jus' put') and pauses (lines 83–93). The tutor withholds response or evaluation at each possible completion point (lines 85, 89, 92, 94), and Tom tries to continue until he fails to add more at line 93. The tutor does a non-committal receipt at line 95. The delivery of Tom's turn is similar to patterns of 'mitigated knowledge display' we have observed elsewhere in our data (Benwell and Stokoe 2004).

Overall, we can see how CA's attention to sequential, turn-constructional and prosodic detail reveals a number of interesting features. An asymmetrical relationship between the tutor and students is displayed in numerous turns, such as in lines 44–9 in which the tutor embodies a 'tutor identity' as someone entitled to give instructions and set agendas. Patterns of turn-taking, distribution of turn-types, and category-bound obligations differ when compared to everyday talk (see examples in Chapter 2), and display the emerging institutional nature of the interaction and its incumbent identities. Whilst familiarity with the institutional setting, in terms of its usual roles and goals, might prepare an analyst for these findings, it is clear that these are things that are *produced* and *oriented to* by the participants in the talk itself. CA attends to how such things as institutional tasks and identities are managed in the machinery of talk-in-interaction, and can identify what is treated as normative and accountable in institutional settings.

A possibly unexpected pattern to emerge from our analysis is the way students appeared to resist the tutorial task, displayed in a number of interactional glitches. The tutor's responses to these long pauses, reports of lack of preparation, and unmitigated dispreferred turns, included reformulating the task into a smaller and more manageable one ('skimming', imagining a lay audience). Whilst the students fulfilled their 'discourse identities' (see Chapter 2) by taking turns in the interaction, they did not fulfil their category-bound obligations as 'students'. It is perhaps surprising that the tutor avoids explicit admonishment of students for their lack of preparation and engagement: as the incumbent of the institutional identity category 'tutor' it might be expected that he would do so.

One issue for CA is how to move from an analysis of a specific interaction to generalisations about teaching and learning in the university. This is generally done by collecting a corpus of data, and attempting to identify sequential patterns through which regular actions are accomplished. Deviant cases are analysed for what they reveal about the robustness or otherwise of the patterns identified. However, as we will see in the next section, CDA does generalisation another way, by moving between theory and normative characterisations of education's macro-social functions, and micro-level detail. We now turn to CDA for our second analysis to produce a different kind of reading. This analysis illustrates one dimension of the full 'triangulated' account that would ideally be prescribed in a CDA programme of research.

Critical discourse analysis

The traditional structures of HE dictate that there is a hierarchically organised relationship between tutors and students in almost all aspects of university life. The role of tutors as 'expert' bearers of knowledge and facilitators of learning means that they may adopt a regulative mode (associated with defining and guiding the task) and an instructional one (associated with the transfer of knowledge; see Christie 2004). These modes can be observed in our example: the tutor initiates sequences (lines 1–4, 44), defines the task parameters, content and timing (lines 1–15, 29, 39–40), guides student responses (lines 13–5, 71) and evaluates them (lines 19, 27, 69, 95). Students in a post-compulsory education setting might be expected to be invested in their own success and achievement, and therefore to align with institutional goals and identities. But this is only partly borne out: students display elements of resistance, both to the task at hand, and to the easy acceptance of an 'intellectual' or 'academic' identity (Benwell and Stokoe 2002). Some consideration of sociological and educational theory may explain these observations.

Earlier in this chapter, we noted that shifts in relations between the state, university and students have resulted in new identities for students as clients or consumers of the commodity of education. In turn, the institution and its representatives are service providers of knowledge and skills. The economic transaction that means students are the main source of income for most universities, and must therefore be wooed, has led to a shift in authority relations. Within this context, we can hypothesise about the interactional patterns observed in this extract. The hedging, mitigation and 'politeness' exhibited by the tutor, and the challenging moves of the student may constitute evidence of a shift in power – a democratisation of the tutorial setting (for example, lines 13–5). The tutor seems reluctant to express criticism overtly or to sanction the students for their lack of preparation and inadequate responses to the task (for example, line 21). We also see the tutor being positioned as accountable for the task-setting ('I did say at the lecture'), an orientation to a wider culture of accountability measures that are increasingly implemented in universities, from the relatively informal 'student evaluation forms', to 'staff–student committees', to national institutional assessments.

Another interesting observation is the tutor's colloquial reformulation of the task with reference to 'home' (lines 13–4). He asks how 'somebody at ho:me' might formulate the task ('↑↑what's ↑↑that ↓sto:ry abo:ut ↑you're ↑reading.'), highlighting the relevance of educational tasks (here, a discussion of a postmodern text) for an 'ordinary' member of the community. This move reflects the current higher education ideology that universities must be accountable to the wider community, a commitment enshrined in many university mission statements.

Finally, this extract reveals the enactment of the ideology of 'student-centred learning', which has become something of an orthodoxy in recent educational research (Christie 2004). It is partly premised upon constructivist work in developmental psychology, in which an interactive (rather than monologic or 'transmission') theory of cognitive development suggests that learners actively co-construct knowledge (cf. Vygotksy 1978). The popularity of 'co-construction' models of learning has resulted in a shift in the usual prescribed moves of teacher-led classroom interaction (Wilcox 1996). In the data above, the tutor enacts this theory by setting a discursive, exploratory task for the students to discover their own understanding of the task's concepts, as well as in his avoidance of explicit evaluation of student responses as 'right' or 'wrong'. Indeed, when interviewed later about his views on pedagogical style, the tutor expressed a clear commitment to this ideology: tutorials should be 'open-ended discussion[s] . . . with no pressure to give a prepared or expected answer'. Furthermore, he advocates the use of presentations whereby 'students can set the agenda'. This 'democratising' may be a deliberate response by tutors to the educational ideology of student-centred learning, although we might note that his displayed orientation to the 'rights' of the tutor to give instructions and set agendas 'in situ' was arguably different from his interview account. Interestingly, the students seem to reject the 'learner empowerment' model (by virtue of their lack of preparation and minimal responses to the task) and instead orient to a 'transmission' model of teaching whereby they reject the option of taking control of, or intervening in the construction of knowledge. Again this becomes a further expression of the view of students as consumers.

CONCLUSION

In this chapter, we have explored what is meant by 'institutionality' and 'institutional identity', filtering the questions through some of the debates between the contrasting approaches of CA and CDA. Whilst CDA is epistemologically invested in exploring the kinds of contextual sites in which institutionality might be thought to reside, it was striking that CA studies revealed emergent orientations to normative identities, procedures and obligations specific to institutions, as well as systematic contrasts with ordinary talk. Indeed, the procedures of CA constitute important analytical resources for CDA practitioners studying the same data. Speculative leaps from macro theorising to micro contexts are embraced by CDA but rejected by CA. Equally, CDA researchers reject the limitations of CA's focus on short extracts of transcribed talk and lament the lost opportunities to relate the local enactment of institutional identities to the broader texture of political, economic and social discourse within which they are situated. These analytical and methodological debates continue in the next chapter, Narrative Identities.

CHAPTER 4

Narrative Identities

We begin this chapter with some conversational data, which come from the start of a neighbourhood mediation session. Three neighbours (Henry, Gilbert and Margaret), involved in a dispute about their communal garden, have met with two mediators (Joe and Lucy). The purpose of the meeting is to attempt to resolve the dispute:

Extract 4.1: Mediation session

Joe:	So do you want to look at, what hasn't worked with the old agreement? Or do you want to sort of say what has happened since?
Henry:	Well, there's quite a bit that hasn't worked really.
Gilbert:	Well, you know what pampas grass is, that razor grass . . .
Joe:	Are we going to start from the beginning, yeah?
Lucy:	I think we'll probably start afresh.
Joe:	Yeah, so three stories . . .
Gilbert:	THIS WOMAN – this woman is trying to nick the garden from the other tenants in the house . . .
Joe:	Hold on, wait a minute, you can't use that 'this woman is trying to' . . .
Gilbert:	Well that's what she's doing, that's why we are here.
Joe:	Yeah, I know, but you must speak for yourself, your problems. You've got to talk about the behaviour she's doing, you can't tell her that's what she thinks. So are you going to make a start first, okay?
Gilbert:	All right, well, she planted the garden like a minefield, y'know, it's a dangerous garden. She put dangerous plants in there, right, spiky teary plants from the razor weeds that she grows to all the other little things ((continues with story))

We can see from the transcript that their meeting will involve a series of stories and counter-stories. We can also see that the participants' story-telling will be embedded in a particular set of institutional rules about who gets to speak and from whose perspective. We can further point to the mediator's orientation to what, in this context, constitutes an appropriate narrative telling. This brief stretch of interaction illustrates several issues that will be explored in this chapter, including how we might *define narrative*, on what sorts of *occasions* narratives get told, how analysts *find identity* in instances of storytelling, and what people are *doing* when they tell stories.

The telling of stories is a prevalent part of social life, through which people recall, recount and reflect on their lives. From the mundane narratives that are produced in conversation, to published (auto)biographies and life histories, from the Internet to other forms of mass communication, we live in a 'storytelling society' through which we make sense of our lives (Denzin 2000). And, as is increasingly argued, it is in *narrative* that we construct identities. Narrative theorists claim that lives are made coherent and meaningful through the 'biographical' work that people do. As Daiute and Lightfoot (2004: xi) suggest, '[N]arrative discourse organizes life – social relations, interpretations of the past, and plans for the future.'

In this chapter, we consider the contribution of narrative theorists to our understanding of the discursive construction of identity. Our path through this literature is necessarily selective. We start by exploring the interdisciplinary development of narrative studies and the numerous *definitions of narrative* that have emerged in sociology, literary theory, psychology and linguistics. Next, we investigate how researchers, writing from these different disciplinary backgrounds, have theorised the link between *narrative* and *identity*, and try to identify the common elements in this diverse literature. We then move on to examine different approaches to *narrative analysis* and explore how such methods provide an empirical purchase on identifying and interpreting identity work in narrative contexts. Throughout the chapter, we cast a critical eye over these different approaches, and make explicit the links between them as well as their points of departure.

NARRATIVE INQUIRIES

The recent roots of narrative inquiry lie in the development, during the 1960s, of the field of *narratology*. Narratologists study the *internal structure of stories*, aiming to define their component parts, distinguish between their different categories, as well as make distinctions between narrative and non-narrative discourse. They also study and identify *different types* of story genres. In Saussurian terms, the focus is on narrative *langue* rather than *parole*: on the abstract identification of universal elements of a narrative rather than on actual story-telling in everyday life (Brockmeier and Carbaugh 2001). For example, Canadian literary critic Frye (1957) produced a grammar of *narrative genres*, claiming that four basic categories capture all the plotlines of literature (comedy, tragedy, romance and satire), and the historian White (1973) applied these modes to his study of historical narratives.

A pioneer analyst of *narrative structure* was Propp [1928] (1968), a structuralist scholar who analysed the 'morphology' of Russian fairy-tales and found that they contained particular plot elements occurring in a regular sequence. Many other writers have identified regular features that define narrative such as psychologist Bruner (1990: 272), who suggested a list of five features: action, scene, actor, instrument and goal, plus trouble: '[S]ome kind of imbalance or conflict between the five elements [which] gives rise to the subsequent actions, events, and resolutions that make-up a coherent, bounded narrative.' Stories about particular events also fall into more general types, such as 'boy-woos-girl' (ibid.). From a linguistic/anthropological perspective, Ochs and Capps (2001: 173) provide another list of narrative components, starting with the *setting* (information about time, physical and psychological location), an *unexpected event* (something unanticipated and problematic), a *psychological/physical response* (a reported change in emotion or psychological state), an *unplanned action* (an unintended and non goal-directed behaviour), an *attempt* (behaviour initiated to solve problematic event), and a *consequence* (the repercussion of the psychological or physiological response).

Labov and narrative coding

The concern with distinguishing narrative components is most famously articulated in Labov's (1972; Labov and Waletsky 1967) classic studies of American oral narratives as a way of comparing verbal skills across socio-linguistic categories. Labov collected a large corpus of interview data, in which narratives of personal experience were elicited using a 'danger of death' question: 'Were you ever in a situation where you were in serious danger of being killed, where you said to yourself – "this is it?"' Labov argued that for a stretch of talk to be a narrative, it must contain two clauses that are temporally ordered. For example, in the illustration below, clauses 2 and 3 are *narrative clauses*, whereas 1 is a *free clause* because it has no temporal junction:

1. I know a boy named Harry.
2. Another boy threw a bottle at him right in the head.
3. And he had to get seven stitches.

Consider the following narrative, which comes from an online collection of paranormal accounts *Narratives of the Weird* (www.notweird.com). We use this example to illustrate Labov's framework:

Extract 4.2: A clear night in October

This is an account of an experience I had that made me more than convinced about the existence of extraterrestrial craft and beings. It was a crisp clear night October 17, 2002 in our little town of El Cajon California, about 20 miles east of San Diego. My wife Rhonda and I had just settled down to watch one of our favourite television programs. It was 8:55 pm and we were sitting in the living room of our second story apartment when our 13-year-old daughter Chelsea had come running in telling us that she was staring at a strange light in the sky. I got up off the couch to see what she was talking about expecting to see a plane or some form of helicopter. What I saw defied any explanation that I could imagine. Rising slowly in the southeast was a large dark caramel coloured light. The amazing thing about this was that although it was dark in colour it was very bright like a star as the moon was in the background and it was still more luminous. It moved very very slowly upward. By this time my wife had joined me on the steps and my neighbour as well when they heard me freaking out a bit. The object moved in a wobbly fashion (kind of like a top in the sky if you can picture that) and stopped all at once and sat like a star in the sky for about 2 minutes and just did that kind of wobbling again like a top but without travelling in an upward motion. It then proceeded to move again in the same direction that it had previously for about 30 seconds and stopped again. What happened next blew my mind!!! Out of the bottom came a small blinking object that shot off west very very fast, and then about 3 seconds later another one that shot off in the other direction!! Then the large object seemed to fade out, back in brighter than before and then it faded out again, this time for good. All I can tell you is that was the most amazing thing that I have ever witnessed and it made believers out of my daughter, my wife and me!!!!

Labov found that the narratives in his collection contained a number of components. A 'fully formed' narrative 'begins with an orientation, proceeds to the complicating action, is suspended at the focus of evaluation before the resolution, concludes with the resolution, and returns the listener to the present time with the coda' (1972: 369). The *abstract* is comprised of clauses that summarise the whole story and its 'point'. In the extract above, we find it at the start of the narrative: 'This is an account of an experience I had that made me more than convinced about the existence of extraterrestrial craft and beings'. The *orientation* is composed of free and narrative clauses about time, place, persons and the activity of the narrative: the 'who, when, what, where?' (p. 370). In our example, the orientation is: 'It was a crisp clear night October 17, 2002 in our little town . . . and we were sitting in the living room of our second story apartment . . .'.

After this kind of scene-setting comes the *complicating action*; the part of the narrative that tells the audience 'Then what happened?' through the use of a temporal juncture (p. 370). In our narrative, this is 'when our 13-year-old daughter Chelsea had come running in telling us . . .'. Next comes the *evaluation*, which Labov defines as 'the means used by the narrator to indicate the point of the narrative' (p. 366): why the story is told, what its point is, and what the narrator's point of view on events is. The evaluation deals with a possible 'So what?' question from the audience, and different kinds of evaluations tell the audience why the story is reportable and tellable (Polyani 1979). In our example, this is 'What I saw defied any explanation that I could imagine.' The *result or resolution* tells the audience 'what finally happened' (Labov 1972: 370): 'and then it faded out again, this time for good'.

The final component is the *coda*, which signals that the narrative is over. 'All I can tell you . . . it made believers out of my daughter, my wife and me!!!'. The coda can provide 'general observations or show the effects of the events on the narrator' and bridge the gap 'between the moment of time at the end of the narrative proper and the present' (p. 365). It is also evaluative, and can serve to recapitulate the *abstract*. Labov (2001) notes further features, including the reporting of *witnesses* to enhance credibility and validation of the reportable event ('By this time my wife had joined me on the steps and my neighbour as well . . .'). Narrators may also *assign praise or blame* for the reportable events by integrating or polarising the characters.

Taken together, the various lists of narrative components share several features. First, narratives have a teller and a trajectory: they are expected to 'go' somewhere with a point and resolution. They have beginnings, middles and ends, and include the recounting of events that are displaced spatially and, crucially, *temporally*. For a stretch of talk or text to be categorised as a 'narrative', it has to incorporate basic structural features including a narrator, characters, settings, a plot, events that evolve over time, crises and resolutions. These features are central to our ability to characterise a stretch of discourse *as* narrative.

Problems with narrative coding schemes

One problem with structural kinds of narrative definitions is that many narratives *simply do not fit* the schemes suggested. Perhaps even more problematically, the fit often seems arbitrary: stories have to be made to fit the ready-made, idealised (and potentially ethnocentric) categories. Most authors claim that not all components are needed to constitute a narrative, or that the components may occur in a different order, or that their schemes only fit prototypical stories. It is in such disclaimers that the frameworks begin to lose their explanatory power. Our paranormal narrative appeared to contain all of Labov's features, and seemed to fit well with the other lists of narrative components we have seen, but sometimes this was a clumsy or forced fit, which could not account for all of its details. For example, the words of the *abstract* 'made me more than convinced about the existence of extra-terrestrial beings . . .' could also be coded as an *evaluation*. Edwards (1997a: 273) summarises this point:

> Are the differences minor and terminological, or are they
> matters that the authors might insist on? How might the
> differences be resolved, or alternatively, by what criteria should
> we prefer one definition to another? It is not simply a matter of
> pointing to actual instances of stories and showing that one
> definition fits better than another, because each definition
> specifies, somewhat circularly, what would count as a good
> ('well-formed') example. Definitions of this kind can be
> understood as analysts' efforts at nailing down common-sense
> categories: efforts at defining what a story or narrative is, as
> distinct from, say, a sermon, lecture, scientific explanation, or
> any other discourse category.

Although many of Labov's features are regularly found in narratives, and his work is undoubtedly influential, Brockmeier and Carbaugh (2001) claim that his project failed, by structuralist standards, to define a universal formal system of narrative. For Barthes (1977: 81), 'narrative analysis is condemned to a deductive procedure, obliged first to devise a hypothetical model of description . . . and then gradually work down from this model towards the different narrative species which at once conform to and depart from the model'.

Another problem with these coding schemes is that they often analyse idealised but decontextualised examples of the narrative format, rather than consider the way narratives are actually told in particular

interactional contexts. The focus on identifying the structural components of narratives, either published stories or those produced in interviews, fails to deal with the interactional business being accomplished in
their telling (Edwards 1997b). As conversation analysts have pointed
out, the interview situation in which Labov collected his narratives
'plays havoc with the motive force of the telling – the action and interactional precipitant of the telling – by making the elicitation itself the
invariant occasion for telling the story' (Schegloff 1997b: 99–100).
Conversation analysts argue that if stories are to be analysed, the interest should be in how they get embedded and are managed, turn-by-turn,
in interaction, rather than in the internal structure or isolated story
events. This is because storytelling accomplishes many different interactional functions: to amuse, inform, accuse, complain, boast, justify, to
build social organisation and (re)align the social order (M. H. Goodwin
1997).

Consider the following example. It comes from Wooffitt's (1992) study
of paranormal accounts told in research interviews, but works from a conversation analytic perspective to analyse *how* paranormal tales are told
and the interactional goals achieved in their telling. There is a focus on
structure, then, but of a different order from Labovian kinds of narrative
coding schemes. The extract comes from one of Wooffitt's participants,
who is part way through describing an out-of-body experience that
happened at a subway train station:

Extract 4.3: EM B 88 from Wooffitt 1992: 117–8

```
 1   I had ear plugs in my ears
 2   'cz I couldn't stand all the noise
 3   I had (.) dark glasses on
 4   >because I didn't want
 5   to see anybody<
 6   an' I was standing right there           'I was just doing X ...'
 7   on the platform (.7) waiting
 8   for this damned train to come (.)
 9   all of a sudden
10   (2.3)
11   I (.) began to feel as total             '. . . when Y'
12   totally (.) absolutely (.)
13   insubstantial that is
14   I had no bodily feeling whatsoever
```

An initial observation about this sequence is that it contains Labovian
components, an *orientation* (lines 1–8) and *complicating action* (lines

9–14). However, if we use this kind of coding scheme to reduce the narrative to chunks, the content of each chunk remains unanalysed (Edwards 1997a). Wooffitt's analysis of a corpus of such accounts shows us that a focus on the interactional features of the account produces a much richer analysis. For example, Wooffitt demonstrates how these tellings follow a particular two-part format: 'I was just doing X, when Y' (cf. Jefferson 2004b). The X part contains the narrator's mundane circumstances, and Y provides the unexpected event. Wooffitt argues that the X-Y device mediates particular interactional concerns and accomplishes specific tasks. For example, the X part of the device is not a bland description of the speaker's activities; rather, 'these formulations are *designed to achieve* this character' (p. 127, emphasis added). It does normalising work, by contrasting the normal (the speaker does ordinary things like everyone else) with the paranormal (Sacks 1984a). It therefore shores up the authenticity of the speaker's account, and their credibility as an account-giver, by virtue of their concertedly achieved membership of the category 'normal perceiver/reporter'. Packaging these lines together simply as an *orientation* loses sight of the detailed way the story is put together.

Wooffitt's work (see also Widdicombe and Wooffitt 1995) provides an alternative way of studying narrative data, by focusing on the detailed, interaction-oriented and rhetorically organised structure of stories, rather than on their individual components. As Holstein and Gubrium (2000: 103) note, 'stories – especially those of the self – are now analysed as much for the ways in which storytellers and the conditions of storytelling shape what is conveyed, as for what their contents tell us about the selves in question'. From this perspective, identity ascription is 'occasioned by the specifics of the interactions' and 'is part of the dynamically emerging trajectory of the conversation' (Antaki 1998: 85). An important feature of Wooffitt's work is that, 'in the context of analysing personal narratives . . . the notion of a "true self" is discursively managed, rather than being something that is simply available in this kind of talk, lying behind and generating it' (Edwards 1997a: 281). The notion of a 'true self' that lurks behind discourse, as opposed to a multiple, postmodern shifting self that is constructed in talk, is a distinction we discussed in Chapters 1 and 2, and unpack later in this chapter.

So far we have seen that, for many social scientists, narrative is a fundamental construct for understanding the shape of the social world. We have considered one trajectory of work: distinguishing *types of story* and defining the *components of individual narratives*. But we have also started to think of narrative not just as an abstract phenomenon to be coded by philosophers, literary theorists and social scientists, but also as functional, occasioned and constitutive of identity. We move on in the next section to consider the narrative construction of identity in more detail.

THEORISING NARRATIVE IDENTITY

Extract 4.4: BBC 'Panorama' interview

Bashir: And what did you do?

Diana: I swam. We went to um Alice Springs, to Australia, and we went
            and did a walkabout and I said to my husband 'What do I do now?'
            And he said, 'Go over to the other side and speak to them.' I said,
            'I can't, I just can't.' And he said, 'Well, you've got to do it.' And he
            went off and did his bit and I went off and did my bit and
            it practically finished me off there and then. And I suddenly realized I
            went back to our – my hotel room and realised the impact that, you
            know, I had to sort myself out. We had a six-week tour, four weeks
            in Australia and two weeks in New Zealand, and by the end when
            we flew back from New Zealand, I was a different person. I realized
            the sense of duty, the level of intensity of interest, and the
            demanding role I now found myself in.

This is an extract from the interview between journalist Martin Bashir and the late Princess of Wales, broadcast on the BBC 'Panorama' programme in the UK in November 1995. It comes from near the start of the interview. Bashir has asked Diana how she handled the 'transition from being Lady Diana Spencer to the most photographed, the most talked-about, woman in the world'. Diana responds by describing how she had to 'sink or swim' in her new situation. Through the recounting of a story, Diana describes a shift in her identity, from one kind of person to another. Whereas her 'true self' is naïve and reluctant to meet the public, her 'royal role' carries certain cultural expectations concerning what is normative behaviour for principal members of the monarchy. We can see how these identities are managed within the narrative structure of her account (Abell, Stokoe and Billig 2000).

If selves and identities are constituted in discourse, they are necessarily constructed in stories. Through storytelling, narrators can produce 'edited' descriptions and evaluations of themselves and others, making identity aspects more salient at certain points in the story than others (Georgakopoulou 2002). In the example above, Diana makes a variety of identity claims including 'ordinary woman', 'royal princess', 'wife', 'public figure' or 'survivor'. Her story is one of transformation and change. It involves particular narrative details including the voicing of another character, her husband, and implies a particular kind of relationship with him. It is being told to an interviewer, with an overhearing audience, and so it has a particular rhetorical function and accomplishes particular interactional goals (for example, blaming, accusing, establishing relationships).

Narrative researchers ascribe a particular ontological character to people, as *storied selves*, and this notion provides the basis for understanding people's lives. For instance:

> Through life stories individuals and groups make sense of themselves; they tell what they are or what they wish to be, as they tell so they come, they *are* their stories. (Cortazzi 2001: 388)

> We speak our identities. (Mishler 1999: 19)

> We 'become' the stories through which we tell our lives . . . Telling stories configures the 'self-that-I-might-be'. (Riessman 2003: 7)

For narrative researchers, assumptions about the constitutive nature of discourse are supplemented with the specifics of narration as a particular practice through which identity is performed, articulated and struggled over. The process of *narrative* identity construction is theorised in similar ways to the discursive construction of identity more generally, as we observed in Chapter 1. The emphasis is on identity as performed rather than as prior to language, as dynamic rather than fixed, as culturally and historically located, as constructed in interaction with other people and institutional structures, as continuously remade, and as contradictory and situational (May 2004). Thus the practice of narration involves the 'doing' of identity, and because we can tell different stories we can construct different versions of self.

Narrative theorists argue that the idea of storytelling adds something crucial to discourse-based theories of identity construction: the notion of *temporality* (Linde 1993; Ricoeur 1991). Narration produces a sense of identity coherence by incorporating notions of connectedness and temporal unity. Polkinghorne (1991: 141) uses the label 'emplotment' to describe how selves are narratively configured by bringing together different temporal elements and 'directing them towards a conclusion or sequence of disconnected events into a unifed story with a point or theme'. Good examples of how narrative in particular, rather than discourse in general, constitutes identity can be found in a number of interview-based studies of chronic illness. The argument is that illness constitutes an 'ontological assault' on people's sense of who they are (Crossley 2000: 539). It is a 'breach' in the orderliness of everyday life, and highlights the taken-for-grantedness of the 'normal' and unseen experience of narrative coherence (ibid.). It is in accounts of such experiences that we can clearly see a 'narrative wreckage' (Frank 1995), with illness as an interruption that 'divides life into a "before" and an "after"' (Bülow and Hydén 2003: 75). For example, Langellier (2001) interviewed women who had had tattoos over mastectomy scars following breast cancer. She found that the women's narrative performance of identity achieved a transformation from a passive, agentless self who 'got cancer' and 'got tattooed' (that is, scarred) by the radiation therapy to an active, agentive self who subsequently had a tattoo done over the scar. As Crossley (2003b: 295) points out, 'when people talk or write about their experiences of chronic or serious illness, they often characterise themselves as becoming a "totally different person"'.

Another distinguishing feature of narrative identity theories is the notion that the local stories we tell about ourselves are connected in some way to wider cultural stories (or master narratives, cultural plotlines, discourses, interpretative repertoires). The local 'storyworld' that is created in narration provides a 'backdrop of cultural expectations about a typical course of action; our identities as social beings emerge as we construct our own individual experiences as a way to position ourselves in relation to social and cultural expectations' (Schiffrin 1996: 170). This kind of interdependency between personal stories and culturally circulating plot lines is another common focus for narrative theorists.

Narrative and subject positions

The connection between 'on the ground' storytelling and wider cultural narratives is developed in a strand of narrative identity work based on *positioning theory* (cf. Bamberg 2004; Davies and Harré 1990; Harré and van Langenhove 1991; Harré and Moghaddam 2003). We briefly outlined the assumptions of this approach in Chapter 1. Positioning theorists examine the co-construction of identity between storyteller and audience. 'Positioning' refers to the process through which speakers adopt, resist and offer 'subject positions' that are made available in 'master narratives' or 'discourses'. Davies and Harré (1990) provide an example from two lines of a reported conversation and the parties' post-hoc interpretation. Two people, Sano and Enfermada (from the Spanish, meaning 'healthy man' and 'ill woman'), are at a foreign academic conference. Enfermada is ill, so the two are searching for a chemist's shop:

> S: I'm sorry to have dragged you all this way when you are
>   not well.
> E: You didn't drag me, I chose to come.

Davies and Harré argue that in order to identify the speech acts through which positioning takes place we need to identify the wider storylines of which these turns are a kind of intertextual moment. They suggest four readings:

1. Sano's line as perceived by Sano is a story of medical treatment, with Sano positioned as nurse and Enfermada as patient. In this story, the action is *commiseration*.
2. Sano's story line as perceived by Enfermada is a story of paternalism, with Sano positioned as the powerful man and Enfermada as the dependent and helpless woman. Here, the action is *condescension* and indexical offence by Sano to Enfermada.
3. Enfermada's line as perceived by Enfermada is a story of joint adventure, with both participants positioned as travellers in a foreign land.
4. Enfermada's line as perceived by Sano is one of feminist protest, which positions Sano as a chauvinist and Enfermada as a righteous suffragette. Here, the action is *complaint*, with indexical offence by Enfermada to Sano.

Davies and Harré conclude that the two people are trapped in a quarrel because each is living a narrative of which the other is unaware: 'He was not being paternalistic and she was not being priggish yet each was driven by the power of the story lines and their associated positions' (p. 57).

In a later paper, Harré and van Langenhove (1991) note that several forms of positioning can take place at once. People differ in their capacity to position themselves and others, in their willingness and intention to position and be positioned, or in terms of their power to achieve acts of positioning. However, it is unclear in their work precisely what their sense of conversational action amounts to. In the example above, it is not difficult to regard what Davies and Harré call *commiseration* as doing the 'action' of apology. And although they claim that positioning is a conversational phenomenon, they do not use actual conversational data to exemplify their theory, sticking instead to idealistic examples that 'fit' the model clearly – and even then perhaps not clearly enough! As Potter (2001: 46) points out, speech act theory has had 'more success with made-up talk than in applying the ideas to actual speech'. Positioning theory remains unclear and somewhat mystical about what, in talk, *counts* as a position, and what does not. Like narrative theories more broadly, it runs into trouble at the application of its categories to the particulars of actual stories and accounts.

In this section, we have considered a number of different theories of narrative identity. We have seen some brief examples of the kinds of discursive identity work people might do in particular interactional contexts. In the next section, we move on to consider the practicalities of collecting and analysing narrative data, before examining some detailed empirical examples of the analysis of narrative identity.

COLLECTING NARRATIVE DATA

Having discussed the theoretical context of 'narrative identities', we now move on to the practicalities of gathering data and analysing it. The link between narrative and identity has been explored in texts derived from public materials such as published biographies and autobiographies, newspapers, magazines, television and radio programmes, films, fiction, fairytales, myths and legends, cultural texts and songs, film, dance, fiction and poetry. However, the majority of narrative research records, transcribes and analyses narratives obtained in interviews. We can further subdivide interviewing into two types: the standard social science research interview, which is not designed to elicit narrative-type answers yet generates storied answers, and *narrative interviews*.

Narrative interviews

Narrative interviews comprise what some call the new tradition of 'biographical methods' (Chamberlyne, Bornat and Wengraf 2000). Some commentators have argued that standard semi-structured interviews do not produce good narrative data, because the schedule has a determining effect on what participants say, often treating their stories as irrelevancies or diversions. The aim of narrative – or 'life history', 'biographic' – interviews is to elicit extended narrative accounts of a person's life. For instance, in McAdams's (1993) method, participants are asked to think about their lives as a series of *chapters in a book*, and to give each chapter a title and outline. They are then asked to identify and tell stories about a series of *key events* in their lives, including peak, low and turning point events, earliest memory, important childhood memory, important adolescent memory, important adult memory and one more important memory. Next comes a question designed to elicit narratives about the *significant people* in the participant's life, followed by a question about their *future script* and stories-to-come in plans and ambitions for the future. The next question focuses on narrative accounts of *stresses, problems, conflicts and unresolved issues*, and their possible solutions. The penultimate question deals with *personal ideology*, defined broadly to encompass the participant's fundamental religious and/or political orientations. Finally, the participant is asked to consider his defining or central *life theme*.

Another method of narrative interviewing is Wengraf's Biographic Narrative Interpretative Method (BNIM: see Wengraf 2005). In contrast to the 'active interview' (see Holstein and Gubrium 1995), which emphasises the role of the interviewer in the co-construction of accounts given in interviews, the BNIM stresses passivity on the part of the interviewer. The voice of the researcher emerges later, through their 'retelling of the story as a weaver of tales, a collage-maker or a narrator of the narrations' (K. Jones 2003: 61). A related method of data collection is Hollway and Jefferson's (2000) 'Free Association Narrative Interview' (FANI) approach, an adaptation of the BNIM that combines features of narrative theory with the psychoanalytic principle of free association.

The aim of the BNIM is to produce a story that is as unhindered by the norms of social interaction as possible. However, this engages people in an unnatural situation that removes them from their everyday lives in which stories might be told. Moreover, it ignores the ontological nature of the *narrative* interview itself, which assumes that people carry their life stories around in their heads, as if being asked to tell one's life story in an interview is something people are primed to do. And rather than following the shift towards treating interviews as 'topic' rather than 'resource' (cf. Wieder 1988), the narrative interview format takes a backwards step with its emphasis in generating some kind of 'pure' account. Edwards (1997a: 277) argues that interview contexts 'tend to substitute, for the ordinary occasions on which stories might be told, got-up occasions for set-piece performances-for-interview'. Of course, not all analysts treat narrative interview data this way, and some researchers analyse stories as they crop up in everyday and institutional interaction, rather than in response to interview questions (for example, Bülow 2004; Hsieh 2004). This taps into a wider debate about the value of interview materials versus naturally occurring data, which has implications for how one might go about analysing the resulting transcripts (for example, Potter and Hepburn 2005).

Having discussed some ways of obtaining narrative data, we now move on to provide empirical examples of different methods of narrative analysis in use, which show the reader exactly how narrative identity work can be identified and analysed.

NARRATIVE ANALYSIS

There are many different versions of narrative analysis. Each maps onto differing ontological treatments of language data. The structuralist approaches discussed earlier map different structures and ways of telling directly and unproblematically onto sociolinguistic variables such as ethnicity, class and gender (for example, Labov 1972). Some versions claim to be accessing minds and worlds beyond the interview context and behind the narrative discourse data: the phenomenological realm of 'real' experience (for example, Crossley 2003a), or the psychodynamic realm of the unconscious (for example, Hollway and Jefferson 2005). Some of these versions, such as Crossley's, adopt a strange hybrid of constructionist *and* referential understandings of language, in which language is a window on the mind/experience *and* the site of identity construction. Others adopt a more thoroughgoing constructionist approach to narrative interview data as a situated, co-constructed interaction between interviewer and participant, and with identities as their product, or process (for example, Korobov and Bamberg 2004). Others still treat the interview as an interaction in its own right, with the narratives told and identity work done within it, as tied to those narrative moments (for example, Widdicombe and Wooffitt 1995). Finally, we have the analysis of stories by conversation analysts and discursive psychologists, whereby the interest does not stem from 'narrative' per se, but from the wider project of analysing everyday talk (for example, Edwards 1997a; Jefferson 1978; Lerner 1992).

Most broadly, 'narrative analysis' is an interpretative tool designed to examine people's lives holistically through the stories they tell. Narrative analysts ask questions like:

> Why was the narrative developed that way, and told in that order? In what kinds of stories does the narrator place him/herself? How does he/she strategically make preferred identity claims? What other identities are being performed or suggested? What was the response of the listener/audience, and how did it influence the development of the narrative and interpretation of it? (Riessman 2003: 8)

Although there are numerous titles on narrative analysis, a journal dedicated to narrative studies (*Narrative Inquiry*), and countless examples of empirical research, there is no one agreed method for going about analysing narrative data. As Riessman (1993: v) notes, researchers can end up 'drowning in a sea of transcripts' because the literature remains 'largely silent about ways to approach long stretches of talk that [take] the form of narrative accounts'.

One common element of narrative research is that the data, usually interview transcripts, are broken down into coded chunks of one kind or another, and interpreted by the researcher who, in the process of doing analysis, weaves the original story into a wider tapestry with their particular blend of relevant theory, cultural information and politics. As Riessman (1993: 30) suggests, the analyst's 'authorial voice and interpretive commentary knit the disparate elements together and determine how readers are to understand [the informant's] experience . . . Illustrative quotes from the interview provide evidence for the investigator's interpretation of the plot twists.' We present a number of examples of narrative analyses of identity, each working from a different analytic position. First, we discuss Murray's (2003) interview-based research in which he classifies the broad narratives that run through his participants' accounts. The second example is taken from Hollway and Jefferson's (2000) psychoanalytically-inspired 'free association narrative interview' method. Next, we illustrate a variety of narrative analysis based on positioning theory. The first three approaches pay some attention to the detail of the narratives, but mainly ascribe broad macro-level narrative/discourse labels to the participants' stories. In contrast, the fourth example illustrates a micro-level analysis based in conversation analysis. Finally, we discuss two examples that aim to combine CA-inflected micro- and poststructuralist macro-levels of analysis, and discuss some of the issues that arise from this kind of combination.

IDENTIFYING NARRATIVES IN INTERVIEWS

Our first example of narrative analysis comes from Murray's (2003) research. Murray recommends collecting data for narrative analysis via a 'life story interview', which aims to facilitate the telling of an extended personal narrative. Unlike Wengraf, Murray argues that the social context of production is a key part of the analysis, in which the interviewer's turns actively shape the telling. Murray interviewed women with breast cancer, focusing on how they handled the 'disruption' of the disease, integrated it into their everyday life story, and how their stories connected to broader social and interpersonal contexts. Murray describes two phases of narrative analysis. In the first 'descriptive' phase, the researcher familiarises himself with the structure and content of each interview, summarising the stories in terms of beginnings, middles, ends, narrative linkages and subplots connected to the overall narrative. The second 'interpretative' phase involves making connections with broader theoretical literatures used to interpret the participants' stories. The researcher therefore needs a simultaneous familiarity with their data's contents and relevant literature.

One interpretative step is to ascribe a macro–categorical label for the type of narrative being told. For example, accounts of personal crisis might be classifiable as 'tragedy narratives'. Murray discusses Robinson's (1990) study of patients with multiple sclerosis. Robinson identified three different life storylines in his participants' accounts: those who thought their life was over ('regressive narrative'), those who thought that life had changed but was generally all right ('stable narrative'), and those that talked in terms of the illness offering new opportunities ('progressive narrative').

Murray provides short data extracts from one of his own interviewees, Mrs Brown:

Extract 4.5: From Murray 2003: 125–7

When the surgeon told her she had cancer she was very upset:

Mrs B:	It really flipped me right out.
Int:	Yeah.
Mrs B:	It really flipped me out, but it was so quick.
Int:	Hmm, hmm.
Mrs B:	Like, I never had time to stop and think.
Int:	Right.
Mrs B:	Like, he told me, and then I cried for weeks, and then next week I was in hospital and had it all done.

She had a lumpectomy, and on discharge from hospital she found it very difficult to cope:

Int:	Was it a mastectomy or a lumpectomy?
Mrs B:	No, it was just a lumpectomy.
Int:	Ok.
Mrs B:	Right, and so I went through all that, and then I went through a year of chemo and radiation and went through hell, but like by myself.
Int:	Hmm. Hmm.
Mrs B:	You know, no husband and three little kids. They were young then, right.
Int:	Oh, it must have been hard.
Mrs B:	And it was terrible, it was absolutely terrible. I had no moral support. I had no one here to help.

She was very anxious about the implications for her children if there was a recurrence of cancer:

Mrs B: If it happens tomorrow, and he's only 12, I will flip. I will go really, really crazy.

Int: Hmm, hmm.

Mrs B: Yeah, because what's going to happen to him?

Int: Yeah.

Mrs B: Welfare would come and take him [I] always worry about that kind of stuff. I worry about all that kind of stuff.

Murray ascribes a 'stable/regressive' macrostructure to Mrs Brown's narrative. Mrs Brown describes her life as a litany of woes, starting with a difficult childhood. For this participant, cancer is yet another bleak challenge. She had no social support and an ongoing fear of death. In contrast, other participants' stories were categorised as 'progressive'. For instance, one describes giving her heart to the Lord, and treats life as a series of enhancing opportunities.

Murray's method therefore begins by identifying commonalities in narrative structure across the different interview participants. He found that each participant's narrative had a similar structure, starting with a 'beginning', which told of life before cancer. Different women emphasised different aspects of their lives, such as work, or family; and some tried to identify possible links between their early experiences and cancer. In the 'middle' of their narratives came tales of diagnosis, surgery and the reactions of friends and family. In the 'end', the women reflected on their story and redefined their identities as cancer survivors. Murray suggests that three different levels of analysis can be performed on the stories. At a 'personal' level, he discusses the way 'the narrative reflects the different experiences of the women' (p. 128). At the 'interpersonal' level, he focuses on how the story is produced for the interviewer, how it is organised, what comes first and what is emphasised. Finally, at the 'societal' level, Murray makes connections with the broader context, suggesting that their narratives 'mesh with the broader moral universes of the women' (p. 129).

Although Murray stresses the importance of treating the narratives as interactively produced between both interviewer and participant, he does not comment on the interviewer's turns directly in his analysis. One place where the interviewer's turn is interestingly consequential is in his question about the kind of operation Mrs Brown had to treat the cancer:

Int: Was it a mastectomy or a lumpectomy?

Mrs B: No, it was just a lumpectomy.

A mastectomy is a more severe and extensive operation, as it involves the removal of the breast, rather than a lump from it. The interviewer's question prompts Mrs Brown to answer that it was 'just' a lumpectomy. The question therefore offers Mrs Brown an opportunity to see her operation as less severe than it could have been, which could have a number of consequences: It might help her see the cancer as less serious, but it could also be seen as not warranting her extremely negative feelings, or as deserving a lesser amount of sympathy than a mastectomy. Whatever, the important thing to note is the role of the interviewer's turns in shaping the production of the narrative.

PSYCHOANALYSIS AND NARRATIVE

The second method we discuss is Hollway and Jefferson's (2000) 'free association narrative interview' approach, which we introduced briefly earlier. The interview operates on the basis that people's narratives contain unconscious links between ideas, giving the researcher insight into the psychoanalytic meanings of their stories. In contrast to the BNIM, the approach treats people as ill-equipped to give reliable accounts of their lives. Instead, Hollway and Jefferson (2004: 404) argue that research participants are 'defended subjects', whose defences against anxiety 'will potentially compromise interviewees' ability to know the meaning of their actions, purposes and relations'. Only a researcher can access the identity implications of the stories research participants tell, whose discourse is a window to their unconscious, subjectively unknown mind.

A person's identity is as a psychosocial subject, shaped by unconscious desires, defences and conflicts as well as societal discourses that render events meaningful. During analysis, the researcher uses their own 'feelings as data, following psychoanalytic principles of transference and countertransference, in order to identify their own emotional investments' (ibid.). The analyst therefore focuses particularly on moments of incoherence, contradiction, conflict, changes in 'emotional tone' and 'avoidances'. Hollway and Jefferson criticise life story interview approaches (such as McAdams's method discussed earlier) for producing an unnatural coherence and rationality to narrative accounts, which is avoided in their free-associative elicitings.

In our example, Hollway and Jefferson (2001) report on the 'case of Ivy', an agoraphobic woman who lives on a UK housing estate. Ivy has told the interviewer that she had a nervous breakdown that she cannot explain. Hollway and Jefferson treat the unaccounted-for nervous breakdown as a puzzle, the solution to which they suggest is partly revealed in this extract:

Extract 4.6: From Hollway and Jefferson 2001: 112

Ivy: And I used to say 'oh, I'm not going out, people will be talking about me, 'er [daughter Fiona] being pregnant.' He [Albert] used to say 'let 'em talk about you, while they're talking about you, they're leaving somebody else alone.'

Wendy: (laugh). Is that one of the reasons you didn't like to go out?

Ivy: I weren't frightened 'cos I used to show off if anybody said owt. I mean when Fiona were took in 'ospital, er, I 'ad a right go at one of doctors there ... And when she were in 'ospital, when she'd 'ad our Jonathan – I went – she wouldn't – I couldn't keep away. I 'ad to be there all the time. And I went in one day and she were crying. I said 'what you crying for?' She said er, 'two of women have just said – aye that's 'er what's not married.'

In terms of identity, Hollway and Jefferson's (2001) conclusion about this and other extracts is that Ivy's identity is 'invested in respectability', including sexual respectability. They point to Ivy's 'free-associated link' and *unconscious* fear of people talking about her and her daughter. They also suggest that Ivy contradicts *what they know as analysts* is her 'fear' because she says 'I weren't frightened', thus her knowledge of this link is 'difficult'. They propose a relationship between local gossip about her unwed daughter and moving to a different ward, and Ivy's agoraphobia: 'we interpreted her reported behaviour as defensive reactions against the anxiety of her daughter's status as a young unmarried mother' (p. 112). They cite Ivy's routine avoidance of discussing her grandson's illegitimate status as further evidence for this interpretation. Hollway and Jefferson import the psychoanalytic observation that agoraphobia is the result of 'a deeply felt contradiction which cannot be rendered conscious because it is extremely anxiety-provoking' (p. 112). Ivy's agoraphobia meant she did not have to expose herself to the neighbours, an activity which might threaten her identity as a respectable woman. They also claim that Ivy is 'positioned in a contemporary discourse concerning respectability, but . . . escapes the potential determinism of that analysis by showing how she negotiated and resisted this through the inner conflicts which it precipitated' (p. 112).

Hollway and Jefferson move a long way from the data presented to produce their analysis: they claim to look *beneath it*, in a metaphorical sense, *to the psyche* of their participant, *above it*, to wider culturally circulating discourses, and to *their own feelings* about what is 'really' going on in the data. One reason for the first kind of analytic move is linked to a more general dissatisfaction among some narrative analysts with what they see as the inability of discursive approaches (such as discursive psychology and conversation analysis) to deal with the inner psychological world of experience (cf. Craib 2000; Frosh 1999). As Day Sclater (2003: 324) argues, 'it's as if there's little (if anything) more to "the self" than its multiple and shifting positionings in discourse, or language, its presentation in narrative'. As we noted in Chapter 1, although the 'turn to discourse' resulted in a shift away from treating identity as a fixed, unitary product accessed *through language*, towards a postmodern understanding of identity as fluid, dynamic and contingently constructed *in language*, Hollway and Jefferson's work is a good example of the retreat to using language to access the interior world of subjectivity.

Some have argued that the introduction of psychoanalytic theory into narrative analysis (and discourse analysis more generally) results in the kinds of individualistic psychopathologised bases for explaining why people say (or do not say) the things they do that prompted the 'turn to discourse' in the first place (Hepburn 2003). Furthermore, when we examine the empirical work of Hollway and Jefferson, we find that it is *nothing but* language. Edwards (2006: emphasis in original) argues that although it is clear that discourse is not 'all there is' in the world, nor is it the same thing as 'experience', 'feelings' and so on, '*it is the primary work of language to make all those 'other' phenomena accountable.* That includes not only what participants say, but what theorists and analysts write about what participants say, including what people (purportedly) think or feel but do not say.' As we have noted, it is a common criticism that discourse-based approaches 'leave out' the study of experience, the unconscious, subjectivity, and it is these things that writers like Hollway and Jefferson seek to rescue in their approach. However, Edwards (2006) argues:

> There is no realm of subjectivity, unconscious feelings, or objective reality, that language does not reach – indeed, the writings of those who are primarily concerned with such ostensibly language-independent and almost-ineffable matters, is reflexive testimony to the adequacy of language for dealing with them. Beyond that adequacy, as Wittgenstein famously concluded, 'Whereof we cannot speak, thereof we must be silent'.

Edwards further argues that notions such as *surface* and *depth* are 'locative metaphors' which are themselves 'part of the practices of everyday accountability and professional conduct – part of the rich surface (if I may use the metaphor while discussing it) of talk and text. They do not reach, really, beyond the surface of anything at all. Rather, as elements of language use, they are part of the rich surface where experiences and ideas are made accountable, publicly and for social consumption'.

One interesting feature of Hollway and Jefferson's analysis of Ivy is the way that they render her talk in their transcript. While there is no attempt to represent or analyse the delivery of her account, in terms of prosody, pacing and so on, what Hollway and Jefferson *do* build into their transcription is a series of emblematic dropped h's, signalling her working-class identity. In effect, Hollway and Jefferson do some identity work, or positioning, in the way they represent Ivy in their transcript. The authors themselves take up a 'subject position' in relation to Ivy: the 'educated analyst' versus the 'ignorant participant'.

Hollway and Jefferson's method, in addition to invoking the participant's 'psyche', makes a different kind of analytic move, invoking wider discourses that they claim might be informing or positioning their defended subject. This second kind of move is illustrated clearly in the next example.

DISCOURSES, NARRATIVES AND 'SUBJECT POSITIONS'

The third example draws on Harré and colleagues' work on 'positioning theory', analysing identity-relevant 'subject positions'. It comes from an analysis of a magazine interview with a woman called 'Rachel', in an article entitled, 'How I became a lesbian escort' (Swan and Linehan 2000). The authors aim to redescribe the narrative and highlight 'the subtle interplay between the use of cultural elements or discourses in a story and the individual's positioning of self in relation to such elements to create a unique and justifiable identity in that setting' (p. 406).

Swan and Linehan predict that being a lesbian escort may produce difficulties for the storyteller, as this identity position does not sit easily within dominant narratives. They therefore investigate the 'range of narrative strategies that functions to position [Rachel] in a manner which renders cultural norms problematic, and in doing so validates her construction of self' (p. 408). Swan and Linehan first identify sections in the data that deal explicitly with constructing escorting and lesbianism, and analyse how subject positions are created through the account. They note that Rachel's story fits the canonical structure of narratives, in which the 'point' of the story is some obstacle to be overcome. For Rachel, the trouble is her identity, and her story is one of a shift from a 'normal' heterosexual existence to a lesbian escort: '[S]he emplots her breach in terms of a rejection of submission to her boyfriend and move to agency and self determination and as the realisation of her sexuality through lesbian escorting' (p. 410). This is their first extract:

Extract 4.7: From Swan and Linehan 2000: 411

I've never been physically attracted to men. They must pick up on this because they rarely show any interest in me. I don't really know how to define myself but I'm definitely attracted to women. The first time I noticed a woman I was eighteen and working in London as a nanny. I would see this girl waiting at a bus stop every morning and think, 'Mmm, you're lovely.' Then I'd think, 'That's weird.' For years I didn't do anything about my feelings, and I'd had a boyfriend and two children before I knew for certain that my sexual inclinations were towards women.

We report the analytic comments that seem, to us, to pin down what is meant by narrative identity, positioning and so on. To start with, we track the sequence of subject positions that Swan and Linehan point to in their analysis. They claim that Rachel positions herself (pp. 411–13):

1. In relation to men, as not sexually responsive to men: *I've never been physically attracted to men.*
2. In relation to men, as not an object of their desire: *they rarely show any interest in me.*
3. In relation to women, as sexually responsive to them: *I'm definitely attracted to women*, with some warranting work done in an anecdote about finding a girl at bus stop attractive.
4. As not comprehending her own sexuality: *Then I'd think, 'That's weird.'*
5. As sexually interested in women but lacking knowledge of her sexuality: *I didn't do anything about my feelings, and I'd had a boyfriend and two children before I knew for certain that my sexual inclinations were towards women.*

Swan and Linehan suggest that these different positions illustrate the dynamic process of identity construction. They argue that identity-making is a social as well as an individual process, and in the second part of their analysis demonstrate how Rachel's story can be related to macro-level narratives:

1. The *narrative of romance*: Rachel places herself within a particular fragment of this narrative: the 'sexual awakening': *The first time I noticed a woman . . . 'Mmm, you're lovely.'*
2. The *narrative of change*: A popular narrative in Western culture is that of female transformation from the 'monstrous to the beautiful' (for example, in fairytales such as *Cinderella*, or in more contemporary times in the film *Grease*) (see also Chapter 5). The change revolves around the hidden-but-present seeds of the future identity being available in the past identity: 'In Rachel's relation of her sexual response to the girl at the bus-stop, and her positioning of self as sexually responsive to women but lacking awareness of it when with her boyfriend, Rachel begins her overarching genre of change by portraying herself as having the seeds of her later identity as a lesbian escort within her earlier identity' (p. 413).

Swan and Linehan claim that their analysis shows how narrators may challenge master narratives through their positioning work: Rachel includes 'motherhood' and 'marriage' storylines but positions herself in such a way as to challenge the identity options they make available. Thus people are not determined by dominant narratives or the local discourse context, 'but rather a complex self emerges from the teller's relational positionings with respect to both' (p. 424). For Swan and Linehan, this kind of analysis captures the *relational* and *socially constructed* nature of identity.

In their analysis, Swan and Linehan use their knowledge of cultural narratives somewhat to reduce the detail in Rachel's story to a small number of narratives. The next example, which illustrates an approach based in conversation analysis, contrasts sharply with the kind of analysis conducted in 'positioning theory'.

NARRATIVE IN TALK-IN-INTERACTION

Conversation analysts treat storytelling as an interactional accomplishment. It is an activity that requires a long turn, and so analysts have examined *how* stories get told: how they are organised within the turn-taking system and how they get told without interruption (for example, Ryave 1978). Stories can be invited ('Tell us about . . .'), pre-announced ('Guess what . . .') or proposed, ('Well I have something to tell you about her'). Proposals function to tell the audience that 'I'm going to talk for more than a sentence', to keep people listening, and to tell people *how* to listen to a forthcoming stream of talk (Sacks 1992).

A key feature of conversation analytic studies that marks them out as a contrast to most other empirical work on narrative and identity, is that they deal with naturally occurring rather than researcher-produced interview data. These kinds of data allow us to see more clearly how stories are told in a collaborative way between participants, and how the sense of what is being told is displayed in subsequent turns at talk. Below is a short section from a telephone call made to an alcohol abuse helpline. The caller has telephoned because she is drinking large quantities of alcohol and wants a 'detox'. In particular, she wants to know if she can get a detox without going through her own GP. The advice worker has suggested she see another GP and at the same time start her detox on her own by reducing the amount she is drinking. The advice worker has just finished eliciting the caller's narration about her current situation:

Extract 4.8: MT 08–03–1–8

```
 1   AW:   >So it's- so y-< so y'De: toxed you've been
 2           abstinent for five ye:ars,.hhh [an' then] you've
 3   CA:                                     [ °Yeah.° ]
 4   AW:   sort'f started,
 5                 (0.3)
 6   AW:   U::[m
 7   CA:       [Yeah
 8                 (0.7)
 9   AW:   Drinkin' >again an' it's< sort'f crept u:p 'as
10           it. t- th- [t' this] level over the three weeks
11   CA:               [Ye:s. ]
12   AW:   an'.
13                 (0.2)
14   CA:   [Yeah.]
15   AW:   [.Hhh ] Now. I- >I suppose< you'll be findin' now
16   AW:   you've got a bit of physical (.) dependence. an'
17           you- you maybe >d'you get withdra:wal symptoms if
18           y- if y- tr- if you don't drink.
19                 (0.5)
20   CA:   °M:m.°
21                 (0.7)
22   AW:   U:::m,
23                 (1.1)
24   AW:   Tch.hh ↑So- (.) the- (0.4) the- (0.2) f- >an' another
25           thin-< an- (.) >one of the-< (.) there's a few
26           things that I really need to: (.) to mention to you.
```

What is the relevance of this to narrative identity? First, we can observe that storytelling, recounting and identity ascription are practices that happen interactively. We can also see the 'institutionality' of the data emerging in the organisation of the talk (see Chapter 3). Being an 'advice worker' involves 'formulating' (Garfinkel and Sacks 1970) caller's stories, to show understanding and receipt, but also to shift into different actions such as advice-giving or, as we have here, using the formulated story as a basis to interpret or project what the caller may be experiencing. The caller goes along with the first action, which is the advice worker's formulation of her story (lines 3, 7, 11 and 14).

Note, however, what happens at line 15: having done a successful bit of formulating, the advice worker starts a new activity, prefaced by the discourse marker 'Now', shifting to a heavier 'medical' register as he begins to produce a candidate interpretation or projection of what, on the basis of his incumbency of the category 'advice worker', the caller is experiencing. The advice worker is therefore *offering a candidate identity* for the caller: someone who has physical dependence on alcohol and withdrawal symptoms. 'Physical dependence' and 'withdrawal symptoms' might be what Jayyusi (1984) calls 'category-bound predicates', for which the category is something like 'addict' or, in this case, 'alcoholic'. It is the close connection between categories and their predicates that makes 'alcoholic' inferentially available, without it having to be explicitly mentioned. However, the caller does not ratify his interpretation as she did previously. We can see her resistance to it in her delayed response at line 20. Before this, we can observe a number of possible transition relevance places at which a response might be done: after 'dependence.' and 'symptoms'. Moreover, the caller's response, when it comes, is noticeably quieter and uses a different receipt token than her previous turns. Combined with more long gaps, an 'U:::m' from the advice worker and an activity shift to advice-giving at line 24 (which is littered with repair initiators and pauses), we can see some serious interactional trouble following the advice worker's attempt to interpret the caller's experiences and attribute an identity to the speaker.

This brief analysis is of a rather different order from what we have seen so far in the chapter. A macro-level analysis might ascribe the 'discourse of alcoholism' to the sequence, or an 'addiction narrative'. Moreover, one could comment on the asymmetrical 'subject positions' taken up by the advice worker, who has the power to position the caller as an alcoholic. However, by paying attention to the fine detail of interaction, we can see how identity categories are inferred, attributed and resisted in the course of storytelling in a particular setting, done relevantly to interactional and institutional goals. The advice worker, through actions such as formulating, interpreting and advice-giving, ongoingly achieves membership of the relevant professional identity category, as well as ascribing identity categories to the caller.

The next two examples aim to blend macro- and micro-levels of analysis, which we now move on to discuss. We also pull together some of the emerging critical debates about the different methods we have illustrated in this chapter.

COMBINING MICRO AND MACRO NARRATIVE ANALYSES

A theme throughout this book has been the conflict between macro and micro styles of analysis. In Chapter 3, we compared CA and CDA approaches and reviewed the debates between them. In our next example, the author aims to combine a macro analysis of 'discourses' (similar to Hollway and Jefferson, and Swan and Linehan), with close attention to the co-construction of narrative between interviewer and interviewee as we saw in the example above. It comes from Kiesling's (forthcoming) study of interviews with young male members of an American college fraternity. In the extract below, 'Mick' is answering a question about why he was chosen as fraternity president:

Extract 4.9: From Kiesling (forthcoming)

```
 1  Mick:  I:'m just a very:
 2         Tha- the type of person that's goin' somewhere and and uh, whatever I
 3         mean. This is merely just uh
 4         I mean they- I- um
 5         Anything I do I do it . . . the best I can do.
 6         I mean I have I have not watched television in I couldn't tell you how long.
 7         I mean just don't do things that aren't very productive at all. I me-
 8  SK:    (?)
 9  Mick:  No I don't No I don't you're right I don't ha:ng out.
10  SK:    (sit on the couch)
11  Mick:  Not even if I go to the townhouse I'll sit there for a whi-
12         I don't know if you've ever been there when I come in I sit there and I'm like
13         All right. What are we doin'.
14  SK:    He he he he
15  Mick:  's like. I just can't– I can't just do nothing.
16  SK:    Yeah
17  Mick:  I could never, never satisfy my dad.
```

18	SK:	Yeah
19	Mick:	I tore down, wa- we had a chicken coop?
20		That- the end of it burned down.
21		It was, like, on my grandfather's farm
22		it wasn't really our farm it was the closest- our closest neighbor.
23		But ah, it was huge.
24		It was about three times the size of this house
25		It took me a whole summer to tear it down.
26		Hand- by my hand all- hand by-
27		brick by brick I tore the damn thing down.
28		And he was still like- he was bitchin' at me the whole time y'know.
29		Like, if- I'd come in, yeah, What's takin' so long?
30	SK:	Yeah
31	Mick:	Yeah I mean he's- and he's-
32		not that I hate him for that I'm very glad that he was like that, y'know.
33		He built our whole house himself.
34	SK:	Wow
35	Mick:	The entire thing.

Kiesling's analysis focuses on how Mick performs 'hegemonic' masculinity within his narratives. His first observation is that the two narratives (lines 12–13, and 17–35) conform to the Labovian characterisation of a well-formed narrative. The first contains two narrative clauses to describe the typical order of events when he goes to the townhouse ('when I come in I sit there and I'm like'). The identity work done here is to construct himself as somebody who 'just can't do nothing', and as someone who is hardworking. The second narrative contains an *abstract* ('I could never, never satisfy my dad'), a long *orientation* ('wa- we had a chicken coop? That- the end of it burned down. It was, like, on my grandfather's farm it wasn't really our farm it was the closest- our closest neighbor.'). The *complicating action* includes the *resolution* ('It took me a whole summer to tear it down. Hand- by my hand all- hand by- brick by brick I tore the damn thing down. And he was still like- he was bitchin' at me the whole time y'know.'). Finally there is an embedded *evaluation* ('Like, if- I'd come in, yeah, What's takin' so long?') and a *coda* ('not that I hate him for that I'm very glad that he was like that, y'know. He built our whole house himself.').

Having identified the structural properties of Mick's narrative, Kiesling goes on to point out a number of identity-relevant shifts and evaluations, from someone who is 'goin' somewhere' to someone who does 'the best I can do', who doesn't 'do things that aren't very productive', who is excellent at activities and endurance and persistence to, finally, someone who could 'never satisfy my dad'. Kiesling asks: 'What do these narratives index, and how do they do it? If Mick belongs to the hegemonic categories of male, white, middle class do his narratives help him maintain that hegemony?' Kiesling argues that a purely micro-level analysis does not provide enough analytic power to understand Mick's narrative, and the analyst needs to invoke other contexts that are not referred to directly (cf. Wetherell 1998).

For example, in mentioning 'the townhouse', Kiesling argues that Mick assumes the interviewer shares his knowledge of what the place means for fraternity members, and so includes the interviewer as a fraternity member. Kiesling suggests that Mick's story *indexes* (that is, implies, makes reference to) particular fraternity discourses about valued personalities, as well as broader *discourses of masculinity*. Mick evaluates different men in the fraternity in relation to economic and physical/ bodily *discourses of masculine power*. Without access to these wider cultural narratives, he argues, we would not be able to make sense of Mick's account. For example, the story about the chicken coop does not make sense without knowing about a ' "Rocky" masculine cultural model'. Nor can we understand the relevance of Mick's father and the destruction of a building to Mick's election as fraternity president without seeing it as a warrant for his identity *as* president. In order to make sense of this, Kiesling argues, we need to draw on the discourse of masculinity in which 'the disciplining of one's body is valuable'. He suggests that Mick values these kinds of traits in men, and that the interviewer shares his cultural presuppositions.

For Kiesling, then, narrative is a site for the maintenance and negotiation of hegemonic identity categories. Mick's account reworks cultural narratives for a specific purpose, in a specific context, with variations on the dominant theme. Another discourse operating in Mick's narrative is a *discourse of fatherhood*, in which good fathers are demanding and distant, although Mick positions himself in an ambivalent manner towards this discourse. Thus the practice of narration involves the circulation and mutation of discourses: 'Each new recreation (telling) both *relies on* the Discourse, in that it requires a listener to have access to that discourse, and *recreates* the Discourse, by giving it details particular to that telling and that person' (ibid.).

Issues in combining macro and micro analyses

Kiesling's study, with its mix of macro- and micro-levels of analysis, taps into the methodological and theoretical debates about the analysis of talk discussed in earlier chapters. As we have seen in many of our examples, analysts often reach into the intangible world of discourses and narrative genres to explain the local workings of narration. We have seen examples of how master narratives and/or discourses – of romance, change, respectability, tragedy, 'Cinderella' fairytales, stability, regression, masculinity, fatherhood, 'Rocky' masculine cultural models, masculine power – make available particular 'positions' or identity choices for the storyteller. It is argued that such narratives do not determine identity – they are both constituted in talk and constituting of talk – but they are 'out there', shaping identity construction.

There are two problems with this kind of analytic move. First, we might reiterate Edwards's (2006) argument that language is a 'complete cultural system of description and accountability'. As we saw in Kiesling's own data, the speakers did not have any trouble understanding each other's references. It is important to recognise that speakers do not routinely make all their referencing explicit: this is how language works (Edwards 1997a). Analysts cannot pin things down more definitively than language itself does, second-guessing what speakers might have in mind as they tell their story. As we saw in Sacks's (1992) example of the 'old man burden' (Chapter 2), the fact that speakers do not make everything explicit and clear means that language can be an active resource for accomplishing interactional business. If the meaning of some description, interactional style, cultural category, and so on was unambiguous, speakers could not be subtle, make defeasible inferences, be implicit, deny intention, claim they did not say precisely that thing, be suggestive and so on (Stokoe 2005).

The other problem is to do with the analytical process of ascribing theorised labels (for example, discourse of masculinity, narrative of romance) to stretches of text. The criticism is that social interaction (including talk in interviews) is too complex to reduce to discourses. This kind of analysis, therefore, offers 'an impoverished view of human conduct' (Wooffitt 2005: 179). Here, Wooffitt notes that many studies of interview data find a particular, usually small number of 'discourses' (or narratives, repertoires, master narratives, cultural models, and so on), operating within them. For example, as we discussed earlier in this chapter, Robinson (1990) and Murray (2003) identified *three* organising narratives in the talk of patients. Wooffitt asks:

> Given the complexity of the organization of social interaction . . .
> one is forced to ask: is this really all there is to say about those
> stretches of talk? . . . It seems unlikely. A more likely explanation

is that the very nature of the analytic enterprise – the analysis of discourses and repertoires, and the exploration of theoretically derived positions on the oppositional or contested nature of social life – establishes at the outset a set of expectations about what might be uncovered in whatever data the analyst might be examining. (p. 180)

For Wooffitt (see also Widdicombe 1995), attributing gross discourse labels to chunks of talk is problematic because there is no empirical or evidential basis to that attribution. As we noted earlier, Riessman (1993: 30) celebrates the fact that narrative analysis proceeds this way: 'the analyst's authorial voice and interpretive commentary knit the disparate elements together and determine how readers are to understand [the informant's] experience'. This practice appears to rely on the analyst's notion of which gross, culturally familiar plotline might resonate at a particular moment. Let us remind ourselves of one section of Kiesling's data:

25		It took me a whole summer to tear it down.
26		Hand- by my hand all- hand by-
27		brick by brick I tore the damn thing down.
28		And he was still like- he was bitchin' at me the whole time y'know.
29		Like, if- I'd come in, yeah, What's takin' so long?
30	SK:	Yeah
31	Mick:	Yeah I mean he's- and he's-
32		not that I hate him for that I'm very glad that he was like that, y'know.
33		He built our whole house himself.

Amongst other things, Kiesling suggests that this stretch of talk (and we presume it is this section) invokes/produces a *discourse of fatherhood* and a *discourse of masculinity* (with variants to do with labour and physical power). It is not spelled out at which point in the sequence the discourse is relevant, or when it stops being relevant. Nor is it clear why those discourse labels are the most appropriate: why not a 'familial' discourse, a 'construction' plotline, or a 'class' discourse? Is it as simple as spotting some talk about fathers, and ascribing the label 'fatherhood discourse'? As Wooffitt (2005: 183) asks, 'what value is the concept of discourses as an analytic tool if there is no clear method by which to establish the presence of any particular discourse in any specific sequence of talk-in-interaction?'

Kiesling's analytic aim is to study the *narrative production of hegemonic masculinity*, and this is what he finds. What is his warrant for claiming Mick is 'doing masculinity', as opposed to doing 'class', 'sexuality', 'femininity', 'ethnicity'? Interestingly, Kiesling does not comment on the most obvious gender-relevant line of this extract, in which Mick describes his father as 'bitchin'' at him. It appears that the fact that Mick is 'actually' male is the first warrant for analysing his performance as 'masculinity' (Sidnell 2003). Across the social sciences, gender identity is increasingly theorised as a performance. But, as we discussed in Chapter 2, this constitutes another example of a performativity study in which the analyst starts out 'knowing' the relevant identity of the speakers, rather than figuring out what identity work the participants themselves might be oriented to. As Hausendorf (2002: 175–6) asks:

> What exactly is the connection between a certain type of discourse (narration) and certain sets of social categories implied by these notions? . . . [Narrative analysts] focus on the question of *what* is told by *whom* and how these roles (of storyteller, listener and 'neutral' bystander) can be related to the participants' social identity – while the latter is identified by the author who claims what aspect of identity is relevant (from her own point of view).

Along with methods that purportedly 'see through' the data to underlying experience, analytic moves such as ascribing discourse labels and identity positions enable researchers to claim the relevance of things they perhaps wished the participant had said but did not, or make broader, theoretically or politically motivated claims about the data than they actually warrant.

Despite these reservations about the importation of macro discourses to illuminate conversational data, some writers attempt to include a clearer warrant for reaching 'above' the data, and show how an intertextual understanding of identity narratives can enrich the analysis of local identities (Benwell 2005). An example is Wetherell's (1998) research about the construction of masculinities in interviews with groups of 17–18-year-old men (see also Wetherell and Edley 1999). Wetherell (1998: 388) argues that 'conversation analysis alone does not offer an adequate answer to its own classic question about some piece of discourse – why this utterance here?' Her solution is a synthetic meshing of the approaches: the preservation of CA's attention to the 'highly occasioned and situated nature of subject positions' but combined with the more inclusive definition of 'discourse' found within poststructuralist models. The resulting approach is a 'genealogical' one, which aims to trace normative practices, values and sense-making through both historical and synchronic intertextual analysis: 'The genealogical approach . . . suggests that in analysing our always partial piece of the argumentative texture we also look to the broader forms of intelligibility running through the texture more generally' (Wetherell 1998: 403).

Whilst Wetherell adopts a grounded and indexical approach to the identification of these subject positions in the data, she goes further to generalise the 'institutionalised forms of intelligibility' to which these subject positions are culturally attached, such as 'male sexuality as performance and achievement, a repertoire around alcohol and disinhibition, and an ethics of sexuality as legitimated by relationships' (p. 400). She argues that such subject positions are not merely 'taken up' in a passive way, but do highly situated, interactional 'work'. At the same time, they are attached to prior, culturally familiar discourses situated within already-circulating, shared repertoires and thus a *resource* for the micro exigencies of identity work in talk. An example of a 'prior' subject position can be found in Wetherell's analysis of a story about one young man, Aaron, and his night out in which he 'went with' four women. At one point in the narration, one of the other participants, Phil, describes Aaron as being on the 'moral low ground because he was like (.) gigolo Casanova whatever' (p. 397). For Wetherell, the use of the term 'gigolo Casanova' is an instance of how existing narratives and discourses, richly imbued with historical and cultural meanings (a 'gigolo' is a male escort paid for his sexual favours, whilst 'Casanova' was a fictional 'great lover') are invoked as shorthand for particular kinds of ambiguous male sexual and moral behaviour.

Wetherell's (1998) 'synthetic' approach has proved popular with many analysts who criticise conversation analysis for being too 'limited' and 'restrictive' for the kinds of claims they want to make about a stretch of talk (for example, Bucholtz 2003). However, in his response to her paper, Schegloff (1998) criticises Wetherell for misunderstanding some of the fundamental concepts and aims of CA, and thus basing her critique on these misunderstandings (see also Wooffitt 2005). Moreover, we might suggest that there is nothing special about the term 'Casanova' that requires the import of extra-textual discourses to understand it any more than any other word in a culture's language ('cat', 'lift', 'gate' and so on – it is likely that Aaron's friends use this term without knowing its literary etymology). These debates, as we have seen throughout the book, have produced a great deal of commentary over the past few years, and will doubtless continue to do so.

CONCLUSION

We aimed in this chapter to review narrative approaches to the theorisation and empirical investigation of the discursive construction of identity. We have considered a wide range of approaches and examples, and considered some of the limitations of this heterogeneous body of work. Once more, we have drawn out some of the key debates in the study of identity, including the issue of macro- versus micro-levels of analysis, the advantages and disadvantages of particular methods of data collection, and the theory of the subject as pre-, post- or solely a discursive phenomenon.

The first four chapters of the book have covered a wide range of theoretical and methodological literatures within the field of discourse and identity. We have at times been quite polemical in our reviews of different theoretical positions, analytic approaches and illustrative examples. Our aim for the first part of the book has been to outline key approaches, show readers how writers analyse identity, and highlight key debates, criticisms, points of departure and differences between various methods of discourse and interaction analysis. In the remaining three chapters of the book, we focus less on debating methodology, and more on examining three more sites of identity construction, starting with Chapter 5: Commodified Identities.

PART TWO

Contexts

CHAPTER 5

Commodified Identities

In this chapter, we explore the notion of *commodified identity* and introduce a series of tools and frameworks by which to analyse its discursive constitution. We pursue four different interpretations of the term 'commodified identities':

1. Identities of consumers (accounts for and practices of consumption).
2. The process of identity commodification through acts of consumption (How do commercial discourses such as advertisements 'speak' to us and engage us with their message?).
3. Representations of identities in commodified contexts (for example, consumer femininity, commodified 'laddism').
4. Self-commodifying discourses (for example, personal advertisements, job applications/CVs/references, commercial telephone sex lines).

In order to address all of these connotations of 'commodified identity' we draw on critical discourse analysis and critical discursive psychology. In other words, we analyse the linguistic content of advertising or promotional material, but will, in a detailed case study of men's lifestyle magazines, relate this to in-depth interviews and reader-response exercises conducted with groups of male consumers. This kind of two-way analysis captures meanings at the interface between contexts of production, text and consumption and is allied to a growing tradition of research known as a 'circuits of culture' model central to contemporary cultural studies (for example, Du Gay et al. 1997; Johnson 1986). A circuits of culture model acknowledges the importance of a global consideration of all moments in the broader context of commercial culture (that is, production, text, consumption, lived identities of consumers) and the often complex ways in which they may intersect. This is a welcome development in a field that has tended to privilege either the productivist end of the spectrum or the analyst's interpretation of commercial texts and speculation about their probable effects on consumers.

Our decision to include consumers' responses and readings of consumer texts is arguably one way of redressing an imbalance in the traditional account of consumption – a way of returning a little power and 'voice' to the consumer. Furthermore, this two-way approach reflects some of the debates rehearsed earlier in the book about the implications of the structure/agency dualism for identity. The analysis of advertisements as a way of understanding the consumption process assumes that readers are being situated by the positions offered to them in the text. By contrast, the focus on actual readers' *accounts* of this process pays conscious attention to the way in which individuals may engage actively with the available discourses of consumer culture (constructing positions for themselves, negotiating or resisting available meanings) as a form of social organisation (Smith 1990).

Readers may detect a tension running through this chapter between various theoretical accounts of consumption. Some accounts see consumers as controlled and positioned by market forces and advertising – an essentially passive activity (the Marxist or Frankfurt School view); others see consumers as active, autonomous and discerning, whereby consumption is an act of creativity and even production, and consumers derive their own meanings from goods. In our analysis of various sites of consumption we will demonstrate and often reconcile both accounts of the 'active' and the 'passive' consumer and show that an identity that is 'commodified' is not as straightforwardly negative as we might at first assume.

THEORIES OF CONSUMPTION AND IDENTITY

We are at the point where consumption is laying hold of the whole of life. (Baudrillard 1998: 29)

Retail therapy and *shopoholic*: two expressions which have recently entered the English language point to our obsession with consumption and its intimate relationship with lifestyle and identity. Shopping is not simply a utilitarian exchange of money for goods, but is both social vice and palliative; a dependency and a comfort. The very activity of shopping can apparently transform our sense of self, and the promise of such overwhelming emotional experience can in turn lead to a permanent sense of unfulfilled desire and, more practically, crippling debt. Consumerism characterises what critics have termed post-industrial 'late modernity' (Giddens 1991). Featherstone (1991) denotes consumption as a key characteristic of postmodern society and more pessimistic accounts of consumption see it as an all-enveloping force to which, increasingly, all identities are subject – a force which dictates that *anything* is potential substance for consumption, even ourselves.

The relationship between identity and consumption has been widely theorised, particularly during the twentieth century. It was at this point that consumption came to be seen as foundational in society, and to have usurped the power and position of production. Expansion in mass-production of goods led increasingly to a commodification of culture and a rise of culture industries. In a free-market economy, goods are not simply produced to fulfil needs, but needs are stimulated by producers and advertisers, frequently through appeals to identity and lifestyle. Inevitably these processes of commodification have profound implications for identity and a close, symbiotic relationship has developed between consumer and consumable. The fact that identity is so intimately bound up with consumption is not lost upon advertisers and marketers who predominantly employ lifestyle as a concept in their campaigns, rather than categories such as class or income.

Campbell (1987) identifies the roots of consumerism in the eighteenth century and the rise of the Romantic individualism, pointing to an early association between consumption and processes of self-actualisation. According to this perspective, *we consume according to who we are or want to be* and the 'consumption ethic' (in comparison to Weber's 'ethic of production' directed to the greater glory of God) seems to be directed to the good of the individual (Corrigan 1997). Consumption becomes a means of articulating a sense of identity and, perhaps even more crucially, *distinction* from others. The display or overt consumption of goods may function as a sign indicating membership of a particular culture, and consumption practices are socially structured, functioning as an index of, for example, class or gender difference. In this account, according to Campbell (1987: 74), much of the pleasure of modern consumption derives from 'an individualistic ability to manipulate the meaning of objects . . .'. This account of consumption as a builder or symbol of identity is one favoured by Veblen (1899: the author of the term, 'conspicuous consumption'), who argued that consumption was a key means of achieving social differentiation and thus status. Bourdieu (1984) similarly used the concept of 'cultural capital' to describe the way in which different classes use different goods and consumption practices in order to situate themselves in social space.

Using an anthropological approach to consumption, Douglas and Isherwood (1979) also describe how goods are used to construct an intelligible culture and establish and sustain social relations. We will later illustrate this through the example of women's magazines, in which an identity of consumer femininity is constructed. This is achieved not only through the promotion of particular products, such as moisturising cream and tampons, but also through the concepts, skills and 'know-how' acquired through the simulated dialogue of magazine advice – which then enters the realm of the real 'lifeworld' such as women chatting to friends (Talbot 1995). Cosmetic products in these contexts then take on *symbolic* value and illuminate categories of culture. The symbolic function of goods and lifestyle in turn play a more and more central role in modern consumption which is seen increasingly to aspire *beyond* need, and indeed identity and symbol come to be seen to be the driving force behind it. Modern consumption becomes an endless quest for new identities, characterised by a never-sated, infinite desire, 'an endless discontent' (Corrigan 1997).

Bauman (1993) also contributes to the thesis that consumption is a key builder of identity in his work on 'neo-tribes'. He argues that consumption practices are a crucial part of 'belonging' to social groups, and products ('tribe-specific paraphernalia', Warde 1994: 69) are the building blocks of a cohesive lifestyle. This thesis suggests crucially that identities forged through consumption are subject to *interpersonal* constraints. Poststructuralist theorists such as Baudrillard (1998) take the relationship between identity and consumption a stage further arguing that 'we become what we consume' (Mackay 1997: 2). In postmodern accounts, cultural consumption is seen as being the very material out of which we construct our identities. The relationship between consumer and product is not simply one of subject and object; being 'hailed' by producers positions the audience into a relationship of commodification. The audience shapes its identity through the purchase and the consumer becomes a mere token or sign in a transaction.

Baudrillard's (1998) early and largely structuralist account of consumption is particularly influential for this perspective and worth elaborating in more detail. For Baudrillard, commodities and objects, rather like words, constitute a system of signs (cf. de Saussure 1960) – a system that replaces values and classifications with needs and pleasures. The use value of objects is replaced by 'sign value': commodities achieve meaning, not from their utilitarian value, but from their relationship to a whole system of signs. The consumer, through acts of consumption, enters into this same system but is subject to its repressive rules, is 'immanent in the signs he (sic) arranges', unable to transcend or reflect upon the system, absorbed into a 'logic of signs' (Baudrillard 1998: 192). Like Veblen and Bourdieu, Baudrillard (1998: 61) also sees consumption driven by the quest for 'differentiation':

> You never consume the object in itself (in its use-value); you are always manipulating objects . . . as signs which distinguish you either by affiliating you to your own group taken as an ideal reference or by marking you off from your group by reference to a group of higher status.

Baudrillard's (1988) conception of 'a system of signs' – signs relative to one another but with no real signification – leads to his famous cluster of concepts: 'simulation', 'simulacra' (copies without originals) and the 'hyperreal'. The 'hyperreal' refers to an arena of floating signs: imitations unanchored to stable meanings in the 'real' world whose existence often *disguises* the underlying absence of a 'real' referent. Baudrillard's (1988: 172) famous example is Disneyland, which is 'presented as imaginary in order to make us believe that the rest is real, when in fact all of Los Angeles and the America surrounding it are no longer real, but of the order of the hyperreal and of simulation'. Sites of consumption, particularly those tied to the media, are very much associated with simulation. Instability in the *meaning* of goods suggested by Baudrillard's thesis of simulation leads to an infinite process of redefinition or recoding as well as a continuous quest for the 'new'. An example of such semantic arbitrariness is the increasingly outlandish crisp flavours dreamt up by manufacturers, which, like 'hedgehog flavour' or the punning 'Salt and Lineker' (salt and vinegar) and 'Smokey Beckham' (smoky bacon) after British footballers, have no clear or conventional correspondence to the physical product, but evoke connotations of prestige and fashion. Like 'Disneyland', they also suggest that the 'real' flavours (for example, bacon) to which these simulations relate, are indeed real, whilst the discerning consumer will know that most crisp flavours are entirely artificial. The location of consumption within a system of endlessly renewable signs is especially favourable to the imperatives of the producers and a feature of modern advertising that will be clearly demonstrated in the next section.

Baudrillard (1998) also identifies simulation in the pseudo relationship set up between advertiser and consumer – a kind of 'simulated intimacy' lodged in direct address and affective discourse (see also Talbot 1995). 'Simulated solicitousness' is identified in the verbal exchanges between sales people and clients, a field also explored by Cameron (2000) in her study of commodified talk. Many of these examples of simulation are apparently designed to serve as a form of seductive power: simulated intimacy seduces customers into feeling they are being personally addressed; simulated solicitousness pacifies them. However, Baudrillard's account of consumption is undeniably negative, affording little control to consumers and seeing them socialised into a system that is largely beyond their control. Giddens's (1991) notion of 'the commodification of the self' also suggests that consumers become mere subjects of the force of consumption, fashioning themselves into a kind of product. He argues that there has been an *interpenetration* of commercial practices into the lifeworld and into selfhood.

This negative take on the notion of commodification and consumption is very much influenced by a particular school of theory known as the Frankfurt School which provided a *critique* of mass culture and the rise of what was termed 'culture industries'. Within this model, the consumer is viewed as a passive dupe, manipulated by advertising and the production of 'false needs', constructed by the imperatives of production. Furthermore, by virtue of its mass appeal and reach, consumer culture is seen as homogenising and inauthentic. Similarly critical, Fairclough (1992) argues that one consequence of commodification is that it creates uncertainty about the authentic and the promotional and creates an inextricable link between self-identity and self-promotion.

Not everyone, however, is so gloomy about commodification discourses. Later models within cultural studies foreground the active role of the consumer and reject the idea that identity is so malleable and suggestible. Keat, Whitely and Abercrombie (1994) interrogate recent shifts in favour of the 'authority of the consumer' and other work in cultural studies focuses upon the *pleasures* of audiences and the potential for responses to mass culture to be both *creative* and *critical*, whereby consumers themselves are 'cultural experts' (for example, Fiske 1989). In this model, consumption is seen, not as an end, but as a beginning, and in this sense *productive*. Though rejected in its extreme form by many for being naïve, romantic and optimistic about the power of the consumer, it is an important corrective to the mass culture critique, and our own engagement with focus groups of male consumers similarly gestures in this direction.

In this section, we have considered a number of competing accounts of the relationship between consumption and identity. We have identified a tension between two main accounts, what Miles (1998: 147) terms 'the consuming paradox'. The first sees consumers as subject to a form of hegemonic and institutionalising power, trained unwittingly into codes of consumerist behaviour for the continuing expansion of the market. This account therefore sees identity as an element that is cynically *exploited* by the forces of consumerism for self-interested profit. The second account accords the consumer more power and acknowledges that consumption is an activity by which individuals *express* identity and use it to forge solidarity with other members of society, and moreover are sufficiently reflexive and knowing to be able to negotiate, play or even resist its codes

(Smith 1990). Ideally, we need to combine these two perspectives by adopting a model that acknowledges both creativity and constraint for the position of the consumer, a model that views production and consumption as mutually constitutive.

IDENTITY COMMODIFICATION THROUGH TEXTS OF CONSUMPTION

Women are given women to consume. (Baudrillard 1998: 137–8)

In this section, we illustrate in more detail the kinds of linguistic strategies employed by advertisers to draw potential consumers into a relationship of consumption and the implications such strategies have for the commodification of identity, specifically *gender* identity. Gender has a long, historical association with processes of commodification (for example, Andrews and Talbot 2000; Beetham 1996; Benwell 2004; Scanlon 2000). The constructed differentiation between masculinity and femininity as identity categories is significantly supported and perpetuated by the production and consumption of gendered products (clothes, fragrance, make-up, gadgets). In turn, gender identity – and femininity historically more so than masculinity – is the commercial raison d'être of a huge sector of the market, governing and directing the terms of consumption. Our data thus focuses on 'commodified femininity' and are all taken from advertisements in one issue of the women's lifestyle magazine, *Cosmopolitan* (February 2003).

Advertising is a crucial facilitator of consumption and relies heavily upon the social meanings and connotations that may be attached to products: 'Modern advertising concentrates at those points where the individual and society meet' (Corrigan 1997: 67). As we discussed in the previous section, advertisers are keenly aware of the rewarding potential of identity as a key component of their products, and appeals to identity – perhaps the promotion of a 'real you', an 'inner self' or maybe an appeal to group membership – play a prominent role in advertisements. This appeal to the 'real' and 'authentic' amidst a sea of identical products is identified by Baudrillard (1988: 180) in his thesis of simulation: 'What society seeks through production and overproduction, is the restoration of the real which escapes it.'

The promise of fulfilment that characterises almost every advertisement we examined is the key motif of the relationship between product and consumer. In consumer society, inanimate objects are invested with symbolic emotional meaning to take on a fetishistic quality (witness, for

example, the current slogan for Nokia mobile phones: 'A Sign of Passion').
Usually, objects represent bridges to emotions or frequently unattainable
lifestyles: 'For Natural Confidence' (Palmolive anti-perspirant); 'A sign
of ambition . . . a sign of attitude' (Nokia mobile phone); 'Are you an
All Rounder?' (Nike sportswear). Women's magazine advertising frequently promotes an ideology of envy within its readers, who are presumed to desire to attain the image of idealised femininity: 'advertising
falsely links people's internal feelings to an external object through
what comes to be seen as a logical connection; the unattainable is associated with what can be attained – the purchased product' (McCracken
1993: 79).

So we witness in these advertisements the juxtaposition of an impos-
sibly flawless complexion (*unattainable*) and a lipstick product (*attainable*); or the image of a glamorous celebrity (*unattainable*) with perfume
(*attainable*). As Corrigan (1997) suggests, the world of advertising presents an ever-shifting dialectic between pleasurable dreams and social
nightmares, to which, of course, products present solutions.

The commodified body as a symbol of the self

In women's magazine advertising, the body is a key site for identity work.
Not only do bodies, through their aesthetic and sexualised presentation,
sell commodities and services by association, they are themselves an object
for consumption. In most of the advertisements we explore in this section,
the body has this function – it is dressed, fed and disciplined. Baudrillard
(1998: 129) argues that the body has taken over from the soul as 'an object
of salvation'; as a form of capital it is narcissistically invested in as a spec-
tacle and subjected to 'a labour of investment' (p. 132). However, this
apparent self-creation conceals an act of self-consumption. As consumers,
our identities are drawn into a commodity relationship then sold back to us
transformed by Estée Lauder, Dior and Calvin Klein. For this sleight of
hand to prove effective it is necessary for the consumer to make a clear
Cartesian separation between mind and body. For the body to be consumable, it must be 'rediscovered narcissistically' or liberated in order to be
exploited (Ritzer 1998: 13). Texts of commodified femininity facilitate this
act of bodily consumption further via a frequent process of *fragmentation*
(Mills 1995; Talbot 1995), whereby the female body is described in terms
of parts: eyes, lips, breasts, legs, hair. Mills (1995: 171–2) points out that
this has two main effects: 'First, the body is depersonalised, objectified,
reduced to its parts. Second, since the female protagonist is not represented as a unified conscious physical being, the scene cannot be focalised
from her perspective – effectively, her experience is written out of the text'.

In almost all of the advertisements in *Cosmopolitan*, we identified a model of femininity characterised by self-indulgence and narcissism. The female body is a pampered, sensual one, and advertisements for beauty and grooming products are consistently characterised by a type of *subjective, affective* language which links even the most unlikely products to *sensation* or *sexuality*:

* *envelops every strand of your hair in rich, luscious shades* (Clairol Lasting Colour)
* *silky smooth* (Lancôme Skin Balancing Make-up)
* *amazingly soft and supple* (Lancôme Triple Performance Cream)
* *gorgeous colour* (Max Factor lipstick)
* *ecstatic blondes . . . new peaks of blonde intensity* (Clairol Herbal Essences)
* *a seductive design available in nine sensual colours* (Nokia mobile phone)
* *small, sexy, stylish* (Samsung mobile phone)
* *vitamins with passion* (Vitabiotics vitamin pills)
* *masses of lovely, velvety bubbles* (Imperial Leather bath gel)

The almost pathological relentlessness of this discourse of sensuality, permeating even the incongruous spheres of mobile phones and vitamin tablets, is an exhortation to sink helplessly into a soft focus, airbrushed, smooth and infantilised version of femininity. In this version, all products promise some kind of solicitous pleasure or orgasmic sensation which suggests that an ideology of passivation, narcissism and sexual objectification is being aimed at female consumers. Campbell (1987) has argued that a shift from traditional to modern forms of consumption coincided with a shift from seeking pleasure in *sensation* to seeking pleasure in *emotion*. In fact advertising in women's magazines, particularly in the arena of beauty and cosmetics, reveals a synthesis between these two forms of pleasure. The discourse of potentially liberating, sexualised femininity which can be seen in some of these examples ('ecstatic blondes'), and which is generally prevalent in women's magazine advertising, is a discourse which Baudrillard (1998) argues is subsumed and neutered by the consumer imperative – a means, in fact, of controlling or subverting desire.

Assumptions and discourses of commodified femininity

Even a brief engagement with women's magazines reveals a set of tacit 'rules' which underpin the identity and ideology of consumer femininity.

These rules can be inferred from a number of the advertisements under discussion but are also part of a broader knowledge of appropriate consumer femininity. In turn, a knowledge of such 'rules' is frequently necessary in order to decode some of the advertisements' meanings:

1. Ageing is bad and must be striven against or disguised ('the unwatchability of old age' J. Coupland 2003: 129): skin must be smooth, hair must be non-grey and bodies must be slim, supple, toned and erect:

    Prevent, delay and reduce the appearance of ageing. For firmer, younger-looking skin (Almay foundation cream); *Deep lines look lifted away . . . wrinkle-reducing effect . . . Welcome to the ageless future* (Estée Lauder: Perfectionist Correcting Serum); *Stops fine lines in their tracks* (Clarins: Multi-Active Day Cream); *Cover grey perfectly with natural-looking colour* (Garnier: Belle Colour); *Why fade to grey when you can keep your colour young?* (Clairol: Lasting Colour)

2. Fat is bad:

    100% flavour, 0% fat (Amoy soy sauce); *We can effectively remove stubborn fat from the stomach, bottom, thighs, knees, ankles, arms, chin . . .* (The Harley Medical Group)

3. Activity/fitness is good, and we are always busy:

    Are you sick of hearing 'where do you find the time' (Nike sportswear)

4. But inactivity in the form of relaxation or 'indulgence' is equally encouraged:

    Go on, escape for a while (Imperial Leather: Bubbleburst Scentsations)

5. Body hair (except on head) is bad:

    Our latest laser treatment removes unwanted facial and body hair . . . Problem areas treated include the face, under-arms, bikini line, legs, body . . . (The Harley Medical Group)

6. Natural body odour is bad, synthetic fragrance is preferable:

    For natural confidence. 24 hour protection formula (Palmolive deodorant)

7. Bare face (that is, no make-up) is bad, but simultaneously a 'natural' look is prized in all arenas:

   looks flawlessly natural (Maybelline: EverFresh make-up); *keeps long hair naturally shiny* (Trevor Sorbie: Long Hair)

8. Transformation, newness and change are good:

   the big difference maker (Clinique: Clarifying Lotion); *Flush out last year's nasties and make a clean start to 2003* (Evian mineral water)

9. Consistency of appearance is good: deodorant must last, lipstick must not smudge or fade, mascara must not run, hair colour must not fade and skin must look 'even'. This also links to the assumption that we are too busy to reapply products:

   Gorgeous colour after 8 hours, even through eating and drinking (Max Factor lipstick); *Skin stays fresh, make-up looks natural and even all day* (Lancôme Adaptîve: Skin-balancing make-up); *resist fading . . . stays put . . . day to night* (Maybelline: EverFresh make-up); *It stays beautifully shiny* (Garnier Fructis: Intense Anti-Frizz); *Get a shine and moisture control foundation that balances your complexion for even coverage all day long* (Rimmel Doubleact: Shine and Control Make-up)

All of the above examples constitute what Foucault (1972, 1981) has termed *discursive formations* or simply *discourses*. We encountered the concept of 'discourses' in Chapter 4, used near-synonymously with other terms for wider systems of meaning-making (for example, 'master narrative', 'interpretative repertoire'). These naturalised narratives encode and preserve key ideological assumptions and exclude others, and are used frequently in identity construction and negotiation. A number of researchers working within a broadly feminist perspective have attempted to identify such discourses. Sunderland (2004) details a number of 'gendered discourses' such as 'the male sex drive discourse' (Hollway 1989), 'compulsory heterosexuality' (Rich 1980), and the discourse of equal opportunities (Wetherell, Stiven and Potter 1987). Machin and Thornborrow (2003) identify a series of discourses uniting the global 'brand' of *Cosmopolitan*, such as 'pleasing the other' and 'transgressive'. All of these 'discourses' are historical, pre-constituted, ideological narratives implicitly underpinning the construction of talk or text and identifiable via specific linguistic and propositional cues.

Two key discourses of consumer femininity, touched on above, are those of *transformation* and *surface appearance*. Transformation is clearly the lifeblood of consumerism since it relies on consumer products or objects for its facilitation. The verbs, 'improve', 'reduce' and 'reveal' are repeatedly employed in advertising and almost always appear in conjunction with the product name: 'Clinique Clarifying Lotion: The big difference maker that sweeps away dull flakes to reveal smoother, brighter skin'. Female consumers are encouraged to make a connection between cosmetic change (for example, hair colour) and 'inner' change – change which impinges on a more profound sense of identity: 'Celebrate *the new you* in the New Year with fabulous fashion and accessories' (*Cosmopolitan* Collection Fashion and Accessories); '*Find yourself* at nikewomen.com' (Nike sportswear) (our emphases). This ideology of deep transformation ties in with the ideology of 'self-consumption' – female consumers are being exhorted, not simply to invest in image-enhancing products, but to invest in the *whole self*. Once fully clothed or accessorised by 'Cosmopolitan Collections' or 'Nike', the female consumer is sold back to herself – transformed, complete, essential, 'real'.

Similarly 'newness' in the range of available goods on the market is a key imperative of consumerism which relies on an in-built obsolescence for products, a market requirement that newly created 'needs' will necessitate a new product, or, for the more cynically inclined, a newly packaged one. Certain products even incorporate this motif into their product labels, such as Clinique's 'Dramatically Different Moisturising Lotion'. Bourdieu (1984) makes the point that there is a permanent tension between 'distinguished goods' and the popularisation that threatens their distinguished status. This leads to an endless recoding of the 'status' of goods and perpetuates the momentum of the market.

The second discourse is preoccupied with *surface appearance* – an unsurprising theme for consumer femininity – and signalled by the prominence of the verb 'look' or adjective 'looking' ('looks more radiant and eventoned', 'deep lines look lifted away', 'looks flawlessly natural', 'smoother-looking skin'). Paradoxically, this obsession with appearance and surface also embodies, without embarrassment, the principle of duplicity and deception. Skin is not smoother, it only looks so, deep lines are not *actually* lifted away, they only appear to be so. This may, in part, be linked to issues of Advertising Standards Agency guidelines that police unsustainable claims made by producers. However, it is also fortuitously compatible with the ideology of obsolescence and renewal so central to consumerism. These products must not provide *permanent* solutions to cosmetic 'problems'; they must simply temporarily mask or disguise them. One of the key imperatives of consumer femininity is that 'problems' are ultimately insoluble.

So how is it that these normative discourses are sustained and supported? Our next aim is to demonstrate the precise linguistic devices and mechanisms by which advertising texts promote and naturalise their ideological message and 'hail' the identity of the reader into a relationship of commodification (see also Delin 2000; Mills 1995, for useful overviews of these strategies).

ANALYSING COMMODIFIED IDENTITIES

In the sections that follow, we set out a series of useful foci for analysis, including *problem-solution patterns*; *assertion, implicature and presupposition*; *synthetic personalisation and simulated intimacy* and *transitivity*. This kind of linguistic approach combines methods and insights from SFL and CDA (see Chapter 3).

Problem-solution patterns

The consumer imperative necessitates the continual construction of problems (physical, cosmetic, emotional, lifestyle, practical) to which objects are offered as (temporary) solutions. The macrostructure of advertisements commonly adopts what Hoey (1983) has described within a typology of clause-relations as 'problem-solution pattern'. This involves the positing of a series of propositions in a particular order and linked crucially by conjunctions or implicit relations of contrast, justification, or causality (for example, 'but', 'so', 'therefore'). The minimum number of propositions is two: a problem in conjunction with a solution ('With treatment this intense it's the finish for Frizz' (Garnier Fructis)). Here we find a *cause–consequence* relation: if you use this 'treatment' it will smooth out frizzy hair. Also common is the three-part structure 'situation–problem–solution'. In this configuration, a situation is first presented to which a problematic connotation is attached ('Combination skin: Different needs. One balanced solution' (Lancôme: see Figure 1 p. 178).

Advertisements will often present evidence and something akin to a conclusion. In the Lancôme example that follows, the 'perfect make-up solution' is followed by three bullet-points offering further evidence, a discursive pattern reminiscent of an empirical report. Finally, we are offered a conclusion which sums up the positive properties of the product ('RESULT: the ultimate combination – balanced skin and a perfect look – all day').

The ability to recognise problem-solution patterns is often contingent upon vocabulary choice. In the above examples, we are guided to

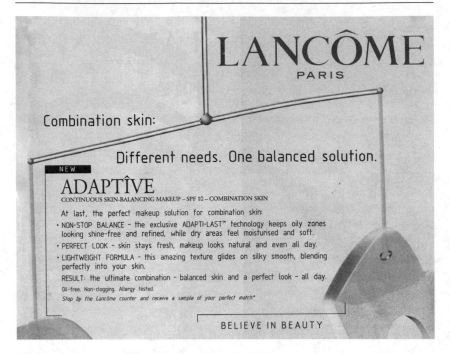

Figure 5.1 Lancôme Adaptive advertisement

our conclusions about what constitutes a 'problem' and what a 'solution' by choice of lexis with positive or negative *connotation*. Delin (2000: 133) demonstrates how a series of 'candidate synonyms' (words denoting the same concept) are distinguished in crucial ways by *connotation*: the cultural associations brought to a word by the reader, such as 'active', 'frenetic', 'lively', 'hyper', 'vital'. In most instances there is a high degree of cultural consensus about whether an item incurs positive or negative associations. 'Lively' is usually positive, whilst 'frenetic' is not, thus signalling the *affective* or *expressive* meaning of the term. In the Lancôme advertisement, we are guided to our attribution of a 'problem' by terms that in the conventional context of skin care are unequivocally negative: 'dry' and 'oily'. However, it is actually more common to be directed to the *positive* qualities of the product by positive lexis such as 'balanced', 'perfect', 'refined', 'fresh', 'natural', 'silky-smooth' which thus allows the reader to *infer* what is problematic by clause relation patterns ('At last, the perfect make-up solution for combination skin'). By positing something 'perfect' as the 'solution' to 'combination skin', we are forced to conclude that combination skin is a 'problem'. This rhetorical device is known as 'implicature', which we elaborate upon below.

Assertion, implicature and presupposition

A key function of advertising is to 'hail' the consumer into a subject position from which they can interpret the 'common-sense' assumptions of the advertisement. One of the most effective ways to position readers to accept the import of advertising messages is via *assertion, implicature* and *presupposition*. Assertion simply states a proposition about the reader in a direct and unmitigated way ('There's a bit of the West in all of us', Wranglers jeans). Implicature is the additional meaning that arises between the surface form of the utterance and its underlying intention, and is *inferred* by the reader as a result of a particular language choice. In the following line from an advertisement for Amoy soy sauce, 'When you add Amoy Dark Soy Sauce to your stir-fry you get our rich distinctive flavour without worrying about adding any fat', the implicature arises that the reader is likely to worry about fat in their diet.

Presupposition is an even more powerful device, since it refers to meaning embedded in one part of the text that must be both understood and accepted for the whole proposition to make sense. In an advertisement for Evian mineral water, we are exhorted to 'flush out last year's nasties and make a clean start to 2003'. Here, it is necessary to accept that we *house* 'last year's nasties' (whatever they may be!) in order to accept the command to flush them out. In an advertisement for mobile phones, we are told, 'The Samsung A800 brings you all the sophistication you demand', which positions the reader as someone who 'demands sophistication'. The power of presupposition over both assertion and implicature is that it cannot be denied without rejecting the whole proposition. Implicature and presupposition are naturally key devices which support the supposition of a supposed 'problem' and presupposition in particular is commonly encoded in a proposition by the use of the 'why' question form. An advertisement for a series of language classes appearing frequently in British newspapers used to read 'Are you shamed by your English?' or 'Does your English let you down?' After a few years the formulation had changed to 'Why are you shamed by your English?' By the subtle insertion of the 'why', the advertisers denied the implied reader the option of answering 'no'. In the second formulation the reader's ineptitude is built into the proposition and must be accepted for it to make sense.

Presupposition of a broader, cultural kind is at work constantly in consumer advertising and serves to construct ideological discourses to which the reader must subscribe in order to make sense of the text (Mills 1995). Many of the *assumptions of commodified femininity* outlined above, for instance, must be presupposed for certain propositions to make sense

('Why fade to grey when you can keep your colour young with lasting color?', Clairol: Lasting Color). For this to make sense we are required to take on board the ideology that ageing is negative and its outward manifestations must be avoided at all costs. The negative connotations of 'fade' obviously support this reading, but knowledge of the broader ideology is also necessary. 'Win his heart this Valentine's day' (Octagon motor sports) implies that the female readers of *Cosmopolitan* will firstly *wish* to win his heart, but also that they in fact *have* a 'him' as a significant other and thus are heterosexual.

Synthetic personalisation and simulated intimacy

The need for advertisements to address the consumer intimately has led to the use of a mode of discourse that Fairclough (1989: 37) has termed *synthetic personalisation*: 'a compensatory tendency to give the impression of treating each of the people handled "en masse" as an individual'. Advertisements commonly attempt to address the potential consumer as an individual, thus invoking their identity, and use a variety of linguistic means to simulate a special intimacy. Synthetic personalisation is closely linked to Baudrillard's (1998) term, 'simulated intimacy': both refer to the paradoxical form of consumerism and its conflicting impulses to be both 'mass' in its appeal and 'intimate' in its engagement with the consumer. It is precisely this synthesis between the mass and the individual, the commercial and the intimate, facilitated by discourses of synthetic personalisation, that plays particularly into the configuration of 'commodified identities'.

Synthetic personalisation is achieved perhaps most commonly through forms of address ('you' second person singular pronoun), but also other features of language emulating natural conversation. In fact, the broader form of cultural presupposition, with its dependence on shared knowledge, is arguably an instance of synthetic personalisation. The simulation of 'ordinariness' and everyday talk in advertising discourse achieves not only the impression of individual address, but also serves to level a potentially unequal power dyad between the knowledgeable producer and the ignorant consumer. Synthetic personalisation is realised via pronoun choice ('you'), simulation of dialogue, the use of an informal register (for example, colloquialisms), vague reference and deixis, positive politeness, humour and graphology (see Talbot 1995). We explicate each term with the following example from *Cosmopolitan*.

In this advertisement, the producers construct a mini-narrative, which relies on a high degree of cultural knowledge for its effects, and unsurprisingly exhibits many features of synthetic personalisation.

Figure 5.2 Imperial Leather advertisement

The advertisement is for a bubble bath mousse and the implication is that the relaxing properties of this product will send the consumer off into a fantasy world: 'Where will your Bathtime take you?' Most obviously, the advertisement adopts a simulated *direct address* to the 'individual' consumer by use of 'you' and 'your', but a similar effect of direct interaction is also produced by the use of *questions*: 'Where will your Bathtime take you?' and *commands*: 'Go on, escape for a while', which seem to require a reply or action from the implied reader. In the fantasy narrative part, the text adopts a *first-person* voice with which readers are intended to identify. So not only does the rest of the advertisement directly *address* the reader, the main part actually *speaks for her*. In this simulated first-person narrative, an *informal register* is invoked by the use of *colloquial words and phrases* that emulate spoken discourse: 'Go on'; 'ickle froggy'; 'wah Shizzam' (presumably the sound of a magical spell being broken), 'What's that you say'?; 'watch yourself'.

Some of the colloquialisms are exclusive to a particular targeted group (young, Western women familiar with television and magazine culture), and blur with *neologisms* (coined words/expressions: 'you *pert-pecked*, Hollywood sex god you'). *Vague reference* is not present here, since 'you' is identified as Brad Pitt/the plastic frog, but we can see an instance of *deixis* being employed in '*those* taps' (our emphases). Deictic items are inexplicit references to time and place which can only be understood from the perspective of the speaker/writer, such as 'here'; 'now' and 'these'. The effect is one of immediacy, of being present in the constructed scenario of the advertisement, of sharing the same visual space with the first person narrator, and of overhearing the conversation. In effect, the advertisement constructs an intimate, specific, exclusive *consumption community*, forging simulated solidarity by like-minded consumers (Machin and Thornborrow 2003). Such consumers will also 'get' the references to Brad Pitt and his (now ex-) wife, Jennifer Aniston, share the assumption that Brad is a worthy object of fantasy, and perhaps even share the same kinds of speech patterns in their *real* communities. Building solidarity with the consumer is also achieved by *humour*, and this, alongside the in-group references and exhortations to the reader to 'Go on, escape for a while', are examples of what Brown and Levinson (1987) have termed *positive politeness*: examples of language behaviour which boost the *positive face* of the addressee and nurture their need to be approved of and supported (see also Chapter 7).

Transitivity: Relations between consumer, the body and the product

A common feature of advertising for consumer femininity is the way the product is *personified*. Shampoo and moisturising cream 'care', 'protect' and 'nourish' one's hair or skin and many products actually incorporate this nurturing function into their brand names: 'Olay Complete Care; Multi-Action Day Cream Protection Plus'. Baudrillard (1998: 167) comments upon the 'ideology of therapy' implicit in this use of solicitous language, but also on the double meaning inherent in the verb, *to solicit* – an act of both gifting and demanding, which he describes as the 'ambiguity and terrorism of solicitude'. So when an advertisement exhorts us to 'Go on, escape for a while' we feel simultaneously indulged and impelled. Baudrillard's unease is perhaps partially founded on the implications for *agency* that such personified solicitude has.

Transitivity (see Chapter 3) refers to the pattern of processes and participants in a clause and involves a focus on who or what assumes *agency* in relation to the verb. Frequently, for consumer femininity, the product *serves* the consumer: it does things *for* but also *to* her making her the *beneficiary*. The following sentences from advertisements in '*Cosmopolitan*' are united by the same transitivity patterns:

Table 5.1 Transitivity in the language of consumer femininity

Product (Actor)	Process (Material verb connoting 'care')	Consumer/Consumer Body Part (Beneficiary)
Impactive . . .	immediately leaves (silky smooth)	skin
Impactive	(is designed to) stimulate and revitalise	your skin
Lasting Color	envelops	every strand of your hair
A cream gel formula . . .	to make (look flawless)	your skin
It	monitors	the balance of your skin

Sometimes the voice is passive and the agent is implied elsewhere ('With just a few drops (of Fructis Intense Anti Frizz) hair is instantly smoothed and nourished').

The ideological implications of such repeated patterns are clear. Despite the real world knowledge that consumers must actually apply these products to themselves, the language choices employed by such texts imply that female consumers are passive recipients who have things done to them, or more precisely, to their disembodied body parts. Power, at least in terms of grammatical agency, resides in the product.

In this section, we discussed a range of linguistics features to explore the process of identity commodification through advertising in a women's magazine, and in doing so, illustrated common characteristics of the construction of consumer femininity. We will now turn to a slightly different realisation of commodified identity: discourses of *self-commodification*.

DISCOURSES OF SELF-COMMODIFICATION

Self-promotion is becoming part-and-parcel of self identity . . . in contemporary societies. (Fairclough 1995: 140)

The relationship between identity and commodification may take the form of processes and discourses of *self-commodification* – literally, the selling or promotion of the self. Likely discursive sites of self-commodification include the job application, the job interview, telephone sex and the personal advertisement.

In an investigation into the discourse of telephone sex workers, K. Hall (1995) examined the linguistic strategies employed by women to sell a verbal and virtual simulation of a sexual encounter over the phone. K. Hall found that the women in her study produced a style of language stereotypically associated with what Lakoff (1975) famously termed 'women's language'. Items such as tag questions, supportive comments, intensifiers (for example, 'so', 'really'), dynamic intonation and breathiness were remarkably consonant with Lakoff's characterisation of women's talk. However, where Lakoff interpreted such features within a deficit paradigm and assigned them a powerless function, K. Hall argues that such 'powerless' language is reinvested with capital by symbolising sexuality, the commodity on sale in this transaction. In telephone sex work, verbal creativity is a marketable tool, and stereotypically 'feminine' language is employed for strategic ends. K. Hall comments that female operators receive positive reinforcement for using a feminine style of discourse throughout life and are now selling it back to culture at large for a high price – a strategic form of cultural capital. Moreover, interviews that K. Hall conducted with fantasy-line operators revealed that they felt *empowered* by their work and entirely in control of the interaction. This conclusion again challenges the dominant and traditional view that discourses of commodification are invariably disempowering to the individual subject.

Self-commodification in personal advertisements

The personal advertisement is another example of self-commodification in the metaphorical marketplace of romance and relationships. It is both a form of self-presentation and description of ideal partner and in this way it represents a likely site for an insight into cultural mediations of identity construction. Studies of personal advertisements have been approached from a number of perspectives but have perhaps most commonly looked at patterns of regular personal traits in order to explore cultural notions of attraction and role expectation. Shalom's (1997) sample, for instance, demonstrates that men seek attractiveness and women seek professionalism. P. Baker's (2003) longitudinal and quantitative analysis of gay personal advertisements over three decades shows that a 'straight-acting' orientation to heterosexuality is prized in a AIDS-aware culture in which gay identity is continuously stigmatised in the popular media. R. Jones (2000) discusses the commodification of race in his study of inter-racial gay personal advertisements in the Hong Kong press and identifies a prevalent pairing of the worldly, older and solvent professional Western man with the younger, dependent, aesthetically pleasing Asian man. All these studies view advertisements as a textual barometer measuring what is deemed to be the cultural capital of particular societies and particular subgroups.

Dating advertisements have also been analysed in terms of their distinctive generic *form*. The *structure*, *semantics* and *pragmatic norms* of personal advertisements are characterised by a high degree of generic predictability. J. Coupland (1996: 193) identifies generic structure as:

1. advertiser
2. seeks
3. target
4. goals
5. (comment)
6. reference

The generic structure and indeed pattern of transitivity here position the *sought-after* participant more obviously as the commodity in this transaction. However, descriptions of both participants make it clear that the advertisement is a two-way exchange with the desirable qualities of both participants emphasising the objectification and marketisation of the self. Types of categorisation label identified by J. Coupland (ibid.) include (in order of frequency): sex 100 per cent; age 87 per cent; location 73 per cent; appearance 60 per cent; personality/behaviour traits 55 per cent; interests 51 per cent; career/solvency/status 34 per cent; generational/marital status 33 per cent; ethnicity 7 per cent. In other words, these are the dimensions (perhaps with the exception of sex and location) which 'can be taken to constitute the conventional repertoire of self-commodifying attributes for self-selling in this medium' (ibid.).

Semantically, advertisements are characterised by a short list of predominantly positive characteristics and occasional creative examples of extended metaphor that tend to emphasise the view that the self is a commodity like any other. In the following example, the advertiser is compared metaphorically to a vintage car.

Extract 5.1: From J. Coupland 1996: 192
CLASSIC LADY limousine, mint condition, excellent runner for years seeks gentleman enthusiast 45 + for TLC and excursions in the Exeter area.

The register of dating advertisements is informal ('guy', 'baldies', 'bubbly'), arguably mimicking the patterns of speech, but equally drawing from a pool of familiar and clichéd resources unique to this register that function to reinforce the sense of synthetic community (for example, acronyms TLC = tender, loving care; GSOH = good sense of humour). Pragmatically, personal advertisements deviate from other relational genres by their *explicit* self-promotion – in politeness terms 'positive face enhancement' (Brown and Levinson 1987) – and what might be regarded as a flouting of 'normative' behaviour in conversational contexts.

A common response to the phenomenon of personal advertisements, both within and outside academia, is similar to that which we rehearsed in relation to marketisation discourses more generally. They are often thought to be reductive and homogenising, limiting personal qualities into a series of 'types'. They also promote 'categoriality, conventionality and social stereotype', and the genre requires a kind of lexical reification of what might be thought of as 'ineffable' personal qualities (J. Coupland 1996: 198). A common source of unease revolves around the fact that appearance is almost always foregrounded, a fact supported by Giddens's (1991: 198, cited in J. Coupland 1996) observation that 'self-actualisation is packaged and distributed according to market criteria . . . Commodification promotes *appearance* as the prime arbiter of value and sees self-development above all in terms of display'.

However, J. Coupland argues against this overwhelmingly negative assessment of the self-commodifying aspects of personal advertisements by focusing on what she calls 'strategies of personalisation'. Advertisers increasingly respond to the homogenising impulses of the personal advertisement by introducing quirkiness, creativity (for example, the *recontextualisation* of a register of legal language, 'I hereby declare') and humour, for example:

Extract 5.2: From The Guardian, *October 2002*
I hereby declare I am 39, slim, feminine, 5'3, bright, talented, attract. Accuracy is another strong point!

Here, the second sentence is a reflexive way of drawing attention to the reputation personal advertisements have gained for *in*accuracy, and thus is a way of challenging the genre whilst preserving the symbolic capital of the advertiser. In the recorded spoken advertisements accompanying the written ones that she examines, J. Coupland also identifies scope for affective meanings and interpersonal engagement:

Extract 5.3: From Coupland 1996: 198
I'm considered to be very attractive or (.) well so people say (laughs)

Here the advertiser *impersonalises* the attribution of a key quality by use of the passive voice with agency deleted ('I'm considered'). This is further shored up by a second clause of *concession* ('or (.) well so people say'), which, although structurally presented as contrastive ('or'), in fact presents a similar semantic proposition: it is not she who has made this observation. Laughter adds a further affective dimension, lessening the impact of what might be seen as a potentially self-promoting act.

This tendency towards an anti-commercial impulse is commonly observed in personal advertisements. Other manifestations of this impulse include humour, uncompromising honesty and even undesirable capital, as in the following examples:

> *Extract 5.4: From* London Review of Books, *October 2002*
> Vibrant, attract F, 25, drinks like a fish smokes like a chimney
>
> Cheerful profess, 38, short, bald, terrible humour
>
> Ugly man seeks ugly F for beautiful relationship

J. Coupland argues that such patterns reveal resistance on the part of the advertiser to the commodification of the self. The mitigation in the earlier example above ('or so people say') allows an attribution of modesty; however, this is still arguably a strategic 'selling point'. Humour, honesty and indeed novelty are all forms of desirable capital. Such strategies by advertisers are no different from the eternal striving towards originality, the relentless pushing at the boundaries of the genre observed in the ever-evolving work of copywriters. As we witnessed in our examination of commodified femininity, newness sells. Resistance to the dominant values of consumer culture gets seamlessly reassimilated back and invested with commodity value. Qualities of 'wit', 'unconventionality' and even 'rebelliousness' may be seen, to use Bourdieu's terms, as forms of 'cultural capital'.

INCORPORATING CONFLICTING DISCOURSES

The previous section ended with a consideration of what might be termed an 'anti-commercial', 'anti-consumption' (Baudrillard 1998: 91) or *counter-commercial impulse* within discourses of commodified identity. The proliferation of commodified discourses in Western society has led to a certain fatigue in consumers accompanied by a backlash. Cameron (2000), for instance, who explored practices of scripting and codifying spoken interaction in commercial settings such as call centres, points to growing scepticism about such styling. Conversation cannot be scripted or styled, she argues, because its very effectiveness relies on sensitivity to context – it is a *locally* managed phenomenon. And this, she argues, is precisely the reason why so many people get profoundly irritated by these kinds of scripted exchanges.

A number of theorists, such as Giddens (1991) and Beck (1992), have described an impulse of *counter-modernity* which responds to the loss of traditional certitudes accompanying the breakdown of industrial society (such as family, life-employment) with a new set of certainties. One possible outcome of counter-modernity may be a return to the personal and 'authentic' and a resistance to discourses of globalisation and commodification. This becomes a means of shoring up a clear and unified sense of identity or ideology and is palpable in the recent popularity of anti-capitalist and green movements. For this reason, a certain degree of *resistance* is creeping into cultures of consumption, and consumer culture is increasingly, simultaneously, about a *disavowal* of commodification. This resistance to commodification may originate with consumers in their critical or creative responses to commercial discourses. However, what is equally common, is that the producers of commercial texts will first anticipate, then attempt to *incorporate* modes of resistance to the anonymising and homogenising effects of commodification into their discourse in a kind of pre-emptive move: 'advertising increasingly parodies itself, integrating counter-advertising into its promotional techniques' (Baudrillard 1998: 195). For example, advertisers will sometimes incorporate resistance to commodification through a kind of reflexive acknowledgement of their constructedness *as* advertisements – perhaps through pastiche or parody, as we saw in the example of the personal advertisements above (Chouliaraki and Fairclough 1999: 15). This is an increasingly common strategy in commercial advertising.

Reconciling gendered discourses and consumption

As well as accommodating the consumer's distaste for explicit commodification, advertisers also increasingly have to accommodate ideological contradictions based on conflicting identities. Sometimes this is unpalatably cynical, as in the case of a recent British television campaign in which the identities of 'hippies' and 'eco-warriors' are used to sell finance. But it also occurs in an apparent attempt to reconcile feminism and femininity in contemporary women's magazines. Goldman (1992) discusses the canny construction of 'commodity feminism' in women's glossy magazines in the 1980s. He argues that growing feminist resistance to images of glamour and the creation of envy in images of consumer femininity led advertisers to incorporate feminism into their texts. If women were to continue to be kept on board in the marketplace of consumer femininity, their political identities and preoccupations needed to be addressed and accommodated. Thus *signs* of feminism (the briefcase, the Filofax, the suit) become commodified and incorporated, perhaps rather cynically, into advertisements for products ranging from perfume to jeans. In so doing, advertisers effected a superficial collapsing of the hitherto binary and exclusive opposition between feminism and femininity. This pattern, though arguably less explicit, is still in evidence in magazines in the 21st century. For example, consider the following advertisement from the edition of *Cosmopolitan* referred to earlier:

Figure 5.3 Ford Fiesta advertisement

The advertisement is a double-page spread. On the left of the page are four cartoons, each depicting traditionally feminine, domestic activities or preoccupations: a wedding cake, an iron, a shopping basket and a baby's pram. Each is contained within a traffic sign symbolising 'no' (a red circle with a diagonal line through it). On the right-hand side is a photograph of a car, which, according to Kress and van Leeuwen (1996) is higher in 'visual modality' and thus more 'real' than the cartoons. In small print beneath the cartoon images, reads 'Don't play "her indoors"' . . . Get out more and get into the all-new Ford Fiesta.' In addition, there is a slogan in bold white letters ('Get out more'). The textual features work together to highlight the division, theorised by feminists, between the 'private' domestic realms ('her indoors') of housework and mother-hood and the 'public' realm ('out') of driving cars. The advertisement therefore exploits *multi-modal semiotic* systems of meaning (cartoons, text, photographs, street signs) to construct its message (see Chapter 6). The private/public split is presented symbolically by the layout of the advertisement: with 'private' on the left, and 'public' on the right. The rejection of symbols of traditional femininity here – an appeal perhaps to a youthful postfeminist identity – has been effectively appropriated by the commercial imperative.

A strategic accommodation of oppositional or conflicting discourses is also prevalent in the newer men's lifestyle magazines. Within men's magazines (and indeed, within the surrounding culture of 'new lad' mas-culinity), one of the defining identities of masculinity is an explicit *rejec-tion* of anything remotely feminine. This pattern not only conforms to the logic of the binary inherent in traditional gender relations, but is also highly compatible with the consumption imperative which dictates that differentiation sells. Indeed, as we have already argued, gender identity itself is realised largely through processes of commodification (Andrews and Talbot 2000). This rejection of the feminine, however, presents a problem for those who wish to position men as consumers, since the trad-itional view of the consumer as *passive* has led to a common thesis which links the discursive role of the consumer to femininity.

As we saw in our analysis of advertisements in *Cosmopolitan*, the pro-ducer frequently occupies the discursive role of authority in adverts whilst the consumer is passive and receptive. This is further compounded by the historical association of shopping, leisure, the domestic sphere and women. This relationship is summarised below:

Subject   →   Object
Active   →   Passive
Producer →   Consumer
Masculine →   Feminine

Mulvey (1988) similarly expresses the idea that in mainstream cinema, the pleasure of the gaze is split into two distinct positions: men look and women exhibit. This 'scopophilic' rule greatly informs the visual imagery in 'new lad' magazines (for example, *loaded*, *FHM*), which largely avoids the objectification and aestheticisation of masculinity (Benwell 2002). The emergence of 'new lad' masculinity in the mid-1990s was a clear reaction to the feminist-friendly, sensitive, but also narcissistic 'new man' of the 1980s, and arguably an attempt to reassert the power of masculin-ity deemed to have been lost by the concessions made to feminism by 'new man' (Benwell 2004). 'New lad' masculinity, most clearly embodied in *loaded* magazine, but also by its competing successors (for example, *FHM*, *Maxim*, *Front*) marked a return to traditional masculine values of sexism, exclusive male friendship and homophobia. Its key distinction from *traditional* masculinity, however, was an unrelenting gloss of know-ingness and irony, and reflexivity about its own condition that arguably rendered it more immune from criticism (ibid.). Men's magazines that espouse the 'new lad' identity are a key site of ambiguous commodified identity and have arguably built their identities on resistance to the feminising connotations of commercial culture. Indeed, the founding editors of *loaded* made much of the 'authenticity' of the magazine at its inception, stressing its close relationship to the real lives and discourse of its readers (Southwell 1998), thus distancing it from the consumer enterprise.

Because of the connotations of passivity associated with conspicu-ous consumption, particularly products traditionally associated with a feminine realm in which appearance is at a premium, selling to men becomes a thorny, troubled proposition that has to be delicately nego-tiated by the text's producers. Nevertheless, a *total* avoidance of asso-ciating men with the passivising and narcissistic connotations of consumption is ultimately impossible for men's lifestyle magazines, whose very existence is underpinned financially and ideologically by the need to position men as consumers. It is for this reason that we commonly encounter familiar strategies combining both accommoda-tion and resistance in such texts. Thus the overtly commercial aspects of the magazine, such as promotional features and advertisements are frequently shot through with irony, humour or even explicitly anti-commercial discourse.

This defensive masculine code concerning commodification, particu-larly in the traditionally feminine sphere of beauty and grooming, can be witnessed in men's magazines in their promotion of grooming, goods and practices. For instance, a recent Nivea advertising campaign preva-lent in many magazines was 'For Men Who Dare To Care', implying a need for courage in using such products. The slogan cleverly posits the paradoxical proposition that to conform to patterns of behaviour deemed feminine actually requires male consumers to exhibit a courage and lack of orthodoxy that is in fact masculine. A similar trope involv-ing humorous, defensive or ironic caveats in relation to men using grooming products threads its way relentlessly through men's lifestyle magazines, especially those identified as 'new lad'. Humour and irony in these instances function simultaneously to distance and include the reader in the activity or values being promoted. A promotional feature

for men's facial and manicure treatments in *Maxim* is also heavily protected by one such example:

> *Extract 5.5: From* Maxim
> A men-only grooming shop for normal, everyday, nothing-funny-about-my-
> testosterone-levels-thankyou-blokes who quite fancy the idea of a de-stressing
> massage, with maybe a facial and, oh what the hell, a manicure while I'm
> here.

Here, the text adopts a kind of dual voicing: the ostensible voice is that
of an overly defensive man whose claims to normative masculinity need
to be defended ('men-only', 'normal', 'everyday', 'blokes'). The activity is downplayed and mitigated by low modality ('quite fancy', 'maybe
a facial') and shown to be spontaneous rather than carefully planned
('oh what the hell'). Conversely, a second voice can be detected, that of
the satirist, who finds such defensiveness ridiculous and this is clear
in the exaggerated qualifier 'nothing-funny-about-my-testosterone-
levels-thankyou'. What this dual voice achieves is a degree of space to
accommodate impulses of anti-consumerism whilst simultaneously
undermining the claims of any real resistance with a gently mocking
tone.

Similarly, but with less irony, in a feature profiling a series of after-
shaves, a hyperbolic, dialogic, vernacular and arguably macho register is
employed:

> *Extract 5.6: From* FHM
> **Crave** by Calvin Klein. You said: 'quite simply, the nuts! Looks mad, smells great.
> And survived a three-storey drop from my balcony!'

In other words, attempting to position male readers *as* consumers
requires a certain negotiation, usually involving some kind of reassur-
ance that such engagement with consumerism will not in any way prove
emasculating.

A more cynical view of all these attempts by producers to *incorporate*
resistance to commodification (the 'honest' personal advertisements,
the 'feminist' discourse promoting consumer femininity, the tongue-
in-cheek 'new lad') would see them as still subject to the processes of
commodification. All that has been achieved has been merely to give the
consumer an *appearance* of control. Capitalism drives the endless renewal
and expansion of the commodity-sign value of consumer goods and the
quest for endless renewal may sometimes involve the strategic recupera-
tion of what seem initially to be acts of resistance to consumer culture. As

Corrigan (1997: 74) wryly observes, 'consumption absorbs politics and re-emerges strengthened'.

A less cynical view might be inclined to attend to the actual experiences of the consumers themselves. How accurate are our attempts to predict the likely responses of consumers to discourses of commodified identity? Are readers and audiences in fact more adept at resisting the strategies employed by these texts to position them as consumers? Or, indeed, are their experiences of engaging with commercial discourse far less coherent and consistent than we might like to presume? Can they anticipate the attempts by advertisements to 'incorporate resistance' and do they disapprove of this? In the next section, we will attempt to answer these questions by presenting the analysis of unstructured interviews with two groups of male readers of men's lifestyle magazines.

READERS, MASCULINITY AND RESISTANCE

A study of readers and their responses and practices involving men's magazines is a useful way of attending to the traditional analytical neglect of the consumer in accounts of commodification. The following example draws on research conducted by Benwell (2005). Her study of male consumers took the form of two lengthy, informal, unstructured interviews led and guided by a male researcher who also circulated reading material to prompt discussion. The first group consisted of two 17-year-old males still at school in Scotland. The second group consisted of four 21-year-old male students at a Scottish university. The interview was set up to elicit the reading habits, practices and accounts of a range of dedicated readers of men's magazines with particular reference to issues of consumption and gender. Responses to specific advertisements, articles and images were also elicited.

The recorded data were transcribed orthographically and analysed using critical discursive psychology (cf. Wetherell and Edley 1999). We analysed the sequential construction of identity categories (for example, 'invested' and 'uninvested reader'; 'new man' and 'new lad') and the rhetorical deployment of interpretative repertoires (for example, 'consumer as passive dupe' versus 'consumer as reflexive critic'). The advantage of a study of consumers' own talk is that it is able to capture the fine-grained and sometimes contradictory or ambivalent accounts and identity work of consumers, which is arguably more fruitful for a discursive study of identity than the many studies which view the consumer in abstract economic terms.

Unstructured interviews and focus groups as data collection methods have been the focus of much debate and discussion across the social sciences, largely due to the way they are often treated as a *transparent* description of opinion or unmediated report of practice. As we discussed in Chapter 4, some commentators argue that interview data must be treated as a researcher-driven, occasioned and situated *account* of identity and practices. Nevertheless, interview data are still useful as a resource for broader social analysis. As C. D. Baker (2004: 163) suggests, 'interviewing is understood as an interactional event in which members draw on their cultural knowledge'. We therefore approach the interview data in two ways. First, they are occasioned 'reports' of the participants' buying and reading habits and their broad dispositions towards the commodified community they are engaging with. Second, we look for evidence of more ambivalent, contradictory and negotiated ways of constructing commodified identities through talk by examining the situated and jointly created accounts by the interviewees.

Invested versus uninvested readers

The younger group reveals a series of insights about their reading practices which is suggestive of an unselfconsciously, unembarrassed *investment* in the magazines. They regularly read *FHM* and *Maxim* and one actually subscribes to *FHM*. They profess to read the magazine systematically, whereas older readers 'flick'. They describe the function of the magazines as 'advice' or 'giving insight' into experiences the readers might not have access to, and they actively fill in polls and questionnaires – sometimes sending these back to the magazines. They pull out the posters and use them to decorate their bedrooms and find articles 'very funny', sometimes singling out regular writers. At one stage of the interview one of them discusses reading practices in terms of a kind of brand loyalty:

Extract 5.7: Younger group

1 F: People can say they prefer *Maxim*. You write in to *Maxim* and slag off
2   *FHM* and vice versa, you kind of pick your team, then you find one
3   more funny than the other.
[. . .]
5   I don't know what it is you kind of feel a loyalty to, more than you like
6   the best. It's almost like a football team.

By contrast, the group of 21-year-olds construct themselves as *uninvested*, referring to a past, younger, invested self (I is the interviewer):

Extract 5.8: Older group

1	I:	Do you actually buy any of these magazines yourselves?
2	M:	Yeah I used to be totally addicted to them and buy most of them . . .
3	I:	Most of them yeah so . . .
4	M:	But I kind of stopped now, and if I buy them at all I generally
5		buy um *GQ* and I'll buy *Esquire* but I kind of got fed up
6	I:	So it's on a fairly irregular basis that you er . . .
7	M:	Well I mean I'll buy y'know one or two of them a month I would think
8		um but just I wouldn't go out an' search for them it's just if I'm y'know in
9		Tesco or whatever,
10	I:	Yeah
11	M:	Or the cover strikes me or something when you're a bit bored.
12	I:	Yeah that's fair enough . . . Gordon?
13	G:	Um I don't buy uh very many any more I used to sort of like buy for like a
14		few sort of like, but now it's sort of like if I'm out I may pick up one or
15		two if I'm just bored something to read. Probably something like *GQ* or
16		*Maxim* or something like more interesting articles sometimes but that's
17		about it really.
18	I:	Um that's good . . . Dan?
19	D:	I'm pretty much the same um I used to read *FHM* and *Maxim*, like pretty
20		much every time they came out and stuff. Now I'll buy them occasionally,
21		every so often, it's just whenever it takes my fancy really.
22	I:	Okay, Jonathan?
23	J:	I only used to uh read *FHM* and again it was just till a couple of years ago
24		I stopped buying it. I tended to buy it for the articles and obviously for the
25		men on the front covers (laughs)
26		(laughter from all)
27	I:	Yeah I mean uh cos as none of you are regular buyers is it on the basis of
28		the front cover that you buy them? Or is it cos you just need something to
29		do?
30	J:	I don't tend to buy them any more at all, so . . .
31	I:	At all?
32	M:	I don't know, I mean, the cover's definitely what strikes you, but,
33		sometimes from buying them so much when we were younger and stuff
34		you tend to go, you're still caught by the cover but I think the sensible part
35		of your brain goes 'that's three quid for something you're going to look at
36		once'

All participants use a past-time perspective in presenting the activities associated with the *former invested reading self*. They echo each other's formulations ('I used to') to describe their former regular engagement with the magazines ('buy most of them'; 'buying them so much', 'every time they came out') and construct any current engagement as specifically superficial, functional and mitigated ('occasionally . . . every so often', 'if I buy them at all', 'if I'm bored just something to read', 'just if I'm y'know in Tesco or whatever'). There is a dichotomy being constructed here between the younger, invested, naïve self ('totally addicted'; 'still caught by the cover') and the current, wiser, experienced self, benefiting from hindsight ('the sensible part of your brain', 'I kind of got fed up', 'I wouldn't go out an' search for them', 'I don't tend to buy them any more at all'). The 'uninvested reader' by default is largely one who *no longer* engages in these activities.

Elsewhere in the interview, and in line with other studies of magazine readers, of both men's and women's magazines (Hermes 1995; Jackson, Stevenson and Brooks 2001), the participants display their 'uninvested' identities by constructing the magazines as trashy, disposable, a bit of fun if there's nothing better to do by using vague formulations ('a bunch of stuff') and mitigation ('a wee while', 'just'). Such dispositions are arguably consonant with the 'counter-commercial' backlash or impulse outlined earlier in this chapter.

'New man' versus 'new lad'

Despite the ostensible rejection of magazine culture, the older readers employed a 'new lad' ideology associated with the magazines themselves. For instance, when asked to comment on 'kinds of women' represented in the magazines (in relation to a specific feature, 'Girls on the Sofa'), the 21-year-olds respond as follows:

Extract 5.9: Older group
1 M: Well, these women are <u>HOT</u>
2 G: (laughing) yeah.
3 D: No yeah (laughing) they are
4 I: (Laughing) yeah.
5 M: It's like they do that sort of single woman like she's sort of available
6 sort of like looking for a date or whatever but it's not always a
7 stereotypical girl it's still a fit woman sort of scantily clad
8 G: But you would-
9 M: They're all five <u>REALLY</u> <u>really</u> hot women.

This extract illustrates the unambiguous collaborative enactment of heterosexual male desire – a cornerstone of hegemonic masculinity and one of the key rationales underpinning 'new lad' magazines. Despite their earlier cynicism and dismissal of these magazines, the humour, lively discourse and joshing of the interview discussion with this group matches the style and ethos of the magazine itself, thus emphasising the way in which these discourses continually circulate between various sites of the 'circuit of culture'.

The older group displays distance from the magazine, but is conversant with its discourse, and affiliated to some of its values. Whilst the 17-year-olds appear to fashion their identities through consumption practices, the 21-year-olds adopt a discourse of resistance, premised on a broader discourse that 'consumers' equals 'passive dupes'.

In the following extract, the interviewer has asked about the older group's reading practices and whether there are parts of the magazine they avoid:

Extract 5.10: Older group

1	I:	Are there parts of the magazine you always ignore?
2	M:	I generally try to skip past the 50 pages worth of adverts
3		(Laughter from all)
4	I:	Mike avoids adverts, is that the same for <u>all</u> of you?
5	G:	Yeah, I try my best not to look at them
6	D:	There's just so much advertising in them anyway turn a page 'oh no not
7		another advertisement' you're like 'is there anything here worth reading'
8	J:	I remember doing a Nivea thing that I bought Nivea after reading it years
9		ago like y'know how they have like articles
10	I:	An article rather than an advert
11	J:	Yeah it was like a sponsored article-
12	M:	(Laughing) Lucky this is anonymous!
13		(Laughter from all)

In his answer, and consistent with his earlier resistance to the consumer values of the magazines, Mike says to much laughter: 'I generally try to skip past the 50 pages worth of adverts.' Laughter from other participants is often a useful gauge of normative values. It is clear that there is a cultural consensus that advertisements are a dominant part of the magazines, perhaps even an implicit acknowledgement that their revenue financially underpins the publication, but that they are not worthy of attention and an irritating distraction. This consensus is worked up during the process of the interview, thus constructing as well as reflecting normative values. The interviewer prompts this consensus by asking 'Mike avoids adverts. Is that the same for <u>all</u> of you?' (line 4). This is taken up by Greg and Daniel, who confirm and elaborate upon Mike's opinion (lines 5–7).

However, note Jonathan's turn (lines 8–11), in which he offers a counter to this consensus that has been collaboratively built so far, in the form of an anecdote. Significantly, Jonathan's turn is not explicitly framed as an *accountable* contradiction to this consensus, although it is arguably mitigated by the vague formulation 'Nivea thing' and by his past-time perspective ('I remember', 'years ago'). This again invokes the earlier group consensus of the 'naïve younger self' invested in magazine culture. The interviewer's response to Jonathan's story is to ask another question to clarify one feature of it. However, Jonathan's story prompts teasing laughter from the rest of the group, as well as an orientation to the fact that their discussion is being recorded ('Lucky this is anonymous'). Why does telling such a story prompt laughter from the other speakers? It tells us that Jonathan has breached some sort of normative code, and is now occupying what Wetherell (1998) calls a 'troubled subject position'. However, the precise kind of 'position' is ambiguous. One reading is that by telling a story that reveals him to be susceptible to the power of advertising, the teasing laughter positions him as susceptible to consumerism. A second reading is that his position is 'troubled' because he has bought a 'feminine' grooming product. This provides evidence of a tension between versions of masculine identities ('new lad' versus 'new man') operating in the cultural sphere of this group. Moreover, the reference to anonymity ('Lucky this is anonymous') implies that the speaker needs to be protected from the potential humiliation associated with being an 'uncritical consumer' or breaching 'new lad' masculinity – or both.

Here, the group polices one member's account of his relationship to the consumption of grooming products, despite a more positive orientation to the idea of male 'grooming' elsewhere in the interview. This sequence is occasioned by the problematic association between 'grooming' and femininity outlined in the previous section, and aligned with 'new lad' masculinity. The discourse surrounding this anxiety reveals a complex sequence of rejection and acceptance of consumerism accompanied by shifts between unselfconscious banter and sophisticated critical commentary. Indeed, this whole exchange can be usefully compared with one later in the interview where the interviewer elicits the same readers' responses to a promotional feature on grooming in one of the magazines:

Extract 5.11: Older group

1　D:　　I think humour is a good way of getting around touchy subjects, like
2　　　　y'know . . . if you asked a normal kind of lad who'd be like 'oh I'm not
3　　　　going to go and have a facial' or something
4　I:　　　Having read it, would any of you be interested in those kinds of product?
5　M:　　Great! If I had the money I'd have a go at it.

This exchange reveals what the assumptions, values and anxieties of a 'normal lad' are. It also implies that the two speakers do not identify with this heteronormative construction. This is done in two ways: firstly by employing third-person, distancing strategies ('a normal kind of lad'), and secondly by an explicit, positive, non-ironic alignment to the grooming feature. All of this is at odds with the normative masculinity built up around the discussion of Jonathan's foray into a traditionally 'feminine' preserve. This analytical approach therefore is able to foreground how the participants' accounts of their reading practices vary rhetorically, particularly in formulations relating to the readers' alignment with the masculine constructions promoted by the magazines.

Across the data, we have identified a pair of organising 'interpretative repertoires' – 'consumer as reflexive critic' and 'consumer as passive dupe' – which the participants shift between. These repertoires open up a range of overlapping, 'troubled' and 'untroubled' subject positions and identity choices, such as 'invested reader' ('you kind of feel a loyalty') versus 'uninvested reader' ('I wouldn't go out an' search for them'), and 'uncritical consumer' (the laughter that greets Jonathan's admission to buying Nivea) versus 'cynical consumer' ('There's just so much advertising in them'). Within this repertoire, the participants also shift between different types of identity positioning related to gender: 'new man' and 'new lad' identities. The 'new man' embraces consumer masculinity ('Great! If I had the money I'd have a go at it') and endorses non traditional gender ideology. In relation to the organising repertoires, this identity cuts across both 'reflexive critic' ('if you asked a normal kind of lad who'd be like "oh I'm not going to go and have a facial"') and 'passive dupe' ('doing a Nivea thing'). The 'new lad' is more dominant across the data, displayed in the rejection of 'female' beauty products (laughing in response to Jonathan's 'Nivea thing') and the routine positioning of themselves as heterosexual ('these women are HOT'). The 'new lad' similarly cuts across both 'reflexive critic' ('Lucky this is anonymous!') and 'passive dupe', uncritically taking on the language of the magazine ('a fit woman sort of scantily clad').

In the preceding analysis, we have found that consumers do not represent a homogeneous constituency with uniform views on consumption. Moreover, the data demonstrated variability within participants' accounts of their practices, occasioned by the micro demands of the interactional context. We found that readers – particularly the older ones – negotiated an interesting line between two positions: one of detachment or disdain, and one of acceptance, defence or even internalisation of the magazines' traditional masculine values. Such patterns are supported by existing research on women's magazines, in which it is argued that readers are easily and unembarrassedly able to accommodate the contradictions thrown up by the magazines and their responses to them (for example, Ballaster, Beetham, Frazer and Hebron 1991; McRobbie 1999). Similarly, these readers both formally endorsed the principle of male consumption in direct exchange with the interviewer, but rejected it in more informal exchanges with one another during the course of the interview. Such an exercise demonstrates that attempting to identify a 'true' or 'singular' position for the consumer is a red herring.

THE AUTHORITY OF THE CONSUMER

So far we have argued that research on commodified identities tends to favour one of two emphases: the consumer as passive recipient of the powerful and manipulative strategies of advertisers and producers, or the consumer as discerning and interactive participant in the consumption process. Furthermore, there is evidence that advertisers are starting to accommodate the voice of the consumer more obviously in their discourse. Fairclough (1994) discusses a discursive shift towards the use of conversational styles in public, political and even institutional discourse. He links this shift to a restructuring of the boundary between public and private orders of discourse (see also Chapter 3). It is a pattern we have observed in this chapter, not only in the 'simulated intimacy' of advertising discourse, but also in the high value accorded to the views and discourse practices of the readers of men's magazines by the producers of those magazines. The process of 'conversationalisation' ('the modelling of public discourse upon the discursive practices of ordinary life') invites a number of interpretations relating to the identity of the consumer (p. 253).

On the one hand, Fairclough argues, conversationalisation could be seen to be a democratic move – a shift in favour of consumers. On the other hand, these discursive practices are generated and imposed by the producers, their authenticity suspect and their motives doubtful. Fairclough (1994: 266) concludes:

> Conversationalisation cannot convincingly be simply dismissed
> as engineering, strategically motivated simulation, or simply
> embraced as democratic. There is a real democratic potential, but
> it is emergent in and constrained by the structures and relations of
> contemporary capitalism.

Fairclough's ambivalence about the apparent democratisation of the marketplace and new-found power of the consumer is similarly reflected in Bucholtz's (1999) research on 'shopping channel' discourse. The shopping channel is popular in the US and available on cable networks in Europe and involves viewer-consumers ringing in to the show to describe purchasing experiences and sometimes to endorse products. In line with Fairclough's observations, it is a hybrid genre that 'combines the intimacies of private conversation with the exigencies of the marketplace' (p. 349). Bucholtz's research was motivated by the desire to insert the audience into the text as active participants in the meaning-making process. However, much of her data revealed the way in which the viewer's identity is positioned and constrained by either the active interventions of the show's host or by the generic conventions of the show. The findings from our interview data, by contrast, represent a direct engagement with the accounts of the usually silent audience, elicited in a context independent from the site of consumption. By adopting an ethnographic and interactive approach to consumption, the profile of the reader and his input in the circuit of culture is afforded a higher degree of meaning. Moreover, the content of these interviews might encourage us to reappraise the consumer as more discerning, resistant and fickle than traditional accounts have hitherto suggested.

However, notwithstanding the growing authority of consumers (apparent or real), and their abilities to engage critically with, or in resistance to, discourses of commodification, engagement with the discourse of daily life continues to support the creeping supremacy of commodified identity over all other identities. Consumers may have increased authority but at the expense of other aspects of their identity. Fairclough (1993) has argued that non-commercial texts are increasingly being 'colonised' by the discourse of advertising, as his study of university prospectuses illustrates. When browsing through the pages of a women's lifestyle magazine, we encountered the surprising pattern of discourses of commodity femininity being used in job advertisements. An advertisement for the police force is headlined in bold large letters with 'RICE CRACKERS, COTTAGE CHEESE AND AN APPLE', the stereotypical diet of a weight-conscious female consumer, and a discourse we associate more commonly with the main pages of the women's magazines. Similarly, an advertisement for the London Underground presents an Andy Warhol-style series of prints of garishly-coloured lipstick tubes accompanied by the headline: 'TUBES THAT'LL SUIT YOU PERFECTLY'. It would seem from this observed pattern that it is the *commodified* identity of the reader (consumer femininity) that is assumed to have a higher recognition value than, say, a work or career identity. Identity continues to enjoy an increasingly intimate relationship with consumption, even to the point where other forms of identity are subsumed within its boundaries.

CONCLUSION

In this chapter we have explored the phenomenon of 'commodified identities', arguing that there are a number of diverse ways in which identity could be said to be 'commodified'. Firstly we examined the way that advertising texts construct particular versions and *representations* of 'commodified identity' (particularly 'femininity' and 'masculinity'). These are underpinned by certain ideological assumptions (for example, 'Real women care about their appearance; real men don't'), which become familiar discourses endlessly reiterated across advertising and other everyday texts. Another 'commodified identity' emerging from our analysis relates to the *process* by which the consumer is 'hailed' into adopting these discourses or positioning themselves in relation to them. A range of linguistic strategies was examined (for example, problem-solution pattern, presupposition) that might be argued to achieve this kind of 'positioning'. This sort of critical discourse approach arguably accords little agency to the audience and tends to theorise the consumer as a mere effect of a set of ideological discourses.

We also examined a particular set of genres or discourse-types united by a function of *self-commodification*, including personal advertisements and telephone sex work. Fairclough (1993) described some of this explicitly self-promotional material (particularly in professional contexts) as part of a broader trend of the marketisation of public life and the reconstruction of professional identities along entrepreneurial lines. Finally, we engaged with *actual* consumers through the employment of unstructured interviews using critical discursive psychology to identify patterns of accounting and identity construction in their versions of themselves as consumers of men's magazines. This analysis enabled us to re-evaluate the consumer as a contradictory and ambiguous entity, at once expressing clear alignments with the commercial imperative and also rejecting it via an explicitly 'anticommercial' stance. The analysis was also a fascinating exploration of the way in which gender was implicated in the negotiation of a consumer or commodified identity.

In the next chapter, *Spatial Identities*, we move on to consider a different site for identity construction, one that moves beyond the textual realms discussed so far.

CHAPTER 6

Spatial Identities

In this chapter, we investigate another aspect of contemporary discourse and identity research: the links between place, space and identity construction. We write against a backdrop of academic theorising about the discursive construction of identity that has recently started to take account of spatial, or place-relevant aspects. In addition to language practices, however, we consider the function of other practices and semiotic domains, such as symbols, embodied movement and gesture, in the production of place/space and identity. In other words, we consider two interrelated themes: (1) place/space as *produced in* and as a *topic of* discourse, and (2) place/space as the *location for* discourse.

We start by considering the links between space, social action and identity – particularly how space channels human activity along identity lines – via photographic representations of people's activities in places. Next, we review the history of the 'spatial turn' across the social sciences and humanities, and the ways that writers have theorised its relevance to identity construction. We then discuss a number of approaches to the empirical study of place-identity, including narrative, ethnomethodological and discursive psychological methods. Throughout the chapter, we examine analyses of both visual and discourse data in order to explicate an emerging theme in discourse and identity literature: the inextricable links between identity and location.

SPACE, SOCIAL ACTION AND IDENTITY

The photograph below is of a British beach in summertime, taken in August 2004:

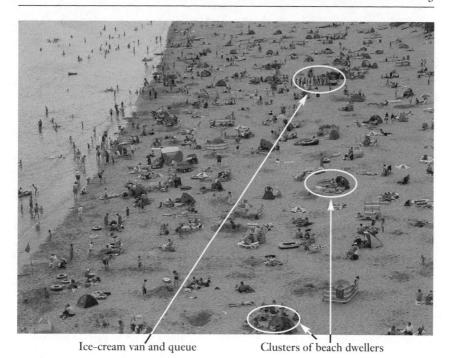

Ice-cream van and queue   Clusters of beach dwellers

Figure 6.1 The beach

One thing the photograph does not show is that, across the proximate stretch of beach, the image represents where most people have located themselves. Numbers fall the further away one might walk from the main beach exit. Despite being a highly populated area of the beach, we can observe that people have positioned themselves in small, separate clusters. The means of separation, in addition to physical distance, include the erection of windbreaks, awnings, deckchairs and umbrellas, which function to partition small areas and stake out territory. Sandpits are dug close to these small territories.

The only break in this pattern is the queue for the ice-cream van, towards the top right-hand corner of the photograph. Here, people are organised into a long, single-person line, one after another. In terms of social action and space, the queue provides an interesting example of a non-discursive but nevertheless accountable activity in which people order themselves according to a culture's rules and maxims. 'Pushing in' or 'jumping the queue' count as (verbalised, accounted for) breaches of those rules. Additionally, one only has to think of two or three different environments in which queuing occurs (for example, the bank, the public toilets, the cinema) to know that not all queues work in the same way: the order of each is a human production done on particular occasions.

There are a number of ethnomethodological studies of queues in which researchers have shown how queues work in different contexts. For example, in Randall and Hughes's (1995) studies of banking, they show how the staff manage their interactions with customers, keeping the queue moving by altering the pace at which they work to prevent a long queue building up. However, although persons acting in space – such as in our beach queue – may be performing a nonverbal activity, it is in discourse that breaches become accountable ('The queue starts here, actually!').

So, what does the photograph tell us about identity? We do not have recordings of the conversations that took place as people came onto the beach and decided where to locate themselves. From the evidence of the photograph, and from our own experience, we might speculate that on arrival at the beach, people weigh up different factors including proximity to the sea, the exit, the toilets and the ice-cream van or other refreshment facilities. But we can also imagine conversations about the appropriate distance to sit from other people, the kinds of people that others want to sit near or avoid, and complaints about new arrivals who sit too close, invading the space of folk already established with their windbreakers and umbrellas ('Why do *they* have to sit so close?').

Beach space and identity

In a recent study, Dixon and Durrheim (2003) investigated patterns of informal segregation on post-apartheid South African beaches. They show how something as seemingly mundane as sitting on the beach can be crucial to understanding identity practices. The theoretical context for their study is the 'contact hypothesis' in social psychology (Allport [1954] 1979). The argument is that intergroup conflict and racism, such as between white and black South Africans, can be reduced if members of the different groups interact with each other, under the right conditions. However, as Dixon and Durrheim point out, intergroup contact does not often happen in everyday social interaction, making 'contact' a tricky thing to study outside of the social psychological laboratory. And despite the abolition of institutionalised segregation, they argue it 'remains a pervasive and adaptable system for ordering social life' (p. 2).

Before the end of apartheid, South Africa's beaches were segregated such that the 'best' beaches were reserved for 'whites', with 'Indians', 'blacks' and 'coloureds' populating smaller and more remote ones. These policies demonstrate how identity is linked to spatiality, constituted in the construction of 'separate spaces for separate races' (Gunn 2002: 8). To investigate the scale and 'ecology' of informal segregation on South Africa's beaches, Dixon and Durrheim plotted the location of beach dwellers on an 'open' beach in Scottburgh, in which members of different 'race' categories could interact freely. They collected observational data during Christmas 1999, the peak holiday season, aiming to track the nature and extent of segregation practices by plotting the patterns of beach occupancy among members of different racial categories. They divided the beach into sectors and, within each of five observation periods over the day, plotted on a map who sat where, distinguishing between race category membership using symbolic markers such as physical, facial and dress cues. In the photograph below, each black triangle indicates one 'Indian' person, each white circle represents one 'white' person, and each black circle indicates one 'black' person:

Figure 6.2 Scottburgh beach (From Dixon and Durrheim 2003: 7)

Close analysis of the photograph revealed particular patterns of social and spatial segregation. As in our photograph of the UK beach, we can see that groups of people clustered in areas Dixon and Durrheim call 'umbrella spaces': territorial spaces that are 'typically marked by personal possessions and act as semi-permanent regions in which activities such as eating, sleeping, talking, sitting and sunbathing can take place' (p. 10). In addition to their role in organising interpersonal relations between small groups of strangers on the beach, however, Dixon and Durrheim argue that these umbrella spaces 'serve as a "legitimate" mechanism for preserving boundaries and distances between groups' (p. 11). The results of coding the racial composition of over 2,500 'umbrella spaces' reveal that over 99.9 per cent are racially homogeneous; that is, exclusively white or black. Dixon and Durrheim conclude that, 'within the intimate preserve of the umbrella space, segregation is virtually complete at Scottburgh' (p. 12).

In addition to observational data, Dixon and Durrheim interviewed groups of 'white' South Africans who were sitting on the beachfront. The interviews were designed to elicit the participants' opinions about changing beach relations, and how they made sense of the patterns of segregation observed in the mapping exercise. The data reveals that people interpreted the closeness of 'others' (that is, 'racial' others) as invading their space and rights to privacy. Overall, informal segregation was achieved in three main ways: at the 'micro-territorial' level of umbrella space, at the broader level of patterns of occupancy on the beach, in which racial groups distributed themselves in particular areas, and in terms of 'invasion-succession' sequences in which the arrival of 'black' holiday-makers was accompanied by the withdrawal of 'white' beach occupants.

We might flag at this point in the chapter an interesting tension in Dixon and Durrheim's study, as well as in research on place and space more generally. In order to study an ostensibly 'non-linguistic' phenomenon such as spatial identity, Dixon and Durrheim ended up interviewing people about it, and, inevitably, producing their own analytic discourse about it. And we ourselves use text throughout this chapter to point out relevant phenomena in various images. It is hard to see how to let pictures 'speak for themselves', 'tell their own stories' (and of course, these are discourse metaphors!) without using language to explicate their meaning – especially in an academic text. We return to this point at the end of the chapter.

This tension notwithstanding, we can begin to see how identity is bound up not 'just' in talk and text, but also in other 'practices-in-interaction' such as bodily movement in physical space. However, 'physical space' is not an objective, neutral phenomenon but inescapably socially constructed by human agents and their semiotic practices. National boundaries, walls around houses, gates to land, roads for traffic and pavements for people are all products of social practices, and have to be continually maintained (that is, re*constructed*) to fulfil their organising functions of channelling human activity. And they have their force and accountability not only by virtue of their brute physical existence, but by virtue of how they are described, categorised, made relevant and enforced in laws, statutes and accounts.

'Geosemiotics' and identity

Consider the sign below, which was, during apartheid years, located in a Cape Town suburb of South Africa, 'District Six'. The black and 'coloured' inhabitants were forcibly removed during the 1970s and it became a 'whites-only' area, under the Group Areas Act, with removals starting in 1968. By 1982, more than 60,000 people had been relocated to the comparatively bleak 'Cape Flats', and the old homes had been bulldozed:

Figure 6.3 District Six sign

The sign demonstrates the interconnectedness of place, identity and discourse. We have the discourse, or words on the sign, which articulates category-based entitlements to occupy the place it refers to. According to Scollon and Scollon's (2003) analytic position of 'geosemiotics', a crucial aspect of signs such as these is their location in the world, or what they *point at in space*. The term 'geosemiotics' therefore refers to 'the social meanings of the material placement of signs' (p. 4).

In our example, the District Six sign would not have made sense *until* it was located in a particular place. Whilst it may have had an abstract linguistic meaning whilst being made in the signmaker's studio, it did not have its referential power until it was posted firmly in a 'place'. Signs therefore are fundamentally *indexical*, acquiring their meaning and power to divide space once they are positioned so as to carve up some space, informing those who read it who is, and who is not, entitled to occupy the place it contains. Once a sign is in place, it operates in aggregate with other signs, in an 'intersemiotic, inderdiscursive dialogicality' (ibid.: 23).

Scollon and Scollon discuss different discourses that comprise the 'semiotic aggregate' of signs in public spaces. We can identify similar discourses in our District Six sign, including 'municipal-regulatory' (controlling the flow of persons in places by carrying some regulatory weight), 'neighbourhood' (dividing up spaces into localities), and 'racial/ethnic' (naming 'whites', but indexing 'blacks', 'coloureds' and other 'non-whites'). We note also its use of two different codes, with English at the top and Afrikaans underneath. The use of these languages, but not South African languages such as Bantu or Zulu, indexes mainly 'whites'. But of course the sign is not really meant for 'whites': it indexes 'non-whites' and tells them that this place is not for them. The sign is a tool of geopolitical power.

Thus space and place, though 'material' and 'physical', is not 'real' beyond the practices that produce it. It is contestable, provisional and contingent *upon* those practices: what *counts* as private land, public space, a county, state or country, the border between one place and another, the national boundary, my land and yours, is, as we will see in the rest of this chapter, accountably up for grabs on a daily basis. Moreover, *who* gets to occupy spaces (in terms of asymmetrically organised identity categories such as gender, ethnicity, sexuality, relationships and age), is a crucial part of understanding identity within the recent 'spatial turn'. It is to these ideas we next turn.

THE SPATIAL TURN

Although much social science research focuses on the study of social life 'in context', Dixon (2005) argues that it has typically disregarded a fundamental contextual dimension of social life – its geographical locatedness. Space and place have been treated as taken-for-granted containers, or 'neutral grids' (Gupta and Ferguson 1992: 7) for the more important social activities taking place within it (Wallwork and Dixon 2004). It is against these sorts of observations that some writers began to theorise the links between space, place and identity, summed up neatly in R. Barnes's (2000) argument that *who* we are is inextricably linked to *where* we are, have been or are going. The centrality of place and space in understanding everyday social life has therefore become an emergent theme in current theorising across the social sciences and humanities. As Dixon (2005: 1) points out, all aspects of our social lives unfold within material and symbolic environments ('places') that are both socially constituted and constitutive of the social. Acknowledgement of this so-called 'spatial dimension' opens up new ways of looking at phenomena such as the formation of social identities and relationships.

The 'spatial turn' has its roots partly in poststructuralist and postmodern theory, drawing on Foucault's (1986: 22) observation that we are currently living in an 'epoch of space'. In other words *space*, rather than *time*, is crucial to contemporary cultural and social analysis. There has been a shift, therefore, from *temporality* and the *historical* to *spatiality* and the *geographical* for theorising social processes (Soja 1989). Prior to this shift, Gunn (2002) notes that space, place and landscape were fundamentally neglected dimensions of social life. Previous historical and geographical sociological studies of, say, the link between class and the spatial structure of cities, treated space as an abstract and uniform category: 'There was little sense that space itself was something that required to be "produced" or that it might be constitutive of historical developments' (pp. 2–3). The linguistic and discursive 'turn' in the social sciences and humanities has brought about new understandings of place and space as 'significant constituent[s] of social processes and bearer[s] of meaning in their own right' (p. 3).

Within postmodern theory, then, space and place are examined not as static, *a priori* or objective phenomena but as ongoingly and dynamically constructed tools of 'thought and action' (Lefebvre 1991: 26). Relatedly, the experiential and cultural significance of space and place in *identity construction* has been examined across a range of disciplines, including cultural and human geography, environmental psychology and sociology (for example, Cresswell 1996; Relph 1976; Tuan 1977). Within this literature, it is argued that not only do *people make spaces*, but also *spaces make people*, by constraining them but also by offering opportunities for identity construction. Institutions such as hospitals, factories and shopping malls, 'rather than containing particular subjects [may] actually and actively create them' (Pile and Thrift 1995: 4). Identity is therefore a fundamentally *spatial* category, 'since the ideas of territory, self and "us" all require symbolic, socio-cultural and/or physical dividing lines with the Other' (Paasi 2001: 10). Spaces and places can 'take on a symbolic significance around which identities are constituted and performed' (Hetherington 1998: 106). Hetherington (pp. 106–7) writes that:

Sites like Stonehenge for New Age travelers, Greenham Common for the women peace campers, festival sites, sacred sites, greenfield sites marked for road development for anti-road protestors, or

> even city centre landmarks around which young people may
> congregate on a Saturday morning to meet their friends, have a
> social centrality for those who are trying to create some alternative
> and expressive identification with one another . . . Such places act
> like shrines for those who live outside the conventions of a
> society . . . because they come to symbolize another set of values
> and beliefs around which groups can order their identities.

An emerging concept in this broad literature is 'place identity', which
focuses on how people make sense of their 'self' via the attribution of
meanings to places (for example, Twigger-Ross and Uzzell 1996). These
meanings are expressed in idiomatic phrases such as 'There's no place
like home' and 'An Englishman's home is his castle'. One example of the
way place-identity is enacted is in the work people do to design, decorate
and personalise the interior and exterior of their individual houses, as well
as their streets, neighbourhoods, villages and cities. Other work focuses
on people's sense of belonging, their attachment to home and away places,
and the contrast between the 'home' and the 'foreign' (for example,
Crouch 1994). The implied essential connection between place and identity is challenged by the notion of *diasporic identities*, in which people
learn 'to "negotiate and translate" between cultures, always unsettling the
assumptions of one culture from the perspective of the other' (S. Hall
1995: 47–8). As Woodward (2002: 65) argues, 'diaspora includes history
and the temporal and spatial specificities of identity formation and the
routes that identities travel'.

Dixon and Durrheim (2004) suggest that place-identity can operate on
a variety of socio-spatial scales, from the home, to the neighbourhood and
beyond to the nation, whose boundaries function as symbolic resources in
identity construction. As Tester (1993: 8) puts it, 'without boundaries,
without direction and location, social and cultural activity would itself be
a pointless thrashing about in the world'. Boundaries not only separate
people, but are also the mediators of contact between them, be they at the
national scale or the much more local level of fences between neighbours.

Spatiality, identity and feminism

A concern with spatiality is also built into second-wave feminism, with
its focus on the structural dichotomies that locate women within domestic spaces: in the private rather than public sphere, inside rather than
outside, at home rather than at work (for example, Ainley 1998). These
traditional dichotomies of place mean that women often live 'spatially
restricted, geographically bounded lives, in a home, in a neighbourhood'

(McDowell 1998: 29–30). In Walkowitz's (1992) study of gender and sexuality in late Victorian London, she investigated how different places in the city were differently used and represented by women and men. She argued that space is active in the constitution of social identities, through the gendering of urban spaces. Women's respectability was often defined spatially, with women and men having access to different kinds of spaces.

Consequently, feminist geographers have developed theories around gender and public and domestic spaces, showing how physical environments maintain and regulate gender identities and relations (for example, Churchman 2000). Massey (1994) argues that women have traditionally occupied marginal positions within urban spaces (and society more generally), although these spaces can become the location of women's resistance to patriarchy. Bowlby, Gregory and McKie (1997) argue that the use of space in everyday activities, such as childcare and housework, constitutes a significant part of the construction of gender and the maintenance of gendered hierarchy at home. For some women, the home may be a site of power, but for others it may be a place of violence. Research with battered women shows that their relationship to residence is particularly complex, and fraught with both positive and negative meanings. As Manzo (2003: 51) notes, 'descriptions of abuse in the residence and the creation of safe space outside of it contrast with romantic recollections of "home"'.

These ideas have been taken up by queer theorists, who note a powerful relationship between space and heteronormativity (for example, Collins 2005). Gunn (2001: 8) explains that heterosexual behaviours are endorsed in public spaces, although this works as an 'unnoticed feature of urban modernity' (see also Chapter 2 on 'unnoticed identities'). Members of other sexual identity categories must restrict their displays of sexuality to particular places (for example, gay clubs and locations of the 'symbolic underworld') or the private sphere. More recently, Gunn suggests, the emergence of 'gay culture' is partly based on claims to gay space – a reterritorialisation and construction of gay space within normative space. Gunn concludes that 'the study of gender and sexuality reveals how public space is regulated by powerful norms, whose force resides partly in the fact that they are implicit, taken for granted' (ibid.).

Space, identity and exclusion

We started this chapter with an example of the centrality of space and place in the exercise of power and social control on South Africa's beaches. Place and space appear to be fundamental concepts – either implicitly or explicitly – in research about the marginalisation (that is, the rendering of people as *out of place*) of many groups: women, the homeless, immigrants, members of particular ethnic groups, prostitutes, young people, gypsies, travellers, old people (for example, Aguilar 2002; Hubbard 2002; Keogan 2002; Kraack and Kenway 2002; Levinson and Sparkes 2004). Membership of these identity categories can affect our interaction in the world, and limit the kinds of places we can connect with. In many Western cities 'race' has spatial connotations in and through the construction of areas like 'Chinatowns', such that 'space becomes saturated with meanings, with ideas of "otherness", that are perceived to be inherent in the identity of the groups concerned' (Gunn 2001: 8). As Manzo (2003: 55) concludes, 'who we are, and where we find ourselves, is distinctly political in nature'.

Space is therefore central to the production and maintenance of ingroups and outgroups in everyday life. Places can be sites of contestation over the rights to use the space, 'particularly when ideologies regarding who "belongs" where clash' (ibid.). Some people, at some times, in some places, will be therefore treated as doing the wrong thing in the wrong place (for example, travellers or gypsies occupying space at the side of a road, young people 'hanging around' on street corners, women entering the 'male members only' golf club). As Cresswell (1996) suggests, the word 'place' implies a sense of the proper, of something belonging in one place but not another. Place and space are simultaneously 'unremarkable yet deeply symbolic of how we define what is right and wrong' (Agnew and Corbridge 1995: 79). Thus a kind of 'place-grounded order' is often used to justify the inclusion and exclusion of particular categories of persons (Wallwork and Dixon 2004: 23), although space can also be the site of transgression and resistance, playing a central role in the reproduction of marginal or outsider identities and alternative moral orders (Sibley 1995).

At the time of writing, the issue of young people and their 'anti-social behaviour' was a key theme in public discourse in the UK. Young people's occupation of public spaces has often been a source of adult concern (see Kraack and Kenway 2002). Here is a brief extract from a local council's 'anti-social behaviour' steering committee meeting, recorded in February 2005, in which the committee chair is summarising a series of complaints about young people's activities in a local shopping precinct:

Extract 6.1: Anti-social behaviour meeting

AC: I went up there two weeks ago, um and I visited um, for those of you
       that don't know, what we've got there is sort of a bit of a shopping mall
       really with four shops on four shop units on one side and four on the

other and a sort of um plaza area, if that's not too posh a word for it, in
the middle. Which of course becomes the real focal point for all the kids.
Um the issues are twofold, we've got complaints of gathering groups of
school children during the lunch hour and there are enormous groups of
children there during the lunch hour and I've got photographic evidence
of that. However, they are just large groups of kids who go down to the
chip shop, buy their chips, eat them and leave. Um the sheer volume
means the noise levels go up and the fact that they're in very close
proximity to a number of, an elderly, a complex of elderly people's
bungalows who are alarmed simply by their presence. That's one
problem and I mean that potentially could be quite easily addressed with
some work with the colleges where the kids are coming from and
possibly even some education of the kids, and also some education of
the elderly residents as well. Then you've got another problem sort of
along side that, there are additional groups of gathering youths in the
early hours of the evening and that was the bit that seems to be more
problematic and where the level of criminal activity perhaps is on the up.
Um there's a whole host of graffiti up there. There's lots of incidents of
minor damage to bar property as well, shutters and windows and
various bit and pieces.

There are a number of interesting features of the Chair's account. She
initially describes the target of their discussion as 'a bit of a shopping
mall', and what constitutes it: its 'four shop units' and 'plaza area'. Note
her ironic orientation to the category 'plaza' as an inappropriate description of the middle of the site, and the moral work it does to cast a particular set of inferences about the place being discussed. The complaints
turn on the *number* of children that 'gather' in 'enormous groups' at a
particular time of day, producing an increase in the level of noise around
the shops. But it is their proximity to another group of residents, 'elderly
people' which produces most of this problem: a clash of identities and
subcultures. The chair minimises the seriousness of the 'problem' in her
description that they are 'just' large groups of kids who engage in the
expectable and legitimate activity of eating at lunchtime. In contrast, the
groups of 'gathering youths' in the 'early hours of the evening' is more
of a problem. Note the different ways that the identity categories are formulated ('youths' versus 'school children'), as well as the temporal situation ('early evening' versus 'lunchtime'). The precise categories used
are important because of their inference-rich nature: 'early evening'
(rather than 'late afternoon') connotes danger; 'youths' rather than
'teenagers' implies something about the possible seriousness of their
offences (see Sacks 1979).

This short extract shows us something of the complex connections between the construction of space, place and identity, and the way these relationships are managed in discourse. Evidence of the 'spatial turn' can be identified in many of the practical approaches to discourse that we have discussed throughout the book, including narrative analysis, ethnomethodology and discursive psychology. We consider each of these in turn, for the ways that the relationship between place-space and identity is articulated and analysed.

NARRATIVE, PLACE AND IDENTITY

Themes of spatiality can increasingly be found within contemporary narrative theory. The basic idea is that tellers express a sense of *who* they are through stories about *where* they are (Johnstone 1991). Some have suggested that the emphasis on time in narrative work, as we discussed in Chapter 4, has led to the sidelining of another defining feature of stories: their spatial component. According to de Certeau (1984: 115), 'every story is a travel story – a spatial practice'. Georgakopoulou (2003) argues that descriptions of spatial organisation are even more crucial to narrative structure than temporality. For example, S. Taylor (2003: 193) writes:

> The places where we live are more than the backgrounds to our
> lives. In the telling of a life story, talk about place and
> relationships to place will be integral to the discursive work
> through which the speaker constructs a personal identity.
> A positioning as someone who is *of* a place can connect a speaker
> to the multiple established meanings and identities of that place.
> This can work as a claim to an identity as, for example, the kind
> of person who belongs there.

The verbal process of narrating allows us to understand the 'physical motions that produce place' (Tuan 1991: 684) which would otherwise be left unarticulated, asocial and meaningless. Sarbin (1983) similarly notes that understanding 'place identity' requires an analysis of its 'emplotment', through which selves are narratively configured by bringing together different temporal and spatial elements, including physical and metaphorical settings.

As people tell stories about places, they can imply or explicitly provide 'a multiplicity of meanings and associations, deriving for instance from its history and from the various ways it can be categorized (for instance,

in terms of its wealth, its weather, visual features, its urban or rural character)' (Taylor 2003: 201). Taylor also notes that people can tell different
stories about places, giving them many potential and contingent identities, depending on how they construct the boundaries around them (for
example, 'where I live' can be described in national, regional, or
city/town/village-based terms, or even in terms of a particular street,
building or room). Crucially, the way a place is described 'carries implications for the identity of a person who claims to be of or not of that place,
or, in other words, to be the kind of person who belongs there or the kind
who does not' (ibid.).

Place and identity in storied accounts

The following example is taken from McCabe and Stokoe's (2004) study
of the narrative accounts of visitors to the Peak Park (in the Peak
District, UK). Participants were interviewed 'in situ' as they walked
within the Peak Park, about their reasons for visiting it. Their accounts
often took the form of stories about different places within the park and
people and their activities within it. Here is an extract from one of the
interviews, which took place during a Ramblers' Association walk in the
Peak Park.

> *Extract 6.2: From McCabe and Stokoe 2004: 609*
> Don: I like the countryside because my mother and my father's side of the
>   family were farming people off the Welsh Borders originally, but then
>   my grandfather came over to Nottinghamshire, and had his last farm
>   just outside Sutton-in-Ashfield, and in fact from my very teens to
>   leaving school I used to go and help out on a farm where my uncle
>   worked and I liked that used to come back with arms prickled from
>   haymaking and straw, and things like that, you know and splatters of
>   shit when you're mucking out stalls and that. But I always used to
>   enjoy it. So I think perhaps I enjoy it because that's where my roots lie.

McCabe and Stokoe found that interviewees often worked up *territorial
warrants* for their activities in the Peak Park through biographical detail,
drawing on, as in Don's account, familial categorisations such as 'father',
'mother' and 'grandfather'. These categorisations are located in an overall
narrative that recounts his past experiences of countryside places. Don
tells us that his mother and father are from the 'Welsh Borders', and that
his grandfather is from 'Nottinghamshire' and has a farm 'just outside
Sutton-in-Ashfield'. These place names index 'the countryside' rather
than urban areas, and his description works to warrant his longstanding

familial connection to countryside spaces. Don's narrative is rich with detail about 'countryside' activities ('haymaking', 'things like that', 'mucking out stalls', 'splatters of shit'), constructing his identity as someone whose 'roots lie in the countryside'. Thus Don's visits to the Park are a 'natural' part of his identity as someone who is continuing a family tradition.

An additional feature of the interviewees' accounts was the telling of familiar stories about past visits to places:

Extract 6.3: From McCabe and Stokoe 2004: 609–10

Larry: It's the old family daytrip thing ... we went to the coast for a week during the summer holidays. We'd go religiously like every summer holiday, we'd go out for a drive and a walk around. Its something we've just always done

Pam: My parents always had a little car, and we always came out every Sunday so er, I can remember lots of places that we picnicked on Sundays they tried to come out in the Peak every weekend if they could. They weren't walkers, you know just the traditional thing you did. Then, you brought a picnic and the Sunday papers and parked somewhere and perhaps have a little walk.

Larry and Pam tell similar stories about the 'family trip', something that happened 'always', 'religiously', 'every summer holiday', 'every Sunday', or 'every weekend'. Both participants emphasise the routine, scripted nature of the trip, establishing an interconnectedness of place and family identity. Although both Larry and Pam include 'walking' as part of the 'family trip', the identity category *walker* is used to imply something different and specific: something that people do in desolate spaces, not on the usual beaten track.

The participants' stories function to construct 'good' places, locating themselves within them, while at the same time constructing 'bad' places and their defining characteristics. Stories of place therefore become stories of morality. McCabe and Stokoe argue that places do not have fixed identities that exist separately from the language practices that produce them. Rather, people flexibly construct places as good or bad, depending on the context in which the account is produced. For example:

Extract 6.4: From McCabe and Stokoe 2004: 612, 614, 616

Emma: People go to get fresh air and exercise, away from their normal everyday lives, and you can have it all different range within a spectrum, so you can have little Sunday afternoon pootlers, and there's so many, within these little towns, it is so obvious that they are so centred around tourism and that is it, because there is like gift shops and tea shops and there doesn't seem to be a lot else.

Emma: Walkers tend to, unless they are serious hikers, tend to swarm around those sorts of centres and only walk half an hour or so round them, it's like when you go up Winnat's Pass, that's really desolate up there.

Pam: Hartington's always, always full of coach loads from Birmingham it's a bit like Gulliver's Kingdom, it always seems to be full of coach loads from Birmingham ... but people seem quite happy just to turn up in a bus in Hartington, get off the bus go and have a cream tea, go and buy something in the shop and get back on the bus and that's Hartington ticked off.

In these extracts, a 'bad' place is one that is 'full' of a certain type of tourist, such as 'Sunday afternoon pootlers', people who 'swarm' and 'coach loads from Birmingham'. These people are casual rather than serious users of places, whose activities breach normative notions of tempo and rhythm: people should not 'swarm' together but walk at an appropriate pace away from other people.

Pam describes the activities of the urban visitors as a kind of repetitive script: they 'turn up in a bus', 'get off the bus', 'have a cream tea', 'buy something in the shop', 'get back on the bus' and 'tick off' the place being visited. Her account is heavy with implicit moral evaluations about the activities of these visitors, and the place that is constructed in and through their activities. 'Bad' places are therefore characterised by their preponderance of gift and teashops for people to eat and shop in. In particular, Hartington is categorised as a 'transitional place' (Schegloff 1972), somewhere that people travel through on their way to somewhere else, spending small amounts of time engaged in the trivial and pointless activities of 'milling' or 'swarming'. As Tuan (1991: 694) argues, 'the "quality" of place is more than just aesthetic or affectional, it also has a "moral" dimension, which is to be expected if language is a component in the construction and maintenance of reality, for language – ordinary language – is never morally neutral'.

In contrast, McCabe and Stokoe's interviewees constructed 'good' places as desolate, isolated and distant ('up there', 'away'). 'Good' places contain few people who stay longer and engage in appropriate activities such as walking, hiking, cycling or looking at and seeing views of empty spaces. This sensory dimension is fundamental to spatiality, such that constructions of visual in- or out-of-placeness can be invoked to warrant the moral categorisation of self and place (Dixon, Reicher and Foster 1997; Rodaway 1994). In the Peak Park, being able to *see* other people constituted a breach of the spatial order. The 'serious' or 'good' visitor to the Park is someone who articulates these understandings of what a place should be like.

Overall, McCabe and Stokoe found that, through their stories about the Park, participants categorised themselves, other people, places and activities in different ways. Thus 'good' places (that is, those that were desirable to locate oneself within) were 'off the beaten track', isolated, untouched by tourist facilities and so on. Conversely, 'bad' places (that is, those to be avoided) were those that 'swarmed with people', were full of traffic queues, and so on, often inextricably linked to notions of temporality (that is, visiting the Park at the weekend was to be avoided; better to go during quiet weekdays). 'Good' visitors were 'serious walkers' and 'hikers', those who could appreciate the Park's beauty, empty space and naturalness. 'Bad' visitors used space inappropriately as 'Sunday pootlers' and 'tourists'. The interviewees described themselves as 'serious' visitors to the Park, by telling stories of their longstanding history of visits to the Park, and using such biographical details to provide their territorial entitlement to 'natural membership' of the place. McCabe and Stokoe concluded that participants' storied accounts simultaneously served to constitute their activities as normal, ordinary, and hence credible social activities, while also setting themselves apart from the masses, as individuals, knowledgeable, and thus warranted in their behaviour. This appeals to what Dann (1999: 162) calls the 'anti-tourist in all of us' (and also echoes formulations of the 'counter-commercial impulse' outlined in Chapter 5).

This section has shown how links between places and persons get connected in narrative accounts, and is an example of how place/space is *produced in*, and as a topic of, discourse. We move on now to consider another analytic framework for the investigation of place, space and identity: ethnomethodology. We address not only how space is topicalised, but also how it functions as the *location for* 'talk-and-other-conduct-in-interaction' (Schegloff 2005).

ETHNOMETHODOLOGY AND MUNDANE SPATIALITY

At the mundane level of *ethnomethodological* inquiry, we find a familiar argument, that although human conduct is always located in a particular space or place, there is very little work that attempts to understand the organisational relationships between space, place and conduct (Crabtree

2000). Like other commentators discussed earlier in this chapter, Crabtree argues that we take for granted the embodied practices through which space is ongoingly organised. The spatial distribution of people and objects passes us by unnoticed.

One limitation of the Foucauldian-inspired poststructuralist work discussed in our earlier review of the 'spatial turn' is that the relationships between space, place and identity can sometimes seem rather abstract and theoretical, trading on the vernacular categories of 'space' and 'place' as resources for theorising (Crabtree 2000). Crabtree therefore recommends a shift from academic *theorising* about the centrality of space towards an engagement with *space as a member's oriented-to concern*; as something that is integral to the accomplishment of everyday activities: 'as activities are, without exception, always embedded "within" space, are always spatially situated, explication of the ways in which situated activities observably "get done" promises to tell us much about the social organisation of space and place'.

For example, Crabtree notes that certain spaces and places are normatively associated with the accomplishment of particular activities: restaurants are for eating, churches are for praying, and supermarkets are for shopping. Members ongoingly make sense of public spaces, and at the heart of the ethnomethodological inquiry is 'the issue of recognizability: how visual scenes are recognized – and made recognizable – by members' (Carlin 2003). Members may display their understanding of people and places by recognising who and what is 'normal' at a certain place such that anyone or anything different or out of place becomes noticeable. Carlin provides an example of 'white' men going to a place to buy heroin in a 'black' neighbourhood (Bourgois 1998: 38, cited in Carlin 2003): 'Our pace was perhaps just a little too fast; our heads were bent a bit too low; and our arms were swinging just a little too fast and wide; but we tried to act like normal white pedestrians strolling innocently through East Harlem at midnight under a freezing December drizzle'.

An ethnomethodological perspective therefore focuses on the explication of 'seeing "just how", and through "just what" ordinary interactional competences, spaces and places come to be implicated in the organisation of practical matters' (Crabtree 2000). Crabtree discusses Rose's ethnomethodologically-inspired study of 'looking' as a mundane activity. Rose reports 'looking' at an everyday scene, in which persons categorisable as 'an adult' and 'a child' walk past a railing upon which Rose is seated, towards a primary school. Crabtree writes:

'Being walked to school' is a category-bound activity, such that when seeing an adult and child walking towards a school, on a

school-day, first thing in the morning, it is inferred 1) that a
parent is walking a child to school; 2) that a parent walks their
child to school, rather than somebody else's child; and 3) that a
child walks to school with their parent, rather than another child's
parent. In this visual scene, Rose recognized the adult as a parent
of the child who skipped around them, and that the child attended
the elementary school that they were approaching. Thus, Rose
'saw' a parent escorting their child to school.

Rose's analysis reveals something mundane yet central to everyday life:
that persons can be seen as belonging or not belonging to particular
spaces and places. Members of identity categories acting in places that are
congruent with those places will generally pass by unnoticed.

Carlin (2003) argues that the visual order is fundamentally *linguistic*, in
that people routinely categorise each other in terms of what they observe,
and where they observe it. Let us consider an example of how these ideas
about spatiality and identity get played out in everyday interaction. The
following extract comes from a neighbourhood mediation interview
between a mediator and two married couples. The couples (Gerald and
Elaine, Louise and Bob) are neighbours and they are all involved in a continuing dispute with another resident in their street:

Extract 6.5: Mediation session

```
 1   Lou:    An' I ca:n't beli::eve that somebody would have
 2           such a sho:wdown in the stre:et.
 3   Ger:    Have you heard her shoutin' at the kids, WHY
 4           don't you Plss off to these little tiny ki:ds.
 5                (0.2)
 6   Ger:    °At the ga:te.°
 7                (0.2)
 8   Ger:    I've ['eard her saying it.]
 9   ?:            [°(Mmm.)° (  )   ] °Mmm.°
10   Ger:    Y'know, this-
11                (1.4)
12   Ger:    °I don't *know:::.*°
13                (0.6)
14   Lou:    It just [seems] so unfa::ir. >I mean=
15   Ger:            [(   )]
16   El:     =That we 'ave to put [u:p with somebody like=
17   Lou:                          [Why don't they just go =
18   El:     =[   t h a t .   ]
19   Lou:    =[and put them,] (0.3) in a street fu:ll of
```

```
20              people of that mentality and then they can all:
21              annoy [each oth:er.
22  Ger:              [Stick 'em in a block of [flats. ]
23  El:                                       [Yeah. ] yeh.
24  Lou:                                      [Why:,]
25          (0.2)
26  Lou:    Put them in with u:s.
```

The neighbours' complaint is overwhelmingly spatial in its basis, and shot through with moral implication. First, they talk about their neighbour's activities, having a 'sho:wdown' and 'shoutin' at the kids', as inappropriate in terms of their *location*: 'in the stre:et' and 'At the ga:te' (lines 1–6). Thus her actions are both available for assessment and complainable because they occur in *public* spaces. Ethnomethodologists explicate culture from within participants' tacit reasoning about social life (Hester and Eglin 1997). Here, we can see a culture of rule-governed spatial behaviour displayed in the participants' accounts of their neighbour's actions. Their complaint turns on a set of common-sense assumptions of what it is appropriate and inappropriate to do in public spaces and, in so doing, maintains a particular moral-spatial order of 'the street'. The location formulations are critical resources in the formulation of talk into a description of the female neighbour's activities, and stand as grounds for the participants' complaint.

Secondly, the participants work jointly to co-construct their neighbour as the 'Other': a category of people who are not entitled to live with 'us' and should instead live in other places. Analysts have explored how the discursive construction of groups functions as part of ongoing identity management and, in particular, how contrasts between normative 'us' and deviant 'them' are mobilised in talk (for example, Dickerson 2000; Smith 1978). The participants describe 'them' and 'they' as people who comprise an alternative culture: 'people of that mentality' (lines 20, 22, 26). And these people do not belong in respectable places, but elsewhere, in a 'block of flats', in a 'street fu:ll of people', and not 'with u:s' (lines 19–26). In other words, the speakers construct their neighbour problem as not simply a 'people' problem, but also as a 'location' problem, thus reinforcing the inextricable links between the identities of people and the places they occupy (Durrheim and Dixon 2001).

'Visibility arrangements of a neighbourhood'

In another study of the neighbourhood context, Laurier, Whyte and Buckner (2002) show how everyday talk can formulate places and occasion the moral accountability of 'being a neighbour'. They take the case

HAVE YOU SEEN JACK?

Jack is our two year old neutered ginger
tom cat who is missing from home. He is
wearing a blue tartan collar with a bell
and he has distinctive ginger markings
and white on his chest and on his paws.
He is micro-chipped so he can be scanned
to identify his owners.
Please let us know if you see him.
REWARD for his safe return.

0131 – 538 - 3079

Figure 6.4 The 'lost cat' sign (Laurier et al. 2002: 335)

of a lost cat ('Jack'), in which the cat's owners ('The Winnings') posted a
'lost cat' notice on street lamps in their neighbourhood (see Fig. 6.4).
Laurier et al. conducted observations of the subsequent interactions
between the cat's owners and their neighbours, in order to explicate what
it means to be a 'neighbour' and what is expectable for incumbents of that
identity category to do for one another. The case of a lost cat provides an
occasion for 'neighbouring' to be done, what Sacks (1992, vol. 2: 194) calls
a 'potential integrative event'. In other words, it produces a public set of
activities to observe, which also have a mundane relevance to the residents
of the street.

The Winnings's immediate next-door neighbour is a woman called
Mrs Munro. Laurier et al. suggest that the spatial organisation of their
adjoining houses is more heavily involved in the way neighbours make
sense of their lives as neighbours than providing simple opportunity to
make small talk, or try to avoid seeing each other:

> Mrs. Munro spends a great deal of time in the summer tending
> her roses whilst also attending to the movements of the street.
> People who walk off the street, up the Winnings's path, and ring
> their doorbell are seen by their sequenced actions by Mrs. Munro
> to be callers. We might note here that such a categorisation's
> criteria will not be fulfilled if the candidate callers do not actually
> go to the door and knock or ring. Indeed, Mrs. Munro would

justifiably become suspicious wondering whether nonknockers were burglars, door-to-door salespeople, or lost people. In doing what they do, from the moment they walk up the garden path, these strangers are seen as callers at the Winnings's. They display their actions as such, and Mrs. Munro sees them as such. It is thus no mystery to either party what Mrs. Munro means when she responds to their action by saying quite loudly to these callers, 'I saw them go out earlier in their car'. (p. 356)

Figure 6.5 The neighbours' houses (Laurier et al. 2002: 356)

Incumbents of the category 'next-door neighbour' are therefore entitled to monitor, to a certain extent, the activities going on next door, and watch out for each other's property. Mrs Munro, as *next-door* neighbour, is a candidate first person to turn to about the lost cat. Laurier et al. argue that while you might turn to 'friends' for *comfort* about your lost cat, they are not likely to be the first people you ask when the cat was last seen (unless your friend is also your neighbour).

Here is an extract from Laurier et al.'s fieldnotes:

Extract 6.6: Vignette 3—Thursday (Laurier et al. 2002: 358)
When Peter Winning called at the door of the old woman's house, he immediately introduced himself as her neighbour Peter whilst also pointing to his back garden ('I live just there') and then quickly added that he was the owner of a ginger tomcat who, he was pretty sure, visited this house. In response, the

woman introduced herself as Moira. 'Yes, your cat comes around quite a lot. I call him Tom the tom.'

Peter asked if she'd seen him recently, to which she replied that she hadn't seen him for a couple of days. After this, Moira apologized for inviting the Winnings's cat into her house, but Peter reassured her that they didn't mind, adding that it was in a cat's nature to be disloyal and that he liked the fact that they made friends with the neighbours. Moira went on to add further justification to her having Tom to visit, saying that she was a cat lover and had had many in the past but was too old herself now to take on a kitten.

We noted in Chapter 2 that, in their study of telephone call openings, conversation analysts have found that an orderly feature of such interactions is that the caller provides a 'reason for call'. Here, Laurier et al. note that neighbours who receive 'a knock at the door from another neighbour also have the expectancy that their neighbour has a reason for calling, more especially if they were previously unacquainted as Peter and Moira are' (p. 358). Before telling Moira his 'reason for call', Peter makes his identity as a neighbour ('I'm your neighbour') available to Moira. Laurier et al. point out that this formulates their common membership of the relational pair 'neighbour–neighbour', which has significant consequences for Moira's obligations towards him. She does not return this greeting with 'I'm your neighbour' – her action of answering the door does the same work.

After establishing common membership of the category 'neighbour', Peter then gestures towards his house. This embodied practice establishes that Peter does not take it for granted that Moira knows him intimately, which might connote something rather noxious about his identity, like 'nosiness'. Although it is common for neighbours to know a great deal about each other, such as the cars they drive, whether they play musical instruments, whether they have children, and so on, it is equally likely that they will not recognise each other's faces. Laurier et al. suggest that Peter's pointing does not just put a name to a face, it puts a face *and* a name to a familiar property: 'In this way, he is orienting to the mutuality of perspectives that unacquainted neighbours should have and no more' (ibid.: 359). Thus we can communicate identities through our movements in space.

Another observation about the interaction between Peter Winning and Mrs Munro is that it is located on her doorstep. Neither party makes a move to take the conversation indoors. Both therefore share a sense of how long such conversations can run, and when Mrs Munro begins to back off the step, the impending end of their conversation is signalled. As Laurier et al. point out, doorsteps are interesting kinds of interactional space, partly because one person owns it – unlike 'table space' in a café, which can be shared equally. The doorstep owner has certain rights to control what happens on it.

Laurier et al.'s research is an interesting example of how to combine the discursive with the embodied and the physical, and the relation of these semiotic realms to identity. Here, the construction of identity, in terms of what two people mean to each other as 'neighbours', is analysed not just in terms of how they talk to each other, but also in their other conduct in space.

We return to the theme of neighbours towards the end of the next section, in which we consider the impact of the 'spatial turn' within discursive psychology.

DISCURSIVE PSYCHOLOGY, PLACE AND IDENTITY

In addition to narrative work and ethnomethodology, the influence of the 'spatial turn' can also be observed in social psychological work, particularly within discursive psychology (see Chapter 1), via a number of key proponents including Dixon, whose work we introduced at the start of this chapter.

A relevant precursor to the discursive study of place and identity is Billig's (1995) work on nationalism and national identity. He starts with the observation that there is no 'readily available term to describe the collection of ideological habits (including habits of practice and belief) which reproduce established nations as nations' (p. 6). The kinds of habits to which he refers include the daily weather forecast (in which weather 'stops' beyond national boundaries!), the text of newspapers (in which the littering of 'small words' like 'us', 'them', and 'we' situate the reader within the – unnamed – homeland in a world of nations), and a host of other overlooked, unnoticed and utterly mundane practices (see also Scollon and Scollon 2003). Billig uses the term 'banal nationalism' to refer to these 'ideological habits which enable the established nations of the West to be reproduced . . . a continual "flagging", or reminding, of nationhood' (pp. 6–8). However, he points out that 'the metonymic image of banal nationalism is not a flag which is being consciously waved with fervent passion; it is the flag hanging unnoticed on the public building' (p. 8). For Billig, the 'nation' is not best understood as an essential phenomenon, existing outside of human practices. Rather, it is a historically, rhetorically constructed – and fundamentally ideological – concept (see also Anderson, 1983). Similarly, he treats national identity not as a psychological identification with the nation, but as a product of the kinds of 'embodied habits of social life' that make up banal nationalism (Billig 1995: 8). The flagging of nationhood, he argues, also flags the 'depths' and 'mechanisms' of our identity that are embedded in the everyday routines of our lives (p. 175).

Concepts of space are fundamental, if implicit, to any study of nationalism and national identity (Paasi 2001). There are many other studies of the discourse of identity and nationalism, and the construction of national identity, across many different contexts including sport, devolution, political debate and the news media (for example, van Dijk 1991; Housley and Fitzgerald 2001; Wodak et al. 1999). Many of these studies focus on the links between nationalism, identity and racism, and their management in discourse. Drawing on Billig's (1995) arguments about nationalism as a spatial ideology, Wallwork and Dixon (2004: 22–3) suggest that:

> to understand how nationalism has operated so successfully, social
> psychologists must attend to how the nation is located in time and
> place . . . nations are, *par excellence*, discursively *located* categories;
> indeed, the very term 'nation' straddles an ambiguity between the
> social and the spatial, denoting both a people (bound together by
> imagined relations of similarity) and a place (the imagined
> country or homeland).

In contrast to the cognitivist formulations of 'place-identity' within environmental psychology, Dixon and his colleagues developed a discursive perspective on place-identity relationships. From this perspective, people's rhetorical constructions of their own and each other's identities are routinely and systematically shot through with the discourse of place. Identification with place is 'a collective construction, produced and modified through human dialogue, that allows people to make sense of their locatedness' (Dixon and Durrheim 2000: 40). Wallwork and Dixon suggest that a discursive approach to the study of place-identity is largely compatible with other social psychological work on nationalism, the rhetorical organisation of national discourse, and the role of place identification in warranting identity construction, exclusion and social practice (for example, R. Barnes 2000; Condor 2000; Hopkins 2001; Taylor and Wetherell 1999). As Wallwork and Dixon (2004: 26) point out, the process of place identification:

> is not merely a matter of 'expressing' a sense of belonging to place
> or of 'perceiving' certain places as arenas of self-expression.
> Rather, in constructing place-identity relationships, individuals
> are often making territorial claims or justifying particular forms of
> sociospatial organisation. In other words, the discourse of place
> and identity may be 'action-oriented'.

Our next and final set of examples of research on 'spatial identities' is mainly rooted in the discursive psychological tradition (cf. Edwards and Potter 2001), but it also ties together some of the ideas about place and identity discussed in this chapter. It is drawn partly from continuing investigations of neighbour disputes conducted by Stokoe and her colleagues, which analyse neighbour-interactional data across a variety of sites including television chat shows and documentaries, and mediation sessions (for example, Stokoe 2003; Edwards and Stokoe 2005; Stokoe and Edwards 2007; Stokoe and Hepburn 2005; Stokoe and Wallwork 2003).

The spatial regulation of neighbour relations

The first extract comes from the BBC audience-participation show 'Kilroy', in which two of the audience members (a married couple, Tim and Janet) have just been describing how they used to be very friendly with their neighbours:

Extract 6.7: 'Kilroy'

```
 1  Host:   When you say frie:ndly neighbours, what- (0.2) what did
 2          you kind of d:o you two.
 3  Tim:    >Well any:thing.< talk over the ga:rden- down the pu:b,
 4          (0.3) anywhere. y'd jus- (0.2) generally conversa·tion
 5          like you wou:ld as neighbours, or frie.nds,
 6  Host:   And Janet, you got on with Ba:rbara to:o.
 7  Jan:    Ye:s ye:s
 8              (0.2)
 9  Jan:    [.hhhhh   ]
10  Host:   [You were] ↑good neighbours.
11  Jan:    WE:ll we used to speak. we never went into one another's
12          hou:ses a lo:t, but (.) I've bin in Dave's and had a cup
13          o' tea when he used to take me to wo:rk in the morning.
14  Host:   Oh he took you to ↑work [in the ↑mo:rning.]
15  Jan:                           [    Years ago.   ] Ye:s,
16          [when I first used to-] when I [( )
17  ?:      [(                          )]
18  Host:                                  [SO you were good
19          neighbours.
20  Tim:    Ye:ah [oh yeh.
21  Jan:          [Ye::ah [yeh
22  Host:                 [Keeping your: privacy and your distance.
23  Jan:    That's correct.
```

A basic point about this sequence is the joint construction, between participants and host, of what it means to be a 'good' neighbour. Within the limited literature on neighbour relationships, an implicit theme is that they are defined as instrumental rather than intimate or communicative relationships, which take place at the 'soft edges' of interactional space (Skjaeveland and Garling 1997). Some of these ideas are displayed above. Tim has previously described the relationship between the two couples as 'friendly'. The activities linked to 'friendly' and 'good neighbours' include talking 'over the ga:rden-', 'down the pu:b,', 'generally conversa:tion', 'keeping your: privacy and your distance.' (lines 3, 4, 22). Taken together, such activities suggest a relationship that occurs *outside*, rather than *inside*, each other's homes. Joan claims that 'we never went into one another's hou:ses a lo:t,', although she establishes that she did go next door for a 'cup o' tea' when her neighbour took her to work. Stokoe and Wallwork (2003) note that although this appears contradictory, entry *into* her neighbour's home is a precursor to going *out*. Thus 'good' neighbour relationships are functional and managed contact; neighbours must be friendly but not *too* friendly.

Embedded in the building of the identity category 'good neighbour' is the participants' use of spatial formulations. For example, Tim says: 'talk *over* the ga:rden- *down* the pu:b, (0.3) any*where*'. However, far from taking place 'anywhere', we can see that neighbour relations are spatially delimited. Janet claims that 'we never went *in*to one another's hou:ses a lo:t,', and the host adds that 'good neighbours' keep their 'privacy' and '*distance*'. Thus, neighbour relations are spatially organised. Stokoe and Wallwork observe this formulation of neighbour relations across their data, where neighbours routinely describe talking 'over the garden fence', 'on the front', 'in the garden' and so on. 'Good' neighbours therefore respect each other's privacy by maintaining distance and spatially restricting the sociability of the relationship. Boundaries such as 'fences' and 'doorsteps', as we saw in our earlier example, are discursive places where neighbour relationships are sustained and, as such, are important sites for the social reproduction of privacy.

Transgressing the spatial order

The negotiation of identity is particularly clear in the next extract, in which we return to the mediation session discussed earlier in the chapter:

Extract 6.8: Mediation session

1	Ger:	THAT was a nice ↑'EDge across the front o' the:re.
2	Lou:	Yea::h,
3	Ger:	*Uh* >go an' 'ave a look< when you go out,
4		(0.2)
5	Ger:	Jus' go (along/an) have a look at that 'edge over there.
6		(0.2)
7	Ger:	What they've <u>do</u>ne at it. [They've (sh-)
8	El:	[You know at one ti:me they were
9		climbin' through the hedge at the bottom an' broke the
10		hedge and [climbin' we got a seat in our garden.]
11	Ger:	[Th- th- THROUGH our garden,]
12	Ger:	Through [next door's garde°°(n),
13	El:	[<u>Th</u>rough our garden.
14		(0.9)
15	Lou:	You see them <u>pi</u>:ling in and out I mean there's- there's
16		times I- (0.2) I'm so <u>wor</u>ried for my property when I
17		he:ar <u>noi</u>:ses I go upstairs and have a look.
18		(0.3)
19	Ger:	Hey [it's got me doing that.]
20	Lou:	[IT'S NOT <u>nos</u>iness] [it's general <u>worry</u> about
21	El:	[Yeah!
22	Lou:	my property.
23		(0.3)
24	Lou:	And:: e- you see GA::ngs of kids coming ↑up and ↓down and
25		into that house.
26		(0.7)
27	Lou:	You know, an' sometimes there's- there's all the <u>lights</u>
28		on and the <u>do</u>::or's open an' people are jus' coming ↑in:
29		an' out [an' ↑in: an' out, ((sing-song voice))
30	Ger:	[Have you noticed the lights are on all ni:ght.
31	El:	°Yeh!°

Stokoe and Wallwork make three main points about this sequence. First, they focus on the participants' descriptions of their neighbours' activities at the boundaries of private space, and how these work to construct the category 'bad' neighbours. In the first part of the extract (lines 1–13), Gerald, Louise and Elaine work concertedly to formulate the activities of 'they', (the neighbour's children) as a problem. Stokoe and Wallwork suggest that it is the terms used to describe the children's *movements in space* that provide part of the basis for their complaint: they climb *through* the hedge, *break* it, and go *through* their garden and next door's garden.

In contrast to 'good' neighbour relations, which are regulated by interactions happening '*over* the fence', 'bad' neighbours pass '*through*' hedges from garden to garden. Appropriate engagement with fences and hedges involves walking 'around' or talking 'over' them. Failing to respect their function as a physical and legal boundary between properties constitutes unregulated entry to space and a violation of the spatial-moral order they represent.

The neighbours' breaches are further marked in Louise's turns between lines 15 and 29. Her complaints about 'them', which include 'pi:ling in and out' and hearing their 'noi:ses', display a culture in which such transgressions reveal the implicit rules of spatial behaviour. People should not 'pile in and out'; entering and exiting a house should be accomplished in the customary way (for example, stopping at a *closed* door). The activity 'piling' is linked to the formulation 'GA::ngs of kids', both of which carry with them connotations of lack of control, excessive movement or irresponsibility. Her description works on a kind of cultural logic that the 'kids' fail to observe the borders constructed to enclose private spaces. In so doing, Louise invokes a particular sense of place and the associated moral order in which these problematic neighbours and their activities are 'out of place' (Sibley 1995).

The repetition (and sing-song delivery) in Louise's description of her neighbours' actions, 'people are jus' coming ↑in: an' out an' ↑in: an' out,', emphasises the (too fast) tempo and rhythm of their activities. It also emphasises the on-going, durable nature of the 'bad' neighbours' activities: these are not one-off events, but regular, over and over again, repeated actions. Further, Louise should not be able to *hear* other people's noises within her own private space. This displays a further sensory dimension to spatiality and the morally acceptable actions of neighbours. Here, noises penetrate the boundaries of private space, such as windows and doors, demonstrating once again how ordered space can become disordered by 'bad' neighbour activities.

Finally, Stokoe and Wallwork examine the 'good/bad neighbour' identity work being performed in dilemmatic talk about spatial threat and surveillance, particularly in lines 16–22. Louise states that she is 'so worried for my property when I he:ar noi:ses I go upstairs and have a look.' and 'IT'S NOT nosiness it's general worry about my property'. As we observed earlier, 'good' neighbours respect each other's privacy. Participants displayed their orientation to this rule through the routine denial of behaviours such as 'spying' or being treated as a 'nosy' person. But activities such as 'going upstairs and having a look' might be construed as spying and so require justificatory work. Here, Louise resists the possible ascription of 'nosiness' by describing her activities as the kinds of 'general'; that is, routine and normal, things that any person would do. Gerald's turn at line 19 does some nice work to reinforce the idea that the activity of 'looking' is not something that they do because of their characters or personalities, but as a response to other people's activities ('Hey it's got me doing that'). Participants routinely resisted the ascription of 'nosy'; they attributed those kinds of characterological inferences to other people as part of legitimate complaints (for example, from elsewhere in our data 'We've watched Mrs Brown spying on us'). These orientations to the moral implications of 'spying' are finely managed. 'Bad' neighbours are those that spy, those that must be spied upon as well as those who make themselves available to spying.

Embodied boundary work in neighbour disputes

Our final extract comes from a documentary series about neighbour disputes. The speakers are engaged in an argument over what constitutes the boundary between their properties. Elsie and Fred are amongst those whose property is bounded by the hedge. Dave is the chartered surveyor who is mediating between Elsie and Fred and their neighbours. The documentary style of the programme means that Dave's first turn takes place with him in the garden alone (lines 1–10). Elsie and Fred talk to the camera (lines 12–25), and all three interact (lines 26–68).

A common criticism of discourse work is that it deletes the embodied, visual and material aspects of interaction. However, this chapter has included several examples of research that uses multi-modal forms of analysis which treat such aspects as central to any analysis of social action, including Dixon and Durrheim's (2003) analysis of beach movements, Randall and Hughes's (1995) studies of queueing, Scollon and Scollon's (2003) 'geosemiotics', and Laurier et al.'s (2002) study of the lost cat. The impact of the 'spatial turn' can be seen in the emergence of new visual methodologies and approaches, such as 'sensuous geography' (Rodaway 1994), visual ethnography, semiology, critical discourse analysis and psychoanalysis (see Bauer and Gaskell 2000; G. Rose 2001). The newly emerging field of 'multi-modal discourse analysis' includes studies of interaction and meaning-making in material and virtual spaces like shopping, electronic discourse, vocational training, and service encounters, (for example, Levine and Scollon 2004; O'Halloran 2004).

Additionally, there is a body of work within conversation analysis that deals with multiple semiotic fields, analysing, for instance, 'pointing' as a situated embodied interactive practice (C. Goodwin 2003). We have attempted to incorporate some of C. Goodwin's ideas about gesture and embodiment into the last part of our analysis. To this end, we have embedded stills from video footage of the neighbour dispute at particular points in the transcript. In the first part of the sequence, Dave, the surveyor, is in Elsie and Fred's garden:

Extract 6.9: The boundary line

```
1    Dave:    Um, (0.2) the bou:ndary line that I've- (0.2)
2             dedu:ced, (0.4) is one foot >eight in:ches< from
3             this pe:g I've put in.
```

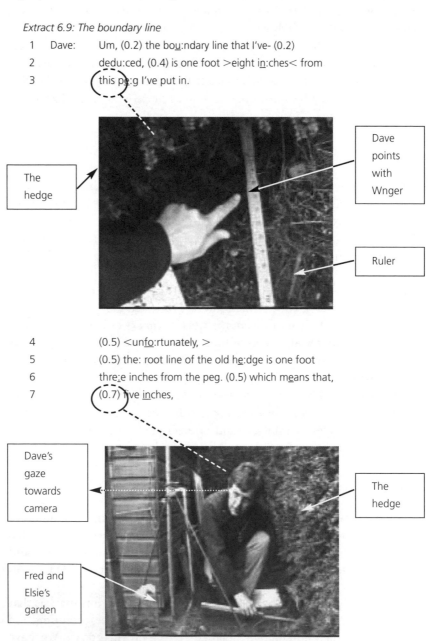

```
4             (0.5) <unfo:rtunately, >
5             (0.5) the: root line of the old he:dge is one foot
6             thre:e inches from the peg. (0.5) which means that,
7             (0.7) five inches,
```

8   on the other side of the root
9   line of the peg, is where I've found the ori:ginal
10   boundary to be.

As suggested by Scollon and Scollon's (2003) framework of 'geosemiotics' discussed earlier in the chapter, Dave's pointing is *indexical*: it
cannot be understood outside of the conversational and physical contexts
in which it happens. The place in which he is pointing is not 'a mere,
undifferentiated space, but a highly structured cultural entity' (Goodwin
2003: 1): the domestic garden. C. Goodwin writes that (p. 218):

> Pointing is not a simple act, a way of picking out things in the
> world that avoids the complexities of formulating a scene through
> language or other semiotic systems, but is instead an action that
> can only be successfully performed by tying the point to the
> construals of entities and events provided by other meaning
> making resources. Rather than being a stepping stone to language,
> pointing presupposes it.

The 'pointing situation' contains at least two participants. In our data,
these are Dave and the camera (which represents the broadcast audience).
Dave points at the increments on his ruler as he says 'this' (line 3), at the
start of the phrase 'this pe:g I've put in.' Thus his pointing works in
tandem with the already-indexical term 'this', elaborating the talk that in
turn elaborates the pointing.

Work environments can be a particularly interesting site for pointing
practices, because it is through these actions that participants 'establish for
each other how a relevant space should be construed in order to perform
the tasks that make up the work of their setting' (p. 219). In our data, Dave
is performing the activities of a 'surveyor', and he is therefore 'doing' membership of the identity category 'surveyor'. His current task is to establish
an objective, uncontestable boundary between two privately owned domestic properties. Lines 1–3 are his report (his deductions) on the outcome of
his calculations, which he has been employed to produce. A number of
semiotic systems work in aggregate to accomplish the actions underway (C.
Goodwin 2003). These include the embodied pointing gesture, using his
finger to indicate the peg he has placed; the 'domain of scrutiny', or place
in the garden that the recipient should look to find the object of the pointing; and the 'graphic field', which includes the peg and the ruler, which
work together to establish the to-the-inch location of the boundary.

Dave continues to explain to the audience what the implications of his
calculations mean for Elsie and Fred: that the original boundary lies

within their garden, and that they are currently claiming land (including the hedge) that 'in fact' belongs to their neighbours. At line 8, the camera angle and orientation provide for Dave to look up from his measurements at the recipient: the audience. It is interesting that this occurs *precisely* after the moment when he finishes explaining his calculations ('which means that,') and formulates their upshot ('five inches,'). The combination of Dave's posture, gestures, gaze direction and talk works to achieve a number of actions, including the warranting of his claim as a surveyor ('identity work'), the establishment of a legal boundary ('boundary work'), conducting the business he has been paid to do ('institutional work') and explicating the practice of establishing a boundary for the overhearing recipient – the broadcast audience. However, boundary lines, despite being deduced in all their mathematical detail, can still be challenged. We return to Elsie and Fred, who are sitting at home discussing a letter in front of the camera:

Extract 6.10: The letter

12   Elsie: Well:, (.) this is a letter from an eighty nine
13

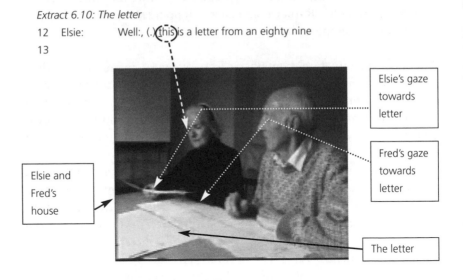

Elsie's gaze towards letter

Fred's gaze towards letter

Elsie and Fred's house

The letter

        year old la:dy. I believe she's eighty nine. .hhh
14   (0.2) and er::, (0.7) this pro:ves that the hedge
15   belongs to u:s. and this is what she uh: has
16   written. (0.2) .hhh to the be:st of my knowledge my
17   husband Leslie W Jarvis, (0.5) planted ↑hedge
18   cu:ttings of <lonicera (.) mathilda, > (0.5) in the
19   autumn of ni:neteen thirty eight in the back
20   garden. on the south side of the property. .hhh
21   that is between ninety nine, and one oh one
22   Oliversbattery Road.

```
23                        (1.2)
24    Elsie:    So:, (0.2) this letter has come forwa:rd and this
25              is proof that ↑it ↑is ↑our ↑hedge
```

Note the way Elsie's and Fred's gaze is directed towards the letter as Elsie holds it up and formulates it ('this') on line 12 ('this is a letter'). The deictic term 'this' works in tandem with the participants' embodied practices of gaze direction and body posture, both of which are oriented towards the letter – the topic of Elsie's talk. The status that Elsie and Fred are affording the letter becomes clear as we move through Elsie's turn, as she reads out the words of a previous owner of the house. There is a similar pattern of evidencing work followed by upshot that we observed in Dave's turn. In Dave's turn, his surveyor's measurements led to one conclusion about the boundary line; in Elsie's a previous owner's letter led to another. In the next sequence, Elsie, Fred and Dave discuss their different findings:

Extract 6.11: The middle of the hedge

```
26    Fred:     So that is the- (.) the I-latest proo:f that we've
```

Gaze directed towards the letter

Points at letter

```
27    Fred:     had from:, from the occupant, [the fi:rst    ]
28    Dave:                                    [And you sent]
29              that to:: the solicitors with [that letter.
30    Fred:                                    [No we didn't. We
31              d- uh:,
32                        (0.2)
32    Dave:     >Y'know I think you should se:nd it. to the
33              *solicitor.*
34                        (0.4)
```

35   Fred: But (they're) [( )
36   Dave: [Which [hasn't happened.]
37   Elsie: [U m ː   ] c̲an I̲
38   i̲:nterrupt [a moment,
39   Dave: [Oh (yes,)
40   (0.3)
41   Elsie: Can I ask y̲ou a questi̲:on, (0.3) If there is a
42   hedge(the̲:re.)why don't you come down >the

Points towards hedge

Gaze towards hedge

43   middle.<
44   (0.9)
45   Elsie: Being a- a chartered surveyor.
46   (.)
47   Elsie: Any other chartered surveyor would come down
48   the mi̲:ddle!
49   (0.4)
50   Dave: °Come [(down-)°
51   Elsie: [Why don't yo̲:u.
52   (0.2)
53   Elsie: ↑↑The ↑middle ↑of ↑the ↑he̲:dge.
54   (0.5)
55   Dave: S- sorry. w- w̲hy don't I,=
56   Elsie: =↑Well ↑why don't you take a straight line down
57   the middle of the [he̲:dge,] and say that's the
58   Dave: [Well-]
59   Elsie: bound'ry=
60   Dave: =Rhight, Well what [I
61   Elsie: [Why do you Wght- fuss
62   about with your little bits of blue:, (0.4)

63		plastic all [up and] down everywhere and bits
64	Dave:	[Mmm:]
65	Elsie:	of roots here and bits of roots there, ↑you're
66		↑wasting ↑your ↑ti:me. .hhh it's the ↑mi:ddle
67		of the <u>h</u>edge. the ordnance survey would say:
68		the <u>mi</u>ddle of the <u>h</u>edge.

Implicit in this kind of 'boundary talk' is an assumption not only that it is possible to find the site at which one piece of space objectively ends and another begins but also that such a finding is an essential component of private space ownership. The speakers in the above extract are orientated to a dilemma. On the one hand, they are attempting to protect personal interests but on the other are striving to maintain the notion of an *interest-free* boundary. For example, Dave's claim to have found the 'real' boundary is warranted by the use of the definite article ('the'), a strategy that, we argue, objectifies and reifies the subject as 'real': '*the* bou:ndary line that I've- (0.2) dedu:ced', '*the* o<u>ri</u>:ginal boundary' (lines 1, 9–10). Similarly, Elsie resists personal claim in the boundary by talking about '*the* hedge' and '*the* boundary' (lines 14, 57–9). Elsie had earlier claimed that the hedge belonged to 'us' (line 25: 'this is proof that ↑it ↑is ↑our ↑hedge'). However, by talking of '*the* hedge' and '*the* boundary', she builds a claim about the legitimate boundary site whilst maintaining the notion that the boundary pre-exists any such claim. Elsie's talk is accompanied by pointing gestures (starting at line 42 on the deictic word 'the:re', and continuing throughout the rest of her turns), which supports the notion that the boundary is objective and physical, rather than up for negotiation.

This sequence is interesting for two reasons. First, the dilemma caused by the contested boundary highlights the arbitrariness of spatial division (Chisholm and Smith 1990). It suggests that neither hedges nor surveyors' lines have the intrinsic power to establish a division in space. Second, it shows the speakers orientating to the need to establish a boundary *as if* it is able to perform that function, *as if* it is possible to establish an 'objective' and therefore incontestable line of division. The category 'solicitors' invokes notions of the law and legality (lines 29, 33).

Yet, even when the law would seem to fix the spatial borders where property ends and begins, boundaries can dissolve into sites of disorder and dispute. The argument develops as Elsie challenges Dave's entitlement to comment as a chartered surveyor as well as the status of his measurement devices: his technical equipment is reduced to 'little bits of blue:, (0.4) plastic', and his precision measuring is formulated as 'all up and down everywhere' (lines 62–3). But rather than use this evidence to claim that '*my* boundary' line is correct, it is mobilised to support the existence of '*the* boundary', which exists free from intervention. In fact, Elsie suggests that such intervention is a 'waste of time' (line 66), because the 'real' boundary speaks for itself.

Underlying these issues is the implication that the respect of boundaries is crucial to the maintenance of the spatial-moral order of neighbour relations. Fences and hedges are normatively treated as reifications of private spatial control: boundaries that perform the work of 'telling' neighbours where their space ends and that of others begins. Although their data regularly illustrates the inability of 'hedges' and 'fences' to exclude determined outsiders from private spaces, Stokoe and Wallwork find that the orientation to boundaries *as if* they have that exclusory power is a crucial discursive resource in neighbour disputes. This requires complicity on the part of neighbours. As shown throughout our analysis, it requires a particular way of interacting not only with each other but also with the materiality of private property ownership (for example, objects in space such as fences, which are talked '*over*' rather than 'run *through*'). Provided the boundary is respected, it deflects attention away from the people who claim their private space on either side of it and becomes, as Sack (1986: 33) suggests, the 'agent doing the controlling'. Once challenged, however, it is revealed for what it is: a symbolic form that is given meaning within culturally situated interaction based on an ideology of private space ownership. It also reveals the inextricable link between claims to personal legitimacy and stake in the spaces we claim as our own.

The analyses of these neighbour disputes illustrate clearly how identity and space are intimately connected in social practices. These practices include not only actions done in *talk*: accusing, defending, justifying, accounting, arguing and so on; but also in and through other *conduct* in interaction, such as gesture and gaze direction (Schegloff 2005). These final examples of neighbour disputes tie together the chapter's related themes of place/space as *produced in* and as a *topic of* discourse, and place/space as the *location for* discourse. In terms of identity, places and boundaries are constructed in order to channel human activity and produce spaces of inclusion and exclusion. Within these places, different categories of people are constructed as belonging or not belonging; as legitimate or illegitimate occupants of space. Across our examples, numerous types of identity categories are occasioned, ascribed and resisted: occupational (co-workers, surveyor, solicitor), characterological (nosy), relational (neighbours, friends), familial (kids, husband), gendered (lady) and group identities (gang members). Each of these categories is put to use in the course of accomplishing some practical action, and is connected to place and space through description and the locatedness of description.

CONCLUSION

In this chapter, we have investigated a range of approaches to the study of place and space as a further context of identity construction. We started by considering the links between space, social action and identity in a mundane setting – the beach – and considered the way people's activities – both discursive and embodied – get channelled in space, as well as construct space and imbue it with the meanings that are then taken-for-granted. We then discussed the spatial turn across several academic disciplines, a key observation of which is that despite writers' best efforts to study social life in context, it is only recently in discourse-based work that the *contexts* of social life themselves have begun to be studied systematically. We examined three sets of empirical work that investigate the space-place-identity-discourse nexus: text-based work in narrative practices, ethnomethodological studies based on observation, and discursive psychological studies of talk and other embodied practices in interaction in space. Throughout these examples, we focused on the way identities were constructed in and through such practices.

At the start of the chapter we noted an interesting tension between theorising and studying spatial identities via a textual medium. Although this chapter contained many images and representations of the locatedness of people's activities, we inevitably used language to explain relevant things about the photographic data. But we conclude the chapter by suggesting that there is no clear distinction to be drawn between the worlds of objects and space, on the one hand, and of discourse on the other. Physical entities (signs, hedges, fences) and places (beaches, streets) are not 'natural' or prior to their human production. Rather, they are designed just like language is, to have social semiotic value through and through.

The next chapter considers another 'environment' for the analysis of discourse and identity – the virtual environment. The crucial role of spatial contexts in talk-in-interaction is evidenced by the way in which communication in 'virtual' environments (such as cyberspace) attempts to build in spatial metaphors and deixis into its talk. The absence of audio-visual context for interlocutors who meet in these environments results in attempts to replicate the embodied actions of those in face-to-face encounters, as we explore in the next and final chapter: *Virtual Identities*.

CHAPTER 7

Virtual Identities

W e start this chapter with the following quotation from a public Internet discussion site describing activities of the members of the board:

Extract 7.1: Internet discussion site
We go on coach trips to Narnia and have Mary Poppins round for tea on a regular basis.

This embodies, in a tongue-in-cheek way, many of the utopian possibilities of virtual identity. In cyberspace, space, time and identity it would seem are no impediment to doing whatever we want to do, or being whomever we wish to be. Identity on the Internet is playful, creative, impressive and limitless, and (so popular discourse would have it) an entirely different proposition from identity in the 'real world'. In this chapter, we critically explore the concept of 'virtual identity' and its relationship to language, and attempt to elucidate its relationship to what is called 'real life' (RL) identity.

After exploring 'virtuality' as a concept, and summarising work that has explored 'identity' and 'community' online, we look at the genre-specific realisations of the language of computer-mediated communication (CMC). We argue that it owes much of its distinctiveness to an attempt to compensate for an absence of audio–visual context in the medium (notwithstanding interactions via 'Webcam'!). This absence has implications for notions of 'embodiment' and space introduced in the previous chapter ('Spatial Identities') and forms a crucial element of identity work online. We illustrate our discussion with data from two message boards, one a soap opera discussion list and the other a graphic novel message board. Using membership categorisation analysis, we examine the way in which identity categories are invoked and negotiated in these online 'chatrooms'. Finally, we apply politeness theory in a study of the category identity 'Newbie' and its rights and obligations, and the way in which entry into online communities is negotiated with other members.

DEFINING VIRTUAL IDENTITY

An incipient, yet burgeoning field, academic studies of 'virtual identity' and Computer-Mediated Communication (CMC) are becoming increasingly numerous and complement the place that cyberspace occupies in the popular imagination (for example, S. Barnes 2003; Bell and Kennedy 2000; Cherny 1999; Crystal 2001; Herring 1996; Jones 1998; Thurlow, Lengel and Tomic 2004; Turkle 1995). Early research on cyberspace and virtual identity was utopian, romantic and élite in flavour, emphasising the limitless freedom and potential that the Internet could offer. However, recent work reflects both the mundane space that the Internet occupies in many people's lives (S. Barnes 2003; Sterne 1999), and also the many moral panics and media debates circulating vigorously around Internet use, such as online dating, child pornography, cybersex, spam, Internet addiction and Internet fraud (Thurlow et al. 2004).

But what do we mean by the term 'virtual identity'? Semantically, 'virtual', is, of course, opposed to 'real', and the semantics of 'virtual' in everyday language has connotations of 'seeming' (rather than being), of potential rather than actuality (Poster 1998), of inauthenticity, simulation and symbolisation (Fornäs et al. 2002), and is a common theme of postmodernity (Baudrillard 1998). This process of simulating the 'real' can be seen at all levels of Internet use including programming that enables 'bots' (robots) to conduct small talk online on your behalf in your absence, and graphical interfaces with icons that attempt to simulate RL experiences (for example, envelopes to simulate electronic mail, a bin to represent deleted items) thus enabling the technologically complex 'inner workings' of the computer to remain opaque (Turkle 1995). In this context, simulation is less about falseness than about what Turkle (1995: 45) terms a 'simulation aesthetic' that undermines the 'truth' beneath the simulacrum and erases the essential connection between the sign and the real (Baudrillard 1998).

Whilst a simulation aesthetic is embraced as an integral aspect of computing, various apocryphal tales abound which highlight the *distinction* between real and virtual identity, the privileging of the 'real', and a profound investment in the stability and 'authenticity' of identities in cyberspace by many participants. For instance, members of one cyber community were outraged to discover that a severely disabled woman, who befriended and inspired many members, was in fact a male psychologist (Stone 2000). Instances of 'cyber-rape' (Dibbell 1999), and 'cyber-violence', whilst morally and emotionally abhorrent in their online contexts, are proven to be legally distinct from physical crimes when challenged in the real-life courts (MacKinnon 1997). And when participants in cyber-romances arrange to meet their online partners face-to-face ('F2F'), the result is sometimes disappointing. In all these examples, what is 'virtual' is crucially *distinct* from the real.

On the other hand, numerous examples of activity online seem to challenge the boundary between the 'real' and the symbolic. Turkle's (1995: 10) ethnography of computer users abounds with testaments to the involving 'realness' of cyberspace: 'this is more real than my real life', says one user. Cherny's (1999) ethnography of the virtual world of 'ElseMOO' demonstrates that the RL events affecting participants offline frequently intrude upon the fantasy narratives of the 'multi-user domain' ('MUD') world, and similarly online events begin to filter into RL contexts (for example, the use of online textual tropes in offline verbal talk, such as 'LOL' = 'laughs out loud').

Not all online participants connect virtual events so intimately to the real, but nor do they see them in a 'deficit' formulation. In relation to identity, 'virtual' takes on a particular complexion, one associated with the anonymising conditions of the Internet, its spatial and temporal indeterminacy, and the escapist, transient, and above all, *postmodern* complexion of cyberspace, a view expressed by D. Bell (2000: 3): 'We can be multiple, a different person . . . each time we enter cyberspace, playing with our identities, taking ourselves apart and rebuilding ourselves in endless new configurations'. This is typical of the theorisation of virtual or cyber-identity to be found in the field. Due to anonymity, freedoms of time and space, and absence of audio-visual context in cyberspace, identity is deemed to be *more* unstable, *more* performed, *more* fluid (and thus prone to inauthenticity and deception). It is a view of cyber-identity that is remarkably consonant with the dominant view of identity as postmodern, constructed and *discursive*, a view that is not confined to cyberspace. In other words, in constructionist accounts, *all* identities are 'virtual': an ongoing production of an imagined, but ultimately intangible 'real' identity (for example, Gergen 1996). In this version of identity, 'virtual' becomes a red herring: a moniker that perpetuates the myth of the authentic, stable and essential identity. With these arguments in mind, we may decide that 'virtual identity' is simply a prosaic term for the identity work that *happens* to occur online.

A key set of questions in this chapter therefore is: is 'virtual identity' – the identities we inhabit and perform online – a viable concept, and how confident can we be that it represents something distinct from RL (offline) identity, given the constructed and provisional nature of 'real' identity? Is the representational quality of the 'virtual' of cyberspace any different from the symbolic properties of language that forge imaginary worlds in the pages of a novel? Is there a *continuum of virtuality*? For instance, face-to-face interactions involve located, embodied actions and audio–visual and verbal modes. Telephone interactions, landline and mobile, are somewhat 'disembodied' but can maintain locational, audio and verbal information. However, many modes of CMC are purely textual and mostly asynchronous. A second, related set of questions might be: is CMC a distinct register, characterised by patterns and configurations of language and communication found nowhere else? And do these particular linguistic characteristics and constraints of the medium come to bear on identity work online? The crux of our investigation into the discursive realisation of virtual identities lies in the interstices between these related questions.

WHAT AND WHERE IS CYBERSPACE?

A Borgesian library . . . billowing, glittering, humming, coursing. (Benedikt 2000: 30)

A common mental geography, built in turn by consensus and revolution. (Benedikt 2000: 29)

A broad process of sociocultural construction set in motion in the wake of new technologies. (Escobar 2000: 57)

A consensual hallucination. (Gibson 1984)

Collectivities which have nothing to do with physical proximity. (Wilbur 2000: 45)

The definitions above represent, with varying degrees of romantic inflection, the range of functions and attributes attached to cyberspace in the popular imagination. It is communal and social ('consensual', 'common', 'consensus', 'collectivities', 'sociocultural'), it is informative and educative ('library'), it is virtual, unstable, ephemeral ('hallucination', 'billowing', 'nothing to do with physical proximity') and it is radical and capable of facilitating innovation ('revolution', 'coursing', 'sociocultural construction', 'new technologies'). Cyberspace is also inextricably bound up with fictional representations – indeed the term 'cyberspace' derives from Gibson's science-fiction writing (especially *Neuromancer*, 1984). Cyber-culture is informed by representations in science fiction literature and film (for example, the *Terminator* trilogy, *Blade Runner*, the *Matrix* trilogy), whose concepts, tropes and images feed back into experience of inhabiting and building cyberspace (Featherstone and Burrows 1995).

Domains of CMC

A more prosaic description of cyberspace identifies the numerous sites and forms of electronic communication in which users actually participate. The various domains of CMC include the *World Wide Web*, *E-mail*, *Chatrooms*, which may be near-synchronous: interacting in real time (for example, *Instant Messenger*: IM; *Internet Relay Chat*: IRC); or which may be asynchronous: interacting with delays between posts (for example, *Posting/Message/Bulletin Board*; *Discussion Lists*); and finally *Virtual Worlds* such as *MUDS* and *MOOs*, which are often fantasy-based and involve the assumption of a 'persona' within an unfolding drama. For instance, discussion lists are often formal and aligned to RL topics, whereas MUDs and MOOs are frequently fantasy-based. In the sphere of the Web, personal web pages are a more monologic way of presenting or displaying identity online. Cyberspace has also been treated as a theoretical domain that encompasses a wider range of practices than simply digital communication, including biomedical technologies, genetic engineering and artificial life. However, for the purposes of this chapter we will focus mainly on the Internet and, to a lesser extent, telecommunications media.

In debating the uniqueness of CMC, we turn to theoretical, conceptual accounts of cyberspace, which have variously characterised it as democratic (Benedikt 2000), decentralised and non-linear (D. Bell 2000). The way in which people, information and communication are linked – haphazard, circular, unbounded by space and time, without apparent beginning or end, hypertextually and without any regard for a central point or authority – has been described as 'rhizomatic' (D. Bell 2000, after Deleuze and Guattari 1972). D. Bell emphasises the ever-expanding, root-like structure of the Internet and its communication networks. It is precisely this unbounded, decentralised, anarchic space, able to accommodate and nurture subcultures and niche interests, and interactive and agentive (rather than passive) which captured the romantic imagination of early researchers and practitioners. Yet how distinctive *is* cyberspace as a communicative domain? Robins (2000: 78) sceptically cautions against such 'cyberhype': 'All this is driven by a feverish belief in transcendence; a faith that, this time round, a new technology will finally and truly deliver us from the limitations and frustrations of this imperfect world.'

Despite the radical, deconstructive potential for identity proclaimed by numerous enthusiasts, cyberspace frequently becomes the location for the enactment of very familiar identities drawn from romance, fairytale, legend and mainstream sci-fi (Robins 2000), as well as revealing an obsession with the visibility and maintenance of traditional, hegemonic gender roles (K. Hall 1996; Herring and Martinson 2004; Squires 2000). Similarly, research by Kendall (1998) into a MUD over two years revealed that people 'persist in seeking essentialised groundings for the selves they encounter and the selves they offer' (Howard 2000: 383). Finally, the decentralised, rootless quality of cyberspace has been interpreted more negatively by some, who see it as individualist and depoliticising (Kolko and Reid 1998).

We might conclude that only a detailed and empirical engagement with the discourse of cyberspace can support or refute both the uniqueness of CMC and its liberatory, progressive potential. A closer look at actual online data, frequently neglected in more abstract, theoretical accounts, reveals the surprising banality of much CMC and its resemblance to RL talk. However, before turning to the language of CMC, we need to consider in more detail the theoretical approaches to the relationship between *cyberspace and identity*, including notions of 'virtual community' and the fictional and theoretical construct of the 'cyborg'.

VIRTUAL COMMUNITY AND IDENTITY

Utopian views of the Internet have tended to emphasise its communal possibilities, and a good deal of academic attention has focused on the notion of the 'virtual community'. Rheingold (1993: 5), a pioneering enthusiast of cyberspace, coined the term 'virtual community' and defined it thus: 'Social aggregations that emerge from the Net when enough people carry on those public discussions long enough, with sufficient human feeling, to form webs of personal relationships in cyberspace.' Virtual communities are 'global villages' – collectivities of people bounded by technology and common interests, unconstrained by geographic distance, based on common interest rather than common location. Cherny (1999) observes that an apt term might be 'community of practice' (Lave and Wenger 1991) or 'discourse community' (Swales 1990), since neither terms imply co-presence. Virtual communities are often framed either as a nostalgic response to the loss of community in RL contexts (S. Jones 1995; Robins 2000), or a location of solidarity and resistance for traditionally marginalised or powerless groups (Poster 1998; N. Watson 1997).

S. Jones (1998) introduces the term 'cybersociety' to describe new forms of community brought about by CMC. Practical attempts to study cyber communities often take the form of 'virtual ethnographies' (for example, Baym 1993; Cherny 1999; Kendall 1998; Turkle 1995). Turkle's (1995) extensive study of computer users was actually conducted offline via interviews with dedicated users and does not focus on a particular site but rather on the quotidian role of the Internet and its culture in users' lives, identities and imaginings. In Baym's (1993, 1995, 1998) study of a fan-based discussion list dedicated to an American soap opera, she theorised an 'emergent mode of online community' (Baym 1998: 38) – behavioural norms and ingroup expressive forms (often humorous) that stabilise over time. Cherny's (1999) study of the virtual world of *ElseMOO* is largely devoted to explicating the linguistic practices and norms of the community that contribute to its ingroup, exclusive character, as well as offering a useful account of more universal features associated with the *register* of CMC.

Cyberspace and identity

There are a number of ways of approaching identity in cyberspace. Firstly we may be interested in the relationship that humans have with computers and/or technology which gives rise to a number of innovative theories about the human–machine interface and 'cyborg' identity. This approach examines the impact of technology on human identity ('technological determinism'), but also the ways in which users have attempted to 'humanise' computers. The second approach sees technology more prosaically as having a mere mediating or facilitating function between remote participants online, but is nevertheless interested in illuminating the formal and linguistic *realisation* of such relations in the distinct and arguably constraining register of CMC. We expand upon this linguistic dimension in the next section, but for now we examine a number of identity issues arising at the human–computer interface.

The position of the *subject* in the human–machine interface is a topic of ongoing debate that has given rise to a number of conflicting theories. One popular view supports the Cartesian mind–body split as the premise upon which virtual identity rests (for example, Coupland and Gwyn 2003, Lupton 2000). In this account, virtual identity utterly depends on a concept of disembodiment. This in turn is linked to utopian discourses about shedding the 'meat' of the human body to exist in a 'pure' domain of technology, a notion supported by the numerous testaments by online users to a feeling of transcendence from RL (Wilbur 2000). Other views argue that the human subject in cyberspace is embodied, thus clashing with theories of 'free' identity play: 'Digital communication . . . remains based on – and repeatedly thematizes – precisely the physical and sensory body so often assumed to be eliminated in cyberspace' (Fornäs et al. 2002: 34). This orientation to embodiment is supported elsewhere (for example, Herring 1996; Schofield-Clark 1998), in particular that *sex* is strongly oriented to by many participants online, despite the opportunities to transcend the body. Even where gender crossing/passing occurs, the preoccupation with gender is still strongly binary in its orientation and essential in its themes and performances.

A midway position argues for a symbiosis between 'meat' and 'metal' with a number of critics arguing that the human–machine dichotomy is a false one (Escobar 2000). Haraway (2000) leads the way with her 'Manifesto for Cyborgs', a deconstructive, post-gender, third-wave feminist project challenging boundary categorisation, totalising narratives, origins and teleology. The cyborg – 'a cybernetic organism, a hybrid of machine and organism' (Haraway 2000: 291) – merges the boundary between human and machine and acts as a *metaphor* for innovative ways of thinking about identity that breaks down traditional binaries (such as male/female). This thesis has clear implications for theories of embodiment as well as structure/agency dualism: 'It is not clear who makes and who is made in the relation between human and machine' (p. 313). Poster (1998: 186) posits a similar mode of deconstruction in his theorisation of 'virtual ethnicity' – an 'alternative to the binaries of particularism and universalism, parochialism and cosmopolitanism'. Both frameworks arise from the unique configuration of space and time embodied by cyberspace.

The mingling of human and machine is symbolised in the way that computers are humanised and users made 'machinic'. Firstly, there is the tendency for people to anthropomorphise computers – talking to them, railing against them and cajoling them when technological problems arise (Turkle 1995). Computers are liable to become 'infected' by 'viruses' – organic metaphors not usually associated with machines (Lupton 2000), humanised icons festoon the screen (animated paperclips offering 'help') and virtual interaction occurs where the user is 'asked' questions as a substitute for programming (for example, online booking forms).

The technologisation of the human subject is exemplified variously in the practices of biomedicine (organ transplants, skin grafts), genetic engineering, plastic surgery (where the body is moulded and sculpted to an aesthetic ideal), and in the arena of 'teledildonics' whereby the human body is physically and sexually yoked to cyberspace via accessories such as visors and body suits (Branwyn 2000). In performance art, the Australian 'posthumanist' artist, Stelarc (2000) has pioneered the 'psycho body', via performances involving cybernetic body art in which his body is wired up to computers and automated prosthetics. More prosaically, most participants in daily life might be deemed 'low-tech' cyborgs (Hess 1995), driving cars, operating machines and working daily with computers: 'The connection with the computer keyboard becomes a prosthetic connection of humanoid body with machinic body' (Kennedy 2000: 471). The once-radical notion that human–machine is a challenging hybrid becomes less plausible as technology is increasingly integrated into our daily lives.

Finally, we may examine cyber-identity from the perspective of a series of recognisable social roles in online communication, such as the 'Newbie' (newcomer), the 'Mod'/'Wizard'/'Op' (Moderator or Operator of the board or domain), the 'Flamer' and the 'Troll' (inveterate troublemakers, deliberately provoking angry responses in cyber communities). Such roles are a fruitful focus for the study of discursive identities online, since we may observe minutely how they are occasioned in ongoing talk, and how they construct themselves and are constructed by others. Our detailed study later in this chapter will involve a close analysis of 'Newbie' identity.

DISCOURSE AND IDENTITY IN CMC

So far we have explored, with broad, thematic brushstrokes, the relationship between cyberspace and identity. But what of the *forms* of CMC, its linguistic and discursive possibilities? How is identity realised discursively online and what are the features that both enhance and limit identity work, deemed to be unique to 'Netspeak' (Crystal 2001)? S. Barnes (2003: 18) describes CMC as 'interpersonal mediated communication' – facilitating the personal, two-way interaction usually associated with orality but with the space/time distanciation more usually associated with written texts. This distanciation is arguably what has the greatest implications for a notion of 'virtual' identity.

A world of text: The implications of an absence of audio-visual context for identity

CMC is often described as a text-only medium, lacking the visual and paralinguistic cues which are a key element of face-to-face communication. A commonly held (albeit increasingly challenged) view is that due to this absence of audio-visual cues or 'cuelessness' (Cherny 1999), 'reduced social cues' (Kiesler, Siegel and McGuire 1984) or 'cues-filtered-out' (S. Barnes 2003), CMC is *lacking* in comparison to face-to-face communication – what Thurlow et al. (2004) describe as the 'deficit approach'. Reduced social cues are deemed to affect 'social presence', leading to psychological distancing, impersonality and even antisocial behaviour due to the 'risk-free' nature of the anonymity guaranteed by an absence of visual context (S. Jones 1998; Kolko and Reid 1998). Conversely, reduced social cues are sometimes deemed to encourage reckless self-disclosure and intense, rapidly developing relationships (Turkle 1995). Following closer scrutiny, many early assumptions about CMC – mostly based on the premise that the Internet is a 'weak' emotional and psychological medium – have been subsequently overturned (Lea and Spears 1995; Walther 2004). The idea that virtual identity would be significantly different from RL identity was therefore based on an incorrect assumption that privileged the significance of nonverbal behaviour in *offline* settings.

A substantial body of work has, nevertheless, investigated the way in which CMC finds means of *compensating* for loss of nonverbal cues and an absence of audio-visual context. In a face-to-face setting, we can gather an immense amount of information simply from the intonation, appearance, facial expressions, gestures and actions of interlocutors – all of which are lacking from cyber contexts. However, the uses of signature files, naming, role adoption, avatars (visual representations of characters on screen), verbal description and self-disclosure are all ways of creating an identifiable personality in an otherwise fairly anonymous environment (S. Barnes 2003; Baym 1998). Many researchers also report on the common practice of verbalising actions, often bounded by a pair of asterisks or angle bracket (for example, *looks*, <says>) and formulated invariably in the third person present tense (Cherny 1999; Crystal 2001). Such actions, or 'emotes', are crucial ways of contributing to identity work online and compensating for an absence of visual context, since they can express relationships (*Mel hugs Bob*), flesh out a dramaturgical space (*Athorn takes the sword from the stone*), reveal inner states or motivations (*cowers in corner pretending he hasn't heard a word said*), or imbue the domain with a surreal cartoonish quality (*cackles till gets whapped upside head by Clooney with her work list/shedual*) – what Cherny terms 'byplay'.

The *performative* quality of these emotes has also been explored (Cherny 1999; Rooksby 2002). For example, a written action can achieve something non-deniable within cyber reality (*Sindy waves to room*). This observation is strengthened by the choice of present tense creating an immediate and dramatic, rather than narratorial, mode (Cherny 1999). Some actions (often *commands* and part of the programming dimension of the domain), are *explicitly* performative and may have consequences either online (for example, cyber 'marriages') or offline (for example, 'toading' – where a mod evicts a participant from the board). Rooksby (2002) addresses the performative status of these actions by asking whether most expressions of action in cyberspace are *literal* or *metaphorical*: actions with real effects or simply textual performances. A virtual *hug*, for instance, may not have the affective power of a *real* hug, but on the other hand may symbolise *real* friendship.

In K. Hall's (1995) study of telephone sex talk (see Chapter 5, *Commodified Identities*), she makes similar observations about the verbal work that is needed to compensate for an absence of visual context in these virtual encounters. She reports that companies go to great lengths to simulate reality – even to the point of having fantasy line operators 'carry' condoms and spermicides to their verbal sexual encounter. In these 'exchanges' (often the message is a pre-recorded, rather than 'live' one), verbal creativity comes to represent the sex act itself. And this, of course, is an observation that supports a commonly expressed view of verbal skill in cyberspace. In a visually impoverished environment, words become a crucial form of cultural capital (Sveningsson 2002).

Like telephone talk, in which the speakers are in an equivalent position to the analyst for understanding the interaction, the purely textual realm of cyberspace presents ideal data for the discourse analyst anxious to present the 'whole picture'. This is also true for the sociolinguist keen to gain the 'whole picture' in a social network study of a single (virtual) community, due to the capacity for *all* interactions to be logged (Paolillo 1999) – an impossibility in face-to-face contexts. The data are also unmediated by the transcription process (unlike speech), making CMC ideal for those concerned with the 'authenticity' or purity of the data. Furthermore, it lacks the problems bound up with the observer's paradox, since the researcher's view is exactly that of a lurker and thus an 'authentic' way of accessing the data.

Deixis: Spatial dimensions

Another important compensatory strategy for an absence of audio-visual context commonly found in CMC is the verbal construction of place and space via spatial metaphors and deixis. Virtual communities invariably construct themselves in terms of physical space, inhabited by physical bodies, and the programming function in most MUD and MOO spaces enables participants to create and save physical spaces and objects within the system. Explicit spatial metaphors abound in cyberspace, and participants of a virtual world take the accuracy of the spatial dimension of cyberspace seriously – if two users simultaneously perform actions that are logically contradictory, this is oriented to and rectified (Cherny 1999).

The examples in Table 7.1, taken from our two message boards ('soap opera' and 'graphic novel' – see *Data: Transcription, Anonymisation and Ethics* at the start of the book), illustrate how metaphors of space and visuality are used. We categorise these references under the following headings: *metaphors of seeing, metaphors of space, creation of virtual objects, creation of 'performative space'* and *creation of virtual space*. Certain examples can belong to more than one category. Examples of deixis are underlined, and this will be explained below. In the category of virtual objects, users sometimes creatively exploit typographical symbols to represent physical objects, such as an asterisk * to represent a bobble on a hat, or a composite graphic: _/, to represent a drink.

Table 7.1 Metaphors of space and visuality in CMC

Types of metaphor		Examples
Metaphors of 'seeing'	–	*looks around*
	–	you won't see me <u>around</u> much
	–	watch out for the crazyness!
	–	Sorry, had to disappear
	–	How lovely to see you my dear, what are doing <u>here</u>?
Metaphors of space	–	Welcome to the place where we celebrate the wonderful addiction of JJ
	–	Can I pop over to <u>your's</u> for tea sometime?
	–	come <u>out</u>, Jake, I know you're <u>there</u>
	–	What a nice place <u>this</u> is
	–	I mostly lurk but I pop up <u>now and again</u>
Creation of virtual objects	–	<u>here</u> have a pretzel
	–	*tosses a tin of caramel and pecan popcorn*
	–	Better send out for extra crumpets
	–	Have <u>this</u> * for your pointy hat ¬Couldn't get the * on quite straight, but I think it looks lovely anyway
Creation of 'performative' space	–	*Clooney kicks her in the shin*
	–	*rolls out welcome banner*
	–	Come and sit <u>over here</u> nicely with your hands in your lap
	–	Hold your glass <u>out here</u> and say 'when' . . . glug glug glug glug . . . etc
	–	¬Flo, I said say 'when' . . . <u>now</u> look <u>what</u>'s happened!
	–	And <u>here,</u> help yourself to one of my crisps. <u>One!</u> And don't say I never give you nothing

Table 7.1 (continued)

Types of metaphor	Examples	
Creation of virtual space (including objects/ furniture etc)	–	Now excuse me while I go chicken out <u>here</u> in the corner X_x
	–	Hiya, come sit with me on ma (blue, the red one is taken in the other thread) couch. Sorry no space fodder in the blue couch, just a load of junkfood. So help ya self and feel welcome!

Deixis refers to markers of reference (usually adverbs, but sometimes pronouns) that signal the spatial, temporal or identity location of a speaker. The full understanding of a deictic marker is dependent on the context of utterance and is thus *indexical*. *Spatial deixis* includes 'here', 'there', 'in', 'out', 'around'. Examples of *temporal deixis* include 'now', 'then', 'tomorrow'. Markers of *identity deixis* include 'I', 'you', 'she', 'it', 'what'. The demonstrative pronouns or determiners 'this' and 'that' are also markers of deixis, signalling either nearness or distance in both time and space. *Proximal deixis* refers to markers suggestive of closeness and includes 'here', 'now', 'this', 'nearby', 'on this spot', 'today'. *Distal deixis* refers to markers suggestive of distance, and includes 'there', 'then', 'that', 'over there', 'far away', 'in the past/future'. Deixis is ubiquitous in the data above, in particular the proximal 'here', which anchors participants in a shared, virtual space.

Deixis generally occurs in contexts where there is a shared understanding or experience of events, since speakers are being presented with inexplicit reference and must have access to contextual information in order to retrieve the full understanding of the utterance (speakers need to know who 'she' refers to, or see the visual referent for 'that'). For this reason, it tends to be more common in speech situations (where there is a shared visual context) and informal registers (where participants are more likely to share assumptions, and thus do not need to 'spell out' all references explicitly). Given our observations about CMC as a medium with strong oral qualities, we therefore might not be surprised to find deixis occurring frequently and as a strategy for recreating some of the immediate, intimate, community qualities of a speech event with a shared visual environment. In cyberspace, markers of *presence* are hugely important: the 'now' of time and the 'here' of space.

Anchors of deixis are arguably a tangible reminder of people's inability to accept a truly different kind of reality – a virtual time and a virtual space – and the use of proximal deixis sits alongside spatial metaphor and the creation of virtual objects in its attempt to recreate the qualities of RL in cyberspace. Occasionally the 'here' of the virtual, shared environment switches confusingly to the 'here' of a member's offline reality (for example, 'We've a long, long way to go here', meaning the member's relationship with her partner in their domestic environment), supporting the idea that users have a sophisticated ability to conceive of, and move between, more than one spatial 'reality' simultaneously.

The ability for members to create virtual objects and dramaturgical spaces are a source of creativity and playfulness. In the extract below, a 'twinkle' becomes a tangible object – a gift – which members collude in visualising in precise, spatial terms. The underlined text within '<< >>' is an embedded quotation from a previous speaker, and the visual layout corresponds to the way that adjacent turns appear sequentially on the screen:

Extract 7.2: Soap opera message board
<Capricorn> :
Actually, Malc, you deserve a twinkle for services rendered. Thanks for looking out for me.
    <Malc>:
    ¬Cheers, Capricorn, you're a real gennleman, so you are! A twinkle, eh?
    I'll put it ... just there I think!
        <Capricorn> :
        ¬<<I'll put it ... just there>>
        There Malc? Are you sure?
            <Malc>:
            ¬Well, it seemed like a good idea at the time. I must admit it
            is beginning to chafe a little. Perhaps I'll just hang it ...
            there?
                <Capricorn> :
                ¬That's much better! Looks lovely there, gives you a
                sort of bohemian look. Very fetching!

Despite the formulation of 'real' objects, the members play here with the arbitrariness of spatial representations. Malc's 'there' (virtual and fictional anyway) is challenged by Capricorn, and relocated in equally virtual and fictional terms.

In the next section, we describe and illustrate the different linguistic levels of CMC, using our message board data, in an attempt to understand 'virtual identity' as identity work that is mediated, constrained and occasioned by the unique properties and limitations of CMC. Many of the observations made rest on the premise that CMC responds in creative ways to the absence of audio-visual context, a dimension traditionally deemed relevant to interpersonal meaning.

DIMENSIONS OF LANGUAGE IN CMC

Crystal (2001) argues that CMC is characterised by unique features, occasioned by their particular functions and contexts of use. We describe these features under a conventional set of language headings (*turn-taking*, *grammar*, *textuality*, *pragmatics*, *graphology* and *lexis*) and show how CMC is realised at these various levels. Many of these unique features are occasioned by the absence of audio-visual context and social cues outlined above, and can be related to the identity work occurring in cyberspace. Whilst most of the headings reveal a contrast with all offline contexts, *grammar* and *lexis* are arguably only deviant in comparison with written modes of language, but have much in common with spoken forms in offline contexts. All spelling, grammar, layout and punctuation in our examples are as they appeared on screen.

Turn-taking

Extract 7.3: From The Guardian, 1 October 2002

Pashmina:	hey room what's up
Bronco:	mullah'omar cursed me
Pashmina:	are those 2 still in ere! Chris2 get them out NOW
Host_Chris2:	I'm afraid I can't. Offensive usernames are only defined as those with swear words in them
Pashmina:	but they been cursin @ Bronco!
Capitalistpiglet:	perhaps it's a sophisticated parody of Western paranoia, but I just don't get it.
Bronco:	no they PUT a curse on me. My hair is fallin out!
Pashmina:	I thought yr GP said that was stress from the call centre
mullah'omar:	osama u still hiding in the same place
Osama_bin_Laden:	yep. u?
Bronco:	I quit the call centre. What does a boil look like?
mullah'omar:	same place. Seen any blasphemous films lately
Osama _bin_Laden:	lilo and stitch
mullah'omar:	yes I condemned it as well
Capitalistpiglet:	is it a political statement? Performance art?

A common understanding of CMC is that its rules for turn-taking will differ from real-time conversation. The above spoof extract from Tim Dowling in *The Guardian* newspaper, with its parallel threads and absence of inter-turn relevance, is a clear demonstration of this difference; indeed Dowling's humour is largely derived from this apparent incoherence and lack of topical relevance. Whilst *technically* there can be no overlap or simultaneous speech in CMC as only one user has access to the channel at a single time (with the exception of the split screen function in Internet Relay Chat), in most synchronous (or near-synchronous) CMC contexts, simultaneity of exchanges is common (Herring 1999). For example, a participant may start a new thread with a different interlocutor, whilst waiting for a response from a previous exchange, or people will often type simultaneously and cross-post so that different conversational strands occur simultaneously (Werry 1996). This is compounded by the practice amongst many users of 'breaking up' their turns and sending them in separate 'chunks' (Baron 2004; Cherny 1999). This creates a sense of 'co-presence' rather than monologue, and is also a practical measure to provide some text for the recipient to begin reading and speed up the interaction; however it means that turn boundaries become difficult to identify.

Any notion of turn-taking is also severely compromised by the absence of non-textual features associated with face-to-face or telephone communication, such as falling intonation signalling the end of a turn. Misunderstanding and turn-taking 'violations' are liable to occur due to the impossibility of identifying 'transition relevance places' (see Chapter 2), and the fact that taking up another turn cannot be allocated by the use of, say, gaze direction. For this reason, in CMC, competition is not so much for the floor or channel, but for having a 'thread' taken up (see also Simpson 2005). A huge proportion of new threads will be ignored on any message board.

The conversational coherence thought to be lacking in CMC is, however, compensated for by a variety of creative means. The ability for people to follow synchronous chat and track conversational threads with all its disruption to sequence and turn-taking is still a source of wonder. Herring (1999: 10) argues that 'standards of local relevance' are weak in CMC, making CMC chat more challenging to process cognitively, but nevertheless not an impediment to successful conversational sequences. Again, the resourcefulness of CMC will compensate for the audio-visual constraints outlined above. In chatrooms and virtual worlds, people will use 'nicks' (nicknames) to make sure their utterance is taken up by a particular person leading to a higher degree of 'addressivity' than one might find in face-to-face communication (Werry 1996). Additionally 'nicks' serve as a virtual 'face' in online encounters, giving an appearance to the users and making them recognisable in subsequent encounters (Sveningsson 2002), as well as facilitating processing of connections between turns when they are out of order. Similarly, where two people reply simultaneously, rather like overlap in talk, they may signal this by typing 'lose' (Cherny 1999) and abandoning their turn – similar to 'cut offs' that occur in real-time conversation. Cherny also comments on the unique function in MUDs of 'whisper' and 'page': commands which allow unseen private conversations between speakers whilst maintaining presence in the group environment. This is an explicit way of controlling turn allocation and a function not available in RL contexts.

Despite a common assumption that turns functioning as continuers, response tokens, or 'back channel' responses (for example, 'mmm', 'yeah', 'really', 'wow') will be rare in CMC, they are very popular in some environments (see Werry 1996). Users are also more prone to cite previous exchanges in order to insert evaluative feedback, which bolsters coherence and interactivity between turns. The example below represents one turn and the underlined text represents the 'quoted' line from the previous turn:

Extract 7.4: Soap opera message board
<u><<fallen woman>></u>
Best kind imho ;-)   [imho = 'in my humble opinion']

Similarly, Rafaeli and Sudweeks (1997) comment on the way users often comment metadiscursively on connections between messages – what they term 'networked interactivity'. This metadiscursive mode provides a way of overcoming or commenting upon the challenge of ambiguous sequences of turns (for example, 'Hey Trish, you read Ned's news above?', 'Why do posts keep getting jumbled up on here?', 'I gave up on our earlier thread – got lost on it!', 'See my answer just now re the crocodile, Fliss', 'Whoa! Almost missed a newbie thread!').

In certain forms of CMC, responses to a turn will be multiple and simultaneous, making a topic difficult to follow. Whereas in real-time conversational turn-taking, multiple responses get abandoned to leave one participant speaking 'in the clear', speaking one-at-a-time is not even an aim in CMC. However, this might be seen as an advantageous distinction of CMC, facilitating more intense, 'hyperpersonal' interaction (Walther 1996). Like Herring (1999) then, we argue that whilst CMC is *conventionally* incoherent in terms of turn-taking (disrupted adjacency, overlapping exchanges, and topic decay), users either adapt to or exploit these 'deficiencies': 'CMC . . . is both dysfunctionally and advantageously incoherent' (p. 2).

Grammar

Grammar is most obviously affected by the rapid-response dictates of CMC, and tends to resemble spoken rather than offline written discourse. The grammar of CMC, particularly in informal media like chatrooms, is characterised by more non-standard, looser constructions and ellipsis, such as subject pronoun or preposition deletion (for example, 'Never tried speaking to them to be honest and not about to start'). In our data, subject deletion was very common, but preposition deletion less so. Contractions are often phonologically related such as 'dunno' 'prolly' (probably: Cherny 1999), or ''sa bit boring if I'm honest . . . 'snot really me, yknow?'. And non-standard grammar is sometimes deliberately employed for comic effect, perhaps to convey an archaic unworldly social dialect (for example, 'Cor a real live Duchess on the radio and I misses it!', 'I nearly drownded in me bath', 'I had the wonderfullest dream', 'You're a real gennleman, so you are'). Again, these are written realisations of what we might more usually expect to encounter in speech, and support the idea that CMC is strongly dominated by an orientation to orality rather than literacy.

However, contrary to such expectations (and a sop to the vanguards of prescriptive grammar), Thurlow's (2003) research into forms of text-messaging found that apostrophes were surprisingly relatively common – carefully inserted in 35 per cent of all messages! Baron (2004) also found abbreviations relatively rare (thirty-one out of 11,718) in her Instant Messanger corpus; and in Cherny's (1999) MUD, subject and article deletion rarely occurs.

Textuality

One of the unique features of certain forms of CMC is that of 'message intercalation' (Crystal 2001). This is also known as 'framing', which involves editing a previous message in order to leave only that which is relevant to the response – a kind of quotation, or intertextuality – but more so than we might find in conventional writing. Message intercalation is facilitated by the technological capacity to log discourse online and retrieve it for future exchanges, another feature unique to CMC. In the following exchange between two users, the second user cuts and pastes from the previous turn (<<underlined>>):

Extract 7.5: Soap opera message board
<Moondust>:
I'll have a pint of Guinness please. Bit quiet round here.

\<Cat\>:

¬sorry don't do pints. Will a skip do? <u><<bit quiet round here>></u> yes – but all the more for us!

This has the function of foregrounding the importance of another's words (particularly notable in multi-party talk), thus attending to what Goffman (1959) calls 'face' and building solidarity. Arguably, from a more functional perspective, it is also a way of rendering an asynchronous mode into something that looks more spontaneous and more like dialogue. It allows a respondent to isolate the elements of the message that have been directly addressed to them, such as questions. Again, we see CMC straining against the limitations of its mode by simulating spatial and temporal immediacy and dialogism – a clear rejection of the thesis that CMC is a socially deficient medium.

Another aspect of textuality is the non-linear way in which chatroom discourse is constructed, which we encountered in our discussion of turn-taking. There is no chronological starting point and individual entry points are arbitrary. In research done on chatrooms, it has been found that people can best conceptualise the formation of topics in spatial rather than temporal terms, and indeed some advocate the development of graphical interfaces to process better the social and conversational dynamics of CMC (Donath, Karahalios and Viégas 1999). The technology used in chatrooms already tends to capitalise on this spatial conceptualisation by use of a *threading* function, which visually sorts exchanges into discrete topics.

Pragmatics

Pragmatics refers to the study of language use from the point of view of its *users* (rather than say, concerns about the formal properties of language) and encompasses a consideration of meaning, communicative intent, social consequences and mutual knowledge of the conventional 'norms' of communication. Grice (1975) has argued that communication is guided by a set of universal principles, which he termed *maxims*, to which the processing of the meanings of conversation are oriented, and the all-encompassing of which is the *cooperative principle*, by which participants make their contribution 'such as is required, at the stage at which it occurs, by the accepted purpose or direction of the talk exchange' (p. 45). More precisely, and in the spirit of *efficient* communication, Grice specified four further maxims: *quantity* (do not say too much or too little for the purposes of the talk), *quality* (do not lie or say that for which you lack evidence), *relevance* (observe relevance to the preceding turn) and *manner* (avoid ambiguity and obscurity, be brief and orderly). When a speaker does not observe (deliberately *flouts*) one of these maxims, it is usually in order to express some underlying meaning or *implicature*. In the following example of a couple choosing paint, B seems to flout the maxim of *manner* and *relevance* by not answering A directly:

A: What do you think of this colour for the kitchen?
B: I've always thought of blue as more of a bathroom colour.

Assuming that speaker B is still guided by a principle of cooperation, we can assume that the implicature is that speaker B wants to avoid causing offence by disagreeing bluntly. In fact, Grice came to realise that indirectness and maxim flouting were actually more *normative* than a strict adherence to maxims, and one of the most common reasons for maxim flouting was in order to observe a further conversational norm: that of *politeness* (cf. Brown and Levinson 1987). We introduce *politeness* as a pragmatic framework for analysis in our case study of the 'Newbie' later in this chapter.

Like the more formal aspects of language, pragmatic norms also differ in significant ways in CMC, particularly with respect to maxims of *politeness* and *efficiency*. The formal and contextual qualities or constraints of CMC arguably intensify the maxim of *efficiency*, whilst sacrificing the maxim of *politeness* in comparison with face-to-face conversation. Thus messages sent quickly in synchronous modes, without the aid of nonverbal cues that might make the tone clearer, are more likely to cause offence because they observe the efficiency maxim so uncompromisingly. Typing is not as gratifyingly instant as speech, and users will attempt to economise by cutting corners and thus losing elements such as 'face work' and mitigation, leading to expression that in other contexts might seem direct and rude. Participants in CMC are often aware of the different 'norms' governing interaction in cyberspace, and adjust their expectations accordingly.

An extreme example of a flout of the politeness maxim that *does* often lead to offence is *flaming*. This is the practice of sending an aggressive or insensitive message designed to offend the sensibilities of others on the board. In these cases it is the *anonymity* of the medium that provides refuge for the habitual troublemaker. A response to such flouts, and indeed to other misunderstandings arising from the idiosyncratic properties of CMC, is the ubiquitous presence of a *moderator* on message boards or virtual worlds – itself a break with the democratic norms of casual conversation, and an acknowledgement that CMC interaction has to be managed in ways appropriate to its context when the pragmatic norms are so different from face-to-face interaction.

Graphology

Graphology and graphological deviation are likely to be very significant in a mode that lacks non-textual social cues, such as paralanguage, prosody and gesture. One of the most familiar graphological devices in CMC is the 'emoticon', such as '☺' ('smiley'), which attempts to compensate for this lack by conveying the mood or attitude of the speaker. Emoticons have an important interpersonal function, conveying to the hearer how the message should be read, and avoiding possible offence. For instance, '☺' or ';-)' ('winking') may be a cue for irony.

Spelling in CMC is frequently non-standard and it has often been noted that it is difficult to distinguish genuine errors (occasioned by the demands of quick typing) from deliberate deviations which contribute to a kind of argot or sociolect. Crystal (2001) comments that non-standard spellings tend to occur without sanction in CMC and it is interesting to speculate that the genre has developed a higher degree of tolerance to such errors as one of its implicit norms. Sometimes deviant spellings are used to approximate idiosyncratic pronunciation (for example, 'schtuff', 'acksherly', 'leddy' (for lady), 'bluudy heck'), to which Thurlow (2003) attributes a playful function. The incidence of 'accent stylisation' via deviant spelling for rhetorical, comic and ingroup purposes was a prominent feature in our data and, along with similarly satirical uses of non-standard grammar, is arguably a significant aspect of an emergent CMC 'register'.

The use of non-standard homophones, where a letter or number stands for a longer word (for example, 'C U l8er' = 'See you later', 'R U there?' = 'Are you there?', 'NE1' = 'anyone'), is both playful and efficient. Thurlow's (2003) research into text ('SMS') messaging (a similar mode to CMC) revealed that number/letter homophones (like 2 for 'to') were less frequent than accent stylisation or phonological approximations. Capitalisation in CMC is rare and for precisely this reason is a marked form. Capitals should only be used to express excitement or a metaphorical raise in pitch and are considered a breach of 'netiquette' if used indiscriminately. Punctuation may also be used in creative ways. Both Crystal (2001) and Cherny (1999) cite the example of an initial exclamation mark expressing negation: *!interesting* ('not interesting').

Lexis

Lexis is one dimension of language which has been profoundly affected within CMC and which links particularly closely to the social and creative dimension of the genre. As a new, technologically distinct medium, CMC has been at the forefront of lexical innovation. Crystal (2001) cites examples of all varieties of word-formation in the creation of neologisms, via the processes of compounding ('bandwidth', 'netspeak'), suffixes ('on-/offline', 'e-zine'), blending ('netiquette', 'cybercide'), coining ('wuggle') and acronyms. Acronyms such as 'LOL' ('laughs out loud') and 'ROFL' ('rolls on floor laughing') compensate for an absence of embodied action and signal a kind of evaluation of the speaker's utterance. Baron (2004), for instance, observes that 'LOL' acts as a phatic filler (like 'cool' or 'OK'). In our data, 'LOL' operates like a discourse marker, albeit with an evaluative function (for example, 'Lol- it's certainly a server with attitude'). Such acronyms may be complex and exclusive to particular domains, contributing to the sense of ingroup identity. Number/letter homophones, as detailed above, are also a common source of lexical innovation and popular in text-messaging, where economy of words is a particular consideration. Crystal (2001) points out that lexical innovation in CMC has had a profound impact offline as well, with the use of @ (found in e-mail addresses) ubiquitous in advertising slogans and brands, and the use of number/letter homophones by young people in academic contexts a common source of hand-wringing by educationalists and parents.

In the table below, we summarise the language features associated with CMC:

Table 7.2 Summary of language features in CMC

Feature	Realisation
Turn-taking	Relative absence of continuers, use of 'nicks' to allocate turns, use of 'lose' to relinquish the floor, 'chunked' turns, lack of local relevance between adjacent turns (simultaneous threads)
Grammar	Non-standard grammar (often for comic purposes), contractions, ellipsis
Textuality	Message intercalation, non-linearity (spatial realisation) of topic – graphical threads
Pragmatics	'Maxims of communication' (e.g. 'relevance', 'efficiency') clash with 'maxim of politeness', hence role of moderators. Anonymity leads to flouts of 'politeness maxim' ('flaming')
Graphology	Non-standard spelling (often approximating pronunciation), capitalisation, punctuation, emoticons
Lexis	Acronyms, neologisms (compounds, suffixes, blends)

Implications for identity

All these observations about the creative, sometimes playful resources of CMC and its ability to 'compensate' for an absence of audio-visual context at all levels of language might lead us to conclude that a highly significant function of CMC is a *social* one (Baym 1995; Werry 1996). Early accounts of Internet language assumed that CMC would lead to patterns of homogenisation and globalisation, but in many ways the opposite has occurred. CMC is increasingly regarded as a highly inter-personal mode, idiosyncratic and creative, and self-disclosure in certain types of domain is rife.

Internet discourse has been characterised as being inherently playful and poetic (for example, Danet, Ruedenberg-Wright and Rosenbaum-Tamari 1997; Sudweeks, McLaughlin and Rafaeli 1995) and set apart from RL concerns in textual and metatextual ways. Herring (1999: 18) comments astutely on the way the unique mode of CMC facilitates this self-consciousness with language:

> The predilection towards meta-humour and meta-play in CMC can be attributed in part to the fact that CMC persists as text on a screen and is subject to conscious reflection in ways that spoken language is not, thereby facilitating a heightened meta-linguistic awareness.

We can observe language play in the form of punning in this example taken from our corpus:

Extract 7.6: Soap opera message board
<Bear>:
Send us the video when you've done with it, Colin!
    <Colin>:
    ¬How would you like it sent, in a plain brown envelope?
        <Bear>:
        ¬just send it through the net!
            <Finn>:
            ¬fish net?
                <Oscar>:
                ¬Did someone mention codpieces, with the ban
                they shouldn't be permitted you know,
                particularly in Fastnet. At least I know my
                plaice.

The puns rely on the textuality of CMC since they play on homophones ('place–plaice') that would be undetectable verbally, and also play with the metaphors coined within CMC ('net'). This reflexive use of language, this playing with form and substance as an end in itself, in turn might contribute to our sense of what is 'virtual' about the identity work that takes place in cyberspace. In a purely textual, disembodied realm, meanings are more apt to reflect emptily back upon themselves, rather than relate referentially to external events or objects.

However, language play and humour – part performative and thus a form of symbolic capital, part invoking solidarity – are also a means of expressing both individual *and* group identity, in ways quite familiar from face-to-face contexts (Baym 1995). Much of CMC is about the replication of a *community* albeit in a virtual sense. Many of the patterns of language behaviour observed in informal CMC replicates those associated with the formation of social groups or communities of practice. This includes a shared lexis exclusive to the group, linguistic accommodation (converging towards the norms of other people), a group history and memory (which is often institutionalised in the form of FAQs), and even evidence of language change within individual chatrooms where particular lexis or spelling shifts are discarded over time.

Walther (1996: 17) has described such communities as *hyperpersonal* rather than interpersonal – where relations in CMC are idealised, intensified and 'more socially desirable than we tend to experience in parallel FtF interaction'. Moreover, the communication transcends the individual exchange and rather is focused on the group and its textual record. This is apparent in the emphasis that many chatrooms and virtual worlds put on *etiquette*, and their own idiosyncratic set of social rules where a certain kind of group pressure may manifest itself when people flout communicative maxims. In the final section, these kinds of issues will be demonstrated by a case study of a particular virtual community and its negotiation of the entry of a new member, or 'newbie'. Before we do this, however, we discuss how common 'categories' of identity (such as 'mod' or 'newbie') are invoked, taken up and employed to accomplish social order in online communities.

CATEGORIES OF VIRTUAL IDENTITY

In a study of identity in chatroom talk, Vallis (2001) uses membership categorisation analysis (see Chapter 2) to illuminate how participants achieve online identities for themselves and others. More specifically, she focuses on the descriptive status of 'ops' (operators or moderators) and their characterisation as either sympathetic (protecters of the integrity and order of the board) or dissenting ('control freaks', 'geeks') (see also Cherny 1999).

In Vallis's data, participants invoke relevant categories by naming them: (for example, 'ops', 'not an op' and 'founder'). Predicates tied to the category 'op' include 'kick' and 'ban'. Vallis notes that there are 'category-generated features' which relate to the specific action being done in the talk, and the identities and motives of those using them. For example, 'being (in the channel) a long time' and 'getting along with other ops' are invoked in response to a discussion about how you get to achieve the status of an op *by someone who is already an op* (p. 91). However, further related categories (for example, 'neo-nazi') and their predicates (for example, requiring 100 per cent agreement and laughter in response to their jokes, being cliquey) are offered up *by non-ops* who display a sceptical stance to the op system. Through her analysis, Vallis explicates how the moral order of the community is organised 'according to the members' claimed incumbencies' (p. 96) and how such competing categorisations may also be crucial in deciphering the motives and identity status of the participants making the categorisation, a process described by Schegloff (1989: 206) as 'categoris[ing] the categoriser'. For instance, an ordinary 'user' who is denied op status is likely to attach negative attributes to an op, which may be inferable as 'sour grapes'.

This view of the tricky and ambiguous status of the mods, and their ascribed status by ordinary users as power-obsessed and territorial, is confirmed by examples across our own data (for example, 'Read the rules of the board . . . it'll help. And NO I'm not taking anyone's "rule-mentioning" job! Just . . . a simple precaution that's all'). Here, the ordinary user's defensive disclaimer displays an orientation to the mod's entitlement to issue reminders of the message board rules, as well as their own lack of category-based entitlement to do so. Elsewhere, an ordinary user warns (albeit light-heartedly) another user about the dangers of 'contradicting' the moderator:

Extract 7.7: Soap opera message board
<Wildebeest>:
Contradicting Mr M [the moderator] is risky Arturo, even for a poster of your calibre. That's the sort of thing that can get you sent into exile on the Gardener's Question Time board if you're not careful.

For the ordinary user, being a 'mod' entails particular category-bound rights and obligations, including 'exercising power'. In the example above, the mod can send users (metaphorically) 'into exile' if they are contradicted. The formulation of the place of exile, 'Gardener's Question Time board', is a hearably 'uncool' online environment, presumably in contrast to the board in which this interaction takes place.

In the next section, our focus is on another category, that of the 'newbie'. However, we employ a different kind of approach to analysing the way in which identities are accomplished and managed in virtual communities. In this analysis, we draw on Brown and Levinson's (1987) theory of *politeness* to describe systematically the process of a 'newbie' 'coming out' online and the subsequent responses they receive from the regulars on the board. This process of initiation, skilfully managed on both sides, is evidence of the complex rules and moral order of a virtual community, particularly where the perceived collective 'identity' of the group is at stake.

VIRTUAL IDENTITY: THE CASE OF THE NEWBIE

The data that follows is taken from our 'graphic novel' message board, and shows a complete sequence in which a 'newbie' introduces themselves to the board. It was collected and transcribed from the Internet, and has been set out below in the sequence in which the 'turns' occurred. However, line numbers have been added for ease of reference. The turns originally appeared in separate, self-contained boxes in asynchronous time and were coloured and animated. Underlined text, enclosed by '<< >>' is quoted from previous turns. '^_^' and '^^^' mean 'smiling face', 'o_O' means 'a nervous tick', '=D' means 'wide grin', 'X_x' means 'the writer is dead', '^_^;' means 'smiling face with a sweatdrop' conveying fear, 'XO' means 'anger or distaste', and '@_@' means 'surprise'.

Extract 7.8: Graphic novel message board

1	<Irene>	Hey, I'm new and stuff ^_^;
2		... And I suck at making topics like this
3		I've been lurking here a while now, and decided to finally
4		register ... I can't write fics that well but I love to read noir
5		shtuffs. Oh and I draw fanart. If you wanna call my crap art,
6		that is o_O
7		Now excuse me while I go chicken out here in the corner X_x
8	<Browndog>	☺
9		Welcome! Oh, I'm the first one here! Coolness! SO you draw
10		do ya? That's great! But don't put yourself down! I'm sure

11   your art isn't as bad as you claim it is! After all an artist is their

12   own worst critic! I should know! My drawing sucks! And by

13   saying this I am being TOTALLY serious! I can only draw

14   what I see. No imagination whatsoever! That is something I

15   save for writing ☺

16   But where are my manners? Have an Oreo and a devilled egg!

17   (not together, mind ya!) Welcome aboard and you better get a

18   vaccination for craziness because it spreads faster than wild fire

19   around here!

20 <Warrior>   WELCOME!! *super wuggle*

21   Wouldja like an Inspiration Duck? They don't bite, but they

22   DO throw themselves repeatedly in your forehead in an attempt

23   to get you inspired (hmmm ... maybe THAT'S why I have so

24   many headaches ...?)!! =D

25   Welcome, welcome, welcome. Have fun, and I promise I won't

26   bite unless you make the Clown too often or think that series 3

27   is horrible. XO

28 <Lina>   Hiya, come sit with me on ma (blue, the red one is taken in the

29   other thread) couch. Sorry no space fodder in the blue couch,

30   just a load of junkfood. So help ya self and feel welcome!

31 <Sprite>   HIIIIIIIIIIIIIIIIIIIIII!!!!!!!!!!!!!!!!!!!!!!!!!!!!!!!!!!!

32   ... uh, yeah ... hehe ...

33   I'm pretty friendly to everyone ... except if you're an avid series

34   4 fan and insist on taking it everywhere you go ... then I don't

35   think I'll like you that much ...

36   But other than that welcome!!!!!!!!

37   Oh yeah, read the rules of the board … it'll help.

38   And NO I'm not taking anyone's 'rule-mentioning' job! Just a

39   simple precaution, that's all! See ya around!

40   *<Kezia>*   Hey there, welcome to the board … uh, here have a pretzel.

41   Welcome!!!

42   *<Irene>*   <u><<SO you draw do ya? That's great! But don't put yourself</u>

43   <u>down! I'm sure your art isn't as bad as you claim it is!</u>

44   <u>After all an artist is their own worst critic!>></u>

45   Greenhorn artists are really good at making you feel like a very

46   crappy artist, y'know? @_@ I'll post some stuff later and let

47   you judge …

48   <u><<Wouldja like an Inspiration Duck? They don't bite, but</u>

49   <u>they DO throw themselves repeatedly in your forehead in</u>

50   <u>an attempt to get you inspired (hmmm … maybe THAT'S</u>

51   <u>why I have so many headaches …?)!! =D>></u>

52   … Inspiration … Duck …? I think I'll stick to my comic book for

53   inspiration ˜;

54   <u><<Welcome, welcome, welcome. Have fun, and I promise I</u>

55   <u>won't bite unless you make the Clown too often or think</u>

56   <u>that series 3 is horrible. XO>></u>

57   Eh, I'm not really fond of that series, sorry ˜; I promise I won't

58   bite you either. ☺

59   And yeah, I read the rules. I'm a moderator elsewhere, so I

60   know it's annoying if people don't read rules first XD

61   Thanks for all the welcomes, and all, I'll come out of my corner

62		now ^_^;
63	<Lou>	Hey, welcome to the board!
64		*looks around* ... well no one's officially said it yet, so I guess I
65		get to do my job. ^
66		[lecture]
67		Please read the rules and regs for the board, and read the stuff
68		at the top of the board. It'll make everyone's lives much easier.
69		^_^
70		[/lecture]
71		<u><<And yeah, I read the rules. I'm a moderator elsewhere, so</u>
72		<u>I know it's annoying if people don't rules first XD>></u>
73		I feel your pain
74	<Rainbow>	HI!!!!!!!!
75		Have a cookie. *read the 'yep the newbie speaks!' thread for
76		info on the cookies, I'm getting sick of writing it over and over
77		and over again ...*
78		Welcome to the forum, and I want to see some of your artwork
79		up here pretty soon, y'hear? Oh and join the Quilted Couch
80		Club, just 'cuz it's fun as hell. ^_^
81	<Jody>	Welcome to the place where we celebrate the wonderful
82		addiction of JJ ☺ I am completely obsessed with series 1 ...
83		Any fics/fanart of that nature will made me very contented,
84		although I can appreciate any of the series (I've been corrupted
85		by several other writers here ... I'm no longer a purist ... lol!).
86		Glad you finally registered, and I hope to see ya 'round ☺
87	<Queen Bea>	New meat!!

88		*Clooney kicks her in the shin*
89		I mean, Newbie! ^_^
90		Welcome to the board!! And if you post any series 1 art here
91		i'll give you a footrub and some more gum! *hands her gum*
92		what flavor do you perfer? ^_^ Don't be shy! (like I am in RL
93		☺ post and reply! Or reply and post … whatever ^_^;
94	*<Dubstar>*	Hiya. *hands a pack of strawberry gum* Enjoy!
95	*<Rainbow>*	<<I've been corrupted by several other writers here … I'm
96		no longer a purist … lol!>>
97		*bows* I can take no credit in that corruption, but I would like
98		to think that Jody's corruption has been a joint effort of
99		everyone on the board. Give yourselves a hand!
100	*<Mack>*	Whoa! Almost missed a newbie thread! *tosses a tin of caramel
101		and pecan popcorn* hehe. With all the goodies ppl have given,
102		you've got quite a spread before you enit?
103		Ooh. Artiste no less! What's your fav series? I'm looking
104		forward to seeing some of your stuff! ☺
105	*<Unruly spirit>*	*rolls out welcome banner*
106		Cool another artist! Welcome you wont see me around much I
107		mostly lurk but I pop up now and again:D have fun watch out
108		for the crazyness!
109	*<Clodhopper>*	Hiya ^_^
110		*waves in greetings*
111		glad you decided to join the rest of us, don't worry … most of us
112		don't bite … well … unless asked nicely *cackles till get's
113		whapped upside head by Clooney with her work list/shedual*
114		Eep!

115		Okay! Gotta go! Welcome!!!
116	*<Folkhero>*	Irene, so glad to see we've another person here in the forum.
117		Don't worry, I'm a newbie too ... (as you can see, from the
118		'Yup the newbie speaks!' string) Anywho ...
119		I hope I get see lots of your fanart. Personally I can't wait! ^_^

Following the previous section on membership categorisation, we note that one method by which participants invoke relevant categories is by naming them, and this occurs in lines 75, 89, 100 and 117, where the term 'newbie' is explicitly invoked. The category 'newbie' relevantly implies a second, 'regular', and thus the 'standardised relational pair' of 'newbie–regular' is strongly suggested, though never explicitly named. Instead, other members categorise themselves collectively, drawing attention to their 'regular' identity in formulations of established membership (for example, 'welcome aboard!', 'welcome to the board/the forum', 'welcome to the place where we celebrate . . .', 'a joint effort of everyone on the board', 'glad you decided to join the rest of us, don't worry . . . most of us don't bite . . .').

The 'newbie's' (Irene) opening turn begins a thread in which she 'comes out' or 'delurks'. Her turn is typical of a widely observed phenomenon that newbies 'do' being cautious (for example, 'I've been lurking here a while now'). What is also notable is the way in which Irene invokes activities of the 'regular' or expert ('making topics'; 'writing fics'; 'reading noir schtuffs'; 'drawing fanart') in order to express her own imperfect but aspiring incumbency of this category ('I suck at making topics like this'; 'I can't write fics that well'; 'if you wanna call my crap art that is').

Newbie identity and politeness

Irene's self-deprecating behaviour can be explained neatly within the framework of Brown and Levinson's (1987) *Politeness Theory*. Brown and Levinson devised their theory as a 'universal' explanation of both anthropological and linguistic phenomena: namely the notion that members of society attempt to preserve their self and others' esteem or 'face' (a term borrowed from Goffman 1967) in interaction. Brown and Levinson argue that we have both 'positive' and 'negative' face wants. 'Positive face' refers to our desire to be approved of and liked, whilst 'negative face' refers to our need to protect our space, territory and autonomy. 'Face threatening acts' are those that threaten our positive face wants, and include criticisms, challenges and insults. 'Face threatening acts' can also threaten our negative face, for example requests, demands, invitations and questions. All of these are routine forms of behaviour that are difficult to avoid in daily social life. Apologies or expressions of thanks are acts that threaten our own face. Interaction is therefore a constant balancing act between protecting our own face and the face of others.

Brown and Levinson thus theorise *politeness* as a phenomenon that *mitigates* the damage we do in issuing face threatening acts. Positive politeness includes expressions of solidarity, praise, flattery, intimacy and empathy (for example, informal language, terms of endearment, humour, seeking agreement, giving 'gifts', both literal and metaphorical) whilst negative politeness usually involves some form of indirectness and deference (that is, the more conventional sense of 'politeness') and may involve giving hints, low modality ('Could you possibly?'), pessimism ('I don't suppose'), apologies, and the minimisation of the imposition (I've just got a small favour'). Whilst positive politeness may mitigate a face threatening act (for example, a compliment prior to asking a favour), it can also function autonomously simply to foster solidarity with others. Negative politeness however, always has a mitigating function.

In the data above, Irene (lines 1–7) employs markers of negative politeness, emphasising social distance, respect to the interlocutor and mitigation of any possible inconvenience or imposition her presence on the board may have caused. She emphasises her 'novice' status ('I'm new', line 1), her lack of ability ('I can't write fics that well', 'I suck at making topics like this', 'my crap art', lines 4–5), her nervousness ('chicken out', the emoticons 'o_O', 'X_x', and '^_^;' meaning respectively a nervous tic, the writer's final exhalation and fear, lines 6–7) and her respect towards regulars ('excuse me', line 7). Her display of negative politeness is suggestive of a social order in which 'newbies' lack status and must 'earn' it from regulars on the board, who may be hostile. Her contributions include vagueness and low *modality* ('and stuff', 'can't . . . that well', lines 1, 4), a common feature of negative politeness which mitigates the otherwise attention-grabbing proclamation of being a new member and active artist. She also uses positive politeness in the form of colloquial language ('suck', 'crap', 'chicken out', lines 2–7), which operates to bolster solidarity with other members.

In this way, Irene exhibits negative politeness: she actively demonstrates a reluctance to enter the virtual 'space' of the other members. By contrast, other members of the board also conform to the moral and social order of the forum by welcoming the 'newbie' in effusive and generous terms, often offering virtual 'gifts' such as popcorn, sweets and biscuits. Indeed, in an example from the soap opera message board, the member draws attention to the *ritual* quality of this behaviour ('Hello. It is tradition for you to have your first drink free – so what is your poison?').

This 'positive politeness' behaviour is a means of enhancing solidarity and attending to the 'face' of others through gifts, compliments, humour and friendship, and a common feature of virtual communities (Harrison 2000). Markers of positive politeness are most explicit in the offer of 'gifts': 'where are my manners? Have an Oreo and a devilled egg! . . . Welcome aboard' (lines 16–17), 'Hiya, come sit with me on ma (blue, the red one is taken in the other thread) couch. Sorry no spacefodder in the blue couch, just a load of junkfood. So help ya self and feel welcome!' (lines 28–30), 'Hey there, welcome to the board . . . uh have a pretzel. Welcome!!!' (lines 40–1), 'Have a cookie' (line 75), '*hands her gum* what flavor do you perfer?' (lines 91–2), 'Hiya. *hands a pack of strawberry gum* Enjoy!' (line 94), 'Whoa! Almost missed a newbie thread! *tosses a tin of caramel and pecan popcorn*' (lines 100–1), and '*rolls out welcome banner*' (line 105).

But positive politeness is also apparent in the performative 'Welcome!', the colloquial language ('Coolness', line 9), the ingroup references ('space-fodder', line 29), the echoic parallelism ('My drawing sucks!', line 12) of a turn following the 'newbie's' admission that 'I suck at making topics like this' (line 2), the 'smiley' emoticons, the exclamation marks, flattery ('I'm looking forward to seeing some of your stuff', lines 103–4) and humour ('a vaccination for craziness', lines 17–18). The ritual, repetitive and unanimous responses of existing members to the 'newbie' establishes further the norms of the group and its expectation of the responsibilities and obligations attached to different members.

So far we have seen that in the phenomenon of a 'newbie' initiation onto a CMC forum, acceptable conversational behaviour of the 'newbie' includes the enactment of negative politeness, and for the 'regular', the enactment of positive politeness. However, a further set of activities of the 'regular' can also be observed. These comprise the articulation of status, ingroup knowledge, expertise, exclusivity and elevated difference from the newbie, partly by consolidating their position as an ingroup: 'you better get a vaccination for craziness because it spreads faster than wildfire around here!' (lines 17–19), 'I'm pretty friendly to everyone . . . except if you're an avid series 4 fan' (lines 33–4), 'Oh yeah, read the rules of the board . . . it'll help' (line 37), '*read the "yep the newbie speaks!" thread for info on the cookies, I'm getting sick of writing it over and over and over again . . .*' (lines 75–7), 'New meat!!*Clooney kicks her in the shin* I mean Newbie' (lines 87–9), and 'don't worry . . . most of us don't bite . . . well . . . unless asked nicely *cackles till gets whapped upside head by Clooney*' (lines 111–12).

In lines 33–4 and 111–12, conditions are attached to the welcomes which ensure that the newbie conforms to the board's rules, and whilst in line 37 the advice is shown to benefit the newbie ('it'll help'), in the other examples the conditions are explicitly oriented to the convenience or preferences of the regular. The conditional clauses of 'well . . . unless asked nicely' and 'except if you're an avid series 4 fan', mitigate the positive politeness gifted in the first clause and the examples in line 37 and 75–7 assert an implicit hierarchy by the use of commands ('read the rules', 'read the . . . thread'). Lines 87–9 invoke an association of 'newbie' with an object for the board to toy with, torment or consume. However, these lines (along with 111–12), though amusingly subversive, and undoubtedly functioning as a form of display by the users, also embed an appeal to the proper moral and politeness obligations of the board to 'newbies' by a virtual, performative enactment of the violent sanctions meted out to those not observing these norms ('*Clooney kicks her in the shins*', '*cackles till gets whapped upside head by Clooney*'). This might be analysed as an example of 'double voicing' whereby the user is able to express two levels of moral accountability: one expressing the 'correct', generous and protective obligations of regulars towards 'newbies' (in this case embodied in a separate persona, 'Clooney'), and the other, an appeal to the existing solidarity, exclusiveness, integrity and status of regular members of the board, which must be defended at all costs, an observation also made by Cherny (1999) about hostility to 'newbies' in her ethnographic analysis of a MUD.

The response of the 'newbie', Irene, to these mitigated, conditional welcomes and displays of expertise, knowledge and membership is to invoke her *own* expertise both as someone familiar with and opinionated about the subject matter discussed on the board ('Eh, I'm not really fond of that series, sorry', line 57), and as one occupying a position of authority (and thus familiar with the normative etiquette) on similar boards ('And yeah, I read the rules. I'm a moderator elsewhere, so I know it's annoying if people don't read rules first', lines 59–60). Furthermore, Irene challenges the authority of established members by invoking her own authority to 'bite' back ('I promise I won't bite you either', lines 57–8), albeit mitigated by the irony-indexing emoticon ('☺'). She uses message intercalation to simulate a synchronous dialogue with one particular user at a time (lines 42–4, 48–51, 54–6), thus enhancing the intimacy and directness of the 'exchange' despite the fact that this is multi-party talk, and her rejection of offers (for example, the virtual 'Inspiration Duck', line 21) is mitigated ('I think I'll stick to my comic book for inspiration', lines 52–3). In politeness terms, this constitutes a face threatening act.

Irene's display of 'counter challenges' to the advice, edicts and gifts of regular members, as well as her positive acknowledgement of their generosity, arguably represents a ritualistic initiation into the membership of the virtual community. To graduate from 'newbie' to 'regular', she must exhibit the authority, exclusive knowledge and shared humour attached to the category, 'regular'. Her passage safe through this process, she is then able to relinquish her self-consciously marginal, 'newbie' status: 'Thanks for all the welcomes, and all, I'll come out of my corner now ^_^;' (lines 61–2).

This analysis of politeness work in the initiation of a 'newbie' to the board reveals how the moral and social order of the forum is jointly accomplished. Expectations about the roles of 'newbie' and 'regular' are inscribed in the talk and users formulate their turns with a ritual appeal to particular attributes. 'Newbies' must be initially deferential and self-effacing and 'regulars' must be generous but uphold the rules, standards and integrity of the board. For a 'newbie' to graduate to 'regular' they must display elements of the same humour, knowledge and expertise that normatively graces the board, and they may even 'challenge' the authority of regulars. With these rituals successfully observed, the order of the board is maintained, and with it, a sense of community.

CONCLUSION

Our analysis of message board interaction demonstrates that identity is a discursive accomplishment: a crucial and relevant phenomenon to which participants explicitly orient. The 'virtuality' of the medium (in the sense that participants do not meet face-to-face) emerges in the specific identity practice of 'gifting' as a way of negotiating the potentially fraught circumstances of a new member joining the group. We observed that 'gifting' took on an especially 'literal' and ritual character involving 'virtual' objects. A second practice in this virtual environment was the way users positioned themselves and each other as 'mods' and 'ordinary users', and 'newbies' and 'regulars', each with different and identity-relevant obligations and attributes.

This leads us back to the question posed at the start of this chapter: is 'virtual identity' (the identities we inhabit and perform online) a viable concept, and how confident can we be that it represents something distinct from 'real-life' (offline) identities? In our opening sections, we surveyed a body of research which characterised cyberspace as a location for the enactment of identities more unstable, creative, liberatory and radical in their mutability than 'real life' (RL) identities could ever hope to be. However, one of the key findings of this chapter was that virtual worlds strive to *recreate* conditions of RL rather than forge radically new ways of conceiving of relations, communities and identity. Furthermore, the virtual nature of the CMC *medium* – particularly the absence of audiovisual context, and the differing pragmatic norms – means that identity work is paradoxically often more rigorously policed and carefully delineated (via, for instance FAQs, mods, the 'toading' function) than offline communication would ever be. This challenges the prediction that virtual identity is somehow 'freer' than RL identity. Arguably, the early, utopian ideals of a transformative medium have been replaced with recognition that the Internet largely facilitates everyday kinds of communication but via a new technological medium. In this sense, we might be reluctant to isolate it as a discrete phenomenon.

Alternatively, 'virtual identity' *is* identity work performed and enacted online. In this sense, it is a unique product of the linguistic qualities and technological properties of CMC. Certain features of CMC, particularly those involving spatial metaphors and deixis, testify to its uniquely 'speech-in-a-written-mode' status. And it is precisely *mode*, and the delicate negotiation between the spoken and written, with the attendant constraints of the latter conflicting with the demands of the former, that most affects and determines issues of identity online. Moreover, mode crucially links the public (non space-bound, anonymous) with the private, encouraging what O'Sullivan, Hunt and Lippert (2004) term 'mediated immediacy' – a mode of communication linked to the hyperpersonal yet synthetic properties of a medium which cultivates psychological closeness, self-disclosure and similarity in spite of (or perhaps because of) its often anonymous and public status.

Finally, these and earlier observations about the properties of online modes suggest that what the 'virtual-ness' of CMC *does* promote is an experimental, resourceful creativity with *language* and other communicative modes (for example, hypertext). At one level, this resourcefulness strives pragmatically to facilitate conventional identity work in the face of the constraints and limitations of the mode. At another, in the disembodied, textual realm of cyberspace, language takes on an especially playful, poetic, metatextual character in comparison to its more referential functions in RL. And in this scenario, identity might be thought to be subordinated to – or a mere by-product of – the substance, the materiality of the flat, two-dimensional forms of language on the screen. At this point, we might be tempted to shift our prediction about the radical potential of virtuality to lie, not in its identity formulations as many assumed, but rather in the materiality of its *language forms*.

References

Abell, J., Stokoe, E. H. and Billig, M. (2000), 'Narrative and the discursive (re)construction of events', in M. Andrews, S. Day Sclater, C. Squire and A. Treacher (eds), *Lines of Narrative: Psychosocial Perspectives*, London: Routledge.

Agar, M. (1985), 'Institutional discourse', *Text* 5 (3), 147–68.

Agnew J. A. and Corbridge, S. (1995), 'The territorial trap', in *Mastering Space: Hegemony, Territory and International Political Economy*, London: Routledge.

Aguilar, M. A. (2002), 'Identity and daily space in two municipalities in Mexico City', *Environment and Behaviour* 34 (1), 111–21.

Allport, G. W. [1954] (1979), *The Nature of Prejudice*, Reading, MA: Addison Wesley.

Althusser, L. (1971), 'Ideology and ideological state apparatuses', in L. Althusser (ed.), *Lenin and Philosophy and Other Essays*, London: New Left Books.

Ainley, R. (ed.) (1998), *New Frontiers of Space, Bodies and Gender*, London: Routledge.

Anderson, B. (1983), *Imagined Communities*, London: Verso.

Andrews, M. and Talbot, M. (eds) (2000), *All the World and her Husband: Women in Twentieth-Century Consumer Culture*, London: Cassell.

Antaki, C. (1995), 'Conversation analysis and social psychology', *BPS Social Psychology Section Newsletter* 32, 21–4.

Antaki, C. (1998), 'Identity ascriptions in their time and place', in C. Antaki and S. Widdicombe (eds), *Identities in Talk*, London: Sage.

Antaki, C. (2002), 'Personalised revision of "failed" questions', *Discourse Studies* 4 (4), 411–28.

Antaki, C. (2003), *Analysing Talk in Interaction: A Course for the University of Southern Denmark, Odense*, available online: http://www.staff.lboro.ac.uk/~ssca1/home.htm

Antaki, C., Condor, S. and Levine, M. (1996), 'Social identities in talk: Speakers' own orientations', *British Journal of Social Psychology* 35, 473–92.

Antaki, C. and Widdicombe, S. (eds) (1998a), *Identities in Talk*, London: Sage.

Antaki, C. and Widdicombe, S. (1998b), 'Identity as an achievement and as a tool', in C. Antaki and S. Widdicombe (eds), *Identities in Talk*, London: Sage.

Atkinson, J. M. and Drew, P. (1979), *Order in Court: The Organization of Verbal Interaction in Judicial Settings*, London: Macmillan.

Austin, J. L. (1962), *How to Do Things with Words*, Oxford: Clarendon Press.

Baker, C. D. (2004), 'Membership categorization and interview accounts', in

D. Silverman (ed.), *Qualitative Research: Theory, Method and Practice*, 2nd edn, London: Sage.

Baker, P. (2003), 'No effeminates please: A corpus-based analysis of masculinity via personal adverts in *Gay News/Times* 1973–2000', in B. Benwell (ed.), *Masculinity and Men's Lifestyle Magazines*, Oxford: Blackwell.

Bakhtin, M. (1986), *Speech Genres and Other Late Essays*, Austin, TX: Texas University Press.

Ballaster, R., Beetham, M., Frazer, E. and Hebron, S. (1991), *Women's Worlds: Ideology, Femininity and the Woman's Magazine*, London: Macmillan.

Bamberg, M. (2004), 'Positioning with Davie Hogan: Stories, tellings, and identities', in C. Daiute and C. Lightfoot (eds), *Narrative Analysis: Studying the Development of Individuals in Society*, London: Sage.

Barker, C. and Galasiński, D. (2001), *Cultural Studies and Discourse Analysis: A Dialogue on Language and Identity*, London: Sage.

Barnes, R. (2000), *Losing Ground: Locational Formulations in Argumentation over New Travellers*, unpublished Ph.D. thesis, University of Plymouth.

Barnes, S. (2003), *Computer-Mediated Communication: Human-to-Human Communication across the Internet*, Boston, MA: Allyn and Bacon.

Baron, N. (2004), 'See you online: Gender issues in college student use of instant messaging', *Journal of Language and Social Psychology* 23 (4), 397–423.

Barthes, R. (1977), *Image, Music, Text*, London: Fontana.

Baudrillard, J. (1988), 'Simulacra and simulations', in M. Poster (ed.), *Selected Writings*, Cambridge: Polity Press.

Baudrillard, J. (1998), *The Consumer Society: Myth and Structures*, trans. C. Turner and intro. G. Ritzer, London: Sage.

Bauer, M. W. and Gaskell, G. (eds) (2000), *Qualitative Researching with Text, Image and Sound*, London: Sage.

Bauman, Z. (1993), *Postmodern Ethics*, Blackwell. Oxford.

Bauman, Z. (2004), *Identity*, Cambridge: Polity Press.

Baym, N. (1993), 'Interpreting soap operas and creating community: Inside a computer-mediated fan culture', *Journal of Folklore Research* 30, 143–76.

Baym, N. (1995), 'The performance of humour in computer-mediated communication', *Journal of Computer Mediated Communcation* 1 (2), available online at http://jcmc.indiana.edu/vol1/issue2/baym.html

Baym, N. (1998), 'The emergence of an on-line community', in S. Jones (ed.), *Cybersociety 2.0: Revisiting Computer-Mediated Communication and Community*, Thousand Oaks, CA: Sage.

Beck, U. (1992), *Risk Society: Towards a New Modernity*, London: Sage.

Beetham, M. (1996), *A Magazine of her Own?: Domesticity and Desire in the Woman's Magazine, 1800–1914*, London: Routledge.

Bell, D. (2000), 'Cybercultures reader: A user's guide', in D. Bell and B. Kennedy (eds), *The Cybercultures Reader*, London: Routledge.

Bell, D. and Kennedy, B. (2000), *The Cybercultures Reader*, London: Routledge.

Benedikt, M. (2000), 'Cyberspace: First steps', in D. Bell and B. Kennedy (eds), *The Cybercultures Reader*, London: Routledge.

Benwell, B. (1996), *The Discourse of University Tutorials*, unpublished Ph.D. thesis, University of Nottingham.

Benwell, B. (2002), 'Is there anything "new" about these lads? The textual and visual construction of masculinity in men's magazines', in L. Litosseliti and

J. Sunderland (eds), *Gender Identity and Discourse Analysis*, Amsterdam: John Benjamins.

Benwell, B. (2004), 'Ironic discourse: Evasive masculinity in British men's lifestyle magazines', *Men and Masculinities* 7 (1), 3–21.

Benwell, B. (2005), ' "Lucky this is anonymous" – Ethnographies of reception in men's magazines: a "textual culture" approach', *Discourse and Society* 16 (2), 147–72.

Benwell, B. M. and Stokoe, E. H. (2002), 'Constructing discussion tasks in university tutorials: Shifting dynamics and identities', *Discourse Studies* 4 (4), 429–53.

Benwell, B. M. and Stokoe, E. H. (2004), 'University students resisting academic identity', in P. Seedhouse and K. Richards (eds), *Applying Conversation Analysis*, Cambridge: Cambridge University Press.

Bersani, L. (1995), *Homos*, Cambridge, MA: Harvard University Press.

Bertelsen, E. (1998), 'Ads and amnesia: Black advertising in the new South Africa', in S. Nuttall and C. Coetzee (eds), *Negotiating the Past: The Making of Memory in South Africa*, Cape Town: Oxford University Press.

Bhabha, H. (1994), *The location of Culture*, London: Routledge.

Bhatia, V. (1993), *Analysing Genre: Language Use in Professional Settings*, London: Longman.

Billig, M. (1987), *Arguing and Thinking: A Rhetorical Approach to Social Psychology*, Cambridge: Cambridge University Press.

Billig, M. (1995), *Banal Nationalism*, London: Sage.

Billig, M. (1999a), 'Whose terms? Whose ordinariness? Rhetoric and ideology in Conversation Analysis', *Discourse and Society* 10 (4), 543–58.

Billig, M. (1999b), 'Conversation analysis and the claims of naivety', *Discourse and Society* 10 (4), 572–6.

Billig, M. (2005), *Lacan's Misuse of Psychology: Evidence, Rhetoric and the Mirror Stage*, unpublished ms., Loughborough University.

Blumer, H. (1969), *Symbolic Interactionism: Perspective and Method*, Englewood Cliffs, NJ: Prentice-Hall.

Bourdieu, P. (1984), *Distinction: A Social Critique of the Judgement of Taste*, London: Routledge.

Bowlby, S., Gregory, S. and McKie, L. (1997), 'Doing home: Patriarchy, caring and space', *Women's Studies International Forum* 20 (2), 343–50.

Branwyn, G. (2000), 'Compu–sex: Erotica for cybernauts', in D. Bell and B. Kennedy (eds), *The Cybercultures Reader*, London: Routledge.

Brenkman, J. (1994), *Straight, Male, Modern: Cultural Critique of Psychoanalysis*, London: Routledge.

Brockmeier, J. and Carbaugh, A. (eds) (2001), *Narrative and Identity: Studies in Autobiography, Self and Culture*, Amsterdam: John Benjamins.

Brooker, P. (1999), *Concise Glossary of Cultural Theory*, London: Hodder Arnold.

Brown, R. (2000), 'Social identity theory: Past achievements, current problems and future challenges', *European Journal of Social Psychology* 30, 745–78.

Brown, P. and Levinson, S. (1987), *Politeness: Some Universals in Language Usage*, Cambridge: Cambridge University Press.

Bruner, J. (1990), *Acts of Meaning*, Cambridge, MA: Harvard University Press.

Bucholtz, M. (1999), 'Purchasing power: The gender and class imaginary on the shopping channel', in M. Bucholtz, A. C. Liang and L. A. Hutton (eds), *Reinventing Identities: The Gendered Self in Discourse*, Oxford: Oxford University Press.

Bucholtz, M. (2003), 'Theories of discourse as theories of gender: Discourse analysis in language and gender studies', in J. Holmes and M. Meyerhoff (eds), *The Handbook of Language and Gender*, Oxford: Blackwell.

Bucholtz, M. and Hall, K. (2005), 'Identity and interaction: A sociolinguistic cultural approach', *Discourse Studies* 7 (4–5), 585–614.

Bucholtz, M., Liang, A. C. and Sutton, L. A. (eds) (1999), *Reinventing Identities: The Gendered Self in Discourse*, Oxford: Oxford University Press.

Bülow, P. H. (2004), 'Sharing experiences of contested illness by storytelling', *Discourse and Society* 15 (1), 33–53.

Bülow, P. H. and Hydén, L-H. (2003), 'In dialogue with time: Identity and illness in narratives about chronic fatigue', *Narrative Inquiry* 13 (1), 71–97.

Butler, J. (1990), *Gender Trouble: Feminism and the Subversion of Identity*, New York: Routledge.

Butler, J. (1997), *The Psychic Life of Power: Theories in Subjection*, Stanford, CA: Stanford University Press.

Buttny, R. (1993), *Social Accountability in Communication*, London: Sage.

Button, G. (1991), 'Introduction: Ethnomethodology and the foundational respecification of the human sciences', in G. Button (ed.), *Ethnomethodology and the Human Sciences*, Cambridge: Cambridge University Press.

Button, G. and Sharrock, W. (2003), 'A disagreement over agreement and consensus in constructionist sociology', in M. Lynch and W. Sharrock (eds), *Harold Garfinkel* (Sage Masters in Modern Social Thought Series), London: Sage.

Cameron. D. (1997), 'Demythologizing sociolinguistics', in N. Coupland and A. Jaworski (eds), *Sociolinguistics: A Coursebook and Reader*, Basingstoke: Macmillan.

Cameron, D. (2000), *Good to Talk? Living and Working in a Communication Culture*, London: Sage.

Cameron, D. and Kulick, D. (2003), *Language and Sexuality*, Cambridge: Cambridge University Press.

Campbell, C. (1987), *The Romantic Ethic and the Spirit of Modern Consumerism*, Oxford: Blackwell.

Carbaugh, D. (1996), *Situating Selves: The Communication of Social Identities in American Scenes*, New York: State University of New York Press.

Carlin, A. (2003), 'Observation and membership categorization: Recognizing "normal appearances" in public space', *Journal of Mundane Behavior* 4 (1), available online at http://www.mundanebehavior.org/index.htm

Carter, R. and McCarthy, M. (1997), *Exploring Spoken English*, Cambridge: Cambridge University Press.

Chamberlyne, P., Bornat, J. and Wengraf, T. (2000), *The Turn to Biographical Methods in Social Science*, London: Routledge.

Cherny, L. (1999), *Conversation and Community: Chat in a Virtual World*, Stanford, CA: CSLI Publications.

Chisholm, M. and Smith, D. M. (eds) (1990), *Shared Space, Divided Space: Essays on Conflict and Territorial Organization*, London: Unwin Hyman.

Chouliaraki, L. and Fairclough, N. (1999), *Discourse and Late Modernity*, Edinburgh: Edinburgh University Press.

Christie, F. (2004), 'Authority and its role in the pedagogic relationship of schooling', in L. Young and C. Harrison (eds), *Systemic Functional Linguistics and Critical Discourse Analysis*, London: Continuum.

Churchman, A. (2000), 'Women and the environment: Questioned and unquestioned

Assumptions', in S. Wapner, J. Demick, T. Yamamoto, H. Minami and C. T. Yamamoto (eds), *Theoretical Perspectives in Environment-Behaviour Research*, London: Plenum.

Cicourel, A. (1992), 'The interpenetration of communicative contexts: Examples from medical encounters', in A. Duranti and C. Goodwin (eds), *Rethinking Context: Language as an Interactive Phenomenon*, Cambridge: Cambridge University Press.

Clayman, S. (1992), 'Footing in the achievement of neutrality: The case of news interview discourse', in P. Drew and J. Heritage (eds), *Talk at Work. Interaction in Institutional Settings*, Cambridge: Cambridge University Press.

Coates, J. (1996), *Women Talk*, Oxford: Blackwell.

Coates, J. (1997), 'Women's friendships, women's talk', in R. Wodak (ed.), *Gender and Discourse*, London: Sage.

Coates, J. (1999), 'Changing femininities: The talk of teenage girls', in M. Bucholtz, A. C. Liang and L. A. Sutton (eds), *Reinventing Identities: The Gendered Self in Discourse*, Oxford: Oxford University Press.

Coates, J. (2003), *Men Talk*, Oxford: Blackwell.

Coates, J. (2004), *Women, Men and Language*, 3rd edn, London: Longman.

Cohen, S. (2002), *Folk Devils and Moral Panics*, London: Routledge.

Collins, D. (2005), 'Identity, mobility, and urban place-making: Exploring gay life in Manila', *Gender and Society* 19 (2), 180–98.

Condor, S. (2000), 'Pride and prejudice: Identity management in English people's talk about "this country" ', *Discourse and Society* 11 (2), 163–93.

Corrigan, P. (1997), *The Sociology of Consumption: An Introduction*, London: Sage.

Cortazzi, M. (2001), 'Narrative analysis in ethnography', in P. Atkinson, A. Coffey, S. Delamont, J. Lofland and L. Lofland (eds), *Handbook of Ethnography*, London: Sage.

Couper-Kuhlen, E. and Selting, M. (eds) (1996), *Prosody in Conversation: Interactional Studies*, Cambridge: Cambridge University Press.

Coupland, J. (1996), 'Dating advertisements: Discourses of the commodified self ', *Discourse and Society* 7 (2), 187–202.

Coupland, J. (2003), 'Ageist ideology and discourses of control in skincare product marketing', in J. Coupland and R. Gwyn (eds), *Discourse, the Body and Identity*, London: Palgrave Macmillan.

Coupland, J. and Gwyn, R. (eds) (2003), *Discourse, the Body and Identity*, London: Palgrave Macmillan.

Coupland, N. and Nussbaum, J. F. (eds) (1993), *Discourse and Lifespan Identity*, London and Beverly Hills, CA: Sage.

Crabtree, A. (2000), 'Remarks on the social organization of space', *Journal of Mundane Behavior* 1 (1), available online at http://www.mundanebehavior.org/index.htm

Craib, I. (2000), 'Narratives as bad faith', in M. Andrews, S. Day Sclater, C. Squire and A. Treacher (eds), *Lines of Narrative: Psychosocial Perspectives*, London: Routledge.

Cresswell, T. (1996), *In Place/Out of Place*, Minneapolis, MN: University of Minnesota Press.

Crossley, M. L. (2000), 'Narrative psychology, trauma and the study of self/identity', *Theory and Psychology* 10 (4), 527–46.

Crossley, M. L. (2003a), ' "Let me explain": Narrative emplotment and one patient's experience of oral cancer', *Social Science and Medicine* 56 (3), 439–48.

Crossley, M. L. (2003b), 'Formulating narrative psychology: The limitations of contemporary social constructionism', *Narrative Inquiry* 13 (2), 287–300.

Crouch, D. (1994), 'Home, escape and identity: Rural cultures and sustainable tourism', *Journal of Sustainable Tourism* 2 (1–2), 93–101.

Crystal, D. (2001), *Language and the Internet*, Cambridge: Cambridge University Press.

Curl, T. (2005), 'Practices in other-initiated repair resolution: The phonetic differentiation of "repetitions"', *Discourse Processes* 39 (1), 1–43.

Daiute, C. and Lightfoot, C. (eds) (2004), *Narrative Analysis: Studying the Development of Individuals in Society*, London: Sage.

Daly, M. (1978), *Gyn-ecology: The Metaethics of Radical Feminism*, Boston, MA: Houghton Mifflin.

Danet, B., Ruedenberg-Wright, L. and Rosenbaum-Tamari, Y. (1997), '"Hmmm . . . where's that smoke coming from?" Writing, play and performance on Internet Relay Chat', *Journal of Computer Mediated Communication* 2 (4), available online at http://jcmc.indiana.edu/vol2/issue4/danet.html

Dann, G. (1999), 'Writing out the tourist in space and time', *Annals of Tourism Research* 26 (1): 159–87.

Davies, B. and Harré, R. (1990), 'Positioning: The discursive production of selves', *Journal for the Theory of Social Behaviour* 20, 43–63.

Day Sclater, S. (2003), 'What is the subject?', *Narrative Inquiry* 13 (2), 317–30.

de Certeau, M. (1984), *The Practice of Everyday Life*, Berkeley, CA: University of California Press.

de Fina, A. (2003), *Identity in Narrative: A Study of Immigrant Discourse*, Amsterdam: John Benjamins.

Deleuze, G. and Guattari, F. (1983), *Anti-Oedipus: Capitalism and Schizophrenia*, trans. Brian Massumi, Minneapolis: University of Minnesota Press.

Delin, J. (2000), *The Language of Everyday Life*, London: Sage.

Denzin, N. K. (2000), 'Foreword', in M. Andrews, S. Day Sclater, C. Squire and A. Treacher (eds), *Lines of Narrative: Psychosocial Perspectives*, London: Routledge.

Derrida, J. (1976), *Of Grammatology*, Baltimore, MD: Johns Hopkins University Press.

de Saussure, F. (1960), *Course in General Linguistics*, ed. C. Bally and A. Sechehaye, trans. W. Baskin, London: Peter Owen.

Dibbell, J. (1999), 'A rape in cyberspace; or how an evil clown, a Haitian trickster spirit, two wizards, and a cast of dozens turned a database into a society', in P. Ludlow (ed.), *High Noon on the Electronic Frontier: Conceptual Issues in Cyberspace*, Cambridge, MA: MIT Press.

Dickerson, P. (2000), '"But I'm different to them": Constructing contrasts between self and others in talk-in-interaction', *British Journal of Social Psychology* 39 (3), 381–98.

Dixon, J. (2005), Homepage, available online: www.psych.lancs.ac.uk/people/JohnDixon.html

Dixon, J. and Durrheim, K. (2000), 'Displacing place-identity: A discursive approach to locating self and other', *British Journal of Social Psychology* 39 (1), 27–44.

Dixon, J. A. and Durrheim, K. (2003), 'Contact and the ecology of racial division: some varieties of informal segregation', *British Journal of Social Psychology* 42, 1–23.

Dixon, J. A. and Durrheim, K. (2004), 'Dislocating identity: Desegregation and the transformation of place', *Journal of Environmental Psychology* 24, 455–73.

Dixon, J. A., Reicher, S. and Foster, D. H. (1997), 'Ideology, geography and racial exclusion: The squatter camp as "blot on the landscape"', *Text* 17, 317–48.

Donath, J. Karahalios, K. and Viégas, F. (1999), 'Visualizing conversation', *Journal of*

Computer Mediated Communication 4 (4), available online at
http://jcmc.indiana.edu/volume4/issue4/donath.html

Douglas, M. and Isherwood, B. (1979), *The World of Goods: Towards an Anthropology of Consumption*, London: Allen Lane.

Drew, P. (2005), 'Conversation analysis', in K. L. Fitch and R. E. Sanders (eds), *Handbook of Language and Social Interaction*, Mahwah, NJ: Lawrence Erlbaum.

Drew, P. and Heritage, J. (eds) (1992), *Talk at Work. Interaction in Institutional Settings*, Cambridge: Cambridge University Press.

Drew, P. and Sorjonen, M. (1997), 'Institutional dialogue', in T. A. van Dijk (ed.), *Discourse as Social Interaction*, London: Sage.

du Gay, P., Hall, S., Janes, L., Mackay, H. and Negus, K. (1997), *Doing Cultural Studies: The Story of the Sony Walkman*, London: Sage/Open University Press.

Durrheim, K. and Dixon, J. A. (2001), 'The role of place and metaphor in racial exclusion: South Africa's beaches as sites of shifting racialization', *Ethnic and Racial Studies* 24, 433–50.

Eagleton, T. (1996), *Literary Theory: An Introduction*, 2nd edn, Oxford: Blackwell.

Eckert, P. (2000), *Linguistic Variation as Social Practice*, Oxford: Blackwell.

Eckert, P. and McConnell-Ginet, S. (1998), 'Communities of practice: Where language, gender and power all live', in J. Coates (ed.), *Language and Gender: A Reader*, Oxford: Blackwell.

Edwards, D. (1991), 'Categories are for talking: On the cognitive and discursive bases of categorization', *Theory and Psychology* 1 (4), 515–42.

Edwards, D. (1997a), *Discourse and Cognition*, London: Sage.

Edwards, D. (1997b), 'Structure and function in the analysis of everyday narratives', *Journal of Narrative and Life History* 7 (1–4), 139–46.

Edwards, D. (1998), 'The relevant thing about her: Social identity categories in use', in C. Antaki and S. Widdicombe (eds), *Identities in Talk*, London: Sage.

Edwards, D. (2004), 'Psicologia discursiva: Teoria da ligação e método com um exemplo', in L. Iñiguez (ed.), *Manual de Análise do Dircurso em Ciências Sociais*, Brazil: Editora Vozes.

Edwards, D. (2006), 'Discourse, cognition and social practices: The rich surface of language and social interaction', *Discourse Studies* 8 (2), in press.

Edwards, D. (forthcoming), 'Managing subjectivity in talk', in A. Hepburn and S. Wiggins (eds), *Discursive Research in Practice: New Approaches to Psychology and Interaction*, Cambridge: Cambridge University Press.

Edwards, D. and Potter, J. (1992), *Discursive Psychology*, London: Sage.

Edwards, D. and Potter, J. (2001), 'Discursive psychology', in A. McHoul and M. Rapley (eds), *How to Analyse Talk in Institutional Settings: A Casebook of Methods*, London: Continuum International.

Edwards, D. and Stokoe, E. H. (2004), 'Discursive psychology, focus group interviews, and participants' categories', *British Journal of Developmental Psychology* 22, 499–507.

Edwards, D. and Stokoe, E. H. (2005), 'God helps those who help themselves: Self-help as a topic in calls to neighbour mediation centres', paper presented at the International Pragmatics Association conference, Riva del Garda.

Eglin, P. and Hester, S. (1999), 'Moral order and the Montreal massacre: A story of membership categorization analysis', in P. L. Jalbert (ed.), *Media Studies: Ethnomethodological Approaches*, Lanham, MD: University Press of America; and International Institute for Ethnomethodology and Conversation Analysis.

Ellman, M. (ed.) (1994), *Psychoanalytic Literary Criticism*, London: Longman.
Erikson, E. (1968), *Identity, Youth and Crisis*, New York: W. W. Norton.
Escobar, A. (2000), 'Welcome to cyberia: Notes on the anthropology of cyberculture', in D. Bell and B. Kennedy (eds), *The Cybercultures Reader*, London: Routledge.
Fairclough, N. (1989), *Language and Power*, London: Longman.
Fairclough, N. (1992), *Discourse and Social Change*, Cambridge: Polity Press
Fairclough, N. (1993), 'Critical discourse analysis and the marketization of public discourse', *Discourse and Society* 4 (2), 133–59.
Fairclough, N. (1994), 'Conversationalisation of public discourse and the authority of the consumer', in R. Keat, N. Whitely and N. Abercrombie (eds), *The Authority of the Consumer*, London: Routledge.
Fairclough, N. (1995), *Critical Discourse Analysis*, London: Longman.
Fairclough, N. (2003), *Analysing Discourse: Textual Analysis for Social Research*, London: Routledge.
Fairclough, N. (2004), 'Critical discourse analysis in researching language in the new capitalism: Overdetermination, transdisciplinarity and textual analysis', in L. Young and C. Harrison (eds), *Systemic Functional Linguistics and Critical Discourse Analysis: Studies in social change*, London: Continuum.
Fairclough, N. and Wodak, R. (1997), 'Critical discourse analysis', in T. van Dijk (ed.), *Discourse as Social Interaction*, London: Sage.
Fanon, F. (1952), *Black Skin, White Masks*, New York: Grove.
Featherstone, M. (1991), 'The body in consumer culture', in M. Featherstone, M. Hepworth and B. Turner (eds), *The Body: Social Processes and Cultural Theory*, London: Sage.
Featherstone, M. and Burrows, R. (eds) (1995), *Cyberspace/Cyberbodies/Cyberpunk: Cultures of Technological Embodiment*, London: Sage.
Fiske, J. (1989), *Understanding Popular Culture*, London: Routledge.
Fitzgerald, R. and Housley, W. (2002), 'Identity, categorisation and sequential organisation: The sequential and categorial flow of identity in a radio phone-in', *Discourse and Society* 13 (5), 579–602.
Fornäs, J., Klein, K., Indendorf, M., Sundén, J. and Sveningsson, M. (2002), *Digital Borderlands: Cultural Studies of Identity and Interactivity on the Internet*, Oxford: Peter Lang.
Foucault, M. (1972), *The Archaeology of Knowledge*, London: Tavistock Publications.
Foucault, M. (1977), *Language, Counter-Memory, Practice: Selected Essays and Interviews*, ed. D. F. Bouchard, trans. D. F. Bouchard and S. Simon, Ithaca, NY: Cornell University Press.
Foucault, M. (1981), *History of Sexuality*, vol.1, Harmondsworth: Penguin Books.
Foucault, M. (1986), 'Of other spaces', *Diacritics* 16, 22–7.
Fowler, C. (2005), *Chasing Tales: Travel Writing, Journalism and the History of British Ideas about Afghanistan*, unpublished Ph.D. thesis, University of Stirling.
Fowler, R. (1991), *Language in the News*, London: Routledge.
Fowler, R., Hodge, B. Kress, G. and Trew, T. (1979), *Language and Control*, London: Routledge.
Francis, D. (1994), 'The golden dreams of the social constructionist', *Journal of Anthropological Research* 50 (2), 1–22.
Francis, D. and Hester, S. (2004), *An Invitation to Ethnomethodology*, London: Sage.
Frank, A. (1995), *The Wounded Storyteller: Body, Illness and Ethics*, Chicago, IL: University of Chicago Press.

Frankel, R. (1990), 'Talking in interviews: A dispreference for patient-initiated questions in physician–patient encounters', in G. Psathas (ed.), *Interactional Competence*, Washington, DC: University Press of America.

Freud, S. (1927), *The Ego and the Id*, London: Hogarth.

Frosh, S. (1999), 'What is outside discourse?', *Psychoanalytic Studies* 1 (4), 381–90.

Frosh, S., Phoenix, A. and Pattman, R. (2003), 'Taking a stand: Using psychoanalysis to explore the positioning of subjects in discourse', *British Journal of Social Psychology* 42, 39–53.

Frye, N. (1957), *Anatomy of Criticism*, Princeton, NJ: Princeton University Press.

Garfinkel, H. (1967), *Studies in Ethnomethodology*, Englewood Cliffs, NJ: Prentice-Hall.

Garfinkel, H. and Sacks, H. (1970), 'On formal structures of practical actions', in J. C. McKinney and E. A. Tiryakian (eds), *Theoretical Sociology: Perspectives and Developments*, New York: Appleton-Century-Crofts.

Georgakopoulou, A. (2002), 'Narrative and identity management: Discourse and social identities in a tale of tomorrow', *Research on Language and Social Interaction* 35 (4), 427–51.

Georgakopoulou, A. (2003), 'Plotting the "right place" and the "right time": Place and time as interactional resources in narrative', *Narrative Inquiry* 13 (2), 413–32.

Gergen, K. J. (1996), 'Technology and the self: From the essential to the sublime', in D. Grodin and T. R. Lindlof (eds), *Constructing the Self in a Mediated World*, London: Sage.

Gibson, W. (1984), *Neuromancer*, New York: Ace Books.

Giddens, A. (1981), *A Contemporary Critique of Historical Materialism*, vol.1, London: Macmillan.

Giddens, A. (1991), *Modernity and Self-Identity*, Cambridge: Polity Press.

Gil, T. (2000), 'The hermeneutical anthropology of Charles Taylor', in H. Häring, M. Junker-Kenny and D. Mieth (eds), *Creating Identity*, London: SCM Press.

Gilbert, G. N. and Mulkay, M. (1984), *Opening Pandora's Box: A Sociological Analysis of Scientists' Discourse*, Cambridge: Cambridge University Press.

Goffman, E. (1959), *The Presentation of Self in Everyday Life*, Harmondsworth: Penguin.

Goffman, E. (1967), *Interaction Ritual: Essays on Face-to-Face Behavior*, New York: Random House.

Goldman, R. (1992), 'Commodity feminism', in R. Goldman (ed.), *Reading Ads Socially*, London: Routledge.

Goodwin, C. (2003), 'Pointing as situated practice', in S. Kito and M. Planck (eds), *Pointing: Where Language, Culture and Cognition Meet*, Mahwah, NJ: Lawrence Erlbaum Associates.

Goodwin, M. H. (1990), *He-Said She-Said: Talk as Social Organization among Black Children*, Bloomington, IN: Indiana University Press.

Goodwin, M. H. (1997), 'Toward families of stories in context', *Journal of Narrative and Life History* 7 (1–4), 107–12.

Gough, B. (2004), 'Psychoanalysis as a resource for understanding emotional ruptures in the text: The case of defensive masculinities', *British Journal of Social Psychology* 43 (2), 245–67.

Gramsci, A. (1971), *Selections from the Prison Notebooks of Antonio Gramsci*, ed. and trans. Q. Hoare and G. Nowell Smith, London: Lawrence Wishart.

Grant, D. and Iedema, R. (2005), 'Discourse analysis and the study of organizations', *Text* 25 (1), 37–66.

Greatbatch, D. (1992), 'On the management of disagreement between news interviewees', in P. Drew and J. Heritage (eds), *Talk at Work, Interaction in Institutional Settings*, Cambridge: Cambridge University Press.

Greatbatch, D. (1998), 'Conversation analysis: Neutralism in British news interviews', in A. Bell and P. Garrett (eds), *Approaches to Media Discourse*, Oxford: Blackwell.

Grice, H. P. (1975), 'Logic and conversation', in P. Cole and J. Morgan (eds), *Syntax and Semantics 3: Speech Acts*, New York: Academic Press.

Grodin, D. and Lindlof, T. R. (eds) (1996), *Constructing the Self in a Mediated World*, London: Sage.

Gubrium, J. F. and Holstein, J. A. (eds) (2001), *Institutional Selves: Troubled Identities in a Postmodern World*, Oxford: Oxford University Press.

Gumport, P. J. (2000), 'Academic restructuring: Organizational change and institutional imperatives', *Higher Education* 39 (1), 67–91.

Gunn, S. (2001), 'The spatial turn: Changing histories of space and place', in S. Gunn and R. J. Morris (eds), *Identities in Space: Contested Terrains in the Western City since 1850*, Aldershot: Ashgate.

Gunnarsson, B-L., Linell, P. and Nordberg, B. (eds) (1997), *The Construction of Professional Identities*, Harlow: Addison Wesley Longman.

Gupta, A. and Ferguson, J. (1992), 'Beyond "culture": Space, identity and the politics of difference', *Cultural Anthropology* 7 (1), 6–23.

Habermas, J. (1987), *The Theory of Communicative Action, Volume 2: Lifeworld and System: A Critique of Functionalist Reason*, London: Heinemann.

Hadden, S. C. and Lester, M. (1978), 'Talking identity: The production of "self" in interaction', *Human Studies* 1, 331–56.

Hak, T. (1999), '"Text" and "context": Talk bias in studies of health care work', in S. Sarangi and C. Roberts (eds), *Talk, Work and Institutional Order: Discourse in Medical, Mediation and Management Settings*, Berlin: Mouton de Gruyter.

Hall, D. E. (2004), *Subjectivity*, London: Routledge.

Hall, G. and Danby, S. (2003), 'Teachers and academics co-constructing the category of expert through meeting talk', paper presented to the Australian Association for Research in Education/New Zealand Association for Research in Education annual conference, Auckland.

Hall, K. (1995), 'Lip service on the fantasy lines', in K. Hall and M. Bucholtz (eds), *Gender Articulated: Language and the Socially Constructed Self*, New York: Routledge.

Hall, K. (1996), 'Cyberfeminism', in S. Herring (ed.), *Computer-Mediated Communication: Linguistic, Social and Cross-cultural Perspectives*, Amsterdam: John Benjamins.

Hall, S. (1982), 'The rediscovery of "ideology": Return of the repressed in media studies', in M. Gurevitch, J. Woollacott, T. Bennett and J. Curran (eds), *Culture, Society and the Media*, London: Methuen.

Hall, S. (1995), 'New cultures for old. A place in the world?', in D. Massey and P. Jess (eds), *Places, Cultures and Globalization*, New York: Oxford University Press.

Hall, S. (2000), 'Who needs identity?', in P. du Gay, J. Evans and P. Redman (eds), *Identity: A Reader*, London: Sage.

Halliday, M. A. K. (1994), *An Introduction to Functional Grammar*, 2nd edn, London: Edward Arnold.

Haraway, D. (2000), 'A cyborg manifesto: Science, technology and socialist-feminism in the late twentieth century', in D. Bell and B. Kennedy (eds), *The Cybercultures Reader*, London: Routledge.

Hare-Mustin, R.T. and Maracek, J. (eds) (1990), *Making a Difference: Psychology and the Construction of Gender*, New Haven, CT: Yale University Press.

Harré, R. (1998), *The Singular Self: An Introduction to the Psychology of Personhood*, London: Sage.

Harré, R. and van Langenhove, L. (1991), 'Varieties of positioning', *Journal for the Theory of Social Behaviour* 21 (4), 393–407.

Harré, R. and Langenhove, L. van (eds) (1999), *Positioning Theory*, Oxford: Blackwell.

Harré, R. and Moghaddam, F. (eds) (2003), *The Self and Others: Positioning Individuals and Groups in Personal, Political and Cultural Contexts*, Westport, CT: Praeger.

Harris, S. (1991), 'Evasive action: Politicians and political interviews', in P. Scannell (ed.), *Broadcast Talk*, London: Sage.

Harrison, S. (2000), 'Maintaining the virtual community: Use of politeness strategies in an e-mail discussion group', in L. Pemberton and S. Shurville (eds), *Words on the Web: Computer Mediated Communication*, Exeter: Intellect Books.

Hausendorf, H. (2002), 'Social identity work in storytelling: Methodological remarks', *Narrative Inquiry* 12 (1), 173–9.

He, A. W. (1995), 'Co-constructing institutional identities: The case of student counselees', *Research on Language and Social Interaction* 28 (3), 213–31.

Hegel, G. W. F. [1807] (1977), *Phenomenology of Spirit*, trans. A. V. Miller, Oxford: Clarendon Press.

Hepburn, A. (2003), *An Introduction to Critical Social Psychology*, London: Sage.

Heritage, J. (1984), *Garfinkel and Ethnomethodology*, Cambridge: Polity.

Heritage, J. (2005), 'Conversation analysis and institutional talk', in K. L. Fitch and R. E. Sanders (eds), *Handbook of Language and Social Interaction*, Mahwah, NJ: Lawrence Erlbaum.

Heritage, J. C. and Atkinson, J. M. (1984), 'Introduction', in J. M. Atkinson and J. Heritage (eds), *Structures of Social Action: Studies in Conversation Analysis*, Cambridge: Cambridge University Press.

Heritage, J. and Greatbatch, D. (1991), 'On the institutional character of institutional talk: The case of news interviews', in D. Boden and D. H. Zimmerman (eds), *Talk and Social Structure: Studies in Ethnomethodology and Conversation Analysis*, Cambridge: Polity Press.

Hermes, J. (1995), *Reading Women's Magazines*, Cambridge, Polity Press.

Herring, S. (ed.) (1996), *Computer-Mediated Communication: Linguistic, Social and Cross-Cultural Perspectives*, Amsterdam: John Benjamins.

Herring, S. (1999), 'Interactional coherence in CMC', *Journal of Computer-Mediated Communication* 4 (4), available online at http://jcmc.indiana.edu/vol4/issue4/herring.html

Herring, S. and Martinson, A. (2004), 'Assessing gender authenticity in computer-mediated language use: Evidence from an identity game', *Journal of Language and Social Psychology* 23 (4), 424–46.

Hess, D. (1995), 'On low-tech cyborgs', in C. Gray (ed.), *The Cyborg Handbook*, London: Routledge.

Hester, S. and Eglin, P. (eds) (1997), *Culture in Action: Studies in Membership Categorization Analysis*, Boston, MA: International Institute for Ethnomethodology and University Press of America.

Hester, S. and Francis, D. (1997), 'Reality analysis in a classroom storytelling', *British Journal of Sociology* 48 (1), 95–112.

Hester, S. and Francis, D. (2000), 'Ethnomethodology, conversation analysis and "institutional talk"', *Text* 20 (3), 391–413.

Hester, S. and Francis, D. (2001), 'Is institutional talk a phenomenon? Reflections on ethnomethodology and applied conversation analysis', in A. McHoul and M. Rapley (eds), *How to Analyse Talk in Institutional Settings*, London: Continuum.

Hetherington, K. (1998), *Expressions of Identity: Space, Performance, Politics*, London: Sage.

Hoey, M. (1983), *On the Surface of Discourse*, London: HarperCollins.

Hollway, W. (1989), *Subjectivity and Method in Psychology*, London: Sage.

Hollway, W. and Jefferson, T. (2000), *Doing Qualitative Research Differently: Free Association, Narrative and the Interview Method*, London: Sage.

Hollway, W. and Jefferson, T. (2001), 'Free association, narrative analysis and the defended subject: The case of Ivy', *Narrative Inquiry* 11, 103–22.

Hollway, W. and Jefferson, T. (2004), 'The free association narrative interview method', in M. Lewis-Beck, A. Bryman and T. Futing Liao (eds), *Encyclopedia of Social Science Methods*, London: Sage.

Hollway, W. and Jefferson, T. (2005), 'Panic and perjury: A psychosocial exploration of agency', *British Journal of Social Psychology* 44 (2), 147–64.

Holmes, J. and Meyerhoff, M. (eds) (2003), *The Handbook of Language and Gender*, Oxford: Blackwell.

Holstein, J. A. and Gubrium, J. F. (1995), *The Active Interview*, London: Sage.

Holstein, J. A. and Gubrium, J. F. (2000), *The Self We Live By: Narrative Identity in a Postmodern World*, Oxford: Oxford University Press.

Hopkins, N. (2001), 'National identity: Pride and prejudice?', *British Journal of Social Psychology* 40, 183–6.

Housley, W. and Fitzgerald, R. (2001), 'Categorisation, narrative and devolution in Wales', *Sociological Research Online* 6 (2), available online at http://www.socresonline.org.uk/

Howard, J. (2000), 'Social psychology of identities', *Annual Review of Sociology* 26, 367–93.

Hsieh, E. (2004), 'Stories in action and the dialogic management of identities: Storytelling in transplant support group meetings', *Research on Language and Social Interaction* 37 (1), 39–70.

Hubbard, P. (2002), 'Maintaining family values? Cleansing the streets of sex advertising', *Area* 34 (4), 353–60.

Hutchby, I. (2005), 'Conversation analysis and the study of broadcast talk', in K. L. Fitch and R. E. Sanders (eds), *Handbook of Language and Social Interaction*, Mahwah, NJ: Lawrence Erlbaum Associates.

Jackson, P., Stevenson, N. and Brooks, K. (2001), *Making Sense of Men's Magazines*, Cambridge: Polity Press.

Jayyusi, L. (1984), *Categorization and the Moral Order*, London: Routledge.

Jefferson, G. (1978), 'Sequential aspects of storytelling in conversation', in J. Schenkein (ed.), *Studies in the Organization of Conversational Interaction*, London: Academic Press.

Jefferson, G. (2004a), 'Glossary of transcript symbols with an introduction', in G. Lerner (ed.), *Conversation Analysis: Studies from the First Generation*, Amsterdam: John Benjamins.

Jefferson, G. (2004b), '"At first I thought": A normalizing device for extraordinary events', in G. Lerner (ed.), *Conversation Analysis: Studies from the First Generation*, Amsterdam: John Benjamins.

Johnson, R. (1986), 'The story so far: And other transformations', in D. Punter (ed.), *Introduction to Contemporary Cultural Studies*, London: Longman.

Johnson, S. and Meinhof, U. (eds) (1997), *Language and Masculinity*, Oxford: Blackwell.

Johnstone, B. (1991), *Stories, Community, and Place*, Bloomington, IN: Indiana University Press.

Jones, K. (2003), 'The turn to a narrative knowing of persons: One method explored', *Nursing Times Research* 8 (1), 60–71.

Jones, R. (2000), 'Potato seeking rice: Language culture and identity in gay personal ads in Hong Kong', *International Journal of the Sociology of Language* 143, 33–61.

Jones, S. (ed.) (1995), *Cybersociety: Computer-Mediated Communication and Community*, Thousand Oaks, CA: Sage.

Jones, S. (ed.) (1998), *Cybersociety 2.0: Revisiting Computer-Mediated Communication and Community*, Thousand Oaks, CA: Sage.

Joseph, J. (2004), *Language and Identity*, London: Palgrave Macmillan.

Keat, R., Whitely, N. and Abercrombie, N. (eds) (1994), *The Authority of the Consumer*, London: Routledge.

Kendall, L. (1998), 'Meaning and identity in "cyberspace": The performance of gender, class and race online', *Symbolic Interaction* 21, 129–53.

Kennedy, B. (2000), 'Cyberbodies: Introduction', in D. Bell and B. Kennedy (eds), *The Cybercultures Reader*, London: Routledge.

Keogan, K. (2002), 'A sense of place: The politics of immigration and the symbolic construction of identity in Southern California and the New York Metropolitan area', *Sociological Forum* 17 (2), 223–53.

Kerby, J. and Rae, J. (1998), 'Moral identity in action: Young offenders' reports of encounters with the police', *British Journal of Social Psychology* 37, 439–56.

Kiesler, S., Siegel, J. and McGuire, T. (1984), 'Social psychological aspects of computer-mediated communication', *American Psychologist* 10, 1,123–34.

Kiesling, S. F. (forthcoming), 'Hegemonic identity-making in narrative, in A. de Fina, D. Schiffrin and M. Bamberg (eds), *Discursive Construction of Identities*, Cambridge: Cambridge University Press.

Kitzinger, C. (2000), 'Doing feminist conversation analysis', *Feminism and Psychology* 10, 163–93.

Kitzinger, C. (2005), 'Speaking as a heterosexual: (How) does sexuality matter for talk-in-interaction?', *Research on Language and Social Interaction* 38 (3), 221–65.

Kolko, B. and Reid, E. (1998), 'Dissolution and fragmentation: Problems in online communities', in S. Jones (ed.), *Cybersociety 2.0: Revisiting Computer-Mediated Communication and Community*, Thousand Oaks, CA: Sage.

Korobov, N. and Bamberg, M. (2004), 'Positioning a "mature" self in interactive practices: How adolescent males negotiate "physical attraction" in group talk', *British Journal of Developmental Psychology* 22, 471–92.

Kraack, A. and Kenway, J. (2002), 'Place, time and stigmatised youthful identities: Bad boys in paradise', *Journal of Rural Studies* 18, 145–55.

Kress, G. and Hodge, B. (1979), *Language as Ideology*, London: Routledge and Kegan Paul.

Kress, G. and van Leeuwen, T. (1996), *Reading Images: The Grammar of Visual Design*, London: Routledge.

Kulick, D. (1999), 'Language and gender/sexuality', *Language and Culture Mailing List: Online Symposium*. http://www.language-culture.org/archives/subs/kulick-don/index.html

Labov, W. (1972), *Language in the Inner City: Studies in the Black English Vernacular*, Philadelphia, PA: University of Philadelphia Press.

Labov, W. (2001), 'Uncovering the event structure of narrative', in *Georgetown University Round Table 2001*, Washington, DC: Georgetown University Press.

Labov, W. and Waletzky, J. (1967), 'Narrative analysis', in J. Helm (ed.), *Essays on the Verbal and Visual Arts*, Seattle, WA: University of Washington Press.

Lacan, J. (1977), *Écrits. A Selection*, New York: W. W. Norton.

Laclau, E. (1990), *New Reflections on the Revolution of our Time*, London: Verso.

Laclau, E. and Mouffe, C. (1985), *Hegemony and Socialist Strategy*, London: Verso.

Lakoff, G. and Johnson, M. (1980), *Metaphors We Live By*, Chicago, IL: Chicago University Press.

Lakoff, R. (1975), *Language and Woman's Place*, New York: Harper and Row.

Langellier, K. M. (2001), ' "You're marked": Breast cancer, tattoo, and the narrative performance of identity', in J. Brockmeier and D. Carbaugh (eds), *Narrative and Identity: Studies in Autobiography, Self and Culture*, Amsterdam and Philadelphia, PA: John Benjamins.

Latour, B. (1993), *We Have Never Been Modern*, Hemel Hempstead: Harvester Wheatsheaf.

Laurier, E., Whyte, A. and Buckner, K. (2002), 'Neighbouring as an occasioned activity: "Finding a lost cat" ', *Space and Culture* 5 (4), 346–67.

Lave, J. and Wenger, E. (1991), *Situated Learning: Legitimate Peripheral Participation*, Cambridge: Cambridge University Press.

Lazar, M. M. (ed.) (2005), *Feminist Critical Discourse Analysis: Gender, Power and Ideology in Discourse*, London: Routledge.

Lea, M. and Spears, R. (1995), 'Love at first byte? Building personal relationships over computer networks', in J. Wood and S. Duck (eds), *Under-Studied Relationships: Off the Beaten Track*, Thousand Oaks: Sage.

Lecourt, D. (2004), *Identity Matters: Schooling the Student Body in Academic Discourse*, New York: State University of New York Press.

Lefebvre, H. (1991), *The Production of Space*, Oxford: Blackwell.

Lerner, G. H. (1992), 'Assisted storytelling: Deploying shared knowledge as a practical matter', *Qualitative Sociology* 15 (3), 247–71.

Leudar, I., Marsland, V. and Nekvapil, J. (2004), 'On membership categorization: "Us", "them" and "doing violence" in political discourse', *Discourse and Society* 15 (2–3), 243–66.

Levine, P. and Scollon, R. (eds) (2004), *Discourse and Technology: Multimodal Discourse Analysis*, Washington, DC: Georgetown University Press.

Levinson, M. P. and Sparkes, A. C. (2004), 'Gypsy identity and orientations to space', *Journal of Contemporary Ethnography* 33 (6), 704–34.

Linde, C. (1993), *Life Stories: The Creation of Coherence*, New York: Oxford University Press.

Litosseliti, L. (2006), *Gender and Language: An Introduction and Resource Book*, Oxford: Oxford University Press.

Livia, A. and Hall, K. (eds) (1997), *Queerly Phrased: Language, Gender and Sexuality*, Oxford: Oxford University Press.

Lupton, D. (2000), 'The embodied computer/user', in D. Bell and B. Kennedy (eds), *The Cybercultures Reader*, London: Routledge.

Lynch, M. (1993), *Scientific Practice and Ordinary Action: Ethnomethodology and Social Studies of Science*, Cambridge: Cambridge University Press.

Machin, D. and Thornborrow, J. (2003), 'Branding and discourse: The case of *Cosmopolitan*', *Discourse and Society* 14 (4), 453–71.

Mackay, H. (1997), *Consumption and Everyday Life*, London: Sage.

MacKinnon, R. (1997), 'Punishing the persona: Correctional strategies for the virtual offender', in S. Jones (ed.), *Virtual Culture: Identity and Communication in Cybersociety*, Thousand Oaks, CA: Sage.

Mäkitalo, A. and Saljö, R. (2000), 'Talk in institutional context and institutional context in talk: Categories as situated practices', *Text* 22 (1), 57–82.

Malone, M. (1997), *Worlds of Talk: The Presentation of Self in Everyday Conversation*, Cambridge: Polity.

Manzo, L. C. (2003), 'Beyond house and haven: Toward a revisioning of emotional relationships with places', *Journal of Environmental Psychology* 23, 47–61.

Massey, D. (1994), *Space, Place and Gender*, Cambridge, Polity Press.

Matoesian, G. M. (2001), *Law and the Language of Identity: Discourse in the William Kennedy Smith Rape Trial*, Oxford: Oxford University Press.

May, V. (2004), 'Narrative identity and the re-conceptualization of lone motherhood', *Narrative Inquiry* 14 (1), 169–89.

Mayr, A. (2004), *Prison Discourse: Language as a Means of Resistance and Control*, London: Palgrave Macmillan.

McAdams, D. (1993), *The Stories We Live By: Personal Myths and the Making of the Self*, New York: Morrow.

McCabe, S. and Stokoe, E. H. (2004), 'Place and identity in "day visitor" narratives', *Annals of Tourism Research* 31 (3), 601–22.

McCracken, E. (1993), *Decoding Women's Magazines: From Mademoiselle to Ms*, London: Macmillan.

McDowell, L. (1998), *Gender, Identity and Place*, Cambridge: Polity Press.

McIlvenny, P. (ed.) (2002), *Talking Gender and Sexuality*, Amsterdam: John Benjamins.

McRobbie, A. (1999), 'MORE! New sexualities in girls' and women's magazines', in A. McRobbie (ed.), *In the Culture Society: Art, Fashion and Popular Music*, London: Routledge.

McRobbie, A. (2004), 'Notes on "What Not To Wear" and post-feminist symbolic violence', *Sociological Review* 52 (2), 99–109.

Mead, G. H. (1934), *Mind, Self, and Society*, Chicago, IL: University of Chicago Press.

Mehan, H. (1979), *Learning Lessons: Social Organization in the Classroom*, Cambridge, MA: Harvard University Press.

Michael, M. (1996), *Constructing Identities: The Social, the Nonhuman and Change*, London: Sage.

Miles, S. (1998), *Consumerism: As a Way of Life*, London: Sage.

Mills, S. (1995), *Feminist Stylistics*, London: Routledge.

Mills, S. (1997), *Discourse*, London: Routledge.

Mishler, E. G. (1999), *Storylines: Craftartists' Narratives of Identity*, Cambridge, MA: Harvard University Press.

Mulvey, L. (1988), 'Visual pleasure and narrative cinema', in C. Penley (ed.), *Feminism and Film Theory*, New York: Routledge.

Murray, M. (2003), 'Narrative psychology', in J. A. Smith (ed.), *Qualitative Psychology: A Practical Guide to Research Methods*, London: Sage.

Nikander, P. (2002), *Age in Action: Membership Work and Stage of Life Categories in Talk*, Helsinki: Academia Scientiarum Fennica.

Ochs, E. and Capps, L. (2001), *Living Narrative*, Cambridge, MA: Harvard University Press.

O'Halloran, K. L. (ed.) (2004), *Multimodal Discourse Analysis: Systemic Functional Perspectives*, London: Continuum.

O'Sullivan, P. B., Hunt, S. K. and Lippert, L. R. (2004), 'Mediated immediacy: A language of affiliation in a technological age', *Journal of Language and Social Psychology* 23 (4), 464–90.

Oxford English Dictionary (2002), second edition on compact disc, Oxford: Oxford University Press.

Paasi, A. (2001), 'Europe as a social process and discourse: Considerations of place, boundaries and identity', *European Urban and Regional Studies* 8 (1), 7–28.

Pacagnella, L. (1997), 'Getting the seat of your pants dirty: strategies for ethnographic research on virtual communities', *Journal of Computer Mediated Communication* 3 (1), available online at http://www.jcmc.indiana.edu/vol3/issue1/pacagnella.html

Paolillo, J. (1999), 'The virtual speech community: Social network and language variation on IRC', *Journal of Computer Mediated Communication* 4 (4), available online at http://www.jcmc.indiana.edu/vol4/issue4/paolillo.html

Parker, I. (1997), 'Discourse analysis and psychoanalysis', *British Journal of Social Psychology* 36, 479–95.

Parker, I. (2004), *Qualitative Psychology*, Buckingham: Open University Press.

Perry, J. (2002), *Identity: Personal Identity and the Self*, Indianapolis, IN: Hackett.

Phillips, V. (1989), 'Students: Partners, clients or consumers?', in C. Ball and H. Eggins (eds), *Higher Education into the 1990s*, Buckingham: Open University Press.

Pile, K. and Thrift, N. (eds) (1995), *Mapping the Subject*, London: Routledge.

Polanyi, L. (1979), 'So what's the point?', *Semiotica* 25, 207–41.

Polkinghorne, D. E. (1991), 'Narrative and self-concept', *Journal of Narrative and Life History* 1 (2 and 3), 135–53.

Pomerantz, A. (1984), 'Agreeing and disagreeing with assessments. Some features of preferred/dispreferred turn shapes', in J. M. Atkinson and J. Heritage (eds), *Structures of Social Action: Studies in Conversation Analysis*, Cambridge: Cambridge University Press.

Pomerantz, A. and Mandelbaum, J. (2005), 'Conversation analytic approaches to the relevance and uses of relationship categories in interaction', in K. L. Fitch and R. E. Sanders (eds), *Handbook of Language and Social Interaction*, Mahwah, NJ: Lawrence Erlbaum Associates.

Poster, M. (1998), 'Virtual ethnicity: Tribal identity in an age of global communications', in S. Jones (ed.), *Cybersociety 2.0: Revisiting Computer-Mediated Communication and Community*, Thousand Oaks, CA: Sage.

Potter, J. (2001), 'Wittgenstein and Austin', in M. Wetherell, S. Taylor and S. Yates (eds), *Discourse Theory and Practice*, London: Sage.

Potter, J. (2003), 'Discourse analysis and discursive psychology', in P. M. Camic, J. E. Rhodes and L. Yardley (eds), *Qualitative Research in Psychology: Expanding Perspectives in Methodology and Design*, Washington, DC: American Psychological Association.

Potter, J. (2005), 'A discursive psychology of institutions', *Social Psychology Review* 7, 25–35.

Potter, J. and Hepburn, A. (2003), ' "I'm a bit concerned" – Early actions and psychological constructions in a child protection helpline', *Research on Language and Social Interaction* 36, 197–240.

Potter, J. and Hepburn, A. (2005), 'Qualitative interviews in psychology: Problems and prospects', *Qualitative Research in Psychology* 2 (4), 281–307.

Potter, J. and Wetherell, M. (1987), *Discourse and Social Psychology*, London: Sage.

Propp, V. [1928] (1968), *Morphology of the Folktale*, Austin, TX: University of Texas Press.

Psathas, G. (1999), 'Studying the organization in action: Membership categorization and interaction', *Human Studies* 22, 139–62.

Rafaeli, S. and Sudweeks, F. (1997), 'Networked interactivity', *Journal of Computer-Mediated Communication* 2 (4), available online at http://jcmc.indiana.edu/vol2/issue4/rafaeli.sudweeks.html

Rampton. B. (1995), *Crossing: Language and Ethnicity among Adolescents*, London: Longman.

Randall, D. and Hughes, J. A. (1995), 'Sociology, CSCW and working with customers', in P. Thomas (ed.), *The Social and Interactional Dimensions of Human–computer Interaction*, Cambridge: Cambridge University Press.

Rapley, M. (1998), ' "Just an ordinary Australian": Self-categorisation and the discursive construction of facticity in "new racist" political rhetoric', *British Journal of Social Psychology* 37, 325–44.

Readings, B. (1997), *The University in Ruins*, London: Harvard University Press.

Reisigl, M. and Wodak, R. (2001), *Discourse and Discrimination: Rhetorics of Racism and Anti-Semitism*, London: Routledge.

Relph, E. (1976), *Place and Placelessness*, London: Pion.

Reynolds, J. and Wetherell, M. (2003), 'The discursive climate of singleness: The consequences for women's negotiation of a single identity', *Feminism and Psychology* 13 (4), 489–510.

Rheingold, H. (1993), *The Virtual Community: Homesteading on the Electronic Frontier*, Reading: Addison Wesley.

Rich, A. (1980), 'Compulsory heterosexuality and lesbian existence', *Signs* 5 (4), 631–60.

Ricoeur, P. (1991), 'Life in quest of narrative', in D. Wood (ed.), *Paul Ricoeur: Narrative and Interpretation*, London: Routledge.

Riessman, C. K. (1993), *Narrative Analysis*, London: Sage.

Riessman, C. K. (2003), 'Performing identities in illness narrative: Masculinity and multiple sclerosis', *Qualitative Research* 3 (1), 5–33.

Ritzer, G. (1998), 'Introduction', in J. Baudrillard, *The Consumer Society: Myths and Structures*, London: Sage.

Roberts, C. and Sarangi, S. (1999), 'Introduction: Revisiting different analytic frameworks', in S. Sarangi and C. Roberts (eds), *Talk, Work and Institutional Order*, Berlin: Mouton de Gruyter.

Robins, K. (2000), 'Cyberspace and the world we live in', in D. Bell and B. Kennedy (eds), *The Cybercultures Reader*, London: Routledge.

Robinson, I. (1990), 'Personal narratives, social careers and medical courses: Analysing life trajectories in autobiographies of people with multiple sclerosis', *Social Science and Medicine* 30, 1173–86.

Rodaway, P. (1994), *Sensuous Geographies: Body, Sense and Place*, London: Routledge.

Rooksby, E. (2002), *E-mail and Ethics: Style and Ethical Relations in Computer-Mediated Communication*, London: Routledge.

Rose, G. (2001), *Visual Methodologies*, London: Sage.

Rose, N. (1990), 'Psychology as a "social" science', in I. Parker and J. Shotter (eds), *Deconstructing Social Psychology*, London: Routledge.

Ryave, A. (1978), 'On the achievement of a series of stories', in J. Schenkein (ed.),
  Studies in the Organization of Conversational Interaction, New York: Academic Press.
Sack, R. D. (1986), *Human Territoriality: Its Theory and History*, Cambridge:
  Cambridge University Press.
Sacks, H. (1972a), 'On the analysability of stories by children', in J. J. Gumperz and
  D. Hymes (eds), *Directions in Sociolinguistics: The Ethnography of Communication*,
  New York: Rinehart and Winston.
Sacks, H. (1972b), 'An initial investigation of the usability of conversational data for doing
  sociology', in D. Sudnow (ed.), *Studies in Social Interaction*, New York: Free Press.
Sacks, H. (1979), 'Hotrodder: A revolutionary category', in G. Psathas (ed.), *Everyday
  Language: Studies in Ethnomethodology*, New York: Irvington.
Sacks, H. (1984a), 'On doing "being ordinary"', in J. M. Atkinson and J. Heritage
  (eds), *Structures of Social Action: Studies in Conversation Analysis*, Cambridge:
  Cambridge University Press.
Sacks, H. (1984b), 'Notes on methodology', ed. Gail Jefferson, in J. M. Atkinson and
  J. Heritage (eds), *Structures of Social Action: Studies in Conversation Analysis*,
  Cambridge: Cambridge University Press.
Sacks, H. (1992), *Lectures on Conversation*, vols 1 and 2, ed. G. Jefferson, Oxford:
  Blackwell.
Sacks, H., Schegloff, E. A. and Jefferson, G. (1974), 'A simplest systematics for the
  organization of turn-taking for conversation', *Language* 50 (4), 696–735.
Sarbin, T. R. (1983), 'Place identity as a component of self: An addendum', *Journal of
  Environmental Psychology* 3, 337–42.
Sarbin, T. (ed.) (1986), *Narrative Psychology: The Storied Nature of Human Conduct*,
  New York: Praeger.
Scanlon, J. (ed.) (2000), *The Gender and Consumer Culture Reader*, New York: New York
  University Press.
Schegloff, E. A. (1972), 'Notes on a conversational practice: Formulating place', in
  D. Sudnow (ed.), *Studies in Social Interaction*, New York: Free Press.
Schegloff, E. A. (1989), 'Harvey Sacks – lectures 1964–65: An introduction/memoir',
  Human Studies 12 (3–4), 185–209.
Schegloff, E. A. (1991), 'Reflections on talk and social structure', in D. Boden and
  D. Zimmerman (eds), *Talk and Social Structure*, Berkeley, CA: University of
  California Press.
Schegloff, E. A. (1992a), 'In another context', in A. Duranti and C. Goodwin (eds),
  Rethinking Context: Language as an Interactive Phenomenon, Cambridge: Cambridge
  University Press.
Schegloff, E. A. (1992b), 'Introduction', in G. Jefferson (ed.), *Harvey Sacks, Lectures on
  Conversation*, Oxford: Blackwell.
Schegloff, E. A. (1996a), 'Issues of relevance for discourse analysis: Contingency in
  action, interaction and co-participant context', in E. H. Hovy and D. R. Scott (eds),
  *Computational and Conversational Discourse: Burning Issues – an Interdisciplinary
  Account*, New York: Springer.
Schegloff, E. A. (1996b), 'Turn organization: One intersection of grammar and
  interaction', in E. Ochs, S. Thompson and E. A. Schegloff (eds), *Interaction and
  Grammar*, Cambridge: Cambridge University Press.
Schegloff, E. A. (1996c), 'Some practices for referring to persons in talk-in-interaction:
  A partial sketch of a systematics', in B. Fox (ed.), *Studies in Anaphora*, Amsterdam:
  John Benjamins.

Schegloff, E. A. (1997a), 'Whose text? Whose context?', *Discourse and Society* 8 (2), 165–87.

Schegloff, E. A. (1997b), 'Narrative analysis: Thirty years later', *Journal of Narrative and Life History* 7 (1–4), 97–106.

Schegloff, E. A. (1998), 'Reply to Wetherell', *Discourse and Society* 9, 413–16.

Schegloff, E. A. (2000), 'When "others" initiate repair', *Applied Linguistics* 21 (2), 205–43.

Schegloff, E. A. (2002), *Tutorial on Membership Categorisation*, unpublished manuscript.

Schegloff, E. A. (2005), 'On integrity in inquiry . . . of the investigated, not the investigator', *Discourse Studies* 7 (4–5), 455–80.

Schenkein, J. (1978), 'Identity negotiations in conversation', in J. Schenkein (ed.), *Studies in the Organization of Conversational Interaction*, New York: Academic Press.

Schiffrin, D. (1996), 'Narrative as self-portrait: Sociolinguistic constructions of identity', *Language in Society* 25, 167–203.

Schofield–Clark, L. (1998), 'Dating on the net', in S. Jones (ed.), *Cybersociety 2.0: Revisiting Computer-Mediated Communication and Community*, Thousand Oaks, CA: Sage.

Schutz, A. (1962), *Collected Papers, Volume I: The Problem of Social Reality*, The Hague: Martinus Nijhoff.

Scollon, R. (2001), *Mediated Discourse: The Nexus of Practice*, London: Routledge.

Scollon, R. and Scollon, S. W. (2003), *Discourses in Place: Language in the Material World*, London: Routledge.

Sedgwick, E. K. (1993), 'Queer performativity', *GLQ: A Journal of Lesbian and Gay Studies* 1, 1–16.

Seymour-Smith, S., Wetherell, M. and Phoenix, A. (2002), ' "My wife ordered me to come!": A discursive analysis of doctors' and nurses' accounts of men's use of general practitioners', *Journal of Health Psychology* 7, 253–67.

Shalom, C. (1997), 'That great supermarket of desire: Attributes of the desired other in personal advertisements', in K. Harvey and C. Shalom (eds), *Language and Desire: Encoding Sex, Romance and Intimacy*, London: Routledge.

Shotter, J. and Gergen, K. J. (eds) (1989), *Texts of Identity*, London: Sage.

Sibley, D. (1995), *Geographies of Exclusion*, London: Routledge.

Sidnell, J. (2003), 'Constructing and managing male exclusivity in talk-in-interaction', in J. Holmes and M. Meyerhoff (eds), *The Handbook of Language and Gender*, Oxford: Blackwell.

Silverman, D. (1999), 'Warriors or collaborators: Reworking methodological controversies in the study of institutional interaction', in S. Sarangi and C. Roberts (eds), *Talk, Work and Institutional Order: Discourse in Medical, Mediation and Management Settings*, Berlin: Mouton de Gruyter.

Simonds, W. (1996), 'All consuming selves: Self-help literature and women's identities', in D. Grodin and T. R. Lindlof (eds), *Constructing the Self in a Mediated World*, London: Sage.

Simpson, J. (2005), 'Conversational floors in synchronous text–based CMC discourse', *Discourse Studies* 7 (3), 337–61.

Skjaeveland, O. and Garling, T. (1997), 'Effects of interactional space on neighbouring', *Journal of Environmental Psychology* 17, 181–98.

Smiles, S. W. (1882), *Self Help*, London: John Murray.

Smith, D. (1978), 'K is mentally ill: The anatomy of a factual account', *Sociology* 12, 23–53.

Smith, D. (1990), *Texts, Facts and Femininity: Exploring the Relations of Ruling*, London: Routledge.

Soja, E. W. (1989), *Postmodern Geographies: The Reassertion of Space in Critical Social Theory*, London: Verso.

Southwell, T. (1998), *Getting Away With It: The Inside Story of* loaded, London: Ebury Press.

Speer, S. A. (1999), 'Feminism and conversation analysis: An oxymoron?', *Feminism and Psychology* 9 (4), 417–78.

Speer, S. A. (2005), *Gender Talk: Feminism, Discourse and Conversation Analysis*, London: Routledge.

Spivak, G. (1990), *The Post-Colonial Critic: Interviews, Strategies, Dialogues*, London: Routledge.

Squires, J. (2000), 'Fabulous feminist futures and the lure of cyberculture', in D. Bell and B. Kennedy (eds), *The Cybercultures Reader*, London: Routledge.

Stelarc (2000), 'From psycho-body to cyber-systems: Images as post-human entities', in D. Bell and B. Kennedy (eds), *The Cybercultures Reader*, London: Routledge.

Sterne, J. (1999), 'Thinking the internet: Cultural studies versus the millennium', in S. Jones (ed.), *Doing Internet research: Critical Issues and Methods for Examining the Net*, London: Sage.

Stokoe, E. H. (2000a), 'Towards a conversation analytic approach to gender and discourse', *Feminism and Psychology* 10 (4), 552–63.

Stokoe, E. H. (2000b), 'Constructing topicality in university students' small-group discussion: A conversation analytic approach', *Language and Education* 14 (3), 184–203.

Stokoe, E. H. (2003), 'Mothers, single women and sluts: Gender, morality and membership categorization in neighbour disputes', *Feminism and Psychology* 13 (3), 317–44.

Stokoe, E. H. (2004), 'Gender and discourse, gender and categorization: Current developments in language and gender research', *Qualitative Research in Psychology* 1 (2), 107–29.

Stokoe, E. H. (2005), 'Analysing gender and language', *Journal of Sociolinguistics* 9 (1), 118–33.

Stokoe, E. H. and Edwards, D. (2007), 'Mundane morality and gender in familial neighbour disputes', in J. Cromdal and M. Tholander (eds), *Children, Morality and Interaction*, Hauppague, NY: Nova Science.

Stokoe, E. H. and Hepburn, A. (2005), ' "You can hear a lot through the walls": Noise formulations in neighbour complaints', *Discourse and Society* 16 (5), 647–73.

Stokoe, E. H. and Smithson, J. (2001), 'Making gender relevant: Conversation analysis and gender categories in interaction', *Discourse and Society* 12 (2), 243–69.

Stokoe, E. H. and Smithson, J. (2002), 'Gender and sexuality in talk-in-interaction: Considering a conversation analytic perspective', in P. McIlvenny (ed.), *Talking Gender and Sexuality*, Amsterdam: John Benjamins.

Stokoe, E. H. and Wallwork, J. (2003), 'Space invaders: The moral-spatial order in neighbour dispute discourse', *British Journal of Social Psychology* 42, 551–69.

Stokoe, E. H. and Weatherall, A. (2002), 'Gender, language, conversation analysis and feminism', *Discourse and Society* 13 (6), 707–13.

Stone, A. R. (2000), 'Will the real body please stand up? Boundary stories about virtual cultures', in D. Bell and B. Kennedy (eds), *The Cybercultures Reader*, London: Routledge.

Sudweeks, F., McLaughlin, M. and Rafaeli, S. (eds) (1995), *Network and Netplay: Virtual Groups on the Internet*, Cambridge, MA: AAAi/MIT Press.

Sunderland, J. (2000), 'Parenthood discourses: The construction of fatherhood and motherhood in parentcraft literature', *Discourse and Society* 11 (2), 249–74.

Sunderland, J. (2004), *Gendered Discourses*, London: Palgrave Macmillan.

Sveningsson, M. (2002), 'Cyberlove: Creating romantic relationships on the net', in J. Fornäs, K. Klein, M. Indendorf, J. Sundén and M. Sveningsson (eds), *Digital Borderlands: Cultural Studies of Identity and Interactivity on the Internet*, Oxford: Peter Lang.

Swales, J. (1990), *Genre Analysis: English in Academic and Research Settings*, Cambridge: Cambridge University Press.

Swan, D. and Linehan, C. (2000), 'Positioning as a means of understanding the narrative construction of self: A story of lesbian escorting', *Narrative Inquiry* 10 (2), 403–27.

Tajfel, H. (1982), *Social Identity and Intergroup Relations*, Cambridge: Cambridge University Press.

Tajfel, H. and Turner, J. (1986), 'The social identity theory of intergroup behaviour', in S. Worchel and W. G. Austin (eds), *Psychology of Intergroup Relations*, Chicago: Nelson.

Talbot, M. (1995), 'A synthetic sisterhood: False friends in a teenage magazine', in K. Hall and M. Bucholtz (eds), *Gender Articulated: Language and the Socially Constructed Self*, London: Routledge.

Taylor, C. (1989), *Sources of the Self: The Making of Modern Identity*, Cambridge, MA: Harvard University Press.

Taylor, S. (2003), 'A place for the future? Residence and continuity in women's narratives of their lives', *Narrative Inquiry* 13 (1), 193–215.

Taylor, S. and Wetherell, M. (1999), 'A suitable time and place – Speakers' use of "time" to do discursive work in narratives of nation and personal life', *Time and Society* 8 (1), 39–58.

ten Have, P. (1999), *Doing Conversation Analysis: A Practical Guide*, London: Sage.

ten Have, P. (2001), 'Applied conversation analysis', in A. McHoul and M. Rapley (eds), *How to Analyse Talk in Institutional Settings*, London: Continuum.

Tester, K. (1993), *The Life and Times of Post-Modernity*, London: Routledge.

Thornborrow, J. (2002), *Power Talk: Language and Interaction in Institutional Discourse*, London: Longman.

Thurlow, C. (2003), 'Generation Txt? The sociolinguistics of young people's text-messaging', *Discourse Analysis Online (DAOL)*, 1 (1), available online at http://www.shu.ac.uk/daoi/articles/vi/ni/a3/thurlow2002003-paper.html

Thurlow, C., Lengel, L. and Tomic, A. (2004), *Computer Mediated Communication: Social Interaction and the Internet*, London: Sage.

Toolan, M. (1998), *Language in Literature: An Introduction to Stylistics*, London: Edward Arnold.

Tracy, K. (2002), *Everyday Talk: Building and Reflecting Identities*, New York: Guilford Press.

Trudgill, P. (1974), *The Social Differentiation of English in Norwich*, Cambridge: Cambridge University Press.

Tuan, Y-F. (1977), *Space and Place: The Perspective of Experience*, Minneapolis, MN: University of Minnesota Press.

Tuan, Y-F. (1991), 'Language and the making of place: A narrative descriptive approach', *Annals of the Association of American Geographers* 81, 684–96.

Turkle, S. (1995), *Life on the Screen: Identity in the Age of the Internet*, New York: Simon Schuster.

Twigger-Ross, C. L. and Uzzell, D. L. (1996), 'Place and identity processes', *Journal of Environmental Psychology* 16, 205–20.

Vallis, R. (2001), 'Applying membership categorization analysis to chat-room talk', in A. McHoul and M. Rapley (eds), *How to Analyse Talk in Institutional Settings*, London: Continuum.

van Dijk, T. (1991), *Racism and the Press*, London: Routledge.

van Dijk, T. (1998), *Ideology: A Multidisciplinary Approach*, London: Sage.

van Dijk, T. (2001), 'Multidisciplinary CDA: A plea for diversity', in R. Wodak and M. Meyer (eds), *Methods of Critical Discourse Analysis*, London: Sage.

van Leeuwen, T. (1996), 'The representation of social actors', in C. Caldas Coulthard and M. Coulthard (eds), *Texts and Practices*, London: Routledge.

Veblen, T. (1899), *The Theory of the Leisure Class: An Economic Study in the Evolution of Institutions*, New York: Macmillan.

Velody, I. and Williams, R. (1998), 'Introduction', in I. Velody and R. Williams (eds), *The Politics of Constructionism*, London: Sage.

Ventola, E. (1987), *The Structure of Social Interaction: A Systemic Approach to the Semiotics of Service Encounters*, London: Pinter.

Vygotsky, L. S. (1978), *Mind in Society: The Development of Higher Psychological Processes*, London: Harvard University Press.

Walkowitz, J. R. (1992), *City of Dreadful Delight: Narratives of Sexual Danger in Later Victorian London*, London: Virago.

Wallwork, J. and Dixon, J. (2004), 'Foxes, green fields and Britishness: On the rhetorical construction of place and national identity', *British Journal of Social Psychology* 43, 21–39.

Walther, J. B. (1996), 'Computer-mediated communication: Impersonal, interpersonal and hyperpersonal interaction', *Communication Research* 23, 3–43.

Walther, J. B. (2004), 'Language and communication technology: Introduction to the special issue', *Journal of Language and Social Psychology* 23 (4), 384–96.

Warde, A. (1994), 'Consumers, identity and belonging: Reflections on some theses of Zygmunt Bauman', in R. Keat, N. Whitely and N. Abercrombie (eds), *The Authority of the Consumer*, London: Routledge.

Watson, D. R. (1978), 'Categorization, authorization and blame-negotiation in conversation', *Sociology* 12 (1), 105–13.

Watson, D. R. (1983), 'The presentation of victim and motive in discourse: The case of police interrogations and interviews', *Victimology: An International Journal* 8 (1–2), 31–52.

Watson, D. R. (1997), 'Some general reflections on "categorization" and "sequence" in the analysis of conversation', in S. Hester and P. Eglin (eds) (1997), *Culture in Action: Studies in Membership Categorization Analysis*, Washington, DC: University Press of America, 49–75.

Watson, D. R. and Weinberg, T. (1982), 'Interviews and the interactional construction of accounts of homosexual identity', *Social Analysis* 11, 56–78.

Watson, G. (1992), 'When Orietta visits, reflexivity is not a trouble', paper presented at the Discourse Analysis and Reflexivity Group, Brunel University.

Watson, G. (1994), 'A comparison of social constructionist and ethnomethodological descriptions of how a judge distinguished between the erotic and the obscene', *Philosophy of the Social Sciences* 24 (4), 405–25.

Watson, N. (1997), 'Why we argue about virtual community: A case study of the Phish.net fan community', in S. Jones (ed.), *Virtual Culture: Identity and Community in Cybersociety*, London: Sage.

Weiss, G. and Wodak, R. (eds) (2003), *Critical Discourse Analysis: Theory and Interdisciplinarity*, London: Palgrave Macmillan.

Wengraf, T. (2005), *The Biographic-Narrative Interpretative Method: Short Guide*, (version 23), Middlesex: Middlesex University.

Werry, C. (1996), 'Linguistic and interactional features of Internet Relay Chat', in S. Herring (ed.), *Computer-Mediated Communication: Linguistic, Social and Cross-Cultural Perspectives*, Amsterdam: John Benjamins.

West, C. (1984), 'Not just "doctor's orders": Directive-response sequences in patients' visits to women and men physicians', *Discourse and Society* 1, 85–112.

West, C. and Fenstermaker, S. (1993), 'Power, inequality, and the accomplishment of gender: An ethnomethodological view', in P. England (ed.), *Theory on Gender/Feminism on Theory*, New York: Aldine de Gruyter.

Wetherell, M. (1998), 'Positioning and interpretative repertoires: Conversation analysis and post-structuralism in dialogue', *Discourse and Society* 9 (3), 431–56.

Wetherell, M. (2001), 'Themes in discourse research. The case of Diana', in M. Wetherell, S. Taylor and S. Yates (eds), *Discourse Theory and Practice: A Reader*, London: Sage.

Wetherell, M. and Edley, N. (1999), 'Negotiating hegemonic masculinity: Imaginary positions and psycho-discursive practices', *Feminism and Psychology* 9, 335–56.

Wetherell, M., Stiven, H. and Potter, J. (1987), 'Unequal egalitarianism: A preliminary study of discourses concerning gender and employment opportunities', *British Journal of Social Psychology* 26, 59–71.

White, H. (1973), *Metahistory: The Historical Imagination in Nineteenth-Century Europe*, Baltimore, MD: Johns Hopkins University Press.

Widdicombe, S. (1995), 'Identity, politics and talk: A case for the mundane and the everyday', in S. Wilkinson and C. Kitzinger (eds), *Feminism and Discourse*, London: Sage.

Widdicombe, S. (1998a), ' "But you don't class yourself": The interactional management of category membership and non-membership', in C. Antaki and S. Widdicombe (eds), *Identities in Talk*, London: Sage.

Widdicombe, S. (1998b), 'Identity as an analyst's and a participant's resource', in C. Antaki and S. Widdicombe (eds), *Identities in Talk*, London: Sage.

Widdicombe, S. and Wooffitt, R. (1995), *The Language of Youth Subcultures: Social Identity in Action*, Hemel Hempstead: Harvester Wheatsheaf.

Wieder, D. L. (1988), 'From resource to topic: Some aims of conversation analysis', in J. Anderson (ed.), *Communication Yearbook 11*, Beverly Hills, CA: Sage.

Wiggins, S. and Potter, J. (2003), 'Attitudes and evaluative practices: Category vs item and subjective vs objective constructions in everyday food assessments', *British Journal of Social Psychology* 42 (4), 513–31.

Wilbur, S. P. (2000), 'An archaeology of cyberspaces: Virtuality, community, identity', in D. Bell and B. Kennedy (eds), *The Cybercultures Reader*, London: Routledge.

Wilcox, S. (1996), 'Fostering self-directed learning in the university setting', *Studies in Higher Education* 21 (2), 165–76.

Wilkinson, S. and Kitzinger, C. (2003), 'Constructing identities: A feminist

conversation analytic approach to positioning in action', in R. Harré and
F. Moghaddam (eds), *The Self and Others: Positioning Individuals and Groups in Personal, Political and Cultural Contexts*, Westport, CT: Praeger.

Williams, R. (2000), *Making Identity Matter: Identity, Society and Social Interaction*, Durham: Sociologypress.

Wilmsen, E. N. and McAllister, P. (1996), *The Politics of Difference: Ethnic Premises in a World of Power*, Chicago: University of Chicago Press.

Wittgenstein, L. (1958), *Philosophical Investigations*, ed. G. E. M. Anscombe and R. Rhees, trans. G. E. M. Anscombe, Oxford: Blackwell.

Wodak, R. (2001), 'The discourse-historical approach', in R. Wodak and M. Meyer (eds), *Methods of Critical Discourse Analysis*, London: Sage.

Wodak, R., de Cillia, R., Reisigl, M. and Liebhart, K. (1999), *The Discursive Construction of National Identity*, Edinburgh: Edinburgh University Press.

Wodak, R. and Meyer, M. (eds) (2001), *Methods of Critical Discourse Analysis*, London: Sage.

Woodward, K. (2002), *Understanding Identity*, London: Arnold.

Wooffitt, R. (1992), *Telling Tales of the Unexpected: The Organization of Factual Discourse*, London: Harvester Wheatsheaf.

Wooffitt, R. (2005), *Conversation Analysis and Discourse Analysis: A Comparative and Critical Introduction*, London: Sage.

Wowk, M. T. (1984), 'Blame allocation, sex and gender in a murder interrogation', *Women's Studies International Forum* 7 (1), 75–82.

Wowk, M. T. (forthcoming), *Another Sociological Chimera: Kitzinger's Feminist Conversation Analysis*, unpublished manuscript.

Zimmerman, D. H. (1984), 'Talk and its occasion: The case of calling the police', in D. Schiffrin (ed.), *Meaning, Form and Use in Context: Linguistic Applications*, Washington, DC: Georgetown University Press.

Zimmerman, D. H. (1992a), 'They were all doing gender, but they weren't all passing: Comment on Rogers', *Gender and Society* 6 (2), 192–8.

Zimmerman, D. H. (1992b), 'Achieving context: Openings in emergency calls', in G. Watson and R. M. Seiler (eds), *Text in Context: Contributions to Ethnomethodology*, London: Sage.

Zimmerman, D. H. (1998), 'Identity, context and interaction', in C. Antaki and S. Widdicombe (eds), *Identities in Talk*, London: Sage.

Zimmerman, D. H. and Boden, D. (1991), 'Structure-in-action: An introduction', in D. Boden and D. H. Zimmerman (eds), *Talk and Social Structure*, Cambridge: Polity Press.

Index